Anonymous

**Trial of William W. Holden**

Vol. III

Anonymous

**Trial of William W. Holden**
*Vol. III*

ISBN/EAN: 9783337172596

Printed in Europe, USA, Canada, Australia, Japan

Cover: Foto ©Suzi / pixelio.de

More available books at **www.hansebooks.com**

# TRIAL

OF

# WILLIAM W. HOLDEN,

GOVERNOR OF NORTH CAROLINA,

BEFORE THE SENATE OF NORTH CAROLINA,

ON

# IMPEACHMENT

BY THE HOUSE OF REPRESENTATIVES

FOR

## HIGH CRIMES AND MISDEMEANORS.

---

**PUBLISHED BY ORDER OF THE SENATE.**

---

## Vol. III.

RALEIGH:
"SENTINEL" PRINTING OFFICE.
1871.

## THIRTY-EIGHTH DAY.

SENATE CHAMBER, March 15, 1871

The COURT met at eleven o'clock a. m., pursuant to adjournment, Hon. R. M. Pearson, Chief Justice of the Supreme Court, in the chair.

Proceedings were opened by proclamation made in due form by the doorkeeper.

The CLERK proceeded to call the roll of senators, when the following senators were found to be present:

Messrs. Adams, Albright, Allen, Battle, Bellamy, Brogden, Brown, Cook, Council, Cowles, Crowell, Currie, Dargan, Edwards, Eppes, Flemming, Gilmer, Graham of Alamance, Graham of Orange, Hawkins, Hyman, Jones, King, Latham, Ledbetter, Lehman, Linney, Love, Mauney, McClammy, Merrimon, Moore, Morehead, Murphy, Norment, Olds, Price, Robbins of Davidson, Robbins of Rowan, Skinner, Speed, Troy, Waddell, Warren, Whiteside and Worth—46.

Senator MOORE moved that the reading of the journal be dispensed with.

The CHIEF JUSTICE put the question on the motion of Senator Moore, and it was decided in the affirmative.

Mr. GRAHAM of counsel for the managers then addressed the court.

He said:—

MR. CHIEF JUSTICE AND SENATORS: I congratulate you that this tedious investigation is approaching its close. The sbuject of impeachment is an important one, and for the first time engages the attention of the legislature of North Carolina. For nearly the century that the constitution of the republic has been in operation, there has been no instance, so far as my information extends, where the representatives of the people have heretofore found it necessary to arraign before the court of impeachment the highest officer of the state or any officer whatever.

Such has been the usual satisfaction of the people with the conduct of their public functionaries, or their forbearance and patience, that until now they have never thought proper to constitute their senate into a court of impeachment and to require at its hands an investigation into the conduct of a public officer. In this instance, the charges are made against the chief magistrate, the person occupying the highest official position and constituting, for the time being, the representative of one department of the government. The matter to be considered therefore, may be expected to be of great moment.

Before I proceed to its consideration, perhaps it may be necessary to mention some things that have been incidentally brought to attention and which may deserve a passing notice. It has been remarked that it was extraordinary that counsel should appear in such a case. I think if precedents are examined in other states, it will be found that it is not unusual. I think that upon reflection it will likewise be conceded that the honorable members in the house of representatives having their necessary duties there to perform, and their usual communication to keep up with their constituents could not, in the length of time usually devoted to the session of the legislature of North Carolina, have fulfilled those duties, and conducted this prosecution without some assistance. The matters themselves have been such as to require the almost undivided attention of counsel for a period of thirty-eight days, and I do not see how it would have been possible for any gentleman of the board of managers on the part of the house of representatives to have been faithful and diligent in his legislative office, and at the same time borne an active part in the conduct of this impeachment. In congress, with its long sessions and its larger number of members it has not been usual, but it certainly has always been allowable to bring in counsel on behalf of the people. But in our mode of proceeding and in the short sessions usually held here, it is not only convenient but it is in the highest degree proper. As I have remarked this is the first occasion, and the subjects are novel, the matters to be investigated are somewhat voluminous and it required more time than could conveniently be devoted to it by the members of the house in person. Besides, it would be no small drawback on the proceedings of the house if seven of its most active and most useful members were withdrawn from their ordinary duties there in order to be obliged to carry on the prosecution here.

I deem it proper also to speak in regard to another observation that has been thrown out in some way in the course of this proceeding, namely that the action of this high court in North Carolina may in some mode or other provoke dissatisfaction elsewhere: and that there may be in consequence new measures of reconstruction, or new movements on the part of congress to the detriment of the state provided the judgment of this court shall be as I think it ought to be. In regard to that. I must say that I do not believe the congress of the United States will depart from that constitution under which we are now living in harmony; and that when the state of North Carolina renewed her constitutional relations to the federal government, she come back with all the rights and privileges of a sovereign state: and that her state senators and representatives when charged with duties by the people, are to perform their functions under the same responbilities and with the same privilege and immunities that belong to the senators and representatives of any state of the union.

I notice this, because by some, it may be supposed that provacation may be given by this proceeding which would subject us to less favorable treatment as a member of the union than we should otherwise receive. For my own part, I have to say to every public man in regard to his public life, what the great poet represents the angel as having said to our first ancestor, in regard to his natural life,

> "Nor love thy life, nor hate,
> But what thou livest live well—
> How long or short to Heaven permit.

Our duties are to be done: to be done candidly, prudently, and at the same time fearlessly.

Mr. Chief Justice and Senators, the representatives of the people, from a deep sense of the high duties which they owed to their constituents, and in answer to complaints made by a respectable portion of the people, have arraigned the governor of North Carolina upon certain specific charges which you are required to try. It is for you, upon the evidence which you have heard; upon the facts and attending circumstances of the occurrences detailed, and the constitution and the law applicable thereto, to say whether he is guilty or not guilty upon the charges preferred. They are charges of the perversion and abuse of high official powers. The first of these charges is that he unlawfully and from improper motives, and falsely, declared certain counties of the state to be in insurrection, when no insurrection existed in fact, and having thus, as he supposed, put them in a state of insurrection, he caused their leading and best citizens to be arrested, imprisoned, tortured, deprived of their liberties for thirty days or more; and that all this he did under the color of his office. They charge that that official power, which had been placed in his hands for the purpose of giving security to society and promoting the public good, was applied to the most outrageous, opprobrious injury and wrong; and they state the fact to be that the respondent having, as he alleged, found that in the county of Alamance, with a population of more than eleven thousand souls, certain crimes had been committed, instead of resorting to the law as established by our ancestors and as it has been known to us in the generation in which we have lived, for the punishment of these crimes and for the prevention of like offences in the future, chose to disregard the law of the land and the constitution of the state, to raise an armed force, unlawfully and without authority, and to march them into those counties, and without making a bow or asking a question, without conferring with any judicial magistrate, high or low, he proceeded, by means of this armed force to seize and arrest men indiscriminately without regard to whether they had been individually guilty, or were even suspected of crime. The object seemed to be to strike terror into the country by seizing men of known respectability and character and holding them up to the world as examples of the criminals who had committed assassinations and other crimes of like nature.

The second charge alleges that he was guilty of a similar course towards the county of Caswell, with a population of more than sixteen thousand; that having declared it in a state of insurrection and proceeding under cover of the insurrection which he himself created—for it had no existence except upon paper in his proclamation—that he sent there an armed force on the day when the people had assembled together to hear those who aspired to represent them in congress discuss the state of the country, an occasion when of all others the people had a right to be free and to have all the information which these gentlemen were capable of imparting to them in order to judge of their qualifications to represent them in the councils of the nation: that this armed force entered that peaceful and orderly assembly and there without authority, or civil officer of the law, without pretence that anybody had made any affidavit, without warrant upon which a man could be deprived of his liberty, first seized Doctor Roane, one of the most respectable gentlemen in that; or any other county in the state and then successively the Hon. John Kerr, the Hon. S. P. Hill, William B. Bowe, Esq., the sheriff, the coroner and others of the prominent citizens of the county, many of them the pillars of society, both in church and state and men above reproach in every respect. They were assaulted and seized in the most rude and violent and insulting manner. They were not accosted in language that might be expected from those who were acting in obedience to law—such as that: "I am sent "here to arrest you; I beg you to understand I intend you no "harm." But when it was asked, "By what authority?"—words that would instinctively issue from the mouth of an American citizen anywhere, upon being told that he was a prisoner, the answer was, "Here is my authority,"—referring to the men with bayonets in hand, with oaths and imprecations disgraceful to civilization. These citizens are taken and imprisoned. They are charged afterwards by the respondent with being assassins and murderers, or with participating in or being accessory to those crimes.

The respondent in his answer admits, "That the said named "parties were arrested and detained and held for examination "in the said county of Caswell, by officers commanding the "organized body of militia therein, and that this respondent "was informed and believes and so charges that the aforesaid "persons, and each of them were arrested on probable cause, "and were either suspected persons, or persons accused of being "accessories or principals in offences against the laws."

And the same admission is made in regard to the citizens of Alamance.

"This respondent admits, "That under the aforesaid order, "the persons named in said first article, were arrested and "detained and held for examination by the officers com- "manding the said organized body of militia in the county of "Alamance and that this respondent, as governor of North "Carolina, did approve of their said arrest and detention, but "this respondent was informed and believes and so charges that "the said persons and each of them were suspected persons, and "arrested on probable cause, for crimes alleged to have been "committed by them and each of them."

Therefore, as to the crime charged in the first article, of falsely declaring the county in insurrection and the arrest of these persons without any cause whatever and their imprisonment and maltreatment; their arrest is admitted in the answer, and the injury done by the arrest, is aggravated by the accusation that each of these persons was arrested as one suspected of crime and held to answer for it. I beg to know where is the evidence against any one of them to prove him guilty of the crime charged. Why, sir, as to the Binghams, the Mebanes, the Scotts and others in Alamance, the Roanes, the Kerrs, the Bowes, the

Hills in Caswell—who has sworn to a word of accusation against any one of them? It is alleged in the answer that crimes had been committed in the county. Certainly there had: but is the fact that a man lives in the county where crime has been committed sufficient to authorize his arrest by the governor or by anybody else? It is alleged in the answer or it is to be inferred from it that nobody was arrested except a suspected man against whom probable cause had been shown. Those arrested in the process of time were brought before the chief justice of North Carolina or before the district judge of the United States for the district of North Carolina on writs of *habeas corpus*, and were discharged—every one of them. Where stood the governor then? Where was the evidence to show that they were lawfully captured or lawfully detained? The whole proceedings show that there was no evidence there against any one of the eighty odd in Alamance or twenty or more from Caswell. The respondent was at perfect liberty to go before these legal tribunals to show, that any one of them was not entitled to be discharged as they all were without any imputation whatever, yet he offered no such proof.

The third article charges the imprisonment of Josiah Turner, a citizen of the state, residing in the county of Orange, which it was not pretended was in a state of insurrection and therefore was in like condition with the county of Wake or any other county. Yet he was assaulted by the governor's troops with cocked muskets, and seized in the town of Hillsboro, his house was invaded while he was held as a prisoner, his bed chamber entered and the arms which he had in the house taken off and never have yet been restored. He himself was hurried off to Yanceyville, was detained there many days and afterwards carried to Alamance and for the purpose of gratifying private malice, of wreaking personal vengeance, committed to jail with other of those persons in a loathsome cell amid vermin and among condemned criminals, one of whom was about to suffer the penalty of death. The answer denies that the respondent ordered the arrest, but admits that he approved it. But the proof is that he not only ordered it, and ordered it to gratify a private grudge on the very day when the election was pending, saying that Turner is responsible for a good many of these troubles, "and he has published me to-day as a coward," or something of that sort. That is a new law of libel in this country by which a newspaper editor is liable to be thus summarily and severely dealt with, for a criticism or denunciation upon a man in authority—by which a governor of a state can order the person who thus assails him to be taken and committed to jail, imprisoned and maltreated and degraded, as was the lot of Mr. Turner at the hands of the respondent in this instance.

There is a law of libel as well as other laws. It is to be enforced through courts of justice as others are; but that a man can be taken and incarcerated instanter without trial, because he has said hard things of a public officer is a new doctrine of *scandalum magnatum* never known in this country or even in that from which we derive our institutions.

The fourth article alleges that the respondent did procure and command G. W. Kirk and Burgen, his so-called military officers, and other evil-disposed persons to seize and imprison divers good citizens who are named, and are residents in the county of Caswell. And the proofs are in substance the same as those applicable to article second.

The fifth and sixth articles charge that whereas, a citizen of Alamance and sundry citizens of Caswell had been arrested without lawful authority and by this armed force thus unlawfully raised, the person thus arrested made application to the chief justice of the state for the writ of *habeas corpus*—that great writ of right which Doctor Johnson, a century ago, said was "the single advantage which the government of "England had over that of all other countries," and which Lord Macauley, in our time pronounces to be the most stringent curb that legislation ever imposed on tyranny. It is the right which every man has, who is imprisoned, whether at the instance of a private individual or of a public functionary, to be brought before a judicial tribunal immediately, to the end that the cause of his commitment may be inquired into and that he may be enlarged without or with bail, except in cases of capital crime where the proof is positive or the presumption of guilt violent. This great remedy is dear to the American people. It is the tenure by which they hold their liberties.

When that writ went out it was the state of North Carolina speaking over the signature of her highest judicial officer, commanding George W. Kirk to bring before him the bodies of Adolphus G. Moore and John Kerr, and others whom he was alleged to have in custody, in order that the cause of their capture and detention might be inquired into. It was sent to Kirk. What answer does he make? He contemns it and defies it. "Such papers are played out—I am acting under "the direction of Governor Holden. I am holding these men "under his order. I don't intend to surrender them to the "order of the chief justice. I intend to obey only a military "superior. I am a military man, and I do not intend that the "civil officers of this state shall inquire into this matter at all. "On the contrary a court has been appointed by the governor "for their trial." He not only refuses to surrender these persons to have their cases examined by a lawful court, but he announces there is another court, which it appears clearly from the evidence, was to be a military commission, and that those persons were to go before that court to be tried. And yet these things occurred in the state of North Carolina—a state with a constitution a century old which had guaranteed the privilege of the writ of *habeas corpus* in all that time; and which those who framedit had had guaranteed to them for centuries preceding. A military officer proclaims that he will not surrender these citizens, nor bring them before the court to have their case inquired into. He is not content with that justice which the constitution and the laws have provided but he and the governor have got a justice of their own, "sharp, quick, and decisive," I think are the words—

something out of the usual channel. They intend that these men (among them, those of the highest esteem and reputation in their respective counties) against whom no crime had been imputed, in any legitimate manner, shall not be tried by the ordinary courts of law, that they shall not have a judge and jury to pass upon their case, but that they shall be tried by a military commission, which, as it turns out in the further development, is to be composed of newly fledged generals, and colonels and captains, without commands, or boundaries of authority, appointed by the Governor in order that they might be detailed to seats in that court: Major Gen'l W. D. Jones, Brig. Gen'l C. S. Moring, Brig. Gen'l W. R. Albright, Col. H. M. Ray, Maj. G. W. Hardin, Capt. Robert Hancock, and other high functionaries of this class, who were supposed to be superior to chief justices, judges and juries in that jurisprudence which Kirk was to administer as military justice under the orders of his chief. What followed next? By a grave judicial error the respondent was brought upon the stage by correspondence where he had no right to appear (the main design of *habeas corpus* being to protect men from oppression by executive power) and avows that he has directed that these men shall be detained notwithstanding the process of the court, that he has directed Kirk to arrest and detain them; and that they shall not be surrendered until he thinks proper to restore civil authority in the counties of Alamance and Caswell.

That is the avowal made by the chief magistrate of North Carolina in reply to a command in the name of the state by its highest officer to Kirk; (which is equally a command to all who had control over him) to bring these men before the chief justice in order that they might have their case enquired into;—not that they should be turned loose necessarily, but that it might be shown whether they were guilty or reasonably suspected or innocent; and if they were just grounds of suspicion that they might be permitted to give bail. But no. Kirk says they shall not come, and the respondent avows that he will not permit them to be brought until such time, as he thinks proper to restore the civil authority in the counties in question. And he does not say that then they shall come before the chief justice. For although it may be inferred that he desired it to be understood by the chief justice that they should in time come before him, he is at the same time carrying on a correspondence "*aside*" with Kirk, in which he tells him that a military court is to sit for their trial on the 25th of July (it is now the 16th or 17th) and subsequently, he writes that although it was postponed from that time, it would certainly be convened on the 8th of August. This double dealing was carried on that while the judicial officer is entertained with the idea that these prisoners may eventually be brought before him, Kirk is advised of the names of six or seven learned members of the court and that his command will furnish six or seven more: that the court would certainly assemble and try the prisoners. And it is implied of course, that such as of them as this court found guilty were to suffer death by hanging or shooting or such penal ties as this wise military commission should impose. And then perhaps it was intended to re-open the correspondence with the chief justice, by advising that the writs of *habeas corpus* had abated by the death of the applicants.

I say, Mr. Chief Justice and Senators, that there never has been such an outrage on the constitution and laws of any free country. I say that a military officer, a major-general for instance in the army of the United States who should have acted as did the governor of this state in refusing to obey the *habeas corpus* and going on to provide a military commission for the trial of citizens that he held in defiance of the writ, if tried by a court martial, would have been sentenced to be shot. At least he would have been deprived of his commission and probably even of his life. Such an outrage on the constitution, and upon our instinctive ideas of personal liberty, would not have been tolerated by even military justice in any court either in America or in England, a moment longer than should be necessary to enable a court to ascertain the truth and pronounce judgment. To make arbitrary arrests of the best citizens, without any legal accusation was bad enough: to disobey and contemn the writ of *habeas corpus* issued to inquire into the cause of their detention—to carry into effect "the most stringent curb that legislation ever imposed on tyranny"—was an enormous aggravation; but to attempt to supersede the whole code of criminal justice, with all its safe-guards to accused pesons, by the agency of learned judges and jury trials, and subject civilians to condemnation by a military commission, a court as Mr. Webster characterized it "appointed to convict," selected by the governor, was an infatuation in guilt, without a precedent or parallel. Although there has been a studied attempt to conceal and suppress the evidence of this iniquitous design, it plainly appears in this cause, that the machinery was all prepared and the plot matured for this inquisition of blood. Having paralized the judicial power of the state by intimidation the respondent was in full tide towards the successful accomplishment of this design when he was interrupted by the beneficent and resolute interposition of his honor Judge Brooks, the district judge of the United States.

Mr. Chief Justice and Senators, the next allegation is that the respondent arrested John Kerr and a large number of other persons, charging a good deal of the same matter as in the first article without the allegation of having proclaimed insurrection, and that he refused to bring them before the Chief Justice in the same manner that he refused in the case of the Alamance prisoners.

The 7th article charges that he raised an unlawful force, and drew large sums of money from the treasury for the purpose of sustaining that force contrary to law.

The 8th article charges that when a citizen of the state, a tax-payer in the name of himself and other tax-payers of North Carolina, applied to a court of justice alleging that these monies were about to be improperly disbursed in paying off this unauthorized force, and an injunction had been granted by a judge restraining the person in whose custody the money had been placed, so that the matter could be kept in suspense till there should be a judicial investigation, the Governor thought proper to cut that gordian knot also with the sword. He has no use for the refinements of judicial decision—no care as to what equity in its injunctions may decree, but in a summary way he chooses to take the defendant out of court, or to take the money out of the hands of this defendant, and put it in other hands before a new restraint can be imposed against its disbursement—another contempt of a court of justice, not however so great or so enormous as the refusal to permit Kirk to obey the writ of *habeas corpus*.

These, Mr. Chief Justice and Senators, are the charges which are made against the respondent, and I submit that he is guilty upon them all.

I have already said the respondent admits by his answer that he did arrest all the citizens named in these articles; that he did commit the acts charged as the gravamen of the offence, and he says, that he did it by reason of their being persons suspected of crimes, residing in counties which he had declared in a state of insurrection. Let me ask again what evidence has he brought forward against any one of them. Were they guilty of assassination, or other offences which are denounced in his proclamation? And if they were suspected, could they not have been readily arrested by process from a civil magistrate? He aggravates the maltreatment and the injury done them by imprisonment and torture, and stands, before this high court as an accuser, yet not sustained by a particle of evidence. And, let me remind you here, senators, that men are not condemned in this country by classes. Every man stands before the law upon his individual conduct, not upon that of the neighbors around him. Each is to answer for himself. The fact that a crime has been committed in a neighborhood, in a county, or in a state is no reason why the first citizens of that neighborhood, or county or state who happened to be met by an avenging power shall atone for it. The freedom of this country requires that, before any person shall be arrested or brought to trial he shall have an opportunity for an investigation of the charge before a judicial magistrate, and that his guilt shall be shown, to the extent at least of probability: and that then he shall have a proceeding before a grand jury to determine whether it is worth while to put him upon his trial, and a final trial before a petit jury of his peers to determine his ultimate fate.

I have shown, on a former occasion, and I shall not repeat the argument now, that the executive of the state has no power to make arrests; that in the distribution of powers under our constitution, the legislative, executive and judicial departments of the state have each their several duties and powers: that the personal liberty of the citizen is under the especial care of the judiciary—and whether the matter may pertain to the arrest of persons accused of crime, or the enlargement of those complaining of having been illegally captured or detained, the question is solely of judicial cognizance. I cited to you authority to show that the King of England could not authorize the arrest of the meanest of his subjects on his warrant or order: that while "the King can do no wrong" according to the British constitution, and cannot be made to atone for such an act by indictment, or in damages, yet the man who should undertake in his name to arrest the meanest subject of the realm would be liable to indictment and an action for assault and battery. I have read authority, also, that when the courts of justice of the country are open it is a time of peace—and if there be a time of peace the executive has no power to make arrests by military force.

As to the matter of making arrests, it is hardly necessary before so intelligent a tribunal as this to call attention to those numerous provisions in the declaration of rights intended for the security of personal liberty. It is there declared that *habeas corpus* shall never be suspended; that no man shall be arrested upon a general warrant, that no man shall be deseized of his liberties or privileges except by due process of law; and other declarations to the same effect are accumulated in order that this great subject of personal liberty shall not be misunderstood, and that he who runs may read. After all that has been proved, I am yet in doubt whether the magnitude of the offences committed by the respondent is fully realized ; that it is not distinctly seen that every essential security for the freedom of the citizen in the declaration of rights, over and besides the privilege of *habeas corpus*, were set aside and annulled. Violent arrests by rude soldiers, colored and white, without the presence of any peace officer, without any semblance of legal warrant--bail refused—*habeas corpus* defied—confinement continued—torture by imprisonment—torture by threats of speedy death of the prisoners and of their women and children as well, with the burning of their dwellings in certain contingencies, and no hope held out of ultimate deliverance except through the tender mercies of a military court. And even after new light had dawned from an unexpected quarter by the issue of the writs of the federal judge, then thrusting a part of them into the common jail amid filth and vermin, as if to consummate the last act of revenge and degradation before the victims are wrested out of his hands.

Senators, the atrocity of these crimes could not but call into exercise the power of impeachment, which has slept for a century in North Carolina.

They are without official precedent within that period in the history of America or England. Our position then, is, that there was no insurrection in the counties of Alamance and Caswell. The governor declared insurrection when none existed. Doubtless there had been crimes committed in these counties, a few of them of a very flagrant character. These, neither the board of manrgers nor their counsel have any disposition to palliate or excuse, whenever the perpetrators can be traced out or identified. But the abhorence in these cases of great aggravation, has been made much less intense, by reason of the exhibition of the long procession of the alleged wrongs of harlots, adulterers, thieves and other vicious characters, not unfrequently subjects of unlawful treatment in any community, by which they have been accompanied. To repeat a saying of Bonaparte, much "foul linen has been brought out to be washed in public." I trust no inference will be drawn from this, unfavorable to the general state ot records in these counties; since it is apparent that every scene of low vice and petty crime there, has been searched by the respondent to swell the throng of sufferers from unlawful outrage, and to sustain his charge of insurrection, made against the whole people. Doubtless he has brought forward all of this description ot characters, that could be found, and it is fair to presume, that the whole herd has been presented before this court. He would even exalt into martyrs, the abandoned votaries of lewdless, who confess their faults in this public assembly, and acknowledge that they got no more in the way of punishment than they deserved. Great pains have also been taken to show, that no prosecutions had been instituted for the outrages complained of, and the inference is sought to be drawn, that this resulted from fear of further violence; and that in some cases the sufferers left the county from apprehensions of this nature—some abatement must also be made in the cases on this head, since it is manifest, that no small number of the alleged sufferers were unwilling to enter a court ot justice, had exposure and punishments of themselves for vice or crime should accompany or follow the vindication of the wrongs, of which they complained.

But it is perfectly manifest that when that proclamation was issued on the 7th of March, 1870, there was no insurrection in Alamance. There had just occurred an atrocious act of assassination; there had also been a number of lesser offences before that time; but as to the eleven thousand people in the county—as to the great majority of the citizens there is no evidence that any individual of them participated in these crimes, save in the cases of some of the misdemeanors, and these could have been dealt with by the courts of justice as suchcases require. But there is evidence before you that the state of society there was generally tranquil, and so far as regards the colored race for whom the respondent appears to have manifested so much interest—their relations with the whites were peaceful and friendly; the usual business relations existing between them, work being given on the one hand and compensation on the other, either in money or by a share of the productions of the labor. And if there had been any state of society requiring military interposition, military aid was there ready. Simultaneously with this proclamation by the governor, there went to that county and encamped at its court house, and stayed there five or six months, a company of troops of the United States. With this company stationed at the court house there was perfect tranquility in the county. From that time forward crime ceased. There is no evidence of the commission of a single crime of any nature, from the time the United States troops arrived there, until Kirk's departure if I may except the single case of Puryear who disappeared within a week or two after the arrival of these troops. With that exception, there is no evidence before this court of any disorder whatever and no semblance of anything approaching to insurrection. And when the proclamation of insurrection was issued it was issued, not with a view to the condition of things then, but to what subsequent events might develop as expedient for the party ends whichthe respondent had in contemplation in the course of the summer.

What is insurrection? What is the meaning of placing a people in insurrection? We have had some experience on the subject during the recent war. Certain states or sections were declared by acts of Congress to be in insurrection. What followed? Why, military lines were established, intercourse between these sections and the people on the other side of the lines ceased and the public law in relation to the treatment of enemies was enforced against them. The people thus denounced were treated for the time being as if not a part of the national family. But what did the governor's proclamation in this instance amount to for three month's after it was issued? No more than the paper on which it was written. From March

7th, when it bears date, down to June 6th, when another proclamation was issued, it was treated by himself as of no significance, and up to the 15th July, when Kirk went there and commenced his arrests what was done towards these people indicating that they were regarded as in a state of insurrection, and were to be treated as insurgents? Nothing at all. They bought and sold, they transacted all business as usual, they went and came and held their usual intercourse over these county lines as if no proclamation had been issued. The judge of probate of the county kept open his court, writs were executed and returned to court, regular terms of the superior court were held, cases were tried if there were any for trial—civil and criminal—not a word heard in regard to an insurrection or in regard to the people of Alamance being on a different footing from any other people in North Carolina, until the arrival of Kirk's command among them on the 13th of July. The proclamation had been issued merely as a preparatory step to the violent, threatening and tyrannical course of action, to be adopted just before and at the time of the election in July and August. This proclamation went forth. But what then? Why, nothing more than if it hadn't gone forth. Nothing was done to distinguish these people from the people of any other county in the state. Every man was in the enjoyment of the same rights he had before, and all the intercourse across their county lines on each of the four sides was carried on precisely as it had been in prior time.

Then I say this proclamation was issued not with the view of any present effect but that the governor might be in a position as military men would say, to be ready for operations towards the first Thursday in August and at as convenient a period before that time as the troops that were intended to be raised could be brought into the field. It was a proclamation without any results, with none of its legitimate consequences being insisted upon, until midsummer, and then, it is used not as a means of security and peace to the country, but as a cover and a license for the outrages of a lawless soldiery headed by equally lawless and unprincipled officers. Meanwhile the company of United States troops which arrived early in March were still at their post, within a stone's throw of the courthouse, keeping guard against any recurrence of violence or disorder, and quiet reigned throughout the country. Moreover, the regular term of the superior court, having jurisdiction of all crimes, had been recently held: criminal trials had taken place, and judgments of the most serious nature had been pronounced, and were in the course of being carried into execution, the governor's proclamation of a state of insurrection in the county notwithstanding.

In this condition of affairs, this state of quietness and order, as if by an after-thought, long subsequent to the proclamation, Kirk's expedition, composed of "desperate and lawless men," as has been fully shown by proof—a body of men, calculated to produce disorder and provoke violence and resistance anywhere, is suddenly gotten up; and his men turned loose upon the people without any warrant of authority, except secret orders and lists of names furnished by the respondent as governor, to seize, vilify, imprison, torture and maltreat all whom he had denounced as proper subjects for such usages.

Why, with the United States troops there, where there was no resistence, and really no need of any military force, it was like carying coals to Newcastle—it was more—it was piling Pelion on Ossa to raise and send thither, five hundred more armed men under Kirk. And the sequel proves that they were not sent to act in the preservation of order and the enforcement of the law, but to override and subvert the law; to deal with the people, as Sir Francis Head, in a work of his on military topics, tells us conquered cities are dealt with, when delivered over to be sacked by victorious armies. Without law and against law, from the mere caprice of the governor, or upon the accusation of detectives and informers, whose names are not yet known, the citizens are pounced upon as if they had been decreed to such a fate; domiciliary visitations are made into all sections of the country by armed bands of white and colored men intermixed, no process shown, no questions asked except to identify the persons sought for capture; and from eighty to one hundred men, in the county of Alamance alone, many of them the most exemplary characters in their several communities, were taken without notice, at any hour in the day or night, in many instances with horrid oaths, imprecations and threats of instant death, and hurried off to prison at a military camp. No explanations are given, no inquiries answered except by fresh insults. No time allowed for changes of clothing from that in which they had been surprised while threshing their harvests—and they are to be detained, in defiance of *habeas corpus*, in mysterious reticence as to the doom impending over them, except they had been placed outside of the protection of the civil law and were to undergo the ordeal of a military commission—some, as in the case of that decrepid man and worthy citizen, Henderson Scott, were permitted to pay their way out by a *douceur* of fifty dollars in cash to Lieut. Col. Burgen, the commandant at the post, and others by barrels or other measures of Whisky, as in the instance of the Messrs. Curtis, to the same high functionary. These means of deliverance from the emissaries of the governor, then dominant over that devoted country, were far more potential than *habeas corpus*, the great boast of American jurisprudence.

Now, for what purpose were these troops of Kirk levied, and marched to that county? Certainly not to aid the civil authority. That had met no resistance; and if it had, the U. S. troops were ample to sustain it. They went, as if in a campaign purely military, and against so many Indians who were alleged to have committed hostilities, and whom they were going to chastise as a tribe, by fire and sword, without distinction of persons as to guilt or innocence. If there was any other object of the expedition, to be inferred from the manner of conducting it, besides this, of reducing the people to desperation and provoking them to resistance and war, it would seem to have been, the procurement of evidence of crimes already committed, by duress and torture, a practice forbidden by the common law from the earliest ages. And the feeble admonition of the respondent to Kirk by letter when he heard that the witness Patten had been hanged by the neck by Burgen, to extort confessions, is prefaced by the information, that such evidence would be worth nothing, and is so pointless of reproof, as to amount to more than half an approval. The respondent says in his answer that the civil law had failed of effect—was incapable of detecting and punishing crime; and therefore he resorted to the military. Is there any rule of law known by our system by which military power is able to obtain evidence in cases of crime imputed to citizens, which the civil courts cannot elicit, or by which the governor is to supercede the civil authority in cases where offenders cannot be discovered by legal evidence? The whole pretension is but wicked and wanton usurpation.

And the subjection of the three witnesses, Murray, Rogers and Patten, to torture and intimidation by threats of instant death by the rope and the pistol in the darkess of midnight, in a solitary wood, as practiced by Burgen, was but a part of the plan concocted when the respondent and his partisans determined on raising such a force and setting on foot such an expedition. Although an officer in the regular army under Scott or under Sherman would have forfeited his life, or at least his commission, by thus maltreating citizens who were his prisoners, Burgen suffers no penalty for these fiend-like atrocities. On the contrary, it is in evidence that after the whole matter became public, the respondent writes to Judge Bond to come to Raleigh and see if he could not be released from the imprisonment to which, by reason of these military cruelties, he had been subjected by Judge Brooks. Entertaining the opinion that the respondent could not justify his conduct in raising this armed force in a time of peace, and making arbitrary arrests of men on his own order as governor of the state or commander-in-chief of the militia, I moved in an early stage of this trial to exclude much of the evidence offered by the defence; because, in case of a plain and palpable violation of the constitution, such as is here imputed, in disregarding and overriding all the most essential principles of our declaration of rights, the proof proposed to be introduced did not amount to a justification. The court, however, admitted the evidence of numerous violations of the law in Alamance and Caswell, but the establishment of any justification of the cause of the respondent in the matters charged in the articles of impeachment is as far off as before. The question still remains, whether the governor of the state, who has been guilty of most unlawful acts by equally unlawful means, can plead in his defence that his intentions were pure, and that there was a necessity thus to act for the preservation of the public peace. In the first place the constitution provides for a state of public disturbance, and even of war, as well as for times of tranquility; and the rules of personal security, freedom from arrest, except upon warrant and probable cause of guilt shown before a judicial magistrate, unless in times of actual resistance to the law, when the courts of justice are not open, obtain under all circumstances. There is no necessity which can authorize the executive to assume the exercise of judicial power and seize the persons of citizens by its own discretionary order. But in the next place, the pretended necessity did not exist.

There was no insurrection in the county of Alamance. That the respondent admitted by the fact that he did not proceed against her people as insurgents until nearly four months after he had issued his proclamation; it is also proved by the circumstance that a military force of the United States, sufficient to preserve order and maintain the peace, was and had been in that county from the very date of the proclamation, and in all this time there had been quietness and order. Kirk's force then was sent into the county for no purpose of peace, but to degrade and if possible to incite the inhabitants to resistance to his authority, to bring on a collision, to produce confusion, and thereby affect the pending election. It was sent not as a military force to aid the *posse comitatus*, to assist in the execution of the law, but for the purpose of being set on the people, as blood hounds were brought from Cuba and set upon the Seminole Indians in Florida. It may be alleged that they were set upon bad men. The law recognizes no such instruments to be employed for making arrests even of bad men, while the civil authority was in the exercise of its functions.

But who have been proven to be bad men? Did they find evidence against any one of those eighty-odd in number who were arrested, to bind him over for a crime? Not a word of it. No proof was attempted on the return of the *habeas corpus* writs. And in the searching examination of a hundred witnesses made here, have they found evidence upon which any man that was arrested could be charged with participation in murder, assault and battery, or other crime? No, sir. Kirk seems to have been sent out in a mere spirit of wantonness without regard to guilt in any individual case, but to deal with the whole community as if every man was a malefactor: guilty even of murder by assassination.

But it is said the respondent declared the county in a state of insurrection under the act of January, 1870, and that having so declared it, he might, by authority of this act, treat all citizens as insurgents. I have suggested, senators, for your consideration heretofore, that the act of 1869 and '70 was intended as a warning to the people of the county, and operated as nothing more than an admonition; because the contrary construction makes it a highly penal act, while the language employed gives authority to the governor merely to declare the county in a state of insurrection, and to call into service the militia to suppress insurrection. But no consequences of such a declaration are set forth. The act does not go on to say that the whole of the citizens in the county shall be treated as insurgents, whereas the acts of congress passed during the war declare that when a state or part of a state is declared in insurrection intercourse should cease, lines should be established of separation, and that the people thus cut off should be no longer treated as a part of the people who are friendly to the government. But if this construction be not tenable the inaction of the respondent for five months after issuing the proclamation as to Alamance, demonstrates that he did not believe there was insurrection nor did he intend to act upon the presumption that there was—not until the 15th of July succeeding does he give any intimation that a state of insurrection will be insisted on in the condition of the inhabitants. He then opens a military campaign against them—he proceeds to make arbitrary arrests and haughtily refuses to show any authority or assign any cause for depriving men of their liberties except executive orders. If he had anything to charge against Bingham, Mebane, the Scotts, and the long catalogue of others, among whom will be recognized many of the most respectable names in that region of the country, it had never been suspected before, and has not been proved since, but he tells this court in his answer that he arrested them all as "suspected persons." If that had been true the least he should have done was to deliver over his prisoners as early as practicable to the civil authority. And here let me remark that it is the duty of the judiciary in such cases not to be content with a proclamation on paper. But if a citizen complains that he has been restrained of his liberty, the judiciary should enquire whether there is insurrection upon a proper traverse of the return to a writ of *habeas corpus*, and should liberate him from custody if his imprisonment be unjust. It is a great measure of our law that in *judicio non cretitin nisi juratis*—in matters of judgment credit is given to no one except those who are sworn. An official communication avowing that he has authorized such things to be done in violation of the rights of the citizens is not to be treated in a court of justice as upon the filing of an affidavit. A peer of England may sit and try his peer without taking an oath. He may, I believe, according to the old practice, put in an answer in chancery upon his honor, but if he wishes to arrest the meanest subject of the realm for poaching his manor, disturbing his game or any trifling crime, he must make an affidavit and incur all the penalties of perjury. So the governor of a state or any other official who seeks to justify the detaining of any man under arrest, must be sworn before he can ask the judge to consider him as responsible for the matter and to continue the imprisonment by his authority.

I beg leave to call the attention of the court to a case on this head in the American Law Register. Congress had suspended the writ of *habeas corpus*, or authorized the president to suspend it, in the year 1863, and it continued suspended until after the surrender of the southern armies in 1865. A man who had been imprisoned under the president's order, in July 1865, applied for the writ of *habeas corpus*. The writ was awarded and when he was brought before the judge, the person who detained him made return that he held him under the order of the president under the act of congress of July, 1863, which authorized the president by his order to detain persons "during the present rebellion." A judge of the supreme court of Pennsylvania, who had awarded a writ determined that he would take judicial cognizance of the real state of facts and ascertain whether the rebellion had not ceased. The southern armies had been surrendered, the war was over and he liberated the prisoners, I cite the case of the Commonwealth on the relation of Cozzens against H. A. Frink, page 700, of American Law Register. The marginal note reads as follows:

"The rebellion being ended, the authority of the president, "under the act of 3d March, 1863, to suspend the privilege of "the writ of *habeas corpus* has expired.

I read from the case:

"The relator, Cozzens, having been tried by court martial "for frauds in connection with contracts for furnishing supplies "to the war department, and the proceedings having been "transmitted to the department, was arrested by the provost "marshal, whereupon he sued out this writ."

The return was as follows:

To the Hon. James Thompson,

*Judge of the Supreme Court of Pennsylvania:*

"The undersigned, one of the respondents in the within writ, "respectfully makes return thereto, that the relator, W. B. N. "Cozzens, was on the 29th of June, inst., arrested by order of "this respondent, and is now detained by him as a prisoner, "under the authority of the president of the United States, and "that the other respondents mentioned in said writ are officers "and clerks under this respondent, and further sayeth not.

"H. A. Frink,
*Col. and Provost Marshal of Philadelphia.*

"July 5th, 1865, the following opinion was delivered by

"Thompson, J.—This return is partly in accordance with the "act of congress of the 3d of March, 1863, § I, that whenever "the privilege of the writ of *habeas corpus* shall be suspended "by the president under the authority of the act, no military "or other officer shall be compelled in answer to any writ of "*habeas corpus* by authority of the president, but upon the "certificate under oath of the officer that the prisoner is de-"tained under and by authority of the president, further pro-"ceedings under the writ shall be suspended by the judge or "court having issued it. This section authorizes the president "during the present rebellion," whenever and wherever in his "judgment the public safety may require it, to suspend the "privilege of the writ of *habeas corpus*, and it is provided, "'that said suspension by the president shall remain in force "'so long as said rebellion shall continue.'

"On this return the important question is, whether on the "29th of June last the rebellion continued or not.

"This is a fact to be judicially determined like any other "fact. It is not for the president only, by proclamation to "determine this. He is not authorized to fix the status of the "country on this point by the act of congress. The power of "suspension depends on the fact of rebellion and its con-"tinuance. It ceases with the rebellion and that fact is as "much within judicial congnizance as is any fact under which "rights exist and are held. As the privilege of the writ of "*habeas corpus* is a constitutional right of every citizen, we are "bound to observe a strict construction of every act which "threatens to deprive him of it.

"We have an expression of legislative intent, which is plain, "that the suspension of the privilege of the writ is only to "continue during the rebellion. When that ceases the right "of the president to continue the suspension ceases. The "courts are bound to give to the citizens his right under the "privilege. There is nothing prescribed as to what shall be "the evidence of it. It is, therefore, to be ascertained like any "other fact, by evidence appropriate to such a fact.

"There is abundant evidence in the current history of the "times that the rebellion no longer continues. We know its "organization is entirely destroyed, its armies captured or sur-"rendered, its officers imprisoned or paroled. In addition, we "know that our own armies are being as rapidly mustered out "as possible. The returning soldiers crowd our streets daily, "and we cease to look for battles and victories as events as "little to be expected as before rebellion commenced. There "is not a single known body of men in arms anywhere under "the once well known organization called the 'confederate "states of America.' It is completely obliterated with all its "forces. Civil government has been set up in all the rebellious "states but one, and trade opened by the proclamation of the "president, with scarcely any restriction. Every fort, navy "yard and port is again under the government and entire con-"trol of the United States; and war has ceased everywhere in "the land. The time has arrived, therefore, when a return to the "enjoyment of civil rights, under civil government, must take "place and when by express limitation the suspension of the "*habeas corpus* should cease."

The judge therefore ordered the prisoners to be discharged.

Now I submit, according to that authority, it is not for the governor of the state of North Carolina to deprive eleven thousand people in one county and sixteen thousand in another of their liberties by an insurrection proclaimed upon paper; and that when the fact is averred that no such insurrection existed they are entitled to traverse the allegations of his agents or of himself and to be released from custody if these allegations be found untrue. But whether that be or not, it is apparent that in this case no such insurrection existed, that at the time it bears date, the legal authority of the county was in full operation. It is apparent that the officers of justice met with no difficulty in serving process and that the only matter which required remedy was that certain offences had been committed in secret and the perpetrators had not been detected. And the question is, whether the governor can make an insurrection out of a state of facts like that; and whether, having proclaimed insurrection, he has a right to go and arrest anybody that he happened to meet, no matter whom, and hold him in custody and make him atone for crimes which have been committed by others. But if the statute bears the construction for which the respondent's counsel contend, and he had authority to arrest according to his judgment, he should be impeached and removed from office for a gross abuse of that power. It is said the power was discretionary. Granted, for the sake of argument. If he abuses discretionary power he is as much liable to be impeached for it is as for any other maladministration: and it may involve greater criminality than other acts of malfeasance because of his taking advantage of a trust reposed in him to the injury of the people over whom he has been appointed to rule. He has a discretion to grant pardons; but, if he grants a pardon from a corrupt motive he is liable to be impeached for it. So a judge has a power to grant new trials; but if he grants one from a corrupt motive, he is liable to be impeached for it and to be expelled from office. So with all other public trusts constituting the offices of government. And here it is proper to remark that the claim set up in his answer at page 25, that his actions within what he conceives to be his constitutional sphere, are not to be questioned by any other department of the government, is a pretension altogether misapplied when he undertakes to assert it against the authority of this high court of impeachment. It reads:

"Further answering, this respondent says that the constitu-
"tion of North Carolina and the laws then in force, vested in
"the government thereof a discretionary power to declare a
"county to be in a state of insurrection, whenever in his judg-
"ment the civil authorities thereof were unable to protect its
"citizens in the enjoyment of life and property, that full faith
"and credit are to be given to the action of this respondent
"as governor of North Carolina in declaring as aforesaid
"the counties of Alamance and Caswell in a state of insur-
"rection, and he submits and insists that his said action cannot
"be questioned by any other department of the government."

I admit that any other department of the government in the usual course of administration will not call in question a pardon he grants. The judiciary will allow the pardon to be pleaded and give the individual the benefit of it; but they may call in question the motives under which the executive granted the pardon, and may find that exercise of power as great a crime as any man can commit in office. So they may call into question the necessary propriety or justice of his making proclamation of insurrection, of his sleeping over it for four months, and then proceeding with an army levied contrary to law, to arrest men of the highest character, on pretence of their complicity in crime, a charge, of the truth of which he has at no time adduced any proof, and oppressed and wronged them in the manner detailed by the evidence in this case. The representatives of the people upon impeachment have a right to question the exercise of the power of any officer whatever, it matters not whether it be a discretionary power or any other power. If they find its exercise has been attended with a corrupt motive, they have a right to treat it as a crime, and to punish it to the extent of the power of the impeaching court. I can only attribute the error into which the repondent's counsel has fallen in this particular, to the fact that the impeaching power has been so seldom brought into action under the government of this old and peaceful state. It is a position which cannot be maintained, and which is in contravention of the very groundwork on which the impeachments were founded in the cases of Judges Chase and Peck, and indeed of every impeachment that has been tried in this country. Nobody questioned the power of Judge Chase to make the ruling which he made in the case out of which arose the charges for which he was tried, though not convicted. Nobody questioned the mere power of Judge Peck to fine and imprison Mr. Lawless on the contempt imputed to him, but the majority of the senate were of opinion that the power had been improperly exercised—not a sufficient majority to produce a conviction it is true, but there was no doubt with any one that it was an impeachable offence if the motive was corrupt.

The respondent attempts to fortify his allegations that there was ground for proclaiming insurrections, by going on to make certain other charges against the people of both Alamance and Caswell, which he has utterly failed to make good by proofs.

He says in his answer: "That a majority of the white adult "male citizens of the said county of Alamance, and also of the "county of Caswell, including the sheriff of said county of "Alamance, were members of the Kuklux organizations afore-"said."

He has proved no such thing; not ten per cent. of the voters of Alamance, and none of the voters of Caswell, have been proved to have had any connection with such an organization. And as to those who had, it is proved by Jacob A. Long, the most intelligent and reliable witness of all those examined on this point, that the organization of the White Brotherhood was dissolved and disbanded in Alamance in May or June, 1869; that it contemplated no hostility to the government or resistance to the laws, and that its dissolution was occasioned by the fact that secret crimes had been committed which were charged on its members as the perpetrators. Almost all the secret offences proved were subsequent to the dissolution, and if not committed by others, under the name of kuklux, as in the case of the colored party under Allen Paisley, were done by parties in their several neighborhoods, without any general concert and, so far as appears, without any political design. And there is no proof that any such organization ever existed in the county of Caswell.

But there is another charge in this answer, a very grave one, made upon the whole people of these counties, which I am gratified to say has not been sustained by any proof. Dr. Johnson somewhere remarks that "He who accuses all man-"kind convicts himself." He who makes accusations against large bodies of people, will generally be found to be himself the author of a calumny.

"Grand juries refused to find true bills against members of "said organization," says this answer.

Where is the evidence of any such thing? You have had the solicitor of that circuit here, what did he prove? Why, that he sent a bill of indictment for a battery, by men in disguise, in one case, before a grand jury constituted of persons from both political parties of the county; and that it was returned not a true bill, and the foreman of the grand jury tells you that there was not a vote among all the members of the jury in favor of it. Now the respondent's accusation is, not that the grand jury *failed* to find true bills,—that is not what is charged in his answer,—but it would appear from this language that the solicitor had sent bills which he was entitled to have found true bills; and that they were returned not true. Sir, there is no evidence of any such thing—on the contrary, the prosecutor in the case of the bill which was ignored, Joseph Harvey, has been examined before this court and admitted here that he had been mistaken as to the identity of the parties charged by him with the offences in that bill. There has been no proof that any bill of indictment failed to be found a true bill which was sustained by proper evidence.

But the answer goes on thus:

"Or if perchance any were found against such members, petit juries refused to convict the same."

Is there an evidence of such a trial? Is there any pretence

of such a state of corruption as that in the counties referred to? Not the first particle.

"Magistrates failed to act."

Well, they appear to have had a pusilaminous magistracy in the town of Graham—in the persons of the two justices there, who say that they were afraid of personal consequences; but it must be remembered that the governor himself in the first place appointed magistrates for the county under the present system; and that his friends afterwards elected these, the only ones in the county who confessed that they were under fear. Yet they would not resign and give up their places to men who would do their duty. It is not, therefore, for him to complain of recreancy of his own appointees and special friends.

In a note to the old edition ot Marshall's Life of Washington—in the account of Shay's rebellion—there is mentioned a judge in Massachusetts, by name Cobb, who had been an officer in the revolutionary army. There was great excitement against judges and lawyers, and interruptions in many places to the holding of the courts. This judge, being informed that there was danger of a mob at a place where it was his duty to hold his court, and advised that it might be prudent not to attend, his propt reply was, "I am determined to sit as a judge or die as a general." Judge Marshall records this noble sentiment as worthy of the best characters in Plutarch, with evident satisfaction. That is the spirit that the judicial officers of this country must manifest if they intend to perform their duties to the people; and if they do not so intend let them give place to others who do and the majesty of the law will readily prevail.

These offices were not established as provisions for the incumbents, but to administer the law and preserve the peace of the community; and an unmanly fear is no more to be tolerated as an apology for failure in duty in these important civil trusts, than it should be in a soldier who deserted his post on the approach of danger.

Again, the answer continues:

"The judge and solicitor of the district attended the courts "merely as a matter of form."

I don't know what the judge would say to that. He has not been brought here, but we heard what the solicitor had to say, and he did not seem to think there had been any great cessation of justice in these counties. He said, there were many complaints of crimes committed by persons in disguise where he could not find evidence on which to found indictments. But to the question whether there were not also many complaints of arson, burglary, larceny and the like crimes done in secret where the perpetrators had not been discovered and prosecuted, his answer was, "Yes, a great many." "You could not find out who did them?" "No." So it was with these offenses. As to the soundness of the people of these counties, as to their integrity in the performance of their duties as jurors or in general as magistrates, there has been no proof of any thing to their disparagement except those two justices of the peace who testified to their own personal fear.

Mr. Stephen White, another justice and a republican in party association, though he thought the relations between the two races were not friendly but the contrary, yet says that he as a magistrate would at all times have issued a warrant against any man if his accusers had come forward and made complaint according to law.

The answer of the respondent goes on to say further,

"That a reign of terror existed and the administration of "justice was wholly impeded."

"In no one instance had the perpetrators of the crimes and "felonies herein detailed and set forth been brought to justice; "men, obnoxious to the illegal organizations aforesaid, dare not "sleep beneath their roofs at night, but abandoning their wives "and children wandered in the woods till day. Murder stalked "abroad in the land, and those whose hands were red with the "blood of their victims remained unnoticed and unpunished."

Meaning that they were known to the county, but that they

were not noticed or punished as criminals. This is all fine rhetoric, but what evidence have you heard of the facts alleged? Are they not all either invented or grossly exaggerated? It is not denied, and is far from being countenanced or approved by the managers or their counsel in this prosecution, that many illegal acts had been done by men in disguise in the county of Alamance, and a few in the county of Caswell, some of those in both counties being of great atrocity; and that being committed in secret, and usually under cover of night as well as under masks concealing the person, the offenders eluded detection and had not been prosecuted. But as to these grave imputa tations of corruption in the magistrates, in the grand and petit juries and the majority of the white inhabitants, so that justice could not be administered in the courts, and that known murderers or other offenders were stalking abroad without arrest or punishment, and that all this proceeded from a political combination to overthrow the government or to counteract its policy as regards the colored population, they are gross calumnies, wholly unsupported by proof.

Fortunately, senators, these things depend not upon what he has alleged, but what has been proved.

It is not proved that any secret organization existeds at all, in the county of Caswell, and it is not proved that in the county of Alamance it affected the administration of justice in the least degree.

No doubt some of the victims of secret violence may have been deterred by fear of further consequences from attempting prosecutions, who were innocent of any offence. These command the sympathy and would have commanded the ready assistance of all good men, upon prompt application for redress. There were others, according to their own acknowlement, and probably not a few, that have made no open admission, who conscious of their vices or crimes, and calculating the chances of their own punishment or exposure, concluded that it was best to submit without complaint.

Others again, I speak now exclusively of the colored people, taught by their leagues that all the whites not of their political party were their enemies, a delusion of which their demagogees will not allow them to be divested, made only a clamor among their immediate associates or in the leagues, who readily caught up the affair to be reported to the governor, a leaguer himself, to swell the list of outrages in the next proclamation; but they sought no vindication by law. Whereas if they could identify the offenders, and had appealed to any respectable neighbor, they might have found friends who would have advised and aided them in obtaining redress.

Henderson Coble, a respectable colored man, readily found such a friend in his neighbor, William Holmes, a former magisrate, and upon his advice readily found the means of bringing to justice and consigning to the penitentiary the colored band calling themselves Kuklux, who wore the disguises and *insignia* of the order, (led by Allen Paisley, a preacher, teacher and member of the Loyal League,) who had inflicted stripes upon him. But not so with the timid magistrates at Graham. Two or three cases are brought before them, where the offenders were successful in concealing their indentity, and all hope of success in such prosecutions is abandoned. "Nobody had been punished," though many offences were rumored to have occurred, say these sworn magistrates of the law, and therefore they determined to issue no more warrants in such cases. Did it never occur to them that our law requires the same activity on the part of those who have suffered injuries or claim its protection—diligence and determination on the part of the sworn conservators of the peace? Surely no offender ever will be punished unless some one is produced to prove the offence against a person charged with it according to law, and unless magistrates shall do their duty in arrest and commitment; nor can grand juries or petit juries perform their office in subjecting criminals to punishment unless evidence is procured of the crimes imputed. The real grievances which occurred in the counties in question, show great need of a reform in the agents of justice there, but none for ignoring the whole machinery of the civil law, as was by done the respondent, making a military expedition into these counties as hostile provinces and substituting his orders for law, in plain violation of the constitution.

The respondent seems to have set out in the execution of his high office with a morbid feeling of partizanship, and a disposition to convert every crime in the calendar which occurred after his accession to power into some kind of political hostility; and very ungraciously, I think, goes back to the protest of Governor Worth at the time he surrendered the office by the order of Gen. Canby, making a change in the government by the authority of congress and the elections held under its direction. True, it is disclaimed on the part of the counsel that any imputation was intended upon the memory of Mr. Worth. I don't think any such disclaimer is made by the respondent in his answer. Yet I think the people of North Carolina, of all parties, now that he has gone beyond the "bourne whence no traveller returns," will say that his action in office was eminently useful and just, and even his exit from it was patriotic and fearless. But when he yielded up the reins of authority, he did it in honor and good faith, and would, as would the friends he represented, have scorned any petty annoyances to regular government, and much less have plotted its overthrow by violence. The idea that any man, at this day, should be so mad as to suppose that the government of the state, and much more the government of the United States, could be overturned by force, is one that could enter into the mind of none except a person of diseased and distempered imagination. It is not within the range of any sane man's calculations. Besides, all who take a philosophic view of it, will, I think, agree that this republican system of ours, even though changes have been made in it that were distasteful to many of us, is now so much better than any other system existing in the world, that no man would think of changing it for an other or incurring the hazards of anarchy for its overthrow. On the contrary, the people expect to live under it, to abide by it, to give to their constitution a fair and honest construction, to reform it in the particulars in which it is not suited to their condition, but without contravening the late requirements of congress, or any curtailment of the rights of the colored race. This is the view of all intelligent men. And yet there is found throughout the respondent's answer a constant complaint, that the freedmen had not been allowed the free exercise of the right of suffrage; and that to secure it to them was a chief end of his military expedition. He states that "proclamation after proclamation has been issued." That is true. There have not been so many proclamations issued by a public functionary since the days of Henry VIII. And what do they contain? Do you ever see in them the word "arson," "burglary," or "larceny," or any offence except something that indicates oppression towards the colored people or to party men? No, sir. These proclamations are issued from time to time and there is complaint made that outrages are committed upon the person in many places.

Parenthetically it is thrown into one of them that the respondent understands there have been some burnings by *way of retaliation*, but the facts and dates are not given to show whether the personal injuries in the burnings were of prior occurrence. Both were great violations of the law, and an impartial magistrate, desirous only of the public peace, would have been very careful in his enquiries, before he assumed that the acts of incendiarism to which allusion is not very pointedly made, were consequences and not causes of the outrages upon persons, which is the only subject of serious denunciation. The proof was, that some of the homicides mentioned in the proclamations and in the answer, all unjustifiable as they were, were committed upon the persons of men accused of burning to ashes three barns in the same neighborhood and at the same moment of time.

Another object of great solicitude in these proclamations is, that all citizens, especially those of the colored race, should be secured in their right to vote as they chose: a privilege, the exercise of which, the reader would suppose, they were in great danger of being deprived. Now we have had a very searching investigation here. Has it been proved that any of the colored people have not been allowed to vote as they wished either in the county of Alamance or Caswell? On the contrary has it not been shown that they voted uniformly the republican ticket *en masse*, with rare exceptions to the contrary,—the very end for which they were marshaled into Leagues, of which the respondent was a High Priest?

This feature in the proclamations was merely one of the old devices of party to hold every colored man to his party-fealty and insure his attendance at the polls, by representing that his right to suffrage was threatened, but that the governor championed his cause. The pretext that an armed force was necessary to secure to the colored men the free exercise of their right of suffrage was as groundless as the calumnies upon the integrity of the grand and petit juries and the general administration of justice in those counties. You had before you, among the best witnesses for the defence, Wilson Carey, a colored member of the late legislature, from the county of Caswell. While he represents that the political feeling between parties was bitter, he at the same time admitted that the black race had the majority of voters in the county, and that they had voted as they pleased; that although some two or three white men, as he understood, had declared that they would employ no one who did not vote the conservative ticket, the elections in general had been fairly conducted, and no troops were needed on that account. It is equally apparent that there was no such necessity in the county of Alamance, where the only interference with elections shown was in the proscription of white men for voting on the conservative side. But let it never for a moment be forgotten that troops of the United States sufficient for any purpose of military aid were stationed in both counties before the arrival of Kirk.

The respondent, instead of devoting himself in his high office to those noble studies by which states are made prosperous and their people happy, seems to have considered himself as the occupant of a garrison in a hostile country, carrying on a warfare with a people who were seeking to overthrow the government by some illegitimate and rebellious means; when in truth and in fact, the hostilities he so much dreaded were not directed against the government, but against the men in power, of whom he was the chief, who had abused their trusts and perverted their power to the injury and well nigh to the ruin of their country. It was the people formed by a sense of enormous abuses on the part of public agents into a more powerful party than had ever before been seen in this state, attempting through the appointed means of an election, to apply the proper correctives, that he affected to consider an enemy in insurrection, requiring a military force under state authority for its suppression in June, July and August, 1870. As to secret outrages they had ceased in Alamance for three months: in Caswell there had been but few cases of the kind altogether, though some in each county had been atrocious assassinations: but the federal force was ample for any military need. Kirk's force, a state army under the command of the governor, was wanted for no purpose but to control the election and make a last desperate effort to preserve the ascendency of party. The dominion of parties in a republic, when elections are free, must often fluctuate; but the hope of the patriot is that the republic itself will endure. The party which formed and put in operation the federal constitution, at the end of twelve years, was ejected from power never again to be restored. And any like period of twelve years has witnessed very considerable changes in the successes or composition of parties. But the country itself has survived all these fluctuations: and looking back upon the past with the eyes of patriots, and not of partisans, we are obliged to confess, that in the main it has been wisely and happily governed. To ensure like results in the future, there must be, as in the past, before the convulsion of the great civil war, a sacred observance of two maxims, first, that elections shall be free and, second, that there shall be an honest acquiescence in the decision of majorities fairly expressed according to the provisions of the constitution, state or federal. These principles are so vital to republican government, that the party which shall resort to force to counteract them will only hasten its own destruction.

But to return to the act of assembly under which the governor had the power to declare a county in insurrection: as originally introduced we have seen there was a clause providing that application should be made to congress for a suspension of the writ of *habeas corpus*. The legislature of North Carolina could not abide that, and they struck it out. They authorized proclamation of insurrection to be made, and allowed the governor to call into service the militia in order to suppress the insurrection. But the act goes on to provide for a judicial trial, and never contemplated any other mode of trial.

By declaring that on motion of the solicitor of the district, or of his own will, the judge may order "the removal of the "trial of any person who has been, or who hereafter may be in-"dicted in any county in the state for murder, conspiracy or viola-"tion of an act entitled 'An act making the act of going masked, "disguised or painted a felony, from the county in which such "offence may have been committed to such other county in "his district or adjoining district as the solicitor may designate."

Granting, then, that after having declared insurrection, the governor had power to make arbitrary arrests upon his own order without warrant, what was to follow? Why certainly to deliver his prisoners over to the civil authority, where the solicitor could take them in hand and prosecute according to the directions of the statute, before a judge and jury in some impartial county. Is this the course he pursued? No, the very contrary. He avails himself fully of the power to make arbitrary arrests, if that was intented, of one hundred persons or more, but sends no one to be tried before a civil tribunal, and holds them all fast for his military judicature, and contemns the writ of *habeas corpus*, to enquire into his proceedings. What ground of pretence for authority does the statute afford for this effrontery and contumacy on the part of the respondent? Even when the privilege of the writ of *habeas corpus* is suspended in time of invasion or rebellion, a warrant of some kind is necessary to authorize arrests. This was demonstrated by Mr. Horace Binney, of Philadelphia, during the late war, when, aroused by the pretensions of the military power, he issued a pamphlet in defence of the right of the citizen to the privilege of *habeas corpus*, in which he demonstrated that the only effect of a suspension of the writ was to place the people of the country in the condition in which our English ancestors were before the passage of the statute of Charles II; that a warrant from some person in authority was always necessary in order to deprive a civilian of his liberty; that a suspension of the privilege of the writ in England was uniformly made by an act declaring that in cases where it appeared the arrest was made by the order of a Privy Counsellor or Cabinet Minister, or it may be some other functionary, there should be no further inquiry into the cause of detention. And Mr. Binney demonstrated, that the only effect of a suspension here, was to give a like consequence to a detention by order of the President of the United States. But no where is such a consequence attached to the orders of a governor of this state—the constitution forbids the suspension of the privilege of the writ under any circumstances. The statute in question, as originally, proposed, designed to procure it through the president, under the authority of congress; but this was stricken out on its passage. He is thus fully apprized, not only of the interdict in the state constitution, but that the legislature, composed in great majority of his party friends, had refused to ask for a suspension; but still eager to get out of the trammels of the declaration of rights and the constitution and to establish a reign of military law, he makes a direct appeal to the delegation in congress from this state in the following letter, dated 16th of March, 1870, which I will read:

"*To the Senators and Representatives in the*
"*Congress of the United States from North Carolina:*

"GENTLEMEN: I have been compelled to declare the county "of Alamance in a state of insurrection. I have called on the "president for aid, but he is restricted by the writ of *habeas* "*corpus*. We want military tribunals by which assassins and "murderers can be summarily tried and shot, but we cannot "have these tribunals unless the president is authorized to sus-"pend the *habeas corpus* in certain localities. Please aid in "conferring this power on the president as the only effective "mode of protecting life and property in Alamance and other "localities in this state."

On the day following he addresses this communication to Mr. Abbott, one of the senators, by telegraph, dated March 17th, 1870:

"What is being done to protect good citizens in Alamance "county? We have federal troops, but we want power to act. "Is it possible the government will abandon its loyal people to "be whipped and hanged? The *habeas corpus* should be at "once suspended, &c."

The congress, as might have been expected in a time of peace, did not grant the application, if any was made. But the respondent with full knowledge of the positive injunction in the declaration of rights, that the legislature of North Carolina had refused to ask any suspension, and that the congress of the United States, notwithstanding his importunity to its members, had failed to respond to his wishes, and in the absence of any pretence of authorization by the president, more than three months subsequently, when the county was in perfect tranquility, undertook himself, by mere executive orders, to make arrests, to hold his prisoners in defiance of the writ of *habeas corpus*, and wonderful to relate! actually proceeded to appoint a military commission to try them as prisoners amenable to military law.

In a letter in his own proper handwriting, among those found in the court house in Graham, dated July 17th, he informs Kirk that "there are more arrests to be made, but the "next list will be furnished to the judge advocate ; the court "will assemble on the 25th of July." Kirk, also, when served with the first writs of *habeas corpus*, told Mr. McAlister, who delivered the process, that "a court had been already appointed for the trial of the prisoners." But in a letter dated August 3d, 1870. introduced by the defence, the respondent addresses Kirk thus : "I should like to have the names of "officers in your regiment, who would be suitable, to compose "a part of the military court. The pending election and the "necessity for some of the officers to be absent on duty have "prevented the meeting of the court as early as I wished it. "It will meet one day next week. It is important to have "all the evidence that can be procured. The following "officers, besides those of your regiment, will compose the "court : Major-General W. D. Jones, Brigadier-General C. "S. Moring, Brigadier-General W. R. Albright, Col. H. M. "Ray, Major L. W. Hardin, Captain R. W. Hancock. This "will leave six to be supplied by your regiment, and the "court will consist of thirteen."

These, Mr. Chief Justice and senators, are the sages who are to supersede the judges and juries appointed by law for the trial of citizens accused of crime ; and their trial is to be conducted, not according to the doctrines of the bill of rights, of Coke, Foster or Blackstone, but by the laws and usages of war as expressed by Turenne or Vanbau, McComb or Halleck—authors who have doubtless been profoundly studied by these *improvised* heroes, some of whom were offered here as witnesses.

Such was the tribunal before which more than one hundred men were to have been tried for offences of the greatest magnitude, but of which they had had no specification up to the time they were delivered out of custody by the timely and beneficent interposition of the federal judge. To this end they had been suddenly and rudely seized and thrust into prison ; to this end they were denied bail, held in close confinement, except in a few instances of military parole, compelled to listen to the low and obscene songs and conversations of a rabble soldiery, who, in the language of one of the witnesses, seemed to be acquainted with civilization only in its vices of profane swearing and gambling; to hear the oaths and imprecations of the commander of the force, with threats to put them to instant death and to burn down their houses and destroy their women and children in certain contingencies, which he deemed of very probable occurrence. And when the respondent and his instruments in this most unlawful and wicked design against the lives and liberty of their victims, found themselves foiled in their purpose, as a last device of cruelty and revenge, a few of those most obnoxious to them were immured amid filth and vermin in a common jail, under the circumstances of indignity detailed in the evidence.

Now, has there been any justification shown for the conduct of the respondent, or even excuse? No citizen of the county of Alamance or Caswell had ever solicited or suggested the sending of such an expedition as a remedy for the outrages which had occurred in those counties. Upon the occurrence of the death of Outlaw, five citizens of Alamance communicated the intelligence to the governor, and recommended that a militia force should be called out from the county, and that Henry M. Ray should be placed in command of it. To this natural and appropriate suggestion he made no response. He was equally reticent in reply to two suggestions made in the letter of Dr. Pride Jones, accepting an appointment of captain of militia in the county of Orange, namely, that if his authority were intended to treat with the Leagues as well as the Kuklux, and into Alamance as well as Orange, he thought he could exert a beneficial influence. The governor, it has been shown, was a propagandist of the League, and therefore may have preferred to attend to that particular association himself; and as for the county of Alamance, he seems to have reserved it for a special and peculiar destiny. With a population of 11,000, it could probably have furnished two regiments of militia, independently of the colored men, now to be added to this organization. It might be objected, that from local causes, such as have been alleged by the respondent, it was not proper to call into service the militia of that county. Well, it has been proved that those who suggested this call were perfectly satisfied with the substitution of federal troops; and no one asked for any addition to this force of one well appointed company, which arrived early in March, within a few days after the murder of Outlaw. Their presence answered every purpose for which a military force could have been desired. With the exception of the case of the disappearance of Puryear, who is as likely to have come to his end by the hands of his own race as by those of the other, and by the connivance of his own family as probably as by that of any known enemies, violence and crimes ceased, and general tranquility prevailed. For the period of three months poor Outlaw and Puryear slept quietly in their graves, without so much notice from the executive as the common tribute of the offer of a reward for the detection of their murderers. Not until about the time of an assemblage of politicians at the governor's office to consult as to raising a state military force, was a proclamation issued, offering a reward of five hundred dollars, and then these cases were included in a collection of others, as if merely to swell the list of such occurrences in the state. Until this time, also, and indeed until the 15th of July following, it never was perceived that the proclamation of the 7th of March, declaring the county of Alamance in a state of insurrection, had had the least effect upon the rights of any of her citizens.

Mr. Chief Justice and senators, much has been said in the discussions of questions of evidence in this trial, upon the intention of the respondent in issuing these proclamations of insurrection, and justifying his arrests by reason of an imputed condition of insurrection therein. I insist, that a paper insurrection, like a paper blockade, amounts to nothing unless the author of it shows that he is himself in earnest in enforcing the consequences of the act he proclaims; and that from the evidence before this court, it is apparent that the respondent at the time he proclaimed the counties in question to be in a state of insurrection, did not believe them to be in that state; and that in fact they were not in such a condition; and that his subsequent trespass upon, and maltreatment of, their inhabitants, were wanton injuries designed to provoke resistance and justify the employment of force to control the election in August, 1870. This is manifest:

1st. From the long delay in treating the citizens of Alamance, especially, as if they were in a state of insurrection; permitting their unrestrained intercourse with other parts of the state; their courts to sit and dispense justice, and all the other conditions of a state of perfect peace.

2nd. From the presence of the United States troops and the absolute demonstration that there was no resistance to the law, nor reasonable ground for any apprehension of resistance.

3d. The ignoring entirely of the civil officers and setting them at naught, from the highest to the lowest; the appointing of a military commission to try the persons arrested, and the disregard and defiance of the writ of *habeas corpus* to carry this object into effect—an object which he had longed for and sought to effect lawfully at first, but which he at last had determined to carry out, with full knowledge of his want of any legitimate authority.

4th. From the character of Kirk and his troops, the last instruments that any sane official would have employed to promote peace. Instead of taking for a commander a man of character from among our own citizens, whose name would have inspired confidence in his purpose to do right, with a body of militia composed of respectable and orderly men, and appointing them to the duty of arresting prisoners and delivering them over to the civil magistrate, the introduction of a stranger with certainly the character of a brigand in this state, with an army composed in great part of foreign mercenaries, and of undisciplined and lawless recruits from the frontier of the state, was an insult and an offence to the pride, manhood and self-respect of the people, calculated to provoke the fiercest collision.

5th. From the savage appeal for recruits to the soldiers in the regiment he lately commanded in the civil war in the name of Kirk, but which we proved to have been written by the hand of the respondent himself. It was published in a placard in large letters and circulated through the country like a battle cry, awakening all the revengeful feelings of border warfare in the late great struggle: or perhaps even more like the war-whoop of the Indian calling his tribes to embark in an expedition in which they were to glut their vengeance in the blood of their enemies. The governor of the state, in the name of Kirk, exhorts the men of the old "second and third regiments," and such others as will enlist with them, to rally against "midnight assassins," yes, and "southern chivalry," the latter being terms of reproachful and contemptuous irony, intended to rekindle the bitter feuds and smouldering embers of sectional hatred. It is difficult to conceive an effusion of a more diabolical spirit and mischievous tendency than this production of the respondent, printed secretly at the *Standard* office in Raleigh, with its array of capitals and catchwords and fiery appeals, to be circulated in East Tennessee and a few counties in North Carolina, in which, during our recent war, the people of neighboring communities had met each other in deadly strife.

6th. The mischievous design of the whole proceeding is further manifest from the suppression and absence from the executive letter book and journals of the office of the adjutant general of all correspondence touching this insurrection, save two letters and one telegram: and the mysterious removal from the state, just after this impeachment was instituted, but a few hours before the telegraphic operators were summoned, of all telegraphic messages from the two stations at Raleigh and Company Shops, obviously to prevent their introduction as evidence. *Omnia presumuntur contra spoliatorem.*

Equally barren is the journal of the council of state, a body provided to advise the governor in the lawful execution of the duties of his office, of all information concerning this military movement. Their consultation or advice seems never to have been sought in any manner whatever.

7th. But certain letters found in the court house of Alamance, just after the departure of Kirk, give us a very full insight into the operations of the governor's mind on this subject. Commencing on the 17th of July, he says to Kirk:

"The company in Dallas, Gaston, will be under your com-"mand, W. S. McKee, captain. He will be mustered in "to-morrow. It will be well to let them remain in Gaston, as "their votes will be needed, and they can have control over "Gaston, Lincoln and Catawba."

"They can have control." What does that mean? That they will bring out the election as we want it.

"Twenty or thirty of your men should be sent to Shelby, "Cleaveland county, to keep an eye on Plato Durham's friends "and prevent intimidation of voters."

He has two objects in view, one to keep an eye on Plato Durham's friends, and the other to prevent voters from being intimidated; whether it is to keep the friends of Mr. Durham from going to the polls as well as to prevent intimidation of his own friends, we do not know; but the hint is sufficient to enable Kirk to construe it to suit his wishes.

The governor in this military correspondence of so essential and important a nature mingles a little politics. He says:

"Our friends in the mountain counties are very much con-"cerned about the loss of votes by the absence of your men. "Send as many as you can spare to Asheville, Marshall and "Burnsville so that they can vote and return. Some men "will be actually needed in Asheville and at Burnsville, to "ensure a free election."

"I would be glad to have a full report of—[rest of this para-"graph lost.]

"The lawyers are exhausting every expedient, but they will "fail. This is their last movement. It is important that the

" chief justice, who is substantially sustaining me, should be " very courteously treated in the person of his messenger.

" You can confide fully in Mr. Neathery, and I wish you to " send me list of prisoners and witnesses together with the " proof in each case.

Sir, he ought to be very much obliged to those lawyers. We see in the argument of Milligan's case that if he had proceeded with his military operations and put any one of those men to death, he would have been hanged for it, just as soon as any murderer guilty of that offence by the law of the land. In that argument is cited the case of Governor Wall, a British colonial governor in one of the West India islands, who undertook to supercede the civil by military law and caused a man to be tried by military commission and put to death. It is said that " the mill of providence grinds slowly but it grinds very fine." Twenty years passed by before it was ascertained in England that this act had been committed; but even after this lapse of time Governor Wall was brought home, tried, condemned and executed. And so it would have been had death been inflicted on any prisoner in this case; and so it ought to be with every man in official position who endeavors to supercede the laws of the land and institute other tribunals to take away the lives of men.

The character of the men arrested show that he had no purpose to detect criminals. If he had seized upon habitual breakers of the public peace, men of low morals and dissipated habits, who might without very violent presumption have been suspected of proneness to crime, there might have been some semblance of excuse for such a proceeding; but to go into a county and seize some of the very best men in the whole community, and who are recognized as such there and elsewhere in the state, evinces a most insane purpose to degrade the people of the country and to provoke strife. He professed that he was in quest of men belonging to those secret organizations and, as such, the authors or instigators of crime. Of the eighty odd men in Alamance whom Kirk arrested, I do not think a dozen are shown to have belonged to these organizations; and among those who did, with all the lights of subsequent disclosures, none are implicated, even by doubtful evidence, in any high crime or misdemeanor.

And the treatment that these prisoners received after they were arrested, shows the design of the respondent further to provoke and bring on strife, were it possible to accomplish it. He cannot disguise his motives by going into a tirade against the secret societies to which the managers in this prosecution and their counsel and the people whom they represent in the other house give no approbation or countenance whatever. He cannot conceal his motives in these transactions by the great zeal he manifests to suppress those organizations. The difference between him and them is but little. Both are gross violators of the law. It is said that "hypocrisy is the tribute which vice pays to virtue,"—secrecy is the tribute which crime pays to justice. They did not dare to come out in open day; they went about their operations in the night, under disguise and concealment; in that way they perpetrated their crimes, if as organizations they intended crime, and those who assumed their name and followed their example, acted in like manner.

But the respondent mounts a Kuklux on horseback, in the person of Kirk, with a rabble around him, with liberty to go forth and commit lawless acts upon the people in open day, under the authority of the highest officer of the state, and supported and paid out of the treasury of the people who are suffering this oppression. These are the points of difference between the disease and the remedy—the offenders and those sent in pursuit of them. The punishment of crimes against society is made a pretext for the overthrow of constitutional liberty, and the destruction of the freedom of elections. Such stratagems are among the old devices of tyranny. It is but a reproduction of the invention of Pisistratis who procured a force to guard his person from a feigned danger of assassination, but soon perverted it to make himself tyrant of Athens.

Men were arrested on a pretended suspicion of their particination in the murder of Outlaw whose names were upon lists, as it appears in evidence, furnished by the respondent, and were threatened with trial and execution by a military court appointed by his order, whom he is obliged to have known were above all suspicion of any such crime: And if his honor Judge Brooks had not opportunely brought the federal power to the relief of the people, or if the August election had not gone against the governor and his partisans, there is no telling how far this course of madness and folly would have been extended, or who would have been secure in liberty or in life. A system of vicarious punishment seems to have been resolved upon, and some offerings were to be sacrificed for the crimes that had been committed—it mattering nothing whether the victims were guilty or innocent.

Mr. Chief Justice and Senators, I have endeavored to expose the conduct of the respondent as being in palpable violation of the constitution and laws. I now proceed to show that his oppressions upon the people were effected by equally unlawful means: that Kirk's army was an unlawful force, both in view of the constitution of the United States, which inhibits any state to "keep troops or ships of war in time of peace," and of the constitution and laws of North Carolina. The only force permitted to be kept or in any way controlled by a state is a militia. The governor is, by the constitution, the commander-in-chief of the militia, and of no other force. He may "call it out to execute the law, to suppress riots or insurrection, and to repel invasion." The militia is to consist of "all able-bodied male citizens of the state of North Carolina, between the ages of twenty-one and forty years, who are citizens of the United States."

The general assembly has power to provide for organizing the militia; and an act authorizing the governor to effect an organization was passed on the 14th of August, 1868; but we have no information that the provisions of the act have ever been carried out. The act of the 27th of January, 1870, commonly called the Shoffner act, authorizes the governor to call into active service the militia "for the purpose of suppressing insurrection," &c. These are the only provisions we have in reference to the composition or the control of the militia. Now, do the troops of Kirk answer the description of militia of North Carolina? His whole force appears by the muster rolls to have amounted to 670 men.

1. Of these 399 were under twenty-one years of age, boys from 13 to 17, 18 and 19, who could not make a valid contract, and every one of whom might have been, at any time, relieved and discharged from service under *habeas corpus* if Kirk had not annulled and set aside the writ of *habeas corpus* for the time being.

2. Sixty-four were over the age of forty years.

3. Two hundred and over came from other states, nearly all these from East Tennessee, with sweepings from Virginia and South Carolina.

4. All the field officers at least were East Tennesseeans.

5. They were all reruited men, as we learn from the testimony of Colonel Clarke, signing similar articles to those prescribed for soldiers in the regular army of the United States, with a substitution of "North Carolina" for "United States."

In the required ages, and citizenship, and mode of enlistment of the men, and the domicil of the officers they had no pretension to the character of militia of North Carolina. They were called "North Carolina state troops," their officers always signing their orders or communications with an appendix of "N. C. S. T.," until Kirk, being subdued into some regard for the law, by the action of Judge Brooks, signed his returns to the writs of *habeas corpus* at Salisbury as "colonel of detailed militia of North Carolina."

It is to be distinctly observed also, that no commission has been produced to Kirk or any of his officers. Why? either because they had none, and were therefore to be regarded outlaws, or what is more probable, because the documents would have shown that they were not commissioned in the militia, but in a regular army raised by the respondent in North Carolina in disregard and defiance both of the constitution of the state and of the national government.

The levying of these troops was itself a great offence deserving of impeachment. Regular armies have been the instruments of usurpurs for the establishment of tyranny in all time. Hence the interdict on standing armies in the declaration rights, and the provision for "a well regulated militia," a force to be made up of citizens of the neighborhood, county, or state, having interests, feelings and sympathies, in common with people of whom they are required to be a part. When the adoption of the federal constitution was under consideration by the American people, the jealousy of standing armies was urged as a reason for not allowing to the president the command of the militia even when called into the service of the United States. In an article of the Federalist by Hamilton, a great soldier as well as statesman, in reply to this suggestion, he describes the true character of militia in these words:

"Where, in the name of common sense, are our fears to end "if we cannot trust our sons, our brothers, our neighbors, our "fellow citizens? What shadow of danger can there be found "in men who are daily mingling with the rest of their coun-"trymen, and who participate with them in the same feelings, "sentiments, habits and interests?"

Sir, did Kirk and his command occupy any such relationship as that to us? Were they people of North Carolina, were they men that expected to face the people after this war was over, and this campaign ended, and meet that public opinion by which more or less every man is affected in this country? Not they. They came here suddenly, and disappeared as suddenly. They had no interest in the state of North Carolina, and were no more to be considered as part of our militia than would be one of the regiments of federal troops that come here upon military service during the war, and returned again when the service was over. Besides, if they were a North Carolina militia, where are their commands now? Militia ordered out for a particular service remain militia still, and when the sevice is over they fall back into the ranks from which they went. But these were a band of foreign mercenaries brought here without authority of law, without any pretence to the character of militia, without sympathies or connections with the people of the state. The officering and organization of such a force was an insult to the entire militia establishment of the state, similar in its nature to that the respondent had cast upon the judiciary department, when he assumed that it was incapable of its duties and took its functions upon himself in making arrests, holding courts and executing sentences by his military authority alone. It was a remark of Mr. Calhoun, who for a long time presided acceptably over the department of war, that an officer who would submit to be overslaughed in the matter of promotion was unfit to serve under the flag of his country. That in a militia numbering not less than one hundred thousand men, no officers could be found in the state fit to command in any of the grades of field officers of this regiment, exhibits a depreciation of the officers by their commander-in-chief truly remarkable.

I neglected in the proper place to mention that the governor's intention in regard to this declaration of insurrection, and his subsequent oppressions of the people, were shown by the additional fact that when he was surprised by a writ from the federal judge he undertook to escape obedience, not by flat refusal, in defiance of consequences, as was his course with the state judiciary, but by seeking the shield of protection from the president of the United States. When he corresponded with the chief justice of the state, he said that he declined to permit the prisoners to be produced as commanded by the writ, but that in a short time he hoped he should restore the civil law in Alamance. He does not say that he expects even when civil law is restored to produce them before him, although he evidently designed that that should be understood. But when early in August, Judge Brooks issued his writ of *habeas corpus*, we find that the governor forthwith addresses a telegram to the president, and informs him that he has in custody certain prisoners charged in substance with murder; that the federal judge has no jurisdiction over murders in the state, and that his design is to resist, unless the federal troops shall come in aid of the marshal. The president referred the communication very properly to the attorney general. The attorney general advises that the governor submit himself to the process issued by Judge Brooks. Forthwith the governor opens his correspondence with the chief justice again; and then he discovers, for the first time, that it had been his design to bring these men before the chief justice from the beginning, and that the moment had now arrived when it could be done. What angel of peace had spread its wings over the land and enabled the civil magistrates again to perform their functions, when he had so recently suspended *habeas corpus*, and driven it out of use in the state, he does not say. But we see when we comes to look at the correspondence, what it was that moved him. He says he is going to bring them before the chief justice now, as he had designed to do before. Until then, he had never said that he had such an intention. His military court was the ordeal he had appointed for them. He had no purpose that they should go elsewhere, until driven from his position by the firmness of the federal judge. Then, to break the humiliation of his fall and cover his retreat, his private secretary is dispatched in his haste for the chief justice to return to the seat of government and receive returns which, but recently, the executive, with the high hand of power, had refused to allow. The chief justice came, but the prisoners having all made application to Judge Brooks, withdrew their petitions. It was then discovered that bench warrants were a process known to the law. Affidavits were made in a few cases, the process issued, citizens of Alamance and Caswell were arrested and the charges against them were examined without let or hindrance, as could have been done at any preceding time without the military or any demonstration of war. There was found to be no insurrection there;

yet there was just as much then as when Kirk's army entered the borders of those counties.

In looking back on those startling events, we have reason to be profoundly thankful that the people were not moved to resistance by all the persecutions to which they were subjected by the respondent. With the law on their side in all these collisions with Kirk and his men, so that if a citizen had been slain the crime would have been murder in them, while if one of them had fallen in the practice to their outrages, it would have been excusable self-defence, no one attempted to repel force by force, but every where there was submission, as if to lawful authority. And even those subjected to bodily torture bore it with heroic fortitude and patience, without being moved from their integrity or swerving from truth.

Their trust, next to that in an overruling Providence, was in the redress provided by the constitution of their country. That redress, senators, is in your hands. The same constitution which guarantees freedom from arrest except in the mode appointed by law; which declares the military subject to and to be governed by the civil power; which assures the privilege of the writ of *habeas corpus* as a right of which the the government of the state, in any and all of its departments, shall never divest a citizen; provides that for any infraction of these great and essential rights by officers entrusted with the powers of government, the remedy by impeachment is the mode of vindication. The house of representatives, by their board of managers and counsel have brought before you the high crimes and misdemeanors imputed to the respondent in his official capacity, and ask of you that judgment which should follow upon the proofs that have been made. They insist that he is guilty upon every one of the articles preferred; that the defence attempted, by proving that crimes had been committed in the counties he invaded, by persons unknown, in disguise and under concealment, afford no justification for his open and causeless arrest, imprisonment and mal-treatment of the innocent citizens who have made complaint, and of his wanton violation in their persons of almost every right secured by the constitution; that he is to be held responsible for the tortures by hanging and other abuses practiced by his lieutenant colonel, Burgen; the more especially since it appears that after these atrocities had all become public, and Burgen was held in prison to answer for them civilly or criminally, the respondent appears as his apologist or advocate in writing to the circuit judge of the United States to procure his liberation; that he is guilty of the arrest and cruel imprisonment in a felon's cell of Josiah Turner; of drawing large sums of money from the public treasury for the support of the troops, the instruments of his cruelties and usurpations, raised and set on foot without authority of law; and of defying and defeating the process of a court of justice issued to restrain the disbursement of public moneys not authorized by law.

*Judex damnatur quum necens absolvitur*—"the Judge is condemned when the guilty escape punishment."

Senators, the last bulwark against oppression by public agents or abuse of official authority is found in the constitution of this high court of impeachment. While no personal or political prejudice should be for a moment permitted to influence your determination against the respondent, I trust that no personal appeal, such as that made by the learned genman, [Mr. Conigland,] who opened the defence, nor any consideration of the consequences that may result from a just discharge of your duty will weigh with you for his acquittal. A fair and impartial but at the same time a fearless judgment, is alike due to yourselves and your country.

## THIRTY-NINTH DAY.

SENATE CHAMBER, March 16, 1871.

The COURT met at eleven o'clock, A. M., pursuant to adjournment, Hon. R. M. Pearson, Chief Justice of the Supreme Court in the chair.

The proceedings were opened by proclamation made in due form by the doorkeeper.

The CLERK proceeded to call the roll of senators when the following gentlemen were found to be present:

Messrs. Adams, Albright, Barnett, Battle, Bellamy, Brogden, Brown, Cook, Council, Cowles, Crowell, Dargan, Edwards, Eppes, Flemming, Gilmer, Graham of Alamance, Graham of Orange, Hawkins, Hyman, Jones, King, Latham, Ledbetter, Lehman, Linney, Love, Mauney, McClammy, McCotter, Merrimon, Moore, Morehead, Murphy, Norment, Olds, Price, Robbins of Davidson, Robbins of Rowan, Skinner, Speed, Troy, Waddell, Warren, Whiteside and Worth—46.

Senator McCLAMMY moved that the reading of the journal of proceedings of yesterday be dispensed with.

The CHIEF JUSTICE put the question on the motion of Senator McClammy, and it was decided in the affirmative.

Senator NORMENT. Mr. Chief Justice, I observe on looking over the published proceedings of the afternoon session of the thirty-sixth day I am not recorded as present. I was present at the session, and I presume the omission to record me was a clerical error. I ask that the fact of my presence then may be noted in the proceedings of to-day.

Mr. Manager SPARROW. Mr. Chief Justice, there is a matter in reference to some witnesses who were subpœnaed to attend on this trial, to which I have been requested to call the attention of the court. Those witnesses who were suppœnaed on behalf of the respondent were not sworn, and hence are not entitled to prove their attendance and get their pay. If they are to be paid, it will be necessary for the court to make some order in reference to them. I call the matter to the attention of the court, as it is not right that witnesses should be summoned and kept here for weeks, and then not be entitled to any compensation. I understand that all three are respectable colored men who can ill afford to lose their time and be on expense beside in attending on the trial.

Mr. BADGER. Mr. Chief Justice, the fact that the witnesses referred to by the manager were not called and sworn was an oversight on our part. Their names were not on the list that was handed to us, or they would have been sworn. The reason of the names not having been furnished us is this: The chief justice will recollect that in the attempt to trace the taking of certain colored men out of the jail of Orange county to men coming from Alamance, we failed because we were unable to show that certain roads in reference to which we proved that horses tracks had been followed connected with each other. These witnesses were called to prove the facts in reference to the taking of those men from the jail and their evidence became inadmissible in the absence of the preliminary proof.

Senator JONES. It seems to me, Mr. Chief Justice, that this is a matter to be disposed of not by the court but by the general assembly. If these witnesses are among those for whose payment provision was made by the general assembly, it is the duty of the clerk to certify them as such. But I do not understand that they are. If I am rightly informed in respect to that, to provide for their payment will require the joint action of the senate and house.

Senator MOORE. The witnesses might be sworn and allowed to stand aside and then they can prove their attendance and get their pay. I make that motion.

Senator GRAHAM, of Orange. I am informed that all of the witnesses referred to are not here. I shall oppose paying them unless certain white witnesses who were subpœnaed and not sworn shall also be provided for.

Mr. Manager SPARROW. I understand that this is an urgent matter with these men. They are here without money to pay their bills or to get away with.

The CHIEF JUSTICE put the question on the motion of Senator Moore, to allow the witnesses referred to be sworn, and it was decided in the affirmative.

Senator JONES called for a division of the senate on the vote.

Senator McCLAMMY. I understand that one of the witnesses has left the city.

Mr. GRAHAM. There were three who were in the city this morning. They live in my neighborhood and they applied to me to know what to do. I told them that the matter would be brought to the attention of the court, and I presumed there would be no difficulty in having their compensation provided for.

The CHIEF JUSTICE announced the pending question to be the motion of Senator Moore to allow the witnesses to be sworn.

Senator WORTH. I desire to know, before I vote, whether the motion of the senator from Craven [Mr. Moore] includes all of the witnesses who have not been sworn, some twenty I understand, or those referred to by the manager? I think it is important that we should cover the whole ground in the action which we take.

Senator GRAHAM, of Orange. I offer this resolution as a substitute for the motion offered by the gentleman from Craven:

*Resolved*, That all witnesses who have been summoned on either side in the impeachment trial be allowed to prove their attendance and be paid out of the treasury.

The ayes and noes were called and a sufficient number seconding the call they were ordered.

The CLERK proceeded to call the roll on the adoption of the resolution offered by Senator Graham, of Orange, as a substitute for the motion of Senator Moore, and it was decided in the negative by the following vote:

Those who voted in the affirmative are :

Messrs. Barnett, Bellamy, Cook, Cowles, Currie, Dargan, Eppes, Flemming, Gilmer, Graham of Alamance, Graham of Orange, Hawkins, Hyman, King, Latham, Lehman, McCotter, Moore, Murphy, Olds, Price and Speed—22.

Those who voted in the negative are :

Messrs. Adams, Albright, Battle, Brogden, Brown, Council, Crowell, Edwards, Jones, Ledbetter, Linney, Love, Mauney, McClammy, Merrimon, Morehead, Norment, Robbins of Davidson, Robbins of Rowan, Skinner, Waddell, Warren, Whiteside and Worth—24.

Senator BROGDEN moved to reconsider the vote just taken.

Senator LOVE moved that the motion to reconsider be laid on the table.

The CHIEF JUSTICE put the question on the motion of Senator Love, and it was decided in the affirmative.

The question then recurred on the motion of Senator Moore to permit the three witnesses to be sworn.

Senator ROBBINS, of Rowan, called for the ayes and noes.

A sufficient number seconding the call, the ayes and noes were ordered.

The CLERK proceeded to call the roll of senators on the adoption of the motion of Senator Moore, and it was decided in the negative by the following vote :

Those who voted in the affirmative are :

Messrs. Bellamy, Brown, Cook, Cowles, Dargan, Eppes, Gilmer, Hawkins, Hyman, King, Latham, Moore, Murphy, Olds, Price, Skinner, Speed and Warren—18.

Those who voted in the negative are :

Messrs. Adams, Albright, Barnett, Battle, Brogden, Council, Crowell, Currie, Edwards, Flemming, Graham of Alamance, Graham of Orange, Jones, Ledbetter, Lehman, Linney, Love, Mauney, McClammy, McCotter, Merrimon, Morehead, Norment, Robbins of Davidson, Robbins of Rowan, Waddell, Whiteside and Worth—28.

The CHIEF JUSTICE. The court is ready to proceed with the hearing.

Mr. BOYDEN. Mr. Chief Justice and senators, I regret to state that I am extremely unwell, so much so that I do not think it will be possible for me to proceed with my argument to-day. It is the first time in forty six years that I ever found myself ill during the trial of a cause. At this moment I am suffering from high fever, and I would be very glad if I could be indulged by an adjournment of the court until to-morrow morning.

Mr. GRAHAM. By all means, sir, so far as the managers are concerned.

On motion of Mr. Graham, of Orange, the court adjourned to meet to-morrow at eleven o'clock, a. m.

# FORTIETH DAY.

SENATE CHAMBER, March 17, 1871.

The COURT met at eleven o'clock, pursuant to adjournment, Hon. R. M. Pearson, Chief Justice of the Supreme Court, in the chair.

The proceedings opened by proclamation made in due form by the doorkeeper.

The CLERK proceeded to call the roll of senators, when the following gentlemen were found to be present:

Messrs. Adams, Albright, Allen, Barnett, Battle, Bellamy. Brogden, Brown, Cook, Council, Cowles, Crowell, Currie, Dargan, Edwards, Eppes, Flemming, Gilmer, Graham of Alamance, Graham of Orange, Hawkins, Hyman, Jones, King, Latham, Ledbetter, Linney, Love, Mauney, McClammy, McCotter, Merrimon, Moore, Morehead, Murphy, Norment, Olds, Price, Robbins of Davidson, Robbins of Rowan, Skinner, Speed, Troy, Waddell, Warren, Whiteside and Worth—47.

Senator JONES moved to dispense with the reading of the journal of proceedings of yesterday.

The CHIEF JUSTICE put the question on the motion of senator Jones, and it was decided in the affirmative.

Mr. BOYDEN, on behalf of the respondent addressed the court. He said:

MR. CHIEF JUSTICE AND SENATORS:

I desire to tender my sincere thanks to the members of this court for delaying the trial by the unanimous vote of its members, in deference to my illness yesterday. I am still feeble, which I regret more on account of my client than from any other consideration; but I trust I will be able by deliberation to fully present my views to the court.

I have a very difficult task to perform. First, I have to justify and to defend military law, in doing which every man speaks to a disadvantage. It is very pleasant to discourse before such an intelligent body as this, and before the country on the great privileges secured to the citizens of the United States and of the state of North Carolina, by those noble principles contained in the federal constitution, and in the bill of rights of the constitution of North Carolina, and to uphold the importance of their preservation to the community. But I have a task to perform directly to the contrary of that. I hope to do it with candor, and to satisfy this court that the views which I shall present are impregnable.

Then there is another part of my duty which has reference to myself and my own feelings. I came to North Carolina nearly half a century ago, without friends or money. I was kindly taken by the hand by the citizens of the good old state and during my whole experience here I have been treated with kindness and consideration, perhaps more than I deserved; and for this I trust in God I shall ever feel grateful. I have never regretted the selection of North Carolina as my home. The people of the state I have found much to my idea of a great, noble and generous people; but though I selected North Carolina for my home, and have entertained for her people this sentiment of love and gratitude, I have not forgotten the land of my nativity, and have never failed to entertain that same deep attachment that every man may be supposed to feel for the home of his childhood and youth. With a flood of fond memories of the people of North Carolina, and with sentiments of affection binding me still to them, it becomes my duty in my relation as counsel to the respondent to hold up to the court and to expose to the world, one of the most wicked and infamous organizations against the peace and good order of society within our state that ever existed in any country; that I have to expose the existence and character of such an organization in our midst, to public scorn and indignation, may well be supposed to be a disagreeable task, but I shall not shrink from any duty. I am a very plain and blunt man, and I often speak in a way, I know, which seems harsh and discourteous, but I wish to say to the court, many of whose members I have known long and well, and for whom I have a high regard for their intelligence, honesty and uprightness, that if I shall say anything in the heat of argument derogatory to any member of the court or to the learned counsel for the managers, it will be unintentional. Nothing could be more agreeable to me, as one of the counsel for the respondent, than to have opposed to me such learned and courteous gentlemen as have been associated with the learned managers in the prosecution of the trial.

The first topic, Mr. Chief Justice and Senators, which I desire to discuss, is the power not only in England at this day, but in the United States and in each of the several states under certain circumstances, to declare martial law, and after discussing that I shall then attempt to satisfy the court as to what is the effect upon any locality and the citizens thereof after martial law has been declared. I maintain and I expect to establish it by the highest authority, that this power of declaring martial law necessarily exists in every community, and that in no country is it more important than in the United States and in the several states of this great republic.

It is said, Mr. Chief Justice and Senators, as I understand the argument of the gentleman who last addressed the court [Mr. Graham] that the power to declare martial law does not exist this day in England; that it does not exist now under the government of the United States, and that it does not exist in the state of North Carolina. I think that in this view the learned gentleman is laboring under a great mistake, and this I trust I shall be able to show by authority to the satisfaction of the court.

I admit that in ordinary times the declaration of martial law should not be resorted to, and when resorted to, it has always been and should be in times of overruling and paramount necessity. It is said that within our state there was no insurrection. But the case for the respondent, sir, it will be remembered, does not stand alone in the idea of insurrection. It is said that nothing amounts to an insurrection but that of an open, armed force attempting to resist the laws of the country. That insurrections usually are of that character no one will deny; but no authority has been produced, and no authority, in my judgment, can be produced to show—when numerous organizations have been formed amounting in the aggregate to thousands of lawless men, banded together to take the law into their own hands and to punish any man, white or black, who has fallen under their displeasure by reason of his political course or moral character, and when this very same organization proclaim themselves the authors of scores of outrages, whippings, scourgings and murders, within the limits of a county, in visiting vengeence upon men and women, and when they have gone to the length of establishing such a condition of terrorism throughout the county, that no poor colored or even white man's house is safe from invasion at the dead hour of the night. I say that when such a condition of society is shown, no authority can be found which will say—that military power may not be invoked to insure the lives and property of the people.

Look at the organization at Graham, in the presence of one of its former chiefs and six or eight others, assembled to carry out one of its decrees, and when this very chief testified here that he was afraid to interfere, to prevent a scene of outrage and murder! Sir, what must have been the fear of other citizens of the county, and especially of republicans, when they saw an array like this in that town? What must have been their fear and dread when a former chief of the whole organization in the county of Alamance dared not lift up his voice to prevent these assassins and cut throats from the perpetration of the murder of poor Outlaw?

Again, at Company Shops, a respectable white woman leaves her home at night, in the streets, screaming for help, her face covered with blood; she is seen by numerous citizens who are aroused from their slumbers by her cries of murder. She tells them of the seizure of her husband by these cowardly wretches in disguise, and yet not a human being dares to follow or attempt to find out the scoundrels engaged in this infamous outrage upon her husband--a crippled white man who had been guilty of what? Is there any senator that has any doubt for what? He had invited a poor colored boy to enter the house of God to hear its pastor call all men to cease their ways of wickedness and to learn and pursue the path of the righteous, that they might be prepared to appear at the alter of that God before whom we are all to account and who has no respect for color or position. That was one offence of Corliss; but he was guilty of another which brought down upon him the decree of this mysterious court of assassins and man-whippers. Corliss, in spite of the prejudices existing on the subject, undertook to teach colored children to read and write and to instruct them in those principles of religion and of government which would tend to make them better and more useful citizens. That was another offence which called for the interposition of this self-elected and self-constituted court, "wise above what is written," and so indifferent to the praise of the world as to modestly seek to be unknown in the annals of judicial decision, though their adjudications were novel and their acts in executing their own decrees manly and brave!

Sir, look back to before the days of the rebellion. Was it ever heard that a slave might not enter the church of God with his master or with any other man, and there to bow together before God and worship him? And does not the fact of Corliss being whipped for inviting a colored boy into a church denote a sad change in the state of public feeling among portions of the white community against colored men and against northern men? I ask senators to dwell with great deliberation before they make up their verdict upon this view of the case which I have presented.

I shall have occasion hereafter to recur to this subject, and to facts which are somewhat similar; but before I do it, I desire, as well as I can, in my feeble state of health, to establish the proposition with which I started, that in England, the United States, and in all the states of the Union, there is the power to declare martial law in those cases where extreme necessity may require it, and that when so declared no civil process can run into such a locality.

In the first place, Mr. Chief Justice and Senators, I shall recur to the case of *exparte* Milligan, reported in 4 Wallace, which has been relied upon by the managers, as I understand it, to establish an entirely different doctrine. I desire, lest all the senators may not have read that case, to read citations from it. What was that case? During the rebellion, while the war was still raging, there was a power vested in the president to arrest and to detain military prisoners under an act of congress. The authority was to arrest and detain. If a prisoner was arrested twenty days before the sitting of the federal court, in the district where the arrest was made, he was to be detained until that federal court had met and adjourned, and if the court took no steps whatever to prosecute these military prisoners, what was to be done? The law expressly provides that in such a case the prisoner had a right, under that very act of congress, to petition a judge of the federal court to take him out of military custody and to discharge him altogether or bind him over to the federal court, as the circumstances of his case might require. When the court met Milligan had been detained some sixty days instead of twenty. The court took no notice of his case, and although it was made the duty of the military officers who held any such military prisoner to report the case to the court, solicitor or district attorney, no such report was made whatever. No notice was taken of Milligan's case in any shape, and of course under the act of congress he had a right to petition a federal judge or the court for his discharge. But the military, notwithstanding this plain provision of the law, expressly provided for that very case, went on and appointed a commission to try Milligan, and that court condemned him to suffer death—exactly what they had no right to do. The law had provided expressly that a prisoner thus arrested, when court met, was to be taken out of the hands of the military and be turned over to the civil tribunals; and if the federal court took no action in his case, he had the right to make his application for a discharge as I have stated.

Now, Mr. Chief Justice and Senators, congress had not declared Indiana in a state of insurrection. In the locality where Milligan had been apprehended and detained no proclamation of insurrection had been made. The courts were open ready to try all militaay prisoners that had been apprehended twenty days before they met; and the court not having tried his case, not taken any notice of it, it was Milligan's right to file a petition to be taken out of the custody of the military and be discharged or bound over as the case might requre. That is all there is in that case, and it went to the supreme court upon these points and upon these points alone; and let me say that every member of the court concurred in every fact and every position of law entitling Milligan to his discharge.

There was no division of sentiment in the court as to any fact or point of law necessary to the decision of the case. What took place? Why, after deciding the cause and all concurring, Mr. Justice Davis, and four of his associates who concurred with him, thought proper to go into a long and learned discussion touching the provisions in the constitution of the United States for the protection of the lives, liberties and property of its citizens—those provisions forbidding arrests without warrants, and among them the writ of *habeas corpus*—which has come down to us from our ancestors and has been maintained in the United States and every state of the Union. But this learned and able discussion was entirely outside of the case before the court—it was mere *obiter dicta*; and, sir, there is nothing better settled in North Carolina, than that, no matter how much is said by the court touching points which have nothing to do with the discussion of the cause, it is not authority. It decides nothing.

Nevertheless, Mr. Chief Justice and Senators, the opinion of Mr. Justice Davis and those who concurred, is the opinion of learned, upright and intelligent jurists, and is entitled to consideration before this learned court; but not being decisions, but mere *obiter dicta*, such opinions are not binding in any court, and should be no authority, except so far as by reason and agreement they appeal to the intelligent understanding of men.

But, sir, what else does this case show? It shows that that learned jurist, Chief Justice Chase, and three of his learned associates, to prevent any misapprehension as to their views of the law, thought proper to deliver their sentiments touching these very points, out sideof the case. And, sir, we say on behalf of the respondent that the judges who joined in the opinion of the chief justice, are as learned jurists, as honest, as intelligent as those who joined in the opinion delivered by Mr. Justice Davis, and therefore, that their opinions are entitled to the same weight before this court on matters outside of the points really adjudicated, as the opinion of Mr. Justice Davis and those who concurred. And, sir, I expect to satisfy this court, beyond all question, from the very highest authority, that the opinion which they delivered in that case is the settled law of the United States. If the majority of the court, in their opinion, meant to declare that in times of great emergency congress could not authorize the president to declare a locality in a state of insurrection, and to authorize military commissions to try and punish any insurgents, which I think a deliberate and careful reading of their opinion will satisfy every senator that the court did not so intend to decide, but if they did, I say they utterly mistook the law.

I desire now to call to the very deliberate attention of this learned court, in which I see many senators capable of occupying with honor to themselves and to their country the very highest judicial position in the land, to the case of Milligan, and to what the learned chief justice said in the opinion which he delivered. I begin at the last paragraph of page 140 of 4 Wallace Reports, and including the opinion of the chief justice from that point to the close:

"We cannot doubt that, in such a time of public danger, "congress had power, under the constitution, to provide for the "organization of a military commission, and for trial by that "commission of persons engaged in this conspiracy. The fact "that the federal courts were open was regarded by congress "as a sufficient reason for not exercising the power; but that "fact could not deprive congress of the right to exercise it. "Those courts might be open"

And I want senators to notice this particularly. I shall have occasion to comment upon it at great length hereafter.

"Those courts might be open and unrestricted in the execu-"tion of their functions, and yet wholly incompetent to avert "threatened danger, or to punish, with adequate promptitude and certainty, the guilty conspirators."

Senators, go with me to the county of Alamance; go to the houses of the poor colored men at midnight, where they are resting with their wives and little ones around them; here they are seized by this band of armed assassins who enter their peaceful dwellings by scores, drag them to the woods. tie them to trees, strip their bodies and whip them as they would hesitate to whip a brute. Yes, in some cases they have not been satisfied with whipping, but have gone on to murder, and this thing has been persisted in for two, three or four years. And. sir, what do the records of the courts of Alamance and Caswell show? Not a solitary violation of law by this band of assassins has ever been punished. I ask senators if the opinion of Chief Justice Chase is not applicable here? Does the fact of having the courts open, and in the exercise of their usual functions, show that these tribunals answer their purpose? I appeal to every senator if the proof of the outrages committed by this cowardly association is not sufficient to satisfy every one that. so far as these organizations are concerned, the arm of the civil power had become utterly powerless, and that there was no means of punishing any one of these vile conspirators? Are senators prepared to say that these things were to go forward; that these vile deeds were to be perpetrated night after night by these cowardly assassins with no power to interpose to protect the unoffending citizens? What glorious and noble deeds!

Seventy-five or a hundred men of the intelligent Caucasian race go forth to the humble dwellings of a poor colored man and drag him from his house. Brave men they be, four score armed with pistols and guns, go forth to conquer one unoffending negro! They dare even to make a night attack. They storm him in his castle; he is taken by surprise. His aged mother only being near to come to his aid, with all her might she tries to beat back the villains and she is knocked down and stamped upon. Her son is taken from his little children, carried off to a tree in full view of the court house, that they might show their contempt for the civil authority, and there he is hung by the neck until he is dead! dead! dead! Brave men indeed, they be, and they should be immortalized in history! Yes, sir, they hanged him before the court house door to show their contempt for all the civil authority of the country. Though they did conceal their persons, they had no intention to conceal their iniquities. They desired it to be proclaimed on the house tops and in the streets that these cowardly deeds were done by men of the brave and noble Kuklux Klan!

Begging pardon for this digression, I will go on with the ballance of this opinion of Chief Justice Chase.

"In Indiana, the judges and officers of the court were loyal "to the government. But it might have been otherwise. In "times of rebellion and civil war, it may often happen, indeed, "that judges and marshals will be in active sympathy with the "rebels, and courts their most efficient allies."

Let me stop here a moment, senators, and ask if you have a recollection of a man by the name of Murray, who is sheriff of Alamance, and who says he was chief of one of these camps of conspirators? Yes, sir, and the night before Outlaw was hung at sunset that perjured wretch was in Graham. For what? I leave it for senators to judge. And, sir, there has been proven here another fact, called out by the prosecution, that he even had a deputy that belonged to this organization of chivalric and brave conspirators. And two or three magistrates in the county were in active fellowship with this organization of cut-throats and assassins. Well might Chief Justice Chase remark that judges and marshals might be in active sympathy. But let me read further:

"We have confined ourselves to the question of power. It "was for congress to determine the question of expediency. "And congress did determine it. That body did not see fit "to authorize trials by military commission in Indiana, but "by the strongest implications prohibited them. With that "prohibition we are satisfied, and should have remained silent "if the answers to the questions certified had been put on "that ground, without denial of the existence of a power "which we believe to be constitutional and important to the "public safety,—a denial which, as we have already suggest- "ed, seems to draw in question the power of congress to pro- "tect from prosecution the members of military commissions "who acted in obedience to their supreme officers, and whose "acting, whether warranted by law or not, was approved by "that upright and patriotic president under whose adminis- "tration the republic was rescued from threatened destruc- "tion."

"We have thus far said little of martial law, nor do we pro- "pose to say much. What we have already said sufficiently "indicates our opinion, that there is no law for the govern- "ment of the citizens, the armies, or the navy of the United "States, within American jurisdiction, which is not contained "in or derived from the constitution. And wherever our "army or navy may go beyond our territorial limits, neither "can go beyond the authority of the president or the legisla- "tion of congress."

Lest I should forget it, I desire here, Mr. Chief Justice, to make a few remarks upon what I regard as a grand mistake which seems to prevail among some, touching a locality declared in a state of insurrection, and what is called the suspension of the writ of *habeas corpus.* I fully concur with the doctrine laid down by the learned gentleman, [Mr. Graham,] who addressed us the day before yesterday—that the suspension of the writ of *habeas corpus* does not authorize the arrest of any man without a warrant, sued out under oath. There never was a greater mistake. And permit me to say that the respondent doubtless fell into this error. It would seem from the letters and telegrams that have been exhibited here that such was the fact, and I am not surprised that he should have so misunderstood the law, as to suppose that although he had declared marshal law in the counties of Alamance and Caswell, unless the writ of *habeas corpus* was suspended, these men might be taken out of custody of the military by the judicial power of the state. and handed over to the judicial tribunal for trial. There never was a greater mistake than that. The declaration of martial law, Mr. Chief Justice and Senators, places at once every citizen, high or low, rich or poor, peaceable or belligerent—every member of society, under the military power: and the judicial power of the state has no sort of authority in such locality and neither the chief justice nor any other judge has any authority to issue a precept to run into any locality declared in a state of insurrection. And, notwithstanding all that has been said in North Carolina against the chief justice in not going further, it will turn out in this investigation that he went beyond his authority; and I am happy to state that upon this subject the opening argument of the learned and distinguished manager [Mr. Sparrow] admits, in so many words, that a writ of *habeas corpus* does not run, and no civil process can run into a locality declared in a state of insurrection.

I admit the opening speech of the distinguished gentleman on the part of the managers is an able and learned one. But, sir, he was forced after having looked into the authorities to admit what is clearly established by all the authorities, that no civil process runs into a locality declared in a state of insurrection. He says:

"Martial law suspends all civil authority, and therefore the "writ cannot run."

I am happy, Mr. Chief Justice, that upon this great question in the cause we are not at issue. We agree on both sides.

There is no getting out of that—that if martial law is declared it suspends all civil authority. I trust, senators now see that all this talk about the writ of *habeas corpus* and about arresting men in the counties of Alamance and Caswell without legal warrant, falls at once to the ground, provided martial law was proclaimed.

But, gentlemen, do they try to get over it anyhow? They say that the governor had no right to make such a proclamation—that there was no insurrection. We are not now upon the question of the right to make the proclamation, but we shall be after a while. We are now upon the question of fact—was an insurrection declared? The governor did declare the counties ot Alamance and Caswell in a state of insurrection, and what does that mean? Why, it has been greatly misunderstood by the people, and I fear by some members of the senate also. And, Mr. Chief Justice, I am free to admit here for myself, that until the investigation in this cause, I have been laboring under the same misapprehension. I shall, before I close, read ample and abundant authority to show the correctness of what the learned manager admitted in his argument. I shall be able to show that the declaration of insurrection not only suspends all ordinary law, but it suspends all those provisions in our constitution and our bill of rights for the protection of the lives, the liberties and the property of the citizen. Yes, sir, the declaration of martial law in any locality overrides all ordinary law, and the provisions in the constitution; and I wonder not a little how it could be supposed that those clauses in our bill of rights which declare that no man shall be apprehended except by warrant under oath, and that no man shall be deprived of his life, liberty, or any of his rights, unless by the law of the land, could be suspended by a declaration of insurrection made by the governor, and that a person might be arrested contrary to those provisions, and yet the respondent be bound to obey a writ of *habeas corpus* issued into such locality. No, sir, the very act of declaring a locality in insurrection suspends all civil jurisdiction. The courts have no power in any shape to meddle with any man, or to issue any process into the locality declared by the proper authority in a state of insurrection; and, sir, what is more than that, it is clearly laid down in the books that when this declaration is made by the proper authority every department of the government is bound thereby, and every citizen is bound to take notice of it and conduct himself accordingly.

And that is not all, sir. When this proclamation of a state of insurrection is once made by the proper authority, it is clearly settled in the books that this identical state of insurrection continues until this same proper authority, to wit, the executive or legislative department of the government, has declared that there is an end of this insurrection. That is the law that I expect to establish.

And here I will take this occasion to reply to an authority—a Pennsylvania case reported in the American Law Register, and read by the gentleman who last addressed the court. I have not the case before me, but it is well settled, as many senators will recollect, that when a state of war during the rebellion—was declared—it continued until the proper authority, the executive or the congress of the United States, the political part of the government, declared it had ceased. Yes, sir, this judge in Pennsylvania had no authority to examine into the condition of the country, and to say whether the war was at an end or not. In law every court in the United States, state or federal, was bound to regard the state of war as existing, although there might not have been a man in arms against it, until the president or the congress of the United States declared it at an end. I am glad that upon this subject I am addressing lawyers quite as learned as the judge in Pennsylvania, and just as competent to pronounce the law as he was, and when they know that that point is perfectly settled, I have a right to expect, and do expect they will be governed by the authorities.

I read further from the opinion of the chief justice in the case of Milligan:

"There are under the constitution three kinds of military

"jurisdiction, one to be exercised both in peace and war, "another to be exercised in time of foreign war without the "boundaries of the United States, or in time of rebellion and "civil war within the states or districts occupied by rebels "treated as belligerents, and a third to be exercised in time of "invasion or insurrection within the limits of the United "States, or during a rebellion within the limits of states "maintaining adhesion to the national government, when the "public danger requires its exercise. The first of these may "be called jurisdiction under military law, and is found in the "acts of congress prescribing rules and articles of war, or "otherwise providing for the government of the national "forces; the second may be distinguished as military govern- "ment superseding as far as may be deemed expedient the "local law, and exercised by the military commander under "the direction of the president, with the express or implied "sanction of congress. While the third may be denominated "martial law proper, and is called into action by congress or "temporarily, when the action of congress cannot be invited, "and in the case of justifying or excusing peril by the presi- "dent in times of insurrection or of civil or foreign war within "the district or locality where ordinary law no longer "adequately secures the public safety and private right."

This is the law which we say existed in Alamance and Caswell at the time of the arrest of all these prisoners; and we say here most emphatically, and I think there is not a senator within the sound of my voice but what must be fully and thoroughly satisfied, that the "ordinary law was no longer adequate to secure the public safety or private right in the county of Alamance or Caswell"—I say most emphatically, in my judgment, every senator must acknowledge that was the condition of things in both those counties.

"We think that the power of congress, in such times and in "such localities, to authorize trials for crimes against the "security and safety of the national forces, may be derived "from its constitutional authority to raise and support armies "and to declare war, if not from its constitutional authority "to provide for governing the national forces."

"We have no apprehension that this power, under our "American system of government, in which all official authority "is derived from the people, and exercised under the direct "responsibility to the people, is more likely to be abused than "the power to regulate commerce, or the power to borrow "money, and we are unwilling to give our assent by silence to "expressions of opinion which seem to us calculated, though "not intended, to cripple the constitutional powers of the gov-"ernment, and to augment the public dangers in times of inva-"sion and rebellion."

I hope all that I have said in reference to the Milligan case will be perfectly understood. I respect and I fully concur in the authority of the case, so far as it is an authority, and so far as it touches any point in that case necessary to a final adjudication of the question involved. But the opinion of the learned majority touching points not necessarily involved in a decision of the case, is not an authority in law, though it may be entitled before this learned assembly to much weight on account of the learning and talents of those exalted jurists who concurred in this opinion outside of the decision in the case. But I do think, and I expect to establish by high authority, that they were certainly in error if they intended to decide what has been urged by the counsel of the managers, which I certainly do not admit, and I expect to satisfy every man that the opinion of the minority on the question not necessarily involved in the decision of the case, is the law of the United States at this day.

I will now proceed to the other authority to establish my position, and will read from Bishop's Criminal Law, volume 1, chapter 4, sections 52 to 64. I have had occasion heretofore to bring that authority before the court in an argument that took place at an early stage of this trial; as I remarked it is a very pleasant position to be in to discuss those high principles of civil liberty, treated at length by the learned gentleman the day before yesterday, and a most disagreeable task to uphold military power. And while men who dare to undertake it are subjected to disparaging views, I will read what this authority says. I shall not read many of these sections, but I wish to read this to show the position that one occupies if he entertains such views of these military and harsh measures and attempts to uphold them before the country.

"Thus we have traced, with some care, the thread of judi-
"cial argument through the various constitutional provisions
"upon which the question of martial law under our govern-
"ment depends. It was not deemed necessary to cite in the
"notes, all the crude utterances which have fallen from judges
"and from legislators on this subject. This is one of those
"questions of constitutional law which the author expects to
"unfold more fully in another connection hereafter.

"It may be here said, however, that, though the constitu-
"tional provisions relating to this subject are, when fully ex-
"amined, plain enough, it is very difficult to tell the truth
"upon it, without subjecting one's self to being misunderstood.
"This matter has been bandied about in politics, and each
"reader is seeking to know whether the author belongs to
"this party, or to that, and he is ready to approve or disap-
"prove, according as he likes or dislikes the answer to this
"question. Yet in the present case, the author belongs
"neither to this nor to that party; but he is one of those few
"persons who hold truth to be superior to party, and who
"seek it alone, without asking or caring whether it pleases
"one party or another."

I read from section 52:

"Martial law is elastic in its nature, and is easily adapted to
"varying circumstances. It may operate"——

I wish to call this particularly to the attention of the senate:

"It may operate to the fatal suspension or overthrow of the
"civil authority; or its touch may be light, scarcely felt, or not
"felt at all, by the mass of the people; while the courts go on

"in their ordinary course, and the business of the community "flows in its accustomed channels."

What have we heard from the prosecution on the other side of this case? Why, that the courts were open; the commissioners held their regular meetings; that the clerk issued writs; and that the magistrates might proceed as they liked. Admit it. The authority that makes this declaration is not bound to visit its severity upon every citizen. "The touch," says this learned writer, "may be light. The great mass of the "people may not feel it at all. All the main business of "the community may flow on in its accustomed channels."

I was not a little amused at one portion of the speech of the learned gentleman [Gov. Graham.] He seemed to think that the respondent had treated the people of Alamance and the people of Caswell in the general, too kindly. He had permitted the great mass of the people not to feel the force of martial law at all. He had permitted them to go on and transact their business as usual, and had only visited this law of necessity upon a smaller number of the citizens, when if it was really martial law and properly declared, the gentleman thinks he ought to let every man feel the weight of it.

Sir, the respondent deserves much credit for taking care that but very few in either of these counties should feel the weight of martial law. But it would seem that he committed a great blunder because he let it fall upon men of high position. If he had visited the weight of martial law upon some few—if it had only been in the lowly walks of society, men of little or no influence—as I understand the argument—there would have been no complaint of that kind of martial law. I will read a portion of section 55.

"This question is not perhaps quite so clear on the face of "our constitution [the right to declare martial law] as are some "others, yet it is believed that the only real difficulty in the mat-"ter lies in the acts of political demagogues who wish to gain "the votes of unthinking people by representing themselves to "be the champions of their rights, and their defenders against "what they call the tyranny of martial law. The truth is that "martial law is the only kind of law which is adapted to those "circumstances in which a reasonable military power will ask "it to prevail, and no people or portion of the people can exist "even for a day without some kind of law governing them."

Now comes that important clause:

"If the civil tribunals in the best of faith endeavor to stretch "their precedents and adapt their processes to the emergencies "which call for martial law, they so change the precedents "which must govern afterwards as to render the jurisprudence "of their courts unfitted for times of peace; and as martial law "necessarily passes away with the emergency which called it "into action, a wise people, a people fit for freedom, will bow "thankfully before it, rejoicing that thus they preserve the law "of the civil tribunal uncorrupted and uncontaminated to enter "again upon its bright work the morning after peace. And "that which designates a people fit for freedom from a people "which must be made slaves is, that the former discerns be-"tween tyranny and law, spurning the one and accepting "thankfully the other, while the latter kicks at the one and "the other alike."

Section 56 says:

"If the reader will turn to the constitution he will there see "that the power conferred on the judges is 'judicial.' It is "not all the power of the government, but only the 'judicial "power.' Says the constitution, 'The judicial power of the "'United States shall be vested in one supreme court, and in "'such inferior courts as the congress may from time to time "'ordain and establish.' Now, here is the power of martial "law because martial law is not a thing pertaining to 'judical "power.' The United States courts cannot establish martial "law on the one hand, nor on the other can they overthrow "or interfere with it in any way."

So that this high authority settles the question, as admitted by the managers, that if martial law is declared by proper

151

authority, the judicial power cannot in any way interfere with it.

Section 57 says:

"There are certain principles laid down in the constitution "to judge the judicial power. In some of the clauses express "words mention the 'judicial' as the power to be guided, "and in others the form of the language is such as merely to "point to this power alone. Of the latter let the fourth and "fifth articles of the amendments serve as samples. They "are read consecutively as follows: 'The right of the people "'to be secure in their persons, houses, papers and effects "'against unreasonable searches and seizures shall not be vio-"'lated, and no warrants shall issue but upon probable cause, "'supported by oath or affirmation, and particularly describing "'the place to be searched, and the persons or things to be "'seized. No person shall be held to answer for a capital or "'otherwise infamous crime, unless on presentment or indict-"'ment of a grand jury, except in cases arising in the land or "'naval forces or in the militia when in actual service in "'time of war, or public danger, nor shall any person be "'subject for the same offence to be twice put in jeopardy of "'life or limb, nor shall be compelled in any criminal case to "'be a witness against himself nor be deprived of life, liberty "'or property without due process of law, nor shall private "'property be taken for public use without just compensa-"'tion.' Perhaps the last clause is properly construed, as it "is by the courts, to be a limitation upon the legislative as "well as the judicial power, and indeed the whole restrains "the legislature from passing any act which shall command "the courts to violate in their proceedings the provisions "thus laid down. But these provisions have nothing to do "with the martial power of war."

Section 60 is in these words: The "President having this "power put into his hands, takes the oath to preserve, protect "and defend the constitution of the United States." In another "clause he is enjoined to 'take care that the laws be faithfully "'executed.' It is obvious that the word 'laws' in this connection does not have any restrictive meaning; it is plural in its form, and, if it were singular it would not be restrictive; it applies not alone perhaps, not primarily, to the laws administered by the judicial power, the judges to whom they are expressly committed being ordinarly competent to execute these laws, but it applies in an especial manner, to the law martial which is executed by the military forces whereof he is the commander-in-chief. If, by reason of insurrection or rebellion at home, or invasion from abroad, there comes a disturbance which the civil power cannot or will not suppress, he is bound to call into action this power of war, carrying with it the law martial."

I will not read any more from that authority, but will read from the opinion of Chief Justice Taney, in the case of Luther *vs.* Borden, reported in 8 Howard. Speaking of the clause in the constitution providing for cases of domestic violence, the learned chief justice says;

"So, too, as relates to the clause in the above mentioned article of the constitution providing for cases of domestic violence. It rested with congress to determine upon the means proper to be adopted to fulfill this guarantee. They might, if they had deemed it most advisable to do so, have placed it in the power of a court to decide when the contingency had happened which required the federal government to interfere. But congress thought otherwise, and no doubt wisely, and by the act of February 28th, 1795, provided that in case of an insurrection in any state against the government thereof, it shall be lawful for the president of the United States on application of the legislature of such state or of the executive, when the legislature cannot be convened, to call forth such number of the militia, of any other state or states, as may be applied for, as he may judge sufficient to suppress such insurrection. By this act the power of deciding whether the exigency had arisen upon which the government of the United States is bound to interfere is given to the president. He is to "act upon the application of the legislature, or of the executive, "and consequently he must determine what body of men con-"stitute the legislature and who is the governor, before he can act. * * * * After the president has acted and called out the "militia, is a circuit court of the United States authorized to "inquire whether his decision was right? Could the court "while the parties were actually contending in arms for the "possession of the government, call witnesses before it, and "inquire which party represented a majority of the people? "If it could, then it would become the duty of the court (pro-"vided it came to the conclusion that the president had decided "incorrectly) to discharge those who were arrested or detained "by the troops in the service of the United States, or the gov-"ernment which the president was endeavoring to maintain. "If the judicial power extends so far, the guarantee contained "in the constitution of the United States is a guarantee of "anarchy and not of order. Yet if this right does not reside "in the courts when the conflict is raging—if the judicial power "is at that time bound to follow the decision of the political, it "must be equally bound when the contest is over. It cannot "when peace is restored punish as offences and crimes the acts "which it before recognized, and was bound to recognize as "lawful. * * * * And in that state of things the officers "engaged in its military service might lawfully arrest any one "who from the information before them, they had reasonable "grounds to believe was engaged in the insurrection, and "might order a house to be forcibly entered and searched when "there were reasonable grounds for supposing he might be "there concealed."

This case goes on and expressly recognizes and confirms the proceedings in Rhode Island declaring the people of that state in a state of insurrection, so that the right to declare a state in insurrection and to enforce martial law is established by that authority.

The next authority which I cite is Finlason on Martial Law, a recent and most learned and exhaustive work on the subject, which I commend to the attention of every senator before he comes to a decision in this case. It is entitled "Considerations "upon Martial Law by William F. Finlason, Esq., of the Mid. "dle Temple, Barrister-at-law, author of the Treatise on Mar. "tial Law." Speaking of martial law he says:

"After the era of the revolution it is true that the exercise "of this prerogative, at all events in its fulness, never arose in "this country, by reason, as Hallam observes, of our standing "army; but in Ireland, where the common law is the same. "and where the necessity for martial law has unhappily arisen "almost within living memory, it was exercised without any "statute to authorize it, and although by reason of horrible ex- "cesses, bills of indemnity were required, and in several in- "stances, as those of Wolfe Tone, J. W. Wright and J. W. "Grogan, its exercise after rebellion was over, or in districts "where it had never been, and where in fact martial law did "not exist, was undoubtedly illegal; yet even when, after the "Union, the Imperial Parliament thought fit permanently to "regulate the subject, it not only did not negative the preroga- "tive of the crown to declare martial law, but distinctly de- "clared it, and carried it further, providing for its exercise, not "only in cases of actual but apprehended rebellion, and in "districts where peace was not so destroyed, but that the com- "mon law could have its course. And so even in our own "time, no later than in the last reign, parliament passed an act "relating to Ireland, in which the prerogative was not only "declared but enacted, and elaborate provisions were laid down "for the regulation of its exercise in times of apprehended re- "bellion, and more especially for the trial of rebels by court "martial, whether civilians or soldiers."

Then at page 6, he says:

"So in India, if not in any of the colonies, regulations or "acts of legislature were passed providing for the exercise of "this important power. In 1846 an act of the legislature of "Jamaica, passed for the purpose, received the sanction of the "crown under the government of Lord Russell, and dis-

"tinctly authorized the governor in council to declare and "exercise martial law for the suppression of rebellion, "without any definition or limitation of the term, without "any restriction of its exercise, and leaving it to be applied "and exercised according to the sense in which it was under-"stood by parliament in the other acts, and in which it was "explained by all text books of military law in the hands of the "British army as the application of absolute military law to "the whole population. Nor was this the doctrine of military "writers alone, nor even of lawyers in this country. It was "equally laid down by the greatest constitutional writers, not "only in this country but America; and while the illustrious "Hallam declared that martial law was the suspension of civil "jurisdiction just as the great Duke declared it to be the will "of the commander, the great Chancellor Kent declared it as "the absolute rule of a military chief."

I now read again from page 6, note C:

"The military law as exercised by the authority of Parlia-"ment and the mutiny act, annually passed, together with the "articles of war, is not to be confounded with that different "branch of the royal prerogative called martial law, which is "only to be exercised in time of rebellion."

He also cites McAuthen and Simmons on Courts Martial:

"There may indeed be times of pressing danger when the "conservation of all demands the sacrifice of the legal rights of "a few; there may be circumstances that not only justify but "compel the temporary abandonment of constitutional power. "It has been usual for all governments during an actual rebel-"lion to proclaim martial law on the suspension of civil juris-"diction. Martial law is quite a distinct thing (i. e., from ordi-"nary military law.) It is founded on paramount necessity, "and proclaimed by a military chief."

At page 8 of this work, note A, he says:

"Martial law is a *lex non scripta*. It arises on paramount "necessity to be judged of by the executive Martial law "comprises all persons—all are under it in the country or dis-

"trict in which it is proclaimed whether they be civil or mili-"tary. There is no regular practice laid down in any work "on military law as to how courts martial are to be conducted "or power exercised under martial law, but as a rule I should "say that it should approximate as near as possible to the reg-"ular form and course of justice, and the usage of the service, "and that it should be conducted with as much humanity as "the occasion may allow according to the conscience and "the good judgment of those entrusted with its execution. "It overrides all other law. It is entirely arbitrary; it is far "more extensive even than ordinary military law.

"The Duke of Wellington said in the House of Lords on "the 1st April, 1851, in reference to the Ceylon rebellion in "1849, that martial law was neither more or less than the "will of the general who commands the army; in fact, mar-"tial law is no law at all! And Earl Grey on the same oc-"casion said, 'that he was glad to hear what the noble Duke "had said with reference to what is the true nature of martial "law, for it is exactly in accordance with what I myself wrote "to my noble Lord Torrington at the period of those transac-"tions in Ceylon. I am sure I was not wrong in law, for I "had the advice of Lord Cottenham, Lord Campbell, and the "Attorney General (Sir J. Jervis) and explained to my noble "friend, that what is called proclaiming martial law, is no "law at all, but merely for the sake of public safety in cir-"cumstances of great emergency, setting aside all law and "acting under the military power? Sir J. W. Hogg, chair-"man of the East India company, said in the House of Com-"mons on the 29th of May, 1851, when an honorable member "was inclined to carp at the statement of the Judge Advo-"cate General (Sir D. Dundas) that martial law was a denial "of all law, but the Judge Advocate was quite correct; it was "a denial of a law, and could not be the subject of regulation; "when martial law was proclaimed, the commanding officer "must use his discretion."

That means, Mr. Chief Justice and Senators, a denial of all

civil law, and that in the locality where the insurrection is declared, the civil law has no force or effect. Martial law overrides all ordinary law, and all constitutional law, and they are to be governed by martial law alone. Speaking this time in 1861 he says, at page 10:

So recently as 1850, "the same doctrines were distinctly and "broadly laid down by Mr. Headlam, the Judge Advocate Gen-"eral at the time, in an official letter which was published, and "which none ventured to challenge, and in which the nature of "martial law as absolute military authority overruling all ordi-"nary law whether military or municipal, was clearly and un-"equivocally maintained with the entire approbation of the gov-"ernment, of parliament and the whole country. And upon "this footing the subject was left as before, except in Ireland "and India, without any other definition, without any restric-"tion or limitation, and without any regulation for the future "exercise of this tremendous power admitted to be vested in "any colonial governor."

A then again:

"Martial law, according to the Duke of Wellington, is "neither more nor less than the will of the general who com-"mands the army. In fact, martial law means no law at all; "therefore the general who declares martial law, and commands "that it should be carried into execution, is bound to lay down "the rules, regulations and limits according to which his will "is to be carried out."

I now read from page 11:

"Accordingly, when on the occasion of the recent rebellion "in Jamaica, the governor, under a local act not defining mar-"tial law, but simply imposing certain conditions or restrictions "upon the power of declaring it, which the statute itself im-"plies was already in the governor, he, under the advice of the "attorney general, and with the assent of the council, declared "it in the form of proclamation, drawn in accordance with "these traditions and doctrines on the subject, and purporting "to place the whole district under military rule, and to em-

"power the troops to use the measures of war against those "found in rebellion. And he, in conjunction with the com- "mander-in-chief, upon that principle appointed an officer to "command the district, who accordingly assumed the entire "and exclusive government of it. On that occasion, when the "governor, under the local act, with the assent of the council, "declared martial law, there were no regulations for its exer- "cise. No instructions have been issued either to colonial "governors or to military commanders by the crown; and in- "deed both parliament and the crown had acquiesced in what "was laid down in the Ceylon case, that no definite instructions "could be issued. At all events none were issued, and on the "breaking out of the rebellion the governor was left to his own "discretion; and he having declared martial law, left its execu- "tion to the military commander."

Mr. BRAGG. Does it say what they did to the governor in that case?

Mr. BOYDEN. No, sir.

Then again on page 47:

"The military law as exercised by the authority of parlia- "ment, and the mutiny act annually passed, together with the "articles of war, is not to be confounded with that different "branch of the royal prerogative called martial law, which is "only exercised in the emergency of invasion and insurrection "or rebellion. Thus Simmons states, that courts martial are "regulated by the mutiny act and the articles of war and gen- "eral orders, and that their practice is moreover regulated on "points where that law is silent, chiefly by the customs of war, "i. e., the usages of the British army. (Simmons on Court "Martials, p. 87.) So it is laid down in that work, p. 97, that "the proclamation of martial law renders every man liable to "be treated as a soldier, that is, he is amenable to courts martial "under the orders of military authority."

And I mention here (and it was cited I think on the part of the managers from the trial of Johnson) the discussion in the house of parliament, touching the trial and the execution of the Rev. John Smith, of Demerara, and I call the attention of senators to the quotation from what Lord Brougham said on that occasion. He declared that every person within the locality declared in a state of insurrection was to be treated as a soldier; and Sir James McIntosh, whose authority is cited in that case, also recognizes the same doctrine, and then there is the case which I will cite now, known as Mrs. Alexander's cotton case, in which it is distinctly laid down by the supreme court of the United States that every person in the locality declared in a state of insurrection is liable to be considered an insurgent, and the case of *ex parte* Moore before the chief justice, and the case of *ex parte* Burgen before Judge Bond, to recognize the same doctrine.

The hour of ten o'clock having arrived, the court on motion took a recess until half past seven o'clock.

## EVENING SESSION.

The COURT re-assembled at half-past seven o'clock. Hon. R. M. Pearson, Chief Justice of the Supreme Court, in the chair.

The CLERK proceeded to call the roll of senators, when the following gentlemen were found to be present:

Messrs—Adams, Albright, Allen, Barnett, Battle, Brogden, Brown, Cook, Council, Cowles, Crowell, Currie, Dargan, Edwards, Eppes, Flemming, Gilmer, Graham of Alamance, Graham of Orange, Hawkins, Hyman, Jones, King, Latham, Ledbetter, Linney, Love, Mauney, McClammy, McCotter, Merrimon, Moore, Murphy, Norment, Olds, Robbins of Davidson, Robbins of Rowan, Skinner, Speed, Troy, Warren, Whiteside and Worth—43.

Mr. BOYDEN resumed his argument in behalf of the respondent. He said:

Mr. CHIEF JUSTICE and SENATORS: I had not got through all the authorities on the point I was discussing when the court took the recess, and I will now proceed. I wish to cite as authority Hough's Practice of Courts Martial, and I will read from pages 383 and 384.

"When martial law is proclaimed, courts martial are thereby "vested with such a summary proceeding, that neither time, "place nor persons are considered. Necessity is the only rule "of conduct, nor are the punishments which courts martial "may inflict, under such an authority, limited to those which "are, under ordinary circumstances, prescribed by the mutiny "act and articles of war; they may inflict the punishment of "death even, where the imperious necessity of the case and "the existing circumstances warrant it, when such a penalty "would not, for such cases, be visited with such severity by "the ordinary common law; but such powers cannot be as-"sumed; they must be duly delegated by proper authority." * * *

"The right of the legislature to adopt this violent but neces-"sary remedy, and to invest the crown with this extraordinary "power of the sword, is likewise pointedly asserted in constitu-"tional principles, that all may perceive its entire legality. It "is there declared, that it shall be lawful for his majesty, or "for any chief governor or commissioner, whom he shall ap-"point during the continuance of the rebellion, and whether "the ordinary courts of justice shall or shall not be open to "issue his or their orders to all officers, commanding his maj-"esty's forces, and to all others whom he or they shall think "fit to authorize, to take the most rigorous and effectual meas-"ures for suppressing the said rebellion in any part of the king-"dom, which shall appear to be necessary for the public safety, "&c., and to punish all persons acting, aiding or assisting in "such rebellion, either by death or otherwise, as to them shall "seem expedient. The statute likewise gives a power to arrest "or detain in custody, all suspected persons, and to cause them "to be brought to trial, in a summary manner, by courts martial, "and to execute their sentences, and release all who act under "its authority from responsibility to the other courts.

I now proceed to read some authorities upon the question

as to how an officer of the government is to be treated where he is intrusted with a discretionary power and has executed that power honestly. The first authority which I cite is from Finlason on Martial Law, beginning at page 147 and 148, as follows:

"At all events, assuming what is admitted on all hands, that "there is a power in the crown or the executive, whether "under the name of martial law or otherwise, to do all that is "necessary for the occasion, that amounts in substance to a dis-"cretionary authority, for it is an authority to do all that the "executive, in their judgment, may deem necessary, and it "follows that, according to all the analogies ot ordinary law "they would not be liable at law for its honest exercise nor "except for an abuse of it. For it is a general principle that "although even a minister of state is legally liable for an act "in excess of his authority, as where in ordinary times he does "an act which, according to ordinary law, he could not do at "all; yet, on the other hand, under ordinary law, the meanest "magistrate or officer of justice is protected, if he acts honestly "in the exercise of a discretionary authority; otherwise, it is "obvious that there would be no safety in actions in the exer-"cise of public functions, and no one would be willing to act "on them, the result of which would be fatal to the great object "of government, the public safety. And if this immunity "attends the humblest officers of justice, how much more would "it in law be deemed to attend the exercise by the executive "of their high functions from which all others derive their "authority."

There is another authority which I have not here but I can state it. It will be found in 2 Sir William Blackstone's Reports, the case of Miller vs. Sears, at page 1144. It is the opinion of Chiet Justice DeGrey, where he lays down the identical doctrine which I have just read from this book. He says expressly that an officer acting honestly in the discharge of the discretionary duty is not liable for any error which he may commit.

I next refer to the case cited by the learned counsel in the opening argument on behalf of the prosecution. It is found in 12 Wheaton, Supreme Court Reports,—the case of Martin vs. Mott. I read from page 32:

"But it is now contended, as it was contended in that case, "that notwithstanding the judgment of the president is conclu- "sive as to the existence of the exigency, and may be given in "evidence as conclusive proof thereof, yet that the avowry is "fatally defective, because it omits to aver that the fact did "exist. The argument is, that the power confided to the presi- "dent is a limited power and can be exercised only in the "cases pointed out in the statute, and therefore it is necessary "to aver the facts which bring the exercise within the perview "of the statute. In short, the same principles are sought to be "applied to the delegation and exercise of his power intrusted "to the executive of the nation for great political purposes, as "might be applied to the humblest officer in the government, "acting upon the most narrow and special authority. It is the "opinion of the court, that this objection cannot be maintained. "When the president exercises an authority confided to him by "law, the presumption is that it is exercised in pursuance of "law. Every public officer is presumed to act in obedience to "his duty, until the contrary is shown; and *a fortiori*, this "presumption ought to be favorably applied to the chief magis- "trate of the union. It is not necessary to aver, that the act "which he may rightfully do, was so done. If the fact of the "existence of the exigency were averred, it would be traversa- "ble, and of course might be passed upon by a jury; and thus "the legality of the orders of the president would depend, not "on his own judgment of the facts, but upon the finding of "those facts upon the proofs submitted to a jury. This view "of the objection is precisely the same which was acted upon "by the supreme court of New York, in the case already re- "ferred to, and, in the opinion of this court, with entire legal "correctness. * * *

"Whenever a statute gives a discretionary power to any person "to be exercised by him upon his own opinion of certain facts, "it is a sound rule of construction that the statute constitutes "him the sole and exclusive judge of the existence of those "facts. But in the present case we are all of opinion that "such is the construction of the act of 1795. It is no answer "that such a power may be abused, for there is no power "which is not susceptible of abuse. The remedy for this, as "well as for all other official misconduct, if it should occur, is "to be found in the constitution itself. In a free government "the danger must be remote, since in addition to high quali- "ties which the executive must be presumed to possess of "public virtue and honest devotion to the public interests, "the frequency of elections, and the watchfulness of the "representatives of the nation, carry with them all the checks "which can be useful to guard against usurpation or wanton "tyranny."

The learned manager, [Mr. Sparrow,] in quoting from the case from which I have read, concludes by saying that the remedy referred to is impeachment. If I understand that case there is no such intimation in it. The remedy expressly stated is that of frequent elections, not impeachment at all.

Those are the principal authorities which I wish to read upon this subject; but there are two authorities in our own courts, I mean upon the question of the presumption of the law being constitutional, and it being the duty of the chief magistrate or other officer to act upon that presumption. The first is the case of Hoke vs. Henderson, 4 Devereux Reports, page 1. I need not read the case. The court there lays down the doctrine expressly that an act of assembly is presumed to be constitutional. And there is another case where that doctrine is laid down in 1 Devereux and Battle, the case of Carney Neal, *qui tam* vs. Mills Roberts. That case adopts the same doctrine. Then we have another authority which I wish to read; it is a series of resolutions introduced into the senate during the present session by one of the distinguished members of this body, [Senator Warren.] I read the fourth and fifth resolutions:

"4th. That the governor of North Carolina has no veto

"power nor any power equivalent thereto, and cannot dispense "with laws or suspend the execution thereof.

"5th. That the governor is not at liberty in his official charac-"ter to feel or to affect constitutional scruples, and to sit in judg-"ment himself on the validity of any act of the general assem-"bly, duly ratified, and to nullify it if he so chooses, but it is "his duty to execute such act until it shall have been declared "unconstitutional in due course of law."

Those are the authorities which I bring to the attention of this court upon that question, and I apprehend that they are perfectly conclusive. It would be difficult to find a gentleman more capable for laying down the law upon that subject than the gentleman who introduced those resolutions. His high character as a jurist is well known throughout the state, and I therefore cite his language as high authority.

I now read section nine of the bill of rights as follows:

"All power of suspending laws, or the execution of laws, "by any authority, without the consent of the representatives "of the people, is injurious to their rights and ought not to "be exercised."

Now what I contend for is this: that the act of the 29th of January, 1870, usually called the Shoffner act, expressly authorizes the governor to declare counties, where life and property are not protected by the civil authorities, in a state of insurrection; in other words, to suspend all the ordinary and constitutional laws of the county. It may be, and has been said on the part of the prosecution, that this act is unconstitutional. I deny that; but the protection of my client does not depend upon that denial, for there is no doctrine better established, and I trust it will not now be denied by the senate, that whether unconstitutional or not, it is the duty and the right of the governor to carry that law into execution; for let me say here to senators, I cannot suppose there is a solitary senator, whatever might have been his opinion when this case was first opened, and before the testimony was offered on behalf of the respondent, who is not satisfied that the identical state of things contemplated by that act existed in the county of Alamance and in the county of Caswell; and I entertain no doubt that it existed in a number of other counties as well.

Let us see by the proof in this case whether that proposition is true or false. Will any man under the sanction of an oath, avow that life and property were protected by the civil authorities in the counties of Alamance and Caswell? Every senator must be satisfied that that question is put beyond all doubt. Life and property safe there! Recur, senators, to the proof in this case; go with me for a moment to the house of those poor and lowly colored men, and see how they have been treated. Have their lives been safe? Has their property been safe? Has there been any protection afforded to them by the civil authorities? Can any man have any doubt upon that subject? Remember the cases of Outlaw, of Puryear, of Morrow, of Holt, of Allen, of Worth, and of scores of others, and I ask have they been protected? And look, too, at the flimsy pretexts which have been set up here before this high court as excuses for these iniquities. This man they say was whipped because he had been stealing. Has any proof been offered before this court that tends to show that in this respect he was not as clear of stealing as any man in this senate chamber? Not a particle, although that has been avowed months since and they have had every opportunity to show such guilt, if guilt existed. And so all the flimsy excuses which they have offered for their outrages fall to the ground. I ask senators to consider, when they come to pass upon these facts, knowing that these outrages have been committed and that the victims have had no redress in any one case, that what does not appear before the court is to be taken as not existing. There is not a particle of proof that the victims of these cruel chastisements have been guilty of any violation of law, and you must take it that every man of them is entirely clear of the charges which have been insinuated against them as excuses for these acts of murder and chastisement. With these facts before him, may God have mercy upon any man who will not say that it is established beyond all manner of doubt, that there was no protectoin by the civil authorities for men in Alamance and Caswell against outrages from this band of cut-throats and assassins—no protection—none at all. Night after night, in more than a score of instances, these poor colored innocent men have had their dwellings burst open and have been dragged from their homes in view of their screaming wives and children and chastised as no humane man would chastise a brute. Yes, sir, they have not only chastised them, but in some instances have fired into their houses and, in one case at least, have laid their victim prostrate with gunshot wounds from which he suffered from three to four months, and to day even he is without redress. Remember the case of Puryear, an humble and deranged man, as the prosecution have proved him to be: he is dragged out of his house by these cowardly miscreants, and with a heavy stone tied to his heels, thrown into a mill pond and drowned. Then remember the testimony of a Kuklux magistrate who appeared before this court and said that if Puryear's case had not been reported to the military he would have issued a precept against Puryear's own wife for the murder of her husband! May God forgive such a man as that witness. There are the facts which show what a horrible state of feeling existed in the county of Alamance.

Nobody knows by whom Outlaw was hung. A Kuklux sheriff, the chief of a camp, was in Graham the night that murder was committed, and he never moved his finger afterwards to ferret out the murderers. Jacob A. Long, a chief of the Kuklux, and other citizens, saw the crowd, and never uttered a word of protest against the crime. Does Long, the chief of the county, and Murray, the sheriff and chief of a camp, expect to satisfy any senator that if they, being in the secrets of the order, had desired to ferret out these guilty wretches, who to show their utter contempt of law had murdered their victim in the view of the court house in the county town, could not have ascertained these murderers? I am talking to men capable of appreciating testimony, who can understand its significance; and any man who, I think, has heard of the object of these organizations, the communications they have among themselves, sees at once that this perjured sheriff attended the inquest, not in the hope of finding out who had committed the deed, but was there to see whether anything would come out to implicate him in this deed of darkness. When he is examined, he says he made efforts to ascertain who had committed the murder. "Did you follow the tracks of the 75 or 100 horses ridden by the men there that night to see where they had gone to?" "No I did not. I did not examine the tracks. I stayed there "till this examination was over before the coroner's inquest "and then I tried to find them out." Does anybody believe that? Where did he inquire? Who is the man he inquired of? Where is any evidence that he asked of a single soul who it was of his brother Kuklux, who had committed this fell deed? The proof is directly to the contrary. He made no such effort. He had the means—being a member of this band of scoundrels, of ferreting out every man of them. Why didn't he do it? Jacob A. Long swears he was afraid to interfere. Does anybody doubt that—he and the sheriff were actually afraid to make any effort to bring these assassins to justice! Have we not proved here that it was a part of this damnable conspiracy, to keep the secrets of the society, and that if any member revealed them the penalty was death? Well might they be afraid, and I have no doubt they were.

Senators will recollect the horrible outrages on two occasions committed upon Caswell Holt, first terribly whipped and a year after shot down in his own dwelling and his family driven to the woods, afraid to remain in their home. Remember, too, the case of Samuel Allen, a peaceful and lonely colored man, as free from guilt as any man in this senate chamber. These villians come to his house to murder him and another man named Joseph Mebane, whose high crime was that he taught a school of children of his own color. They attacked the house, they endeavored to break in, but the brave old Sam Allen met them in a manner which should place his name on the pages of history; with fifty of the armed and disguised cowards on the outside, he thrust a sabre through one of them who was carried off dead, and secretly buried. The villian got what he richly deserved, and it would have been well if his companions in crime had met the same fate. But that was not enough; Samuel Allen's house was to have another visitation from these assassins. Fortunately he was away from home, but Mebane was there and a poor old colored man by the name of Robin Jacobs and another. They heard the approach of the party and ran from the house, two of them in one direction and Robin Jacobs in another. They were pursued. Robin Jacobs, as innocent of any violation of the law as any man in this senate chamber, was overtaken and shot through the body, thrown against a pile of logs, and there he was found the next morning in the agonies of death. Senators, was life and property protected in Caswell? Could the civil power afford protection there?

Go with me, senators, to the house of poor Morrow, and see these cowardly assassins drag him from his bed at midnight, and from his wife and children; see his little babe in his wife's arms, and hear the frantic cry of this poor man's wife, "spare, "spare my husband, for God's sake have mercy upon him for "this one time." It would seem that these wretches had no "hearts but hearts of flint. It produced no effect. He says, "If "you won't spare me, pray let me bid good bye, let me give "my wife a last embrace before you kill me." "We will kill "you if you don't shut your mouth." "Pray let me bid my "baby good bye." But no, they drag him from his wife, they drag him from his little ones, and they hang him to a tree until he is dead! dead! dead! Is that all? This poor heart-stricken colored woman with her children flee to the woods, remain out in the cold all night; when the light of day comes and these murderers have retired to their hiding places, she goes forth to seek her husband and finds him and her brother hanging dead, the victims of this brave and courtly Kuklux judiciary, who have thus carried out their own decrees. Is there any senator who has any apology to offer for such infamy as this?

Is there any senator here who is not prepared to say that life and property were without protection from the civil authorities? Had the humble black man, or humble white man, if he happened to be a republican, any protection if he fell under the displeasure of these murderous bands?

Do senators recollect the number of white men who were scourged and outraged by these wretches? Twenty-one white, men, we have proved before this court, have been outraged and no redress has been had in any case. Let me recur to a few to illustrate:

John Alred, Alamance. House visited by the Kuklux. "If "you don't change your politics and be a white man we will "cut your throat next Saturday night," or "make your throat "red." That is the proof in this case.

John Bason, Alamance, August or September, 1869, postmaster at Haw river, whipped and maltreated.

Mary Gappins. O yes, the gentlemen laugh—why if she were an unchaste woman, have these scoundrels a right to drag her from her house and tear it down? High-toned gentlemen they are to protect the morals of the country against a few incontinent women! That woman's house was torn down, she was turned out of doors with six children on the coldest night of the year, and compelled to live for thirteen months in a tent. Is there any senator that could have justified any such offense as that.

William F. Simpson, Alamance, November, 1869, seized and carried from his house at night, tied to a tree, struck fifteen or twenty times, then four or five times more. Blood was cut from his naked back; charge, "cursing the party" and telling negroes lies and letting negroes live on his lands. He was made to drive the negroes away. Sir, have I not a right to let a colored man live on my land if I please? What is it to these wretches? What have they to do with it? I supposed every man had a right to take on his land just such tenants as suited him. Is it not a fine state of things that a man must get the consent of the Kuklux as to who his tenants shall be? Are senators prepared to justify such conduct as that?

Andrew Murray, Alamance, two of his tenants whipped and he threatened and compelled to leave his home with his family.

Leonard Rippey, of Alamance, whipped at Jack Brannock's, in Caswell county, five licks for being at a negro house. "You are a d—d old radical." Certainly they had a right to whip any white man if he was a radical; nobody can doubt that, I suppose! Rippey was a poor man on his way to Caswell to dispose of some molasses that he had made on his place. His wagon broke down. He went to this blacksmith's (a colored man) just before night. The blacksmith had another job to finish and he could not do this job until the next morning, and this white man, thus unable to proceed, is guilty of the high crime of taking shelter in a colored blacksmith's house until morning! Didn't that fully justify his being scourged!

John Hatterly, Alamance, October 29th, house shot into. He fired at the party, and they found it convenient to leave.

Alonzo Gerringer, Alamance, going to a debate, was met by the Kuklux and carried to the woods, threatened with hanging, made to get down by these wretches and pray for them—made to mock the name of our Savior.

Siddell, Alamance, December, 1869, a carder in the woolen mills, whipped many licks on the back. Yes, sir, they took this man; they gave him a most terrible whipping, but with the purest motives in the world, and hence their actions should not be called in question. It was a part of their creed, we know, that if the courts did not interfere to punish such offences, to take the duty upon themselves.

John Overman, Alamance, white, door burst open, ten persons came in, struck two licks by each; one side of his head shaved.

James Coles, Alamance, fall of 1869, whipped by ten or twelve after being taken from his house and from his wife and two children. I hope the Kuklux informed the prosecution what they whipped him for. I suppose it is well known on the other side, but they kept it back from us for some reason.

Joseph McAdams. In connection with his case, do you recollect the sheriff of Alamance? Do you recollect Jefferson Younger, who did not make a coffin, or anything that looked like a coffin, but he made a box, that is all! He happened to have lumber of that size and he made a box. He made it because the camp had decreed it, of which the sheriff was chief. What was done with this? Why it was carried in the night time and set against McAdams' door, so that if he opened it it would fall in. On it were these comforting words: "Hold "your tongue, or this will be your home; alive to-day, dead "to-morrow."

Green Lankford, Alamance, February, 1870, self and wife dragged from their bed at midnight—at one o'clock, the lock broken. An old man 71 years old, struck fifteen licks after being carried to the woods by seven disguised men, charged that his wife had had it done.

James O. Ringstaff, October 9th, 1869. Eight or nine men come to his house at eleven o'clock at night. Threatened with death by hanging if he went to the Gappins' any more. December, 1869, they came at night, carried off some few things and left a notice, and if he did not leave the county in twenty days he would "pass as if from life to death." I suppose he had quit visiting Gappins', but that wasn't enough—he must leave the county. On the 8th of June they again visited his house in his absence and some things were carried off.

Corliss and wife, badly whipped, eleven o'clock at night, gash over his eyes, bloody water issuing from his wounds, wife cut on her head. But Corliss deserved all he got; he invited a colored man into a christian church and he taught a colored school, and he was a northern man, and therefore they had a right to chastise him!

Senator Shoffner. Now that case is worthy of some little consideration. We have proved here Doctor Moore was informed by M. Boyd that he had heard that a number of men were going to murder Shoffner on a particular night. And Dr. Moore testified here that he saw a member of the present house of representatives and a man by the name of Hedgepeth, and another named Bradshaw, who was the chief of a camp, at Bradshaw's house, near where the murder was to take place, and that he met a crowd of men who stated they were on their way to execute the fell deed. What had Shoffner done? He had introduced this act of the 29th of January, 8701, known as the Shoffner act. I never understood it till now that the official acts of senators were to be called in question in this way. I care not what may be said or proven as to the character of James E. Boyd—and no attempt has been made to attack it—Strudwick was there, and Hedgepeth and Bradshaw were there, and nobody will doubt it until these men come before this senate and deny it—I mean the statement of Moore, as sworn to by Boyd.

And while I am upon that branch of the case I might as well discuss the testimony of John W. Long, of Andrew Shoffner, of Nick Dale and of Tilman Brown, whose characters have been attempted to be impeached. They called up Jesse Gant, apparently a respectable man, but one having very strong prejudices. They called up also Mr. Austin Whitsett, and both of these gentlemen say, that from his youth John W. Long has had a most infamous character. I admit, for the sake of the argument, that he has that character. Yet, senators, in every case where he has deposed to any outrage he has given time and place, and named the men who were engaged in it, and not a man has been brought forward to disprove his statements; and that would have been a vastly better means of disproving his testimony, than any attempt to show he was a man of bad character. It is possible that an unintelligent jury in a county court might disbelieve a witness who has been attacked as Long has, but surely when his testimony stands before a learned court like this uncontradicted, when witnesses might have been produced to disprove every fact he has sworn to if it were false, and when he testified to the same facts months ago, and his statements have remained uncontradicted from that day to this, not a man whom he has named having dared to depose upon oath that Long's statements were not true, I take it that his words will be believed—every one.

And Andrew Shoffner, a colored man, who was whipped by these conspirators and who identified some of those who had thus outraged him, is also testified to as having a bad character; but these very witnesses brought to impeach his testimony, prove that the very morning after the chasetisement was inflicted, they heard of it; and do the managers expect to get rid of his testimony with such corroboration as that? Can senators say they will not believe him when his back shows the marks of the whippings he had received and his statements are confirmed by the neighborhood reports, immediately after the outrage was perpetrated, that it had been done?

Then there is Tilman Brown, a colored mechanic, and Arch. Doll, who overheard the remarks of Hubbard and others at Yanceyville, showing the purpose to kill Stephens that day. This young man Dickey, who had lived in Caswell less than a year when that murder took place, says that these two colored men have bad character. But Dickey himself was a Kuklux, and that fact alone is a significant commentary upon the value of his testimony. Brown and Doll named the men who made the remark they have sworn to—Hubbard, Fowler and Totten,—white men all—and not one of them is brought here to contradict them. I ask if senators expect to get rid of their testimony by the loose impeaching evidence of a member of the Kuklux klan. There is hardly a colored man in the community against whom somebody could not be found to give the same opinion of his character as this man Dickey gives of Brown and Doll. But no amount of discredit that the managers can throw upon the character of these men will weigh a feather in estimating the truth of their testimony, so long as Fowler and Hubbard and Totten who could have been produced were not put upon the stand to disprove the testimony of these two colored men.

I cannot go over all this evidence. Twenty two white men and forty-two colored men have been outraged and not a solitary man in Caswell or Alamance has been punished for it.

And now, senators, go with me for a moment to the town of Yanceyville. The court house there, in the bright month of May, under the full glare of an afternoon sun, is filled with the citizens of the county and listening to harangues of political orators. Stephens, a state senator from that district, is present in the meeting taking notes of the speeches, he being a republican and the speakers his political opponents. At four o'clock he is enticed from the meeting by Wyley and in company with him he leaves the room and is never again, so far as human testimony has divulged, seen alive. At daylight the next morning his body is found with a rope almost buried in the muscles of his neck, and fatal stabs in his breast and neck. Where is Wyley? Where is Mitchell? Both of them, if I recollect aright, were brought here last summer and both of them were bound over by the chief justice to answer a charge of the murder of Stephens. Why have they not been produced here to testify as to what they knew of that assassination? The managers dared not put them on the stand to prove that they were not the perpetrators of this cowardly murder. I ask, senators, if that vile deed was not calculated to shock the whole country? A man, yes a white man, murdered in broad dayling with hundreds of citizens within a few feet of the scene and yet nobody knows how or when! We have ascertained a fact which points at two or three men as having some knowledge of the murder. The are not put on the stand and examined, although they are brought here under subpœna. Look at another fact: a written statement is prepared by citizens who seek to absolve their community from responsibility for the crime, and the brothers of the murdered senator are asked to sign it; and they living in dread of the same fate which had befallen their brother, after vainly resisting the importunity of these citizens, reluctantly put their signatures to the paper, and such a document is expected to have weight before this court! Sir, the circumstances under which that letter was prepared and signed are themselves evidence which leads the mind to the conviction that that murder was perpetrated by men who were attending that meeting.

During this morning I was discussing the rights of martial law, strictly considered; but I wish this court distinctly to understand that no man has a greater repugnance than I have to martial law and to arresting men against whom there was not a probable cause of guilt. I say in strict law the respondent had a right to arrest all men in the counties of Alamance and Caswell; but it was a mistake, in my judgment, to arrest any man against whom there was not strong probable cause of complicity in this conspiracy. And, senators, I have no apology for the cruelty which has been proved to have been exercised upon some of the prisoners by one of the officers of Kirk's regiment. Indeed, no man can denounce it in terms more severely than myself. But let us look at the case and observe how the learned counsel [Mr. Graham] regards it. Gentlemen of high standing, of great respectability and who were clad in purple and fine linen and who fared sumptuously every day, have been taken into custody and detained by the military for a few weeks. But have any of them been murdered or shot or even whipped? They have been deprived of their liberties for a time, and that is all But when white citizens of Alamance and Caswell go to the houses of the colored man and of even humble white men, and drag them from their beds, hang them by their necks until dead, or drown them in mill ponds, or whip them on their naked backs, there is nothing in that to excite the virtuous indignation of counsel!

In view of this fact, I ask how can they denounce the respondent because he happened to apprehend a few of these gentlemen to prevent the entire extinguishment of the black race in the counties of Alamance and Caswell? I think I see numbers of men in this senate here who would not have dilly-dallyed with this matter as this respondent did. They would have crushed them out at once with the military; they would not have waited and waited and waited; they would not have issued proclamation after proclamation; they would not have written letters to distinguished opponents in the different counties and invited them to go abroad and endeavor to stop this vile business, that he might be relieved of the necessity of declaring these counties in a state of insurrection. With them, one proclamation would have been sufficient, and if another death, another outrage occurred after that, which was left unpunished, they would have called in the military and they would have stopped the course of outrage and wrong at once.

I assert that the respondent was in great error in that he did not proceed long before he did to call in the military and put a stop to this carnival of murder and outrage. That is my judgment, senators; I may be mistaken.

Let me say a word or two upon the articles of impeachment. The first and second articles refer to declaring the counties of Alamance and Caswell in a state of insurrection, and of apprehending certain individuals without warrant. If we have succeeded in establishing the position that these localities have been declared in a state of insurrection, then these charges all fall to the ground—they cannot be maintained at all, no matter how innocent, no matter how unoffending any one of these men who were arrested may have been in his conduct—so far as regards this conspiracy.

Passing for the moment the most difficult charge, the arrest of Josiah Turner, Jr., who desired to be arrested and labored with all his might to procure his arrest, I come to the charges of appropriating money to pay the troops, of violating the injunction of Judge Mitchell, in so doing, and will reply to them. Sir, there are plenty of senators here, lawyers of the highest standing, who know that the judiciary cannot enjoin the executive—the judiciary possess no such power. If that were not so, the wheels of government would soon be clogged. Nobody doubts the law that the judiciary cannot enjoin the executive, provided the process was issued against him personally, and that he would not be amenable for disobeyance. This being so, I ask senators how the respondent can be guilt of any offence for disobeying an injunction that was granted against other officers of the government? Nothing is clearer to my mind than that these charges must fail?

But there is this other and most difficult case of all—that of the arrest of Josiah Turner, Jr., a man who labored for months to have have himself arrested by the respondent, and who at last succeeded. Is not that a grave offence! Is it not worthy of an impeachment against the governor and spending the money of the state to endeavor to convict the respondent for placing Mr. Turner in a position he sought more than any thing else in the world! Let me call the attention of the senators to what took place here upon his examination. He was asked if there was not an unkind feeling between him and the respondent, and what, pray, did he reply, "My feelings are "such as you might suppose would exist between a good man and bad man." He went out of his way three times to prove that he was a pious and holy man, and that the respondent was a vile sinner! and held himself as a man whose example was to be followed by all good men!

"I bless an' praise thy matchless might,
Where thousands that were left in night,
That I am here afore thy sight,
    For gifts and grace,
A burnin' an' a shinin light
    To a' this place.

Yes, I am here a chosen sample
To show thy grace is great and ample,
I'm here a pillar in thy temple,
    Strong as a rock,
A guide, a buchler an' example
    To a' thy flock. [Laughter.

Sir, everybody knew that Mr. Turner was this sort of a man, and he need not have gone out of his way to prove what a holy and virtuous person he was. Every man who has read the *Sentinel* since he became its editor knew that he was a shining example of the beauty of holiness and that he had consecrated his talents and his energies to elevating the character of our judiciary and all our state officers! He knew the importance of his powers in this regard, and I am glad that these military men, with all their faults, had an eye to "the eternal fitness of "things." They found in the prison at Alamance a poor wretch condemned to death, who needed ghostly advice, and instead of sending the cursing parson—Yates—to administer unto his spiritual necessities, they sent this good, pious and holy and meek man, Josiah Turner, Jr., [laughter] to perform that spiritual office, and I am suprised that he is not grateful for having accorded to him that exalted privilege. [Laughter.] Yes, sir, and when he returned to Hillsboro' and Raleigh his Kuklux friends offered incense unto his name and consented to become beasts of burden and to carry him in a triumphal procession about the streets. Surely *he* should make no complaint. Wouldn't it be a farce for grave senators to try the governor for doing to Turner of all things earthly what Turner most desired? [Laughter.] That is all I have to say about that charge.

I was about to ask what hope have I for the acquittal of my client? I have practiced law a long time, and I always have been able to ascertain that if the case was one in which parties were divided politically I felt sure I could acquit him, if every juryman was of the opposite party to my client, and had made up and expressed his opinion of the guilt of the accused. But thank God we have not got a common jury; we have got men here of the highest integrity, men who can appreciate testimony, and I entertain the opinion honestly that if what has been proved here before this court had been fully known and comprehended by the house of representatives before these articles of imeachment were prepared, they never dwould have preferred them; and I entertain the further opinion that senators and commoners are utterly astounded at the developments we have made. We have not been permitted to verify our answer in respect to everything we said about these vile organizations and about indictments not being found, and about nobody's being punished in various counties in the State—all that has been excluded. I thought such proof was competent, and I have come to the conclusion that senators have voted to exclude that testimony because they had made up their minds to acquit my client, and they wanted no more of these developments to go forth to the country. I know of no other principle upon which it could have been excluded. I then have hope, and even a belief, that this court will acquit the respondent, and I would be glad that they might immortalize themselves by such action. I say here that a unanimous verdict ot acquittal would immortalize every man in this senate. This case will not cease to occupy the public mind when the verdict is pronounced. When all this feverish excitement, this bitter party feeling which pervades and has pervaded the country for the last several years—when this excitement has passed away, and the second-sober thought comes upon the country, and the people read of these numberless outrages that have been perpetrated upon the humble white and colored men, and for which there has not been a solitary punishment; when they read the vote of acquittal given by any senator, they will say, "Well done, good and faithful servant." They may not say that next week or the week after, but as surely as we are here to-night, the second sober-thought will come, and every man that votes acquittal will feel that he has performed a duty for which the country ought to be grateful—for which I entertain not a doubt it will be.

Let me, before I close, call your attention for a moment to the prosecution of President Johnson. I ask senators, I ask democratic and conservative senators, did you approve of the action of the men who voted for his conviction? Is there a man of you who did not censure the course of the republican members of congress? Is there a senator here who did not say of the pure and upright Fessenden, and of all the other members of the republican party who voted for his acquittal, "Well done, well done; we give you credit for your vote?" I may be mistaken. I entertain the judgment that that was the opinion of every democratic member of this senate. Mr. Fessenden is "gone to that bourne whence no traveller returns," but he has left a record for purity and uprightness that any man might envy. He dared to stand up like a man, and to resist the illegal and improper demands of bitter partizans. He has already got the meed of credit for his action; and I hesitate not to say that the day will come that every man who votes for the conviction of the respondent will have occasion to regret it. In all this I may be mistaken, but that is my judgment.

I desire, Mr. Chief Justice and Senators, frankly and candidly to express here the sentiments I entertain. I come here as no partizan, I come here not as the friend or partizan of the respondent. That he and I have usually been at points upon the great questions before the country is probably known to every senator here. I voted against the present constitution, and advised others to do it. I admit that it has many noble features, but some of its provisions are very unsuited, in my judgment, to the people of North Carolina. I have never approved it, and if I were a member of the legislature to-day (and I always said so) I would vote for an unrestricted convention to reframe our organic law. I am here, as I said before, to express my genuine thoughts and views upon the points in this case. I know that my days are but few. I am near the foot of the hill. I look about me and see the great men of North Carolina, with whom I have been associated at the bar for many years, have all passed that bourne from which no traveller returns. It is with these sad memories crowding upon me, and with a deep sense of the responsibility resting upon me, that I have addressed this learned high court of impeachment on behalf of the respondent, and urged that in my judgment the cause of truth and justice requires his acquittal at your hands of the charges preferred against him. The question of the legality of the organization of the troops embodied by the respondent, (about which I have no doubt,) I leave to my learned associate, who is to follow, as I am too much exhausted to continue the argument longer to-night, and I am unwilling to trespass longer upon the time of the court; and I am unwilling to ask for further indulgence. I must conclude with the full belief that the court will not hesitate, after hearing my learned associate and the counsel who is to follow him, to acquit the respondent of all the charges preferred against him.

## FORTY-FIRST DAY.

SENATE CHAMBER, March 18th, 1871.

The COURT met at 11 o'clock, pursuant to adjournment, Honorable R. M. Pearson, Chief Justice of the Supreme Court, in the chair.

The proceedings were opened by proclamation made in due form by the doorkeeper.

The CLERK proceeded to call the roll of senators, when the following gentlemen were found to be present:

Messrs. Adams, Albright, Battle, Bellamy, Brogden, Brown, Cook, Council, Cowles, Crowell, Currie, Dargan, Edwards, Eppes, Fleming, Gilmer, Graham of Alamance, Graham of Orange, Hawkins, Hyman, Jones, King, Latham, Ledbetter, Linney, Love, Mauney, McClammy, McCotter, Merrimon, Moore, Norment, Olds, Price, Robbins of Davidson, Robbins of Rowan, Skinner, Speed, Troy, Waddell, Warren, Whiteside and Worth—43.

Mr. SMITH, of counsel for the respondent, proceeded to address the court as follows:

MR. CHIEF JUSTICE AND SENATORS: In the arrangement made among the counsel for respondent, it has been assigned to me to perform the last office in presenting the merits of his cause to the consideration of the senate. The case is in many respects one of peculiar features. For the first time in the history of our state has a governor been charged with the high crimes imputed to the respondent, and North Carolina, proverbial for the honesty and integrity of her people, in public and in private life, if she strikes him down, will be the first among all the states to give an example of official profligacy. The trial itself has been protracted over many weeks, and the senate, with great patience, has heard the evidence adduced on either side and now to be passed upon and weighed in determining the question of the respondent's guilt. And towards the respondent himself, his counsel stand in somewhat peculiar relations. He has selected and summoned us from the pursuits of private life, most of us his life-long political opponents, to present to a tribunal, largely of our own political faith, the grounds upon which his acquittal of the charges is asked. In this he has exhibited a confidence in the integrity of our profession which his counsel will endeavour honorably to meet. It will be our purpose, as it has been heretofore, to present the respondent's case in all its legal bearings, with a view of contributing, as far as we can by argument, towards a just and righteous decision of the issues involved.

The constitution originally adopted at Halifax provided for trial of impeachment before a different tribunal, and required the concurrent action of the two houses of the general assembly to frame and pass articles of impeachment, or the prosecution of offenders on presentment of a grand jury of a court of supreme jurisdiction in the state; and the only offences for which an officer could be impeached are therein declared to be for "violating any part of this constitution, maladministration "or corruption." The constitutional convention of 1835 reaffimed (article III, section 1,) those provisions of the old constitution which define and declare what are impeachable acts—but changed the manner of proceeding against offending officers, and directed that the house shall "have the sole power ot impeachment," and the senate "the sole power to try all impeachments." The present constitution retains the machinery for the finding and trial of impeachments, but omits entirely the provisions declaring what shall be an impeachable act and to make any substitute therefor. We were left, therefore, when this constitution went into effect, without any law on the subject, the former having been abrogated and annulled. This defect, it has been proposed to remedy by an enactment of the general assembly, of April 10, 1969, which in section 16 specifies six distinct matters for which an officer may be impeached, to wit:

"1. Corruption or other misconduct in his official capacity.
"2. Habitual drunkenness.
"3. Intoxication while engaged in the exercise of his office.
"4. Drunkenness in any public place.
"5. Mental or physical incompetence to discharge the duties "of his office.
"6. Any criminal matter, the conviction whereof would tend "to bring his office into public contempt."

It might admit of question, if we were disposed to rest upon our extreme rights, whether the general assembly has the power, under the constitution of the United States, to annex conditions of forfeiture to an office which were not attached to it when it was created, nor when the respondent entered upon the discharge of its duties. It certainly seems to be an abridgment of the tenure of an office to annex conditions, by which it may be forfeited and determined, after its creation, by acts which before worked out no such result. But for the purposes of this argument, I shall not deny that there is and must be, independently of legislation, an impeachable offence. The provision of the machinery for its trial, necessarily involves something to be tried, and I look in the constitution to ascertain what is the act, what the circumstances and conditions upon which an officer, aside from positive law, and chosen before its enactment, can be impeached. The punishment prescribed is expulsion from office—and it may be, also, permanent incapacity to hold office in the state. This necessarily presupposes some *official act*—something done or omitted, connected with the discharge of official duty, by which the incumbent has shown himself to be unfit longer to be trusted with the office, and his removal becomes a public necessity; and this view is fortified by the fact that the party while punished by impeachment with the deprivation of office, is still amenable to the criminal law, as if no such trial had taken place. It must, therefore, not be a *mere crime* capable of redress before the criminal courts of the state. It may have the elements of crime, but the act, as we submit, must be one of official depravity—official corruption—official dishonesty—the exercise through improper motives of powers not conferred, or the abuse and misuse of powers that are conferred; and it is in this view that we think the only material aspect in which the case can be presented to the consideration of the senate, arises upon the first of the series of offences designated in the statute as impeachable, and that is "*corruption or other misconduct in his official capacity.*"

The managers, as I understand them, rely on that, and rely on no other provision of the statute, for the conviction of the respondent. We propose, then, to narrow the discussion to those acts of the respondent which are essentially and properly *official*—which are done by virtue of the office which he holds, as distinguished from all others,—acts which under the constitution and according to its requirements unfit the incumbent thereafter to hold the office or to be trusted with the exercise of its functions.

What, then, let us enquire, is essential to the guilt of the accused? It is not every breach of official obligation and duty; it is not every assumption of unauthorized power; it is not every excess of power conferred. These may have been done or omitted, and yet the officer not be liable to impeachment. If the object in view be, and senators so believe upon the evidence, the preservation of greater interests or the defence of greater rights, then although he be amenable to criminal prosecution, we shall insist that he is not amenable, for the charge in this form of procedure. We have abundant examples showing the correctness of this general view of the subject. Senators need scarcely to be reminded of the numerous acts of the president of the United States, in excess of his rightful authority, committed at the beginning of the late civil war, for which he was not called to account, and never would have been held responsible to public justice, whatever may have been the issue of the impending struggle and whatever party may have succeeded to the ascendancy upon its close. The *motives* which prompted the exercise of the power would have furnished full and ample justification, before any tribunal called upon to determine the question of his official guilt. I cannot better illustrate this than by referring to the numerous instances, scattered over the history of the United States in the earlier states of that terrible sectional conflict, of unlawful arrest of persons in parts of the country, where the civil authority was in full exercise of all its powers—the instances in which men were seized and deprived of their liberty, and, when attempted to be released from unlawful restraint under judicial proceedings, were still held in custody by direction of the president. It is fresh in the minds of all that a large number of the members of the general assembly of Maryland, on their return home from Frederick, after adjournment, were arrested by military orders, carried out of the state and imprisoned in one of the northern forts, in a state where the privileges of the writ of *habeas corpus* had not been suspended, and was at the time in full force and activity. We cannot have forgotten the first case, the arrest and detention of Merryman, a citizen of Baltimore, in Fort McHenry, which called public attention to the conflict between the law and arms. He was held in custody by the military authorities and the civil power in the hands of the marshal resisted, notwithstanding the solemn decision of the chief justice of the United States, that the writ of *habeas corpus* was not suspended, and could not be except by an act of the congress of the United States; and he was so held in custody because the president had authorized and sanctioned the detention, and there was no redress under the law.

Not long after, an attorney who sued out a writ of *habeas corpus* from a judge in the District of Columbia, was himself arrested on account of this professional act; and the distinguished judge, (Merrick) who had granted the writ, on his return home after a short absence, found his house surrounded by a squad of soldiers and refused in consequence of duress, to occupy his seat on the bench with his associate justices for the further trial of the cause. These are some of the repeated instances of unlawful arrest, extending over pages after pages of the annals of that period. And yet because of the exigency which then existed in public affairs and the magnitude of the approaching conflict of arms, no one ever supposed or suggested a prosecution of the president and his removal from office because he exercised such extraordinary powers under such extraordinary circumstances. When President Lincoln in his message to the newly assembled congress, on the 4th of July, 1861, communicated to that body his conduct in relation to these various arrests, the language he employs is very emphatic and suggestive:

"Soon after the first call for militia it was considered a duty "to authorize the commanding general, in proper cases according to his discretion, to suspend the privilege of the writ of "*habeas corpus*, or in other words, to *arrest* and *detain without* "*resort to the ordinary processes and forms of law, such individ*-"*uals as he might deem to be dangerous to the public safety*. This "authority has been purposely exercised but very sparingly. "Nevertheless, the legality and propriety of what has been "done under it, are questioned and the attention of the coun-"try has been called to the proposition that one who is sworn "'to take care that the laws be faithfully executed,' should "not himself violate them. Of course some consideration "was given to the question of power and propriety before "this matter was acted upon. The whole of the laws which "were required to be faithfully executed, were being resisted "and failing of execution in nearly one third of the states. "Must they be allowed to finally fail of execution, even had "it been perfectly clear that by the use of the means necessary "to their execution, some single law, made in such extreme "tenderness of the citizen's liberty, that practically it relieves "more of the guilty than of the innocent, should to a very "limited extent be violated? To state the question more "directly, are all the laws but one to go unexecuted and the "government itself to go to pieces, lest that one be violated?"

Soon after the meeting of that congress a bill was introduced declaring the lawfulness of the acts of the president in his proclamations of blockade of the ports of the southern states, in his suspension of the writ of *habeas corpus*, and in his arrest of citizens by military order and without the forms of law, and Senator Sherman while it was under debate declared, (I quote the substance of his remarks and not his words) :

"I will vote for so much of this bill as asserts the right of "the president to declare the blockade, for that is a right of "war; but I will not vote that he has acted lawfully in sus-"pending the writ of *habeas corpus*, for the congress of the "United States alone is competent to do this. And yet I "will say, if I had been in his place, I would have done just "as the president has done. I would have exercised the pow-"er that he exercised, and his justification must be found in "the exigencies of the hour, and the perils of the nation."

And this, senators, is the proper rule alike applicable in all cases of impeachment of public officers. You are not compelled, by an inexorable rule, because the executive has transgressed the constitutional limits which define the powers of his office; you are not compelled, because he has claimed and used an authority not delegated to him, to depose him from office. It is your duty to enquire into the motives of his conduct. Was it an honest effort to discharge his official responsibilities, and execute in good faith his public trusts? Did he act for the protection of the civil rights, and for the preservation of the liberties of the people of the state? If such was his purpose, such the motive which prompted him to act in the manner in which he has acted, it would be the grossest injustice to deprive him of office and consign his name to infamy and disgrace. It is difficult to find a punishment more severe to a high-toned and honorable man than degradation from office for official misconduct; and official misconduct is not predicated of an act, the offspring of an honest and sincere intention to use an office and exercise its powers for the common good and for the well-being of the whole community.

What, then, constitutes an impeachable offence? For what official act should the governor of a state be stripped of his robes of office, and forced from a public position into private life with all the obloquy attaching to the sentence? We are not left without guidance in the principles which have been settled by judicial decision in their application to officers charged with criminal offences, and which must in their nature apply equally to the highest executive officer of a state as to others. What is meant by "corruption or misconduct in one's official capacity" in the language of the statute?

Now to constitute an offence punishable by indictment, in the case of any and all civil officers, it is necessary to charge, and on the trial to show a corrupt purpose accompanying the act, or a party cannot be convicted. For this there is abundant judicial authority and I will read a paragraph from Wharton's American Criminal Law, section 2522.

"It is generally necessary to constitute the offence" (referring to official misconduct) "that the motive should be corrupt."

And in section 2523, the principle is laid down that

"In an indictment against an officer of justice for *misbehav-* "*ior in office*, it is necessary that an act imputed as misbehav- "ior, be distinctly and substantially charged to have been done "with *corrupt, partial, malicious* or *improper motives*; and "above all, with *knowledge that it was wrong*, though there "are no technical words, indispensably required, in which the "charge of corruption, partiality, &c., shall be made."

There are many references made by the author, in support of the proposition enunciated in the text, with the citation of which I will not trouble the senate. But there is a case decided in an adjoining state, reported in 2 Leigh's (Va.) Reports, 709, Jacobs and others *vs* the Commonwealth, in which the principle of official responsibility is so plainly declared, that I shall be excused for calling to your attention the language employed by Judge Brockenbrough in delivering the opinion of the court:

"What is the criminal fact with which it is proposed to "charge these justices? Is it that they formed a court (with "the aid of two others alleged to be innocent) on the second "day of the November term, &c., at which they ordered it to "be entered of record, that Burks, who was nominated to them "by the high sheriff as his deputy, was a man of honesty, "probity and good demeanor, and permitted him to qualify as "deputy? This of itself, so far from being a crime, was, as the "law stood at that day, a legal and valid act." And he proceeds to say:

"But if they do not entertain that opinion, or if they know "that he is not a man of honesty, &c., and certify that he is, "in that falsehood, in that *corrupt conduct* consists their offence, their official misbehavior. The *scienter* is a material "part of the substance of this crime, of which there is no direct allegation in this indictment, and it cannot be supplied "by any implication or intendment whatever."

He then sums up the whole doctrine in these words:

"It is a well established principle that a judicial officer cannot "be prosecuted *criminally* for any judgment rendered by him, "however *illegal*, unless rendered from some motive of *malice*, "*partiality* or *corruption*. Much less can such a prosecution "be carried on where the act done is within the pale of his "lawful authority, without such *corrupt motive*."

We have in our own courts the same principle settled in the case of the State *vs.* Zachary, reported at page 432 of Busbee's Law Rep., wherein Judge Nash says:

"Does the giving the judgment, in the absence of the parties "and without their knowledge, in itself constitute *corruption?* "Certainly not; because it might have been in good faith; "and, if so, an indictment cannot be supported. It is the "*conception*, coupled with the act, the law seeks to punish "criminally. Cunningham vs. Dilliard, 4 D. and B., 351. To "further show the *corrupt motive* of the defendant, the indictment charges that he sold the judgment to one Allman for "a valuable consideration. It is certainly a misdemeanor in "office for a justice of the peace to sell or transfer a judgment "given by himself or any other magistrate. The law makes "the magistrate who gives a judgment its custodian. He "is bound officially to keep in his possession both the war-"rant and judgment, and the evidence of the debt,—in other "words all these papers are in the custody of the law. It was "proper, therefore, that such charge or statement should appear "upon the face of the indictment, and in fact it constituted the "*gist* of the offence said to be perpetrated by the defendant; "and the state was bound to prove it."

The result of our examination of the authorities, then, is to establish the principle that official misconduct necessarily involves *corruption*. There must be the *corrupt intent*—there must be a *guilty purpose*, without which whatever may be the character of the act done by one in his official capacity, it is not the proper subject of criminal prosecution and punishment, neither in this nor in any other form of criminal procedure known to the law. To make a case of guilt, demanding judgment against the respondent, it must be charged, and on the trial it must be proved to the reasonable satisfaction of the court, that his official conduct in the matters we are reviewing, and upon which, in your judgment of them, you are to settle the question whether he shall retain, or be expelled from his office, was prompted by, and associated with, a *corrupt intent*. If this point is made satisfactory to the senate, and accepted as a correct principle—and if, senators, you agreed with us upon the truth of the general proposition, our next step in the progress of the argument will be, to ascertain what are the circumstances preceding and attending the action of the executive, now under consideration, and see what light they shed upon the motives prompting to such action.

Let me then say that a series of outrages, extending through many months after the passage of the act which made it a crime for men to go in disguise, and especially numerous during the fall of 1869, detailed by the witnesses and fresh in the minds of the members of this body, caused the governor, in a message to the general assembly, to invite their attention to the condition of public affairs, and to the necessity of making some provisions, beyond those contained in existing laws, to repress these disorders and put an end to crime and violence. You will remember that we read in evidence his message at the assembling of the legislature in the fall of 1869, advising you to make some enactment to remedy the evils complained of and which pervaded so many counties of the state. What was the response to the recommendation? It is found in the introduction and passage of the bill now known as the "Shoffner act" in January, 1870. This measure was introduced into the senate and passed that body on the same day. It was sent to the other house without delay, and I desire to call the attention of senators to some of the proceedings attending its passage by that body for the purpose of showing—with what purpose it was passed,—what evil it was intended to redress,—and what were the powers it proposed to confer upon the executive. The bill passed the senate on its second reading by a vote ot 28 to 8; and on its third reading by a vote of 28 to 9, on the 16th day of December, 1869.

We have some instructive information in looking at the proceedings which took place in the house, when the bill came up for consideration there, and which will be found on page 185 of the house journal. Mr. Malone moved to amend section 1 by striking out the words "declare such counties "in a state of insurrection." "Mr. Argo moved a reference "of the whole matter to a special committee of five, (to be "appointed by the speaker,) whose duty it shall be to examine "into the condition of those counties, in which insurrection is "alleged to exist." Upon the motion of Mr. Argo, the vote was 37 in the affirmative and 69 in the negative. On the amendment offered by Mr. Malone, to strike from the bill that part of it which authorized the governor to declare a county in insurrection, the vote was yeas 47, nayes 64, thus showing that the house of representatives intended to retain that provision in the bill, and give to the words their full force and effect, after, as we must suppose, a discussion of their import and effect. After the bill had been amended by striking out the clause relating to the suspension of the writ of *habeas corpus*, Mr. Pou, a member, offered a substitute for the bill as amended, and I wish especially to call the attention of senators to a portion of the first section of the proposed substitute. That section is in these words:

"That the governor is hereby authorized and empowered, "whenever, in his judgment, the civil authorities in any "county are unable to protect its citizens in the enjoyment "of life, liberty and property, to declare such county to be in "a state of insurrection, and to call into active service the "militia of the state, to such an extent as may be necessary "to suppress such insurrection: provided, that the military, "when so called into service, shall act *in support of, and in* "*strict subordination to the civil power.*"

Here we have a substitute, offered in place of the original bill, in express terms declaring that, in the employment and use of a military force, it should always be "in strict subordi-"nation to the civil power," and in aid of its process. The substitute was voted down, and the bill passed as it came from the senate so far as this feature of it is concerned. The vote rejecting the amendment is not given, but the bill finally passed by a vote of 63 to 40. The few amendments made in the house were concurred in by the senate and the bill became a law as we now find it upon the statute book.

Now, senators, here is furnished clear and incontrovertible evidence, whatever may be thought of the legal right of the general assembly to pass the act, they did not intend, in making the enactment, that the military, should be used only in subordination to the civil authority. They expressly voted down a proposition which declared, positively and unequivocally, that relation of the military to the civil power, and we are not left in doubt, that the general assembly, in passing the act to meet the pressing difficulties of the case, did not intend that the power to call into active service the militia of the state, conferred upon the governor, was under all circumstances to be exercised in aid of, and subordinate to, the civil authority. Let me not be misunderstood. I am not discussing the constitutionality, nor the policy of this legislation. If it were permitted me to express an opinion, I should say it was a very unwise and impolitic measure, at least; but I am enquiring now into its proper construction and meaning, and for what objects and with what view, it was enacted. What did those members who voted for it intend to accomplish—what was their understanding of its meaning and import? And I have referred to the proviso in the section of the proposed amendment to show, beyond all question, right or wrong—constitutional or unconstitutional—the act was passed with the clear and distinct understanding, manifested by the votes of the house, that it clothed the governor with power to call out and use military force, *not* in subordination to civil process, but independently for the repression of violence and wrong. It delegates to him the right to use such force in aid of the civil authority, but it is not restricted to that use. The attempt to impose such restriction was voted down. The bill was passed with the same provision which was in it upon its introduction. The house refused to substitute in place of the words "declare it in a state of insurrection" the words "declare "it in a state of disorder," upon a motion of Mr. Malone at a later stage in the progress of the bill. And thus we have the clear, positive and unequivocal testimony of the general assembly that adopted the measure, as to what was its purpose and what would be its effect. I have before me the discussion which took place in the house when the bill was under consideration, and with the permission of the senate will read some of the remarks made by Mr. Malone, a distinguished member of that body and of the bar, on the amendment offered by him. The journal of the house does not, it is proper I should say, accord precisely with this report. I read from the *Standard* of January 15th, its report of the proceedings which took place in the house on the day preceding:

"Mr. Malone moved to strike out in the first section the "words which authorize the governor to declare a county in "a state of insurrection, and to change the word 'insurrection' "to 'disorder.'"

He is represented on that occasion to have said:

"He (Mr. Malone) declared that the conservatives did not "endorse the reported outrages of the kuklux. He contended "that the present law was amply sufficient to protect citizens "in their rights. A state of insurrection meant a state of war— "that war existed between the insurrectionary counties and the "remaining counties of the state. He cited as an example the "contest between the United States and the late insurrection- "ary states. The declaration of the existence of a state of in- "surrection implied that a system of passports would be en- "forced, for instance, that no man could pass from Chatham "county to another county without having a passport from "Governor Holden's militia, or from the insurgent portion of "the country, another evil would be that men, as alleged by a "senator, would be tried and sentenced by a drum-head court- "martial, rather than by the ordinary courts."

I refer to this speech for the evidence it affords of the legal construction put on the bill during the progress of its passage through the house by a leading member, and to show that it was passed with full knowledge of its operation and effect and of the extraordinary powers with which it undertook to invest the governor; and so strongly was Mr. Malone's opposition to the bill on this account pressed, that he declared that under its provisions a state of war might exist in a county and its people become subject to all the rigors of martial law, including trial and sentence by military tribunals, and their execution by military authority.

And now let us consider what was the measure of relief intended by the two houses, in their joint action in adopting the statute, and what does the statute authorize and require of the governor to be done under it? To ascertain these we must examine the provisions of the law and give to them a fair and just interpretation.

By the first section the governor is authorized and empowered "whenever *in his judgement* the civil authorities in any county "are unable to protect its citizens in the enjoyment of life and "property to declare such county to be in a state of insurrec-"tion and to call into active service the militia of the state "to such an extent as may become necessary to suppress such "insurrection."

What had rendered life and property insecure? How had the civil authority been rendered incapable of affording protection to both? What was the evil to be remedied, what condition of affairs was to be deemed and declared in a state of insurrection?

Most manifestly the statute had in view the outrages which we have been engaged in investigating, committed in the counties of Alamance and Caswell, and others of a similar kind perpetrated elsewhere in the state. It was intended to arrest this course of lawlessness and crime, and, because judicial process had proved inadequate to afford protection, it was thought an extreme remedy had become necessary. It was therefore to meet the very condition of things which has been disclosed by the evidence in this trial.

Whenever the governor *in the exercise of his own judgment* upon the facts, came to the conclusion that the civil authority was really and truly unable to protect life and property, then was he not only *authorized*, but, as I shall show, it became his *duty*, to declare the county in insurrection, and he would have rendered himself liable to impeachment, before this very court, and removal from office, had he remained idle, and, seeing that property and life were unsafe, and that protection could not be obtained for either under the ordinary forms of law—the very contingency contemplated in the act—had failed to use the power conferred on him for the protection of both.

I have before me, senators, a large number of references which can be cited to support the principle, that whenever a power is conferred for the public good, it involves the *duty* of exercising it, whenever the contingency arises to call it into activity. The point is so distinctly presented in an opinion pronounced by the late Chancellor Kent, in a case reported in Johnson's Reports, that I will read a part of the opinion to the senate:

"Lord Hardwicke observed in Stamper vs. Miller (3 Akt. "212) that the word '*shall*,' or '*may*' when applied to private "trusts, leaves an election to the trustees which is not the case "when the words are used in acts of parliament. And in "respect to statutes, the rule of construction seemed to be that "the word '*may*' means '*must*' or 'shall,' only in cases when "the public interests and rights are concerned, and when the "public or third persons have a claim, *de jure*, that the power "should be exercised. Thus it was held in *Alderman Black-"well's case* (1 Vern. 152) that the chancellor was bound to "grant a commission of bankruptcy, on due application and "proof, though the words of the statute were that he *may* "grant. The creditors had an interest in the application of the "power. So, in the case of the *King vs. Barlow*, as it is re-"ported in *Salkeld* (for in *Carthen* the distinction is not "noticed) the K. B. construed the words, *shall* and *may* as "being mandatory "where the statute directs the doing of a "thing for the sake of justice, or the public good." In that "case, (2 *Salk.* 609, *Carth.* 293) the church wardens were in-"dicted for not making a rate ot assessment, under the statute "of 14 Car. II. chap. 12, sec. 18, for the reimbursement of some "constables. The statute said they "shall have power and "authority to make a rate," and the statute was construed per-"emptory, and the constables had an interest in the exercise of "the power. The court observed in that case, that the statute "23 H. VI, said that the sheriff *may* take bail, which was "construed he *shall*. A similar decision was made in the "case of the *King* vs. the *inhabitants* of *Derby*, (Skinner, 370,) "where it was said, that *may*, in the case of a public officer, "was tantamount to *shall*." So, when the Shoffner act in the contingency contemplated authorized the governor to declare a county in a state of insurrection and to use military force with the view of correcting and putting a stop to those outrages, it in fact, and in truth conveyed a command which he was just as much bound to obey as he was to discharge any other official duty, provided that state of facts existed in his judgment which the statute contemplated when it gave him the authority. If *he really believed*, if his *honest judgment* was, when he issued the proclamation of March 9th, that life and property were not safe in the county of Alamance, and that the civil authority from whatever cause was unable to protect both, then I say he would have been liable to be impeached had he failed to use that extraordinary power conferred upon him to suppress the evil and afford the protection intended by the act. And certainly if this be so, he cannot be held criminally liable for using the power in good faith with a view of executing its commands and making practically effective the remedy it provides for the repression of violence and wrong.

Now, senators, this is aside from the question whether there was, in fact, in Alamance county, when the proclamation was issued, an open and forcible resistance to law. What is insurrection and whether it existed in that county, according to the legal and proper definition of the word, are not questions now to be determined. The general assembly has undertaken to confer upon the governor the right to decide the fact, and to declare that *state of things in which the judicial power proves itself incompetent to afford relief, to be a state of insurrection* for the purpose of bringing into activity the military arm of government, and by its agency to give the protection which otherwise could not be given at all. If, therefore, as we have insisted in a previous stage of the trial, the respondent really and truly believed to exist those facts, to which the statute was designed to apply, and with a conscientious conviction of them, issued his proclamation, to punish him by degradation from office for his act, would be a tyranny without precedent in the annals of criminal jurisprudence. It is altogether apart from the legitimate objects of the discussion to pause and enquire, as the managers and their counsel have done, into the nature and qualities of those offences which in the law books are denominated treason, sedition, insurrection or riot, respectively, and what are their constituent elements. Such questions are not pertinent to the issue depending before the court. Controversies as to the proper meaning of these terms, and the facts of which they consist might arise, if, as legislators, we were considering the *policy* or *unconstitutionality* of the act, but they are wholly irrelevant when the statute is unambiguous in its meaning—when its terms are clear and distinct, and when with or without constitutional sanction it plainly appears that the respondent, in fact and in truth, has exercised the power, and only the power, which the statute confers.

The governor has authority, under the constitution and in the absence of special enabling legislation, to call into service the militia "to repel invasion, and to suppress insurrection, "and riot." In this regard he is clothed with the powers which under the constitution of the United States are delegated to and divided between, the president and congress. He may put a military force in motion to overcome insurrection or riot under a plain provision of the constitution of the state, and requires, for this purpose, no legislative enactment.

The fact of the passage of the Shoffner act itself implies an intent to confer upon the governor something more than he already possessed, a larger and more effective power, and its consideration involves, not the competency of the general assembly to bestow the powers,—not the validity or expediency of the legislation,—but its fair and reasonable interpretation, and the extent and limit of the authority it undertakes to confer.

It might admit of serious doubt, if the point was directly presented, whether the legislature has capacity under the constitution to delegate to an executive officer the large discretion and extraordinary powers that are given the respondent in this act. But the point is not before us and I shall not enter into its discussion.

I beg your attention, senators, for a brief space, to the consequences of a doctrine which makes an officer responsible, criminally, for yielding obedience to the requirements of a statute and for using a power which it confers, on the ground that the statute may be itself in violation of the constitution. My associate, [Mr. Boyden] in his speech yesterday, referred to a resolution introduced into the senate at its present session by one of its most prominent members, now its presiding officer, in which is asserted, in broad and comprehensive terms, and beyond the limits to which I am prepared to give my assent, but with great force of expression, the doctrine that an executive officer, such as was the respondent in executing the Shoffner law, was bound, except in a very clear and palpable case, to obey and execute the requirements of every enactment of the legislature, and not to pass judgment upon its constitutionality; that there was another department of government to which was committed the duty of deciding questions of constitutional and all other law; that the governor was an executive officer, bound to enforce all the laws of the state, and that he had no right, under ordinary circumstances, and certainly not in a doubtful case, to suspend or resist the declared will of the law-making power, because, in his judgment, the enactment was not warranted by the constitution, and was in excess of its authority.

And would it not be very extraordinary, when both houses of the general assembly, then composed of different political elements from those which now have control, concurred with large majorities in passing the law, that the very same body should now proceed to impose an ignominious punishment upon the governor for obeying the legislative demands and giving effect to the expressed legislative will? Still more palpable will this injustice appear when the senate recalls the fact, that unlike the former oath of office, the constitution now requires the governor to swear not only to support the constitution of the United States and of North Carolina, but also "the laws of the United States and of the state of North Caro-"lina," (Art. 3, Sec. 4.) "before entering upon the duties of "his office." Nor is this an inconsiderate and insignificant change in the terms of the oath of office. When the convention which passed the organic law was considering and perfecting the article relating to the executive department, I find on page 148 of the journal the following entry:

"Mr. Forkner moved to amend by inserting after the word "constitution," the words "and laws."

"The amendment was adopted."

On the next day, February 7th, the same matter coming up, a distinguished member of that, as he is of this, body, [Mr. Graham,] moved to restore the article, as it stood before the amendment, and on page 160, the following proceeding is recorded:

"Mr. Graham moved to strike out the word "laws" in the "5th line.

"The yeas and nays were demanded and the motion was lost "by the following vote."

And then the vote is given, 42 voting in the affirmative and 54 in the negative.

Thus it is shown that the change was deliberately made and it was the purpose of the convention to impose other and further obligations upon the executive than were previously imposed. And this was the oath which the respondent was required to take, and did take, on his induction into office and before he entered upon its duties, and he then swore in the language of the constitution, "to support the constitution and "*laws* of the United States and of the state of North Caro-"lina." It is true, that the "laws," which he is to uphold and execute, are *constitutional laws*, and that enactments in conflict with the constitution, are not laws, within the meaning of the oath, and yet it must be conceded, senators, that this addition to the obligations of the oath of office had and has a purpose; that it was intended to have some effect;—to accomplish some end ;—and that end must have been that the executive should not fail, because of his doubts of the compatibility of the enactment of the law-making power with the constitution, to obey its commands and carry into effect its requirements, and that he should, notwithstanding his own doubts, in the absence of judicial decision, execute and enforce the express will, embodied in the form of law, of the law-making department of the government.

If then, senators, I have been successful in maintaining the second proposition ;—to-wit,—that the respondent had the *right*, and that it was his *duty*, to give operation and effect to the act and to call out and to use military force, provided the exigency existed to which it applied; then we are brought to another enquiry arising in the course of the argument. For if we do satisfy the court that the respondent honestly exercised his judgment, there is an end of controversy so far as that part of the charge is concerned. And it can make no difference, in this aspect of the matter, whether you, or myself, or any other person, believe that the contingency had arisen on which the militia was to be called into active service. It is immaterial what may be our belief. The enquiry, and the only enquiry, to be made by the senate, is, was it the conviction and judgment of the respondent? Was it an honest opinion of his? Did he really and in fact come to that conclusion? Is this court satisfied, upon the evidence, that the *respondent believed life* and *property* to be *insecure* in the county of Alamance and "the civil authorities" incompetent and unable to protect them, when he issued the proclamation of March 7, 1870?

And now I proceed to show the good faith in which he did act in declaring the county in insurrection.

I will remind senators of the various appeals made by him to public opinion, before he resorted to this extreme remedy; of proclamation after proclamation issued, in which he invoked active co-operation from the leading men of the counties in which these disorders existed, and sought the aid of a sound public sentiment in putting them down and bringing offenders to justice; that his repeated calls and reiterated appeals were in vain; that crime continued and became more defiant from its immunity; that men were seized at midnight, in their own houses, scourged and maltreated; that life even was taken; and yet for these aggressions was no one convicted or punished.

In the first proclamation issued in the fall of 1868, and bearing date October 12th, the respondent uses this language:

"In view therefore of this condition of affairs, I have deemed "it my duty to issue this proclamation, admonishing the people "to avoid undue excitement, to be peaceable and orderly, and "to exercise the right of suffrage firmly and calmly, without "violence or force of any kind. Every good citizen is gratified "that North Carolina is at present as quiet and peaceable as "any state in the Union. Let us maintain this good name for "our state. Let us frown indignantly on the use of brute force, "or bribes, or threats, to control the election; and let every "officer of the state, civil and military, be prepared to check "instantly any incipient step to sedition, rebellion or treason."

"The flag of the United States waves for the protection of "all. Every star upon it shines down with vital fire into "every spot, howsoever remote or solitary, to consume those "who may resist the authority of the government, or who "oppress the defenceless and the innocent. The state govern-"ment will be maintained, the laws will be enforced, every "citizen, whatever his political sentiments, will be protected "in his rights; the unlawful use of arms will be prevented, "if possible, and if not prevented, will be punished; and con-"spiracy, sedition and treason will raise their heads only to "be immediately subdued by the strong hand of military "power."

When the act was passed making it a felony for disguised men to commit any deed of violence, another proclamation was issued, dated April 16th, 1869, that statute having been passed on the 12th of April preceding. After making this known, the governor, publishing it with his proclamation four days after its enactment, uses, in the conclusion of that proclamation, these words:

"I appeal to the great body of the people to unite with me "in discountenancing and repressing the evils referred to. "Public opinion properly embodied and expressed will be "more effectual in repressing these evils, and in promoting "the general good that will result from the complete establish-"ment of peace and order in every neighborhood in the state, "than the execution of the law itself against offenders in a "few individual cases. I respectfully and earnestly invoke "this public opinion. By the regard which we all have for "the peace of society and the good name of the state, I call "upon every citizen to unite with me in discountenancing "disorders and violence of all kinds, and in fostering and "promoting confidence, peace and good-will among the whole "people of the state."

On October 20th, 1869, when these disorders had multiplied and increased to a very great extent, he issued another proclamation in which he uses the words to which I now invite the attention of the senate, for as the senate will see I am showing what was the disposition of the governor antecedent to the proclamation of March 7th, 1870:

"It is made my duty under the constitution 'to call out the "'militia to execute the law, suppress riots or insurrection and "'to repel invasion.' I deeply regret that it seems necessary "to resort to the military power to enforce the law and to pro-"tect the citizen. But the law must be maintained. I have "waited in vain, hoping that a returning sense of reason and "justice would arrest these violations of the law. But these "evils, instead of diminishing have increased, and no course is "left to me but to issue this proclamation of admonition and "warning to all the people of the counties mentioned, whether "engaged in these flagrant violations of law, or whether indif-"ferent or insensible to what is occurring in their midst. I "now call upon every citizen in the counties aforesaid to aid "the civil power in a fearless enforcement of the laws. No set "of men can take the law in their own hands."

* * * * * * *

"I now give notice in the most solemn manner, that these "violations of law and these outrages in the aforesaid coun- "ties must cease; otherwise, I will proclaim those counties "in a state of insurrection, and will exert the whole power "of the state to enforce the law, to protect those who are as- "sailed or injured, and to bring criminals to justice. In a mat- "ter like this there should be no party feeling. It is my fixed "purpose to protect every citizens without regard to his ante- "cedents, his color or his political opinions; but to do this the "law must be sacred, must be spread over all alike, and must "be inflexibly maintained."

And when, all these measures failing; when warning after warning is disregarded; when crime follows crime, as night follows day, in rapid succession; when private houses are invad ed at the dead hours of night, and those "castles," as they are sometimes called in English law, and so sacred under ours, that every man is armed with power to take human life, if necessary in their defence, no longer afford security against violence within their hallowed precincts; when, time after time, bodies of disguised men are found prowling, in darkness, over the county of Alamance, committing outrages alike upon the guilty and the innocent who may have incurred their displeasure, with entire impunity; even after all these, the governor hesitates, anxious if possible to avert the necessity of a resort to the dire extremity of martial law.

And yet, senators, after the passage of the Shoffner act, Wyatt Outlaw is seized at his own house, near the hour of mid- night, and hanged on a tree at the county seat of Alamance by a band of seventy-five or one hundred men, armed and associa- ted to overcome all opposition, and, as if to defy all law, hu- man and divine, in sight of the courthouse devoted to the ad- ministration of justice. A few days later another poor, help- less, half-witted negro is taken from his home in a similar manner, a stone fastened to his feet, and he buried in the waters of a mill pond, to be recovered only months after when the flesh was fallen from his bones and nothing remained but a shoe and buttons, by which he could be identified.

And again, a senator, the author of the act which bears his name, is doomed to death by a secret tribunal in a decree which directed "Shoffner's *habeas corpus* to be suspended," and his body when life is extinct to be "boxed and sent" to Governor Holden, and the executioners, on their way to his house, at the time appointed, are turned back only by information that he was not in the county.

And I cannot refrain, just here, while upon this topic, from recurring to one of the most touching and tragic scenes which this investigation has disclosed. No one could have listened without a thrill of horror, to the simple and pathetic account given by that colored widowed woman, Lucinda Morrow, of the circumstances of the taking and carrying off of her husband from her bedside at night. I give her own words as she tells the story of her wrongs:

" They put the rope around his neck and took him out of " doors; kicked him about; and knocked him about, awhile, " before they got over the fence. Before they went out of " doors, he said, 'For the Lord's sake let me tell my children " good bye;' One of them says, 'G—d d—n you, we'll tell " you, good 'bye.' The children were all screaming and " hallooing. I said to them, oh! gentlemen, please spare my " husband this time. They said, G—d d—n you, we'll spare " him. Said I, oh! gentlemen, are you going to kill my hus- " band? Well, G—d d—n you, you will see him again. They " got him out of the door, and after they got him out, they " kicked him, and put him over the fence and carried him off: " and we all got into the yard, screaming and hallooing. I " I heard one of them say, after they got down the road apiece, " go back and kill every G—d d—n one of them. We went " into the house and got our clothes, and run out into the field, " and never went back to the house any more. That is all we "saw of him till next morning, when we commenced hunt-"ing for him. We found him then. He was 'dead."'

Yes, senators, his lifeless body was found next morning, with the body of a brother of the wife, both suspended from the tree, with a placard upon the former as if in mockery of the grief of a widowed woman and orphaned children.

And now when persons are found in North Carolina, with the hard and relentless ferocity which inflamed the hearts of the perpetrators of this cruel, wicked and double murder, and urged them on in the midst of the tears and screams of this final parting, insensible to both, shall all this be overlooked and no punishment be awarded for the crime, no measures adopted to prevent its recurrence?

When my friend [Gov. Graham] was indulging in strong and patriotic denunciation of the military outrages upon prominent citizens of Caswell and Alamance, as, one after another, he referred to them by name, I listened to hear from his eloquent lips, words of deep and burning indignation against the perpetrators of this greater outrage upon the person and life of Morris, an outrage which preceded in time those that invoked his severe and deserved reprobation. I thought, as I listened and listened in vain, that some sympathy was due to the victims of this midnight assassination, which far exceeds in atrocity and guilt, any thing brought to light by the prosecution during this long and protracted trial.

These crimes, except the latter, were committed within the short interval between the passage of the Shoffner act and the proclamation of March 7. And now the question confronts us, what could the respondent do? What ought he to have done?

Had the summer's elections resulted differently and had a majority of his political friends been returned to the general assembly, and had the respondent, with knowledge of the facts, refused to issue his proclamation and to enforce security and protection to the people of Alamance, would he not have justly exposed himself to a criminal prosecution and subjected himself to impeachment and condemnation before the senate for his great remissness and dereliction of duty?

Senators, was not life insecure? Let your own conciences answer. Had it not been in several instances taken by lawless violence within the interval seperating the time of the ratification of the act from that when the proclamation was issued? Will you upon your oaths say, there was no insecurity for life, no insecurity for property, and the civil authority was ample and adequate for the protection of both, during that period? And even if you can say all this, have you not charity enough for the respondent, to allow him honestly, upon the evidence, to come to a different conclusion? What would have been your conduct,—how would each one of you have acted, situated as he then was?

Appealing in vain to the people to rise in their might, and, by peaceful agencies, repress crime, no response reaches his ear. Extraordinary powers are given him to meet the emergency. Two outrages resulting in death, unparalleled in the past history of the state, and, I trust, for its honor, not to be repeated in the future, are committed in a single county, one of them under circumstances that must bring the blush of shame to the cheek of every true friend of our state.

Was the respondent to remain silent and inactive—to do nothing? When a company of more than seventy-five mounted and armed men, too strong to be overcome by any force of the civil authority that could be brought against them, arrest and hang, without resistance, an unoffending, quiet colored man, and return unmolested to their homes—when the next day, the sheriff of the county, himself a leading member of the secret organizations by whose decrees these acts of violence are done, sees the lifeless body suspended from the tree, and maks no effort to find the offenders—never summons a posse nor seeks the aid of others, to assist him in tracking the midnight marauders to their den—when every attempt to ferret out the offenders by the use of legal powers proves unavailing, was the respondent to see all this and keep quiet? If he then had honest convictions as to what his duty was under the law and failed to act upon them, his remissness under the circumstances would have been scarcely less criminal than if he were an accessory after the fact to the outrages which he might have prevented. Some forty or fifty cases of gross violence had occurred in a single county, more than twenty of them upon persons of our own color. It was under these circumstances that the proclamation was issued. Was it a crime in the respondent to issue it?

Let us, senators, for a moment reverse the picture and consider the matter in another light.

We are the dominant race in North Carolina, and, while with most of you, probably, I deemed it an unwise and hazardous experiment to elevate at once the colored man and enfranchise him with all the attributes of citizenship, and full political rights, yet the judgment of the people of the United States has determined otherwise and his full civil and political equality are guaranteed under the law. We have acquiesced in the result. Suppose, then, that bodies of armed colored men had been organized into ten companies or camps, extending over the entire county, as was the case before you of white men,—invisible by day, and like prowling beasts of the desert, leaving their hiding places at night, to execute the fell decrees of their secret tribunals upon the helpless and unsuspecting—that one and another of the white people of the county had been dragged from their beds by lawless bands of colored men,—carried to the woods—fastened to trees,—stripped, and their naked backs bruised and lacerated with the lash,—finally released with the threat that if complaint was made and redress demanded through the courts, they would be hung up by the neck, as others had been,—suppose that such acts had been committed by the colored instead of by the white men of the state, (and it is our duty,—your duty and mine,—to protect the colored man with the shield of law, as it is our right and duty to protect ourselves)—suppose, I repeat, all this violence had been committed on us, would the senate be prepared to say that the respondent shall remain with folded arms, and, with means of redress in his hands, make no effort to repress the crime and bring the criminal to justice? I commend, as a just rule of action, that golden precept, uttered from inspired lips: "Do unto others as you would have others do unto you," a lesson of sublime morality, whose observance would free the world from violence and vice and elevate our common humanity. Let us, possessing the legal and political power of the state, by our conduct, show to the colored race, that while we thought them, just emerging from bondage, unfit to be suddenly invested with full political rights,—and they are but children in intellect and knowledge, though men in stature,—until a better training and higher mental and moral culture should have prepared them for the proper discharge of the high trusts of citizenship—let us show them, and be true to our pledges, that the law is the equal protector of the humblest and the highest. Let them feel, under our administration, that the broad shield of the state is ample for their defence against all violence and wrong, committed under all circumstances and by any men, and that they may securely repose in its protecting shadow.

It has been the glory of North Carolina, in the administration and enforcement of her system of criminal jurisprudence heretofore, (as I am sure it will be in the future,) that the negro, when arraigned at the bar of his country, had accorded him every substantial right and privilege on his trial, given by law to the white man. During a period of eight years, in which it was my official duty to prosecute on behalf of the state, I do not recall an instance in which, when demanding the conviction of a colored prisoner, I failed to tell the jury—and such was, I believe, the universal practice of prosecuting attorneys throughout the state—"you must not find the prisoner guilty, "unless, upon the evidence, you would find one of your own "color guilty, and let such punishment only fall upon him, "which, under like circumstances, you would inflict on one of "your own number."

It is our solemn duty, and we should avail ourselves of the

occasion, as a privilege, if we would win them from the pernicious influences which are misleading and prejudicing their minds against their best friends—those who have lived with them and been brought up with them from infancy until the present time, to let them see and know, that in the true and honest people of North Carolina, and not in the strangers who have recently come among them, they must look for and find their truest friends and best protectors. And this we can accomplish better than by words, by frowning down and punishing every form of lawless violence, of which they are the victims, as we would, if we ourselves were the sufferers from it.

Would this senate, would the people of the state have been quiet and calm, had it been known that more than fifty white citizens of Alamance had been taken at midnight from their beds—made to get on their knees and pray for those who held them, mocking high heaven with a form of prayer—fastened by their hands or by their necks to some tree and scourged—each one of the disguised gang inflicting the decreed number of blows, until their vengeance was sated? Would senators sit quetly and unruffled in their places, while this array of wrongs upon persons of our own color was unfolded by the witnesses? And will senators be less just in the enforcement of law for the protection of the weaker, than for the protection of their own, the stronger race?

Here was then a multitude of crimes, and no punishment, no remedy for them. Personal security was constantly violated, and life even taken, and yet the criminal escapes. It is not important, in this connection, to enquire why the remedy was not applied. One thing is quite apparent, great apathy pervaded the public mind in the locality where they occurred; and I will say for that portion of the state in which, until lately, from infancy up, I have had my home, the people would never, for an hour, have tolerated the outrages perpetrated in Alamance and Caswell. Such is not the character of North Carolina—such is not the reputation of her people, and those who have inflicted this stain upon her good name are a bastard progeny, and not her true and legitimate offspring.

But so it was; crime was rampant and defiant from impunity. Men are dragged from their houses, for any and for no imputed offences—scourged and murdered—and no avenging arm is strong enough to protect. The sheriff of the county is commandant of a klan; many leading members of the organization prominent citizens; the arm of justice palsied; the criminal escapes through his disguise in the darkness of night; no one recognizes the perpetrator of the deed and there seems no great disposition to find him out. You will remember, when one of our witnesses [Dr. Moore] was asked as to the identity of those who came to kill Shoffner, and whether he recognized any one of them, his answer was, "No, I did not want to know them, I didn't "desire to mix myself up with any responsibilities for their "acts." There was little apparent inclination to bring offenders to justice. The county was in a condition of duress. Whether it was by a forcible uprising of the people or not, there was, in fact, a new usurping government set up in the county of Alamance. Your courts and your juries did not administer the law, whether from want of evidence or whatever cause. They had become powerless. There was, however, a judicial tribunal, erected within the limits of the county, embracing in its jurisdiction offences against the moral, as well as the civil law. Its sessions were in the shadows of the night, in the woods and in the field. It issued no citation, no notice of trial to the accused, and its judgments were pronounced, without witnesses and upon no other evidence than rumor. Its sentences were recorded and executed with a fatal, and unerring precision. Banded together by an oath which made it the duty of every member, from whom the service should be required, to enforce its decrees, there was no escape from its obligations.

When the witness, [Boyd] was asked, by one of the counsel for the prosecution, the question;—"Did you solemnly swear "that you would not reveal, even under oath in court, the "secrets of the order?" and the witness replied, "So I understood the oath," my friend seemed to regard the answer as conclusive proof that the witness was not worthy of credit.

Let me tell him, however, that we are not left in doubt as to the meaning of the oath, as understood among those who took it, when we know from all the evidence that the behests of the klans were carried out to the letter, when even murder was required, or any other forms of outrage. It may be, that if perjury is not among them, it is merely because of the want of evidence of the fact; and we do know that the obligation extended to the execution of decrees, involving the commission of murder, an offence of much higher grade. When we have thus the practical construction put upon the sworn obligations of the order of the White Brotherhood; when we see the actual workings of the system, it is a mere waste of words to dispute over the question how one, or another, or a third member of the order understood the oath and the obligations it imposed. It is proved, beyond all controversy, that, in consequence of these decrees, human life was sacrificed—the right of personal security, even in a man's own domicil, invaded and violated, and all the bulwarks of the law overthrown by their avenging fury.

There was then another government set up in Alamance,—without responsibility for its acts,—unseen by day, but active and efficient at night,—shrouded in a disguise so impenetrable and effectual, that its agents, like the wild beasts of the forest, disappear at daylight and are tracked only by the ravages they have committed. A new tribunal has usurped the functions of that established by law, and the rightful civil authority is paralyzed and powerless.

I do not care, for the purposes of the argument, whether it was because the judge was inefficient or unfit for his place, or the solicitor incompetent for his official duties; whatever may have been the cause, the fact is clear and indisputable, that public justice was not administered in the courts established by law. What was the respondent to do? Was this to go on and continue? Those who suffered, as they have told you, were intimidated and afraid to complain. If they complained, they dreaded another visitation of disguised men and greater outrages to be put upon them. What was to be done? Must Alamance be left thus without protection? Was no redress to be given, no security to be provided? Was the respondent to sit quietly in his chamber, indifferent to passing events, and insensible to the cries of the injured, charged with the obligation, that rests upon all executive officers, to see the laws enforced, and sworn faithfully and firmly, to discharge a high official trust to the country and to heaven? Was not the governor called upon to give protection? Would he have been excused for withholding it? You have heard evidence of the appeals made to him—you have heard his proclamations read. He finds himself compelled to use an extreme remedy—conferred upon him however by law—and for this he now stands arraigned before this court, and you, senators, his judges, are required to punish him by doing so, by expulsion from office.

When the respondent did at last put forth the power, and declared the county of Alamance in a state of insurrection he did so, as the proclamation shows, with a lingering hope, that the necessity of arming and sending a military force there might be arrested, and peaceful agencies be sufficient for his purpose. The language he employs in that proclamation is that of strong and earnest appeal:

"I have issued proclamation after proclamation to the people "of the state, warning offenders and wicked or misguided viola-"tors of the law, to cease their evil deeds, and, by leading "better lives, propitiate those whose duty it is to enforce the "law. I have invoked public opinion to aid me in repressing "these outrages, and in preserving peace and order. I have "waited to see if the people of Alamance would assemble in "public meeting, and express their condemnation of such con-"duct by a portion of the citizens of the county, but I have "waited in vain. No meeting of the kind has been held. No "expression of disapproval even of such conduct by the great "body of the citizens has reached this department; but on the "contrary it is believed, that the lives of citizens who have "reported these crimes to the executive have been thereby "endangered; and it is further believed that many of the citi- "zens of the county are so terrified that they dare not complain "or attempt the arrest of criminals in their midst."

Was it a crime to issue the proclamation? Will the court so adjudge under all the circumstances attending the act? A crime, to use a power granted by law,—to accomplish the very objects for which it was given?

But, urges one of the counsel on the other side, I regret he is not now in his seat, [Mr. Graham,] "the issuing of the procla- "mation is all that the act authorizes to be done, and the res- "pondent has no right, under its provisions, to exercise a power "or employ a force, which could not have been used before." If this remark had not come from the able and distinguished gentleman, whose sincerity and earnestness in making it I am not permitted to question, I should pass it by without comment or reply. It seems strange indeed that such an argument should be addressed to the consideration of well-instructed legal minds. What, issue the proclamation of insurrection and take no further step! Emit a paper bullet and expect to scatter the ranks of the enemy with such a missile! Why, it reminds me of the plan of attack by *concussion*, so happily alluded to on the impeachment trial of Andrew Johnson, a plan of attack conceived and executed, by one of the managers in that case, during the late civil war, upon one of the forts in this state. He proposed to destroy the fort with its garrison, by exploding a large quantity of gunpowder near its outer walls. The explosion took place and when the military chieftain, whose genius had contrived this novel method of assault, as the smoke was lifted up, looked for evidence of the destructive effects of his artificial tornado in shattered walls and scattered lifeless bodies, there before him stood unharmed the stony battlements of Fort Fisher, ready to meet another assault. And really to issue a proclamation and expect, without further action on it, to accomplish any practical result, is to give a meaning to the act, as idle as the plan of blowing up the fort. And the respondent would have cut quite as reputable a figure had he rested content with its simple promulgation ! The argument, however, is pressed and it is said that it was obviously the intention of the general assembly not to supercede, but enforce the civil authority, inasmuch as the next section provides for the removal of indictments to some other county for trial. A slight examination of the words of the statute will suffice to correct this error.

It gives him power to declare the state of insurrection and then "to *call into active service the militia of the state to such* "*an extent as may be necessary to suppress such insurrec-* "*tion.*" Have these words no meaning ? Was not the issuing the proclamation the fact precedent to the calling out the militia to act in repressing violence? While it is true the statute uses the word "insurrection," it most obviously employs the term to describe, and applies it to, that condition of affairs, in which "the civil authorities in any county are unable to "protect its citizens in the enjoyment of life and property,"— that paralysis of the judicial power, which is attended with all the evils of a physical and forcible uprising of the people in *insurrection.*

Civil government, and the administration of the criminal law, in its ordinary and proper forms, were truly and practically suspended ; whether because of an armed force overawing and deterring the courts from the exercise of their functions, or of those more deadly midnight agencies that operated in secret, it was the same to the victim who suffered.

And now let us consider what followed the proclamation and whether any necessity existed for ulterior measures. For several months thereafter, there was no substantial change. Stephens, a state senator, fell by the hand of assassins, at midday of the 21st of May, in the court house of the county of Caswell, before the insurrection had been there declared. Renewed outrages were perpetrated in both counties. But if none had occurred, the illegal organizations, from which they proceeded, still existed, with all their former capacities for mischief. The same disguised bands are there, in full activity and force. The lion lay crouching in his lair, ready at any moment to spring upon his unsuspecting prey. The remedy was not complete. The temporary cessation of crime does not necessarily imply the eradication of the agencies by which it has been committed. There was the association of the "White Brotherhood"—spread over the entire territory of Alamance—still held together by fearful and impious oaths—still meeting at night—still rendering their illegal decrees against the liberty and life of others--restrained it may be for the moment--and destroyed and broken up only, as all the testimony discloses, when the military force was sent there in July.

And what was the result of the entry of the militia under Kirk into Alamance? You may discuss the propriety and legality of the movement, and the question may be asked, as it has been by the prosecution, over and again, how could the military accomplish what the civil authority could not--what better facilities did it possess to ferret out and trace crime to its source, and vindicate, by penalties, the violated law? The answer is furnished by the simple statement of fact, that from the time when Kirk went to Alamance, these illegal organizations did cease to exist and we have no more of their fruits. Whether the instruments employed were legal and proper or not,—whether the manner in which they were used is to be excused or condemned, the indisputable fact still remains, that the object was successfully accomplished, and the career of wrong and violence arrested and ended.

And here let me say, I have not a word of apology for the military outrages upon the people of Alamance and Caswell, as I have none for those which were perpetrated before the coming of the troops. I have no extenuation for either, and yet was not the result cheaply purchased, even with the attending military excesses, which broke up and dispersed these secret organizations and restored to those counties the quiet and security they so much needed?

The troops, by their presence, seem to have formed a nucleus to which the timid, trembling victim could go with assurances of safety and protection. The vigorous and energetic measures adopted developed the existence and purposes of the conspiracy. the number of its members and its territorial extent. Men began at once to separate themselves from the organization when arrests were made, and to make disclosures concerning it, and thus was put in operation a train of means, which, while no one has been punished for past crime, have resulted in breaking up and dispersing these lawless bands and putting an end to their outrages—in concentrating upon them a universal popular odium. and in an effectual though tardy vindication of violated laws. Were not these valuable results?

Here we find bodies of men bound by ties so strong that human life was the forfeit which disobedience incurred. Of the force of the obligation, as felt by its members, we have a striking exhibition in the evidence of Patten, who, according to his own account of his treatment, suffered himself to be hung up by the neck until he fainted and was almost in the very throes of death before he would disclose his connexion with the order, or that he had any knowledge whatever of it. He denied it, and persisted in his denial up to the very moment, when, apparently, he was about to pass from this world to the solemn accountabilities of another. And shall we be told that organizations, cemented by ties so strong that death seems scarcely able to relax them, can be broken up by the regular and peaceful remedies of the law, and that no other were required?

I do not forget that one of the witnesses (Long,) who was chief and commandant of all the camps in Alamance, has testified to an attempt to disband and break them up in the month of May or June, 1869. But it is little less than idle mockery to tell us they were then dissolved, in the presence of abundant proof that the series of outrages committed after that date and up to the enactment of the Shoffner law, in number and atrocity far exceeds all that had been done before. The organizations did not cease to exist, and whether the witness separated himself from them or not, the same fatal decrees continued to be rendered and executed afterwards as before.

I will not weary the patience of the senate with a minute recital of the various acts of violence and wrong which have been developed in evidence on the examination of the witnesses. I have them in my hands, in tabulated form, from which it appears that twenty white men have been in some way maltreated and abused—most of them by whipping upon the bare back—an indignity at which the spirit of a man revolts as the last to be endured;—and that a similar and often worse punishment has been visited upon forty or more colored men. Among them, more atrocious and horrible in its conception than even the murder of Outlaw, was the attempted assassination of the member of this body, who introduced and secured the passage of the act since associated with his name. In the still hours of the night, professing to have come from a distant place, a body of armed men are on their way to his house, bearing in their hands the decree which dooms him to death, and, in its own expressive language, directs those charged with its execution, "to suspend Shoffner's *habeas corpus*," and "to box up and send his lifeless body to Holden." They are arrested on the way by information of his absence, and return with their fatal mission unfulfilled.

And by what act was the terrible penalty incurred? It was for exercising within these walls, the right of a member,—for nothing more. A peaceful, quiet and popular man, as he is proved to be, sent here as are other senators, by the suffrages of the voters of his district,—for an official act approved by large majorities in both branches of the general assembly, is sentenced to die! And yet so free and independent are your deliberations under the constitution that no representative can be called to account or held responsible criminally or civilly, for acts done or words spoken by him as such, except to the body of which he is a member.

Senators, pause and consider this meditated murder and the refined cruelty of its details—a deed which, if executed, would most probably have consigned husband and wife to one common grave, and then ask yourselves, was all this to be tolerated—was nothing to be done to prevent such acts? Which of you, returning from your official labors here to the bosom of your family, if obnoxious to the members of these secret societies, would for one moment be safe after night fall, even at your own homes? True it is, your home is your "castle," you may take life in defending it against lawless invasion—neither king in England nor other officer here may enter its portals against your will except with process in his hands,—but what do these avail—what are any legal safeguards worth—when men without law, without precept, without authority are found desperate and determined enough to break through all obligation, human and divine, and murder the innocent and unoffending?

And look for a single moment at the inexcusable wickedness of Outlaw's hanging, and how little he merited his fate. A witness [Albright] has told you that the negroes, exasperated at their treatment, and bent on revenge, at one of the meetings, deliberated upon a plan of retaliation by burning barns, a system which determined and carried out by those angry and misguided negroes, would have wrapped Alamance from one end of it to the other in flames, and brought upon its people all the horrors of internicine war. Outlaw was present at the meeting, resisted with all his influence the iniquitous suggestion saying to those assembled: "Resort to no such measure; "trust to the law; it is your only safety, your only defence." His appeals were not in vain, his counsels not unheeded. And now what is Outlaw's reward, after he has done thus much for the public good and the peace of society? He is himself dragged from home and hanged at the court house of the county, and no arm is uplifted to rescue him, no voice pleads for his release!

These things, senators, ought not to be and must not be.

The good name and honor of the state forbid. Let these colored people feel and know, that though the life of their leader was thus lawlessly taken, his words are and shall be true—the law shall be their protection and defence under all circumstances. Let them see that you will not strike down the arm that was interposed, in the hour of trial, for their defence and security.

It is not an excuse that men thus maltreated were charged with stealing, adultery, bigamy or other numerous offences over which jurisdiction was assumed. If they were guilty of crime. the law provides a mode of trial and adequate penalties. Many of the charges if true were susceptible of easy proof. The same evidence and no more should be required to convict before a legal, which is sufficient for an illegal tribunal. The violence and wrong done were not less criminal because the persons suffering had themselves committed an offence, still less if only charged with it. It is for the poor and the criminal even, that the law is specially needed. The strong may be able to take care of themselves without its aid. They may successfully repel assaults upon their persons and property. Let these men who then submitted unresisting, willing to bear upon their bodies the marks of the lash, rather than resort to violence in return, witness in the result of a trial they so intently watch and to which the whole country is looking, that this court will be just to all—protect alike the lowest and highest in the possession of every personal right—and be true and faithful to their trusts.

But Caswell is next the scene of operations, and if the argument of the defence is successful in regard to the other, it will not be difficult to apply it to this county. What then are the facts of the case in regard to Caswell?

Two, if not more, murders were committed in the county before troops were sent there—one of them under circumstances so extraordinary and mysterious that we look in vain in the annals of romance for its parallel.

In the midst of hundreds of people, met for public political debate at the court house in open day, a man who had been, and I think still was, a member of the senate, suddenly disappears from public view, and after all search has proved fruitless, is found next morning in one of the rooms of the court house, stabbed, strangled and dead. It seems impossible that such a deed should be undetected and its authors undiscovered, and yet, from that day to this, there has been no sufficient evidence of either. I shall charge it upon no one until there be proof pointing to the guilty criminal. I know and can say only this: Stevens had become very obnoxious to the people of his county. He was believed by many to have instigated or encouraged the colored people to commit outrages upon the property of white people, and was odious to them in consequence. He was present at the meeting taking notes of what the speakers said, and attention was drawn to him. He left, and soon after fell by the hand of an assassin. Who gave the fatal stroke, what hand drew and tightened the cord around his neck that stifled his cries for help and mercy is known only to the murderer and to that God before whom he and his victim must both hereafter stand.

For this and other crimes unredressed the respondent deemed it his duty to pursue in Caswell the course he had adopted in Alamance, and similar results seem to have followed. Crime ceased to be committed with impunity after Kirk and his men arrived there. True there were federal troops at Yanceyville already, but they were there to aid in the enforcement of civil process when called upon, not to hunt up and arrest offenders. They were not required for the former, for there was no open resistance to overcome.

The soldiers under Kirk, with all their lawless and violent conduct, for which I repeat I have no apology or excuse to make, have, nevertheless, it will be admitted, accomplished one good and wholesome result, and the condition of things no longer exists which preceded their coming.

I omitted at the proper time, and senators will excuse me

now for referring to some further evidence of the respondent's desire for a peaceful solution of difficulties.

You will remember, when the use of military measures had been determined on, under the advice of others, and in accord with his own disposition, the respondent commissioned a leading and influential conservative of Orange, an adjoining county, to adjust, by peaceful means, the disorders there prevailing and to restore peace and quiet to the people.

Dr. Pride Jones, when entering upon the duties of his commission, apprehending the consequences of a policy of coercion, it applied to his own county, writes back in reply, "The Kuklux cannot be put down without bloodshed." Notwithstanding this menace of armed resistance, presented in the state of public affairs, and made known to the respondent, he still hopes for a favorable issue from peaceful agencies, and says to Dr. Jones, "You have authority to promise immunity to all "who will separate themselves from these organizations and be "at peace hereafter. I cannot pardon before a conviction and "sentence. The solicitor may enter a *nol. pros.* or he may pray "judgment. I can interfere, and will interfere, in the latter "case, when in good faith, men separate themselves from the "organizations." I quote from memory and substantially his language.

In like manner Mr. Ramsey was commissioned to act, and with similar powers, in the county of Chatham, as was also Mr. Donaho in the county of Caswell. These instrumentalities, like his appeals to public sentiment, proved unavailing and fruitless of result. And now what is his crime? Wherein has he so grievously offended? In view of all the facts, has his conduct been so flagitious; is he that dark, guilty culprit, in the light of which he is exhibited by the managers to the gaze of an astonished and indignant people? Has full justice been done to the respondent and his motives in this prosecution? Is he the wicked, desperate man, represented by learned counsel, whose sole purpose, throughout his whole conduct, has been to overthrow your and our liberties and those civil institutions which secure them, in order to erect upon their ruins a party supremacy? Can you find no excuse, no extenuation, for what has been done? Must he be personally degrade andd, the stigma put upon him and his children of faithlessness and corruption in the discharge of high official trusts, when the evidence shows his motive from the beginning to have been to vindicate the supreme authority of law, and to interpose, by rigorous and forcible measures only in order to the effectual suppression of crime?

But there is another aspect of the case, which remains to be considered, and that is, the *agency employed*, the *character* and *quality* of *the military force* used by him, to accomplish the object. It is charged that the instrumentality used was not warranted by law; that he has called to his aid a band of foreign mercenaries, if the term may be applied to them; and that, instead of drawing from the regular military organization of the state, he imported from Tennessee, and commissioned as commander, a violent, unscrupulous and desperate man, and organized an army of his own, for the accomplishment of his ends.

To all this I reply at once—the *governor has authority by law to receive volunteer troops* for any and all the purposes for which the militia may be used. Such a force, when raised and accepted, is indeed a part of the militia. The act to organize the militia of the state, ratified August 10th, 1868, section 8, contains these words:

"The governor is hereby authorized to accept and organize "regiments of volunteer infantry, not exceeding six, the same "to be apportioned as nearly as possible through the state, for "which purpose the state shall be divided into three divisions, "which divisions shall constitute a major general's department. "If in the discretion of the governor, it shall be deemed advis-"able, he may also accept and organize volunteer battalions of "cavalry, not to exceed three, and one volunteer battery of "artillery, the same to be equally divided among the divisions "named in this section."

Here, then, is express authority given the respondent to accept regiments of volunteer infantry to a number exceeding those received into service. He possesses, under the law and within its limits, equal right to accept a volunteer force, that he has to call out and use the "detailed militia." Which kind of military force was most suitable to be employed in the repression of violence, is necessarily left to his own sound judgment; and if, in the exercise of his discretion, he believed the former most available and best adapted to the end, it was alike his right and duty to use it. The men constituting this force, when accepted and mustered into service, became and are as truly "militia," in the proper legal sense of the term, as those conscripted under the act between the ages of twenty and forty years. The clause in the constitution, to which we have been referred, and which declares of what persons the militia shall consist, applies obviously to that *coerced, involuntary service*, which is imposed as a duty upon a certain class of the population. It is necessary there should be limitations upon the body of men, from whom the service is to be exacted, and these limitations are founded upon age and presumed physical ability. These limitations do not apply, and are not intended to apply, to persons who *volunteer* and are *willing* to serve, though not within the constitutional age nor the obligations of the constitutional provision. There never was an instance, so far as I know, in which a volunteer was rejected, on such grounds, when he was physically and otherwise competent to perform the duty required; and therefore, we insist, whether the troops, enlisted under Kirk, were within or without the constitutional age, whether they were, as some one describes them, the rough boys of the "mountains" or the more polished people of the interior of the state, wherever they may have come from,—when accepted by the respondent, they became and were part of the militia and could be used for any legitimate and proper service for which any other class of the militia could be used.

It is charged further that officers must be *citizens* and white and colored men cannot be enrolled and associated in the same organizations, and in these respects the respondent has wilfully disregarded the requirements of law.

This charge, also, we submit, is founded on a total misapprehension of the act. The provisions is this:

"All officers and enrolled men in the militia shall take and "subscribe the oath required of officers by the constitution of "the state of North Carolina." And again the act declares:

"The white and colored men in the militia shall be enrolled "in seperate and distinct companies, and *shall never be com-"pelled to serve in the same companies.*"

This section, last quoted, relating to enrolment in companies, plainly refers to *coerced* and *conscripted* companies only. It says that persons of the two races "shall never be *compelled* to serve in the same companies." Their voluntary association in a single company is no where prohibited; and if, in any one of these companies, there was, as alleged, an intermixing of white and colored men, (and the testimony of the adjutant general of the employment of the colored men as teamsters, cooks, and in other menial offices, tends strongly to disprove it,) if this intermixing did exist, it is not in contravention of law, nor is the respondent, had the fact been brought to his notice, criminally responsible for permitting it. And there is sufficient reason for the distinction, in this regard, between *coerced* and *volunteer militia.* In the one case it is a man's own choice to become a soldier and, if he pleases, to associate himself with those of another color; and he cannot rightfully complain of his own free and voluntary act. It is quite a different thing to enforce and compel an association, which disregards the instincts of race and the prejudices of caste and color. It is only where men are *coerced* into military organizations and enrolled *under the law,* that the races are required to be formed into separate companies.

It is further urged that officers of the militia must not only be citizens but *voters,* and as a twelve months residence is necessary to this, the appointment of officers was illegal.

In support of this assertion the 11th section of the act is relied on, the words of which are :—"No man shall be an officer or "private in the detailed militia, unless he be an elector "of the state and first take and subscribe the constitu-"tional oath of office." Mark the words, "*in the detail-"ed militia.*" The act intends to mpose limitations in forming the "detailed militia," providing restrictions both upon officers and men of the "*detailed*," as distinguished from other kinds of militia, authorized under the preceding sections. It has no application to the *volunteer militia* provided for in the eighth section of the act. In the formation of this latter force, as none were deemed necessary, so none are prescribed for either officer or private, who are to constitute it.

We come now to consider the question whether the troops employed by respondent were, under the law, *properly formed* and *officered.*

These companies and the regiment they composed, were duly organized and accepted, and their officers appointed and commissioned, according to law. It was not necessary that an officer of the volunteer militia, as this was, by whatever name called for the sake of distinction, should be a *citizen*, still less an *elector*, when the commission issues to him. It is supposed the volunteers have discretion and will judiciously exercise it, in the selection of those who are to command them, and therefore the statuatory restrictions are not extended to them, which apply to other militia. Even these, however, are required to take the oath of office and swear to support the constitution of the state, and this oath is proved to have been administered to every one, officer and private, of the entire command.

The volunteer organization seems thus to have been formed and brought into service in strict conformity to the requirements of law; and, if it be otherwise, the respondent does not incur the penalty of impeachment for an honest mistake of the extent of his powers. If the court shall be of opinion, that the raising of this military force was unwarranted by law, and that it was not the militia meant in the Shoffner act, still it does not follow, in the absence of evidence of a corrupt purpose, that the respondent shall, for his errors only, be degraded from office.

Who was the master spirit and commander of the expedition which moved forward into Alamance and Caswell? Of George W. Kirk, senators, I know little or nothing beyond the disclosures of the trial. But I do know he has brought before the court testimonials of character I was not prepared to hear, after the severe invectives of the public press and the unsparing denunciations of my friend, sitting before me [Judge Merrimon.] Let us appeal to the evidence and see how he stands before the court.

Mr. Turner testifies that Kirk treated him courteously; offered him his hand, which he declined to take; and, when he spoke of the bucket of water thrown upon him, though I did not think he answered as promptly as he ought to have done, Mr. Turner did finally reply to my question, in substance, that Kirk did disapprove of it. This was the inference he had to draw from the fact that men were placed in his room to prevent a repetition of the indignity.

Judge Kerr testified, with great earnestness and feeling, to a conversation with Kirk, in which Kirk said to him, "I ask "you to do me justice if my name is ever brought up;" and his prompt response was, "I will do it, sir," and added Judge Kerr, speaking to us, "I am going to do him the justice here "to-day to say, that he always treated me with *courtesy;* ex-"cept as I was included in the general denunciatory language "addressed to the prisoners, his conduct towards me was "*courteous* and *becoming* and I have *nothing to complain of* "*him.*

It is further in proof, that, when the storm of war was over and devastation and pillage were rife in the land—when the victorious armies of the United States were passing over our impoverished and desolate country on their return home, the leading and prominent citizens of the town of Asheville, until late the residence of my friend, [Mr. Merrimon,] united in a written application to General Stoneman, to put Kirk in charge of the place to protect it from outrage and plunder, using this strong and emphatic language, "We have been taught to hate "him, but now know to appreciate and love him." I do not know that my friend was among the number of those who put their names to the petition, but as he then resided in Asheville and certainly belongs to its class of "*prominent men*," the expression of the witness will take him in.

Mr. MERRIMON. [*Soto voce.*] No, I wasn't.

Mr. SMITH [resuming]. However this may be, and of course I accept the disclaimer, the witness did swear to the fact that *leading and prominent citizens*—when a man of nerve and courage was wanted to shield the town from pillage and violence—when, as the interrogatories upon the cross-examination seemed to imply, the storm was gathering and about to pour its fire and thunderbolts upon the heads of that people—at this moment of peril and alarm—did ask of the commanding general the appointment of George W. Kirk to take charge of their town and give it protection.

Is it strange that the respondent should select a man, thus endorsed, to put in command of a force intended to protect the people of Alamance and Caswell from violence and outrage?

But, senators, we hold the respondent not to be responsible for acts committed by militay subordinates, unless directed or approved, provided only he exercise *sordinary care and prudence in their selection.* The position of commander of such an expedition was not to be desired by any one. It required a man of true courage and nerve, associated with great prudence and moderation—of ability and energy coupled with sound judgment and a humane temper—qualities so rarely found in unison—that I should not have known where to look for the man possessed of them, and fitted to conduct the enterprise to a prosperous termination. The respondent has selected Col. Kirk, who, if not residing in the state, in the past had exhibited in an eminent degree some of the qualities so desirable in such a commander. And whatever may be said about his fitness for the work, whatever of just reprobation may have been merited by the unnecessary arrest and harsh and violent treatment of prisoners, many of them most exemplary and good men, it is nevertheless certain that his operations did effectually and finally break up those numerous klans from which all the mischief proceeded.

In regard to his general character and conduct, while witnesses have testified to his reputation as a desperate and bad man, others, apparently respectable and credible, who have been with him and under him, and had opportunities to know, have assured us of the utter falsity of the report. Col. Kirk has been proved by men who served in his command during the late civil war, to have been brave in battle and gentle in peace, or in the forcible language of one of them, "a thunderbolt in war, and humane and kind to prisoners." Courage in battle is usually associated with gentleness to the captive, and these are the attributes ascribed by the witnesses to Col. Kirk. True it was, his reputation is different among those of us who were identified with and stood faithfully by the "lost cause" until its banners were forever furled upon the field of Appomatox. But, senators, we are one people now, and our charities must be as broad as the territory of the nation. We must forget the passions and prejudices which the long contest engendered, and do justice to the patriotism of those who espoused the side of the Union as we expect them to do justice to ours. I speake only of what witnesses here testified, knowing nothing, and having a right to know and tell nothing outside of the testimony in the cause. Witnesses in regard to the conduct of Col. Kirk in Caswell contradict many of the reports circulated to his injury, and in executing his most difficult and delicate task, he seems, with a single exception, to have acted with prudence and discretion. And what are the facts of this exception?

It was proved by several of Kirk's prisoners, that, on one

occasion information was brought that he was about to be attacked by an armed party from Danville, and that he declared with great vehemence of manner, if he was attacked he would kill all his prisoners and destroy the town of Yanceyville, with the women and children in it.

It is very apparent this was merely a threat, uttered in a moment of intemperate excitement and intended to intimidate. He made no attempt, no demonstration of a serious purpose, to execute the wicked threat. It was made obviously for no other object than to over-awe and prevent an uprising among the prisoners. No other fair construction can be put upon his words, for a moment afterwards, when Judge Kerr remonstrated with him and asked "why put us to death, we are your prisoners?" the ready answer is returned, "If you will "promise to be quiet, there shall not a hair of your head be "touched; if you will promise me you will do nothing, I shall "not have you hurt."

The language is that of a passionate man, uttered in a moment of great excitement, when he was expecting to engage immediately a hostile force, and wanted no impediment in his rear. And the moment the assurance required was given by Judge Kerr, the prisoners retired to a room, where they were as safe in the midst of bayonets as when they testified in this capitol. Will senators convict and condemn respondent because of a threat made by Kirk, not executed nor attempted to be, and from which, in calmer moments, as the whole of his conduct shows, his heart revolted? What crime then has respondent committed?

Will you tell me that Burgen hung men up by the neck? Will you tell me that he extorted confessions from his prisoners? Will you tell me that he levied black-mail upon them, seizing their persons and letting them go at liberty only for a pecuniary price? He ought to have been shot by some of them for his cruel and wicked acts. I have not a word of apology for this or any similar conduct. But, senators, when you refuse to permit us to show that the governor attempted to arrest and punish him for levying black-mail and for other crimes, I beg you not to remember in judgment against him that which you would not permit us to explain. You allowed us no opportunity to show what he did do. Your ruling was that all this was an after-thought and therefore inadmissible in evidence. I do not complain that you have excluded the evidence, but the respondent could justly complain, if, when you have thus closed his mouth, you should bring up the conduct of Burgen to condemn him.

But we insist that Governor Holden never sanctioned a single act of outrage on the part of these subordinate officers.

You will remember, senators, that when Kirk was dispatched to the scene of military operations, about the 20th or 22d of July, if I recollect the time aright, there was a general order issued, containing instructions as to his conduct, and therein he was expressly directed and enjoined to arrest suspected persons only, and, at the same time, to afford ample protection to the lives and property of the people. These are the instructions for which the governor is responsible, and not for their disobedience. He is not chargeable for acts of officers done in disregard of his directions; for such they and they alone are accountable at the bar of public justice. If Burgen perpetrated the excesses and enormities imputed to him—and the evidence is quite positive that he did perpetrate them—then arraign and try him for crimes as you would any other offender; for, to the extent that he wilfully exceeded his rightful authority and departed from the line of prescribed duty, he is criminal, unprotected by his commission and liable for his acts. It would be a monstrous doctrine, alike unsustained by reason or authority in law, to hold the supreme executive officer of a state chargeable personally with the misconduct of all those whom he appoints and commissions to perform public trusts. He is required to select such persons as he may deem suitable for public office, and then upon them and them alone devolve all the responsibilities of the manner in which its duties are discharged. Nor is the rule less applicable to the acts of military officers outside of the restraints imposed by the order of their superior, which, under the general law, is to them a special law for their guidance and control.

The prosecution has produced in evidence to affect the respondent (and I must express my regret that it was done) harsh and violent paragraphs from a political paper opposed to him, and seeks thereby to charge him with knowledge of what was transpiring, and of the gross outrages, mentioned and commented on therein, and invokes the condemnation of this court in that he did not interpose to prevent them.

But the statements in that paper are in many particulars quite unlike the facts as they come out in evidence on this trial, and we have, in these discrepancies, a forcible illustration of the truth, that we are not to look for a calm and unprejudiced narrative in the teeming columns of an excited partisan press and especially during an animated political campaign. I call attention, for a moment, to one of the cases so greatly misrepresented.

On August 3d, 1870, the respondent addressed to Colonel Kirk a letter, from which I will read only so much as presents the point now before us. He says:

" It is reported that Lieut. Col. Burgen, put a rope around " the neck of William Patton, one of the prisoners, to force him " to confess. Evidence obtained in this way is worthless. All " prisoners, *no matter how guilty they may be supposed to be,* " *should be treated humanely.* From my knowledge of your " character, I am sure it is only necessary to call your attention " to this matter."

This was the language of the respondent's letter of instructions to the commanding officer of the regiment in which Burgen held a subordinate position, when intelligence of the hanging of Patton reached his ears; and it appears from the testimony of Col. Clarke, who communicated the information to the governor, that notwithstanding the publication in newspapers, and notwithstanding the evidence given here, that Patton himself voluntarily sought out Col. Clarke and gave him a very different narrative of the manner of his treatment by Burgen. His statement then was that while it was true the rope was put around his neck, it was not done to punish him—that he did not so understand and it did not hurt him. This was substantially his account of the matter, and this was at once communicated to the respondent. And when the governor learned thus much, he hastened, in the letter from which I have quoted, to express his disapproval of the act, and to say that all prisoners must be treated with humanity and that no coercion must be resorted to for the purpose of eliciting evidence, not only because it was wrong in itself, but because evidence extorted by duress or menace was wholly inadmissible in court. In this connection I read an extract from a general order of July 13th, issued to Col. Kirk, through the adjutant general's office, in which it is said:

"He will take the necessary steps to preserve order, and to "give the best protection to life and property,"

We maintain, then, Mr. Chief Justice and Senators, that all which can be legally demanded of the governor is:—that he select suitable and competent officers,—that he prescribe necessary rules and instructions for their goverment and guidance—and that he interpose, when advised of misconduct, for the protection of the injured and the redress of their wrongs. When the respondent has taken all reasonable precautions, and issued general directions, as in this case, he ought not to be charged, by a fair minded body of triers, with responsibility for those acts of disobedience and lawlessness, which he disapproved and condemned, on the part of that atrocious and guilty man, who seems to have lost sight of the real objects of the military movement and to have made it subservient to the promptings of his own depraved appetite and avarice. As I have before said there is no palliation or apology for the conduct of Burgen, and it is a matter of regret that he has escaped the penalty due for his crimes.

But when this man violates the laws of the country and the

commands of the governor, addressed to his superior officer,—and when the governor promptly interferes, as soon as informed of his misconduct, to prevent its recurrence, I do protest, in the name of common justice, against a doctrine which imposes on respondent that high degree of responsibility for the acts of subordinates necessary to his conviction.

It would be very extraordinary if the president of the United States had been personally charged with every illegal act comcommitted by the infinite number of his officers, military and civil, scattered over the southern states, during the late civil commotion; as, for instance, the hanging of Daniel Bright in the county of Pasquotank, for no other offense than that he belonged to a military force, raised under the laws of this state and commissioned by its governor.

It is upon the authors of outrages like these, and those who, having power, sanction and approve, that public odium should rest, and the vengeance of violated law should fall. But the commanding officer is not a party to, nor liable to public opinion or otherwise, for a departure from the usages of civilized states, the laws of war, or the dictates of a common humanity, in what may be done against his will and without his sanction.

If then, senators, I have been successful in maintaining the propositions discussed,

1. That the proclamation, declaring the insurrection was rightfully issued by the authority and under the requirements of the act; and

2. That the force employed was regularly organized and officered according to law;

I proceed now to consider the *legal consequences of declaring a county to be in a state of insurrection*, and what may be done lawfully therein.

The necessary legal effect of such declaration, it is submitted, was to determine conclusively the fact, by a clear, incontestable and official test, with all the results of an actual subsisting insurrection. Being thus established by law, and declared by competent authority, the agencies, producing and maintaining it, could be lawfully suppressed by force. The effect of *declaring a county* in *insurrection*, was to create, for all legal purposes, a state of insurrection in such county; in other words, the *fact declared* exists, and the declaration is conclusive proof of its existence, for all objects and to admit all proper measures of repression, as if an actual insurrection is otherwise proved.

It is very true that if the governor in the exercise of the extraordinary power conferred upon him, grossly abuses it, as if, without pretext, he should assume to declare the county of Wake in a state of insurrection, he would be responsible for the abuse of his power. But the principle still remains unaltered, to-wit, that there attaches to a county so declared by authority of law, all the incidents and qualities of a state of actual insurrection. In other words the declaration is made by the statute full and conclusive proof of the fact. It is thereafter no longer the subject matter of inquiry and dispute, and, collaterally, it is to be assumed to be true and cannot be contradicted. I am speaking now of the proceeding by impeachment, because, whether the declaration be true or false, becomes a question only when the governor acts *corruptly*,—when he *abuses his trust*,—when he uses his power for *improper and unlawful ends*. If he acts honestly, he is not responsible whether the alleged insurrection exists or not.

Assuming, then, the insurrection to exist, to wit, that state of things in which "the civil authorities are unable" to protect the citizens of a county in their lives and property, what results? The *inability* of the civil authority legalizes the introduction of *force*. The putting down insurrection involves force, can be accomplished only by force and by military agencies; and whatever was that condition of the county, which warranted the respondent in pronouncing it in a state of insurrection, was the very condition of things which he was to correct by the employment of a military force. The general assembly has undertaken to say, that a *county is in insurrection*, and the *governor may so declare*, whenever in his judgment, life and property therein become insecure, and the judicial tribunals, in the use of the ordinary process of law, prove insufficient for their protection. I repeat, and it is the point on which the defence mainly depends, whenever, in the words of the act, "*the civil authorities of any county are unable* "*to protect its citizens in the enjoyment of life and property,*" and, declaring a state of insurrection is to this effect, then the military arm of government may be employed to furnish that protection and that security to both, which do not exist under the administration of the civil law. This being so, it follows, and was so decided by the chief justice, on the hearing of the *habeas corpus* cases last summer, in which all the judges of of the supreme court concurred, as he states at the conclusion of his opinion in one of them, arrests might be lawfully made of suspected persons within the limits of counties declared in insurrection. In other words, the great constitutional privilege of every citizen to be secure in person and property, and not to be interfered with, nor his liberty restrained, except upon affidavit and warrant rightfully issuing thereon, yields for the moment to a paramount law, *the law of force,* which is tolerated by the laws of the country and the usages and necessities of the state as a means of restoring the destroyed authority of the law itself.

My brother Boyden has shown in his quotations from various books, that this is not so much a species of law, but rather a temporary exercise of physical power put forth to bring about the restoration and re-establishment of the temporarily suspended civil power itself. And this being so, we submit that the *right to arrest*, so asserted by the chief justice and his associates, carries with it the *right to detain*, so long as is necessary to accomplish the objects for which the arrest is made. The arrest of suspected persons by military authority is not to bind them over for trial—its purpose is not so much to bring offenders to justice, though this may be one of its fruits, as it is to break up and destroy the illegal organzations which have been the prolific source of crime. It is a species of preventive, not remedial force, coming in to set up the displaced legal authority and restore its rightful jurisdiction. And therefore necessarily, it would seem, until the ends have been attained, the right to arrest and to detain for a limited period rest upon precisely the same grounds.

But it is argued that the respondent contemplated the trial of the prisoners by a military court and had already appointed the judges who were to hold it. It is fortunate for the respondent that this was not done and that better counsels prevailed. He has thus escaped the consequences of a very dangerous error in the construction of the provisions of the law under which he was acting, and from which it would have been a very difficult task to defend him, for the purposes of that law most manifestly were, not to set up new and unheard-of tribunals for the trial of offenders against the civil law, but to warrant the arrest and detention of them, until the insurrection is repressed, its agencies broken up and the supremacy of law and order fully restored. And thus the power given to the respondent by the act is restricted to the arrest and detention of prisoners until, and no longer than, they can be surrendered to the courts recognized by law and invested with jurisdiction to hear and determine the cause. But it is a sufficient answer to the charge to say no such military courts were held, and if the intention was entertained it was not carried into effect, so as in any way to involve the respondent.

We submit, then, senators, that arrest and detention resting upon similar foundations and supported by the same reasoning, if the writ of *habeas corpus* runs into a county in insurrection, because the constitution declares its privileges shall never be suspended, does not the right of *exemption from arrest*, otherwise than under due process of law, equally guarded in the constitution and admitting no abridgment or suspension, exist also in full vigor in such county? The right to the remedy of *habeas corpus* is no greater, nor more strongly fortified and defended, in the organic law than is that other right, to be free from unlawful arrest in the first instance. Not less valuable and important is immunity from arrest than deliverance from it when made. If the effect of the proclamation is to suspend those constitutional guarantees which secure personal freedom and to justify arrests of men upon suspicion only, what violence is there in the supposition that it also suspends the right of immediate release from custody? I am unable to see the principle upon which the two cases can be distinguished, or why the one right should be deemed less sacred than the other.

The same reasoning, which conducted the mind of the chief justice to the conclusion, announced by him heretofore, that the respondent had the right to arrest suspected persons, in a county declared to be in insurrection, would seem to prove also his right to detain for such reasonable time as was required for the suppression of the insurrection even as against this great remedial writ. This view of the subject derives additional strength from the very nature of the insurrection and the means to be used to overcome it.

Suppose there had been in truth a flagrant open armed resistance to the law and its officers,—a large conspiracy and uprising of the people—and bands of desperate men were engaged in the work of overthrowing the government and all its civil agencies, would it be seriously contended that men, thus employed, with arms in their hands, may be arrested, and, as soon as arrested, must be turned loose again to rejoin the insurgents and swell the numbers of the very bands which a military force is sent to overcome and disperse? And yet such is the inexorable result of a doctrine which forbids you to retain those whom you may have rightfully arrested, even for that short interval required for the re-establishment of a subverted civil government and the restoration of public order. And thus we maintain that the respondent finds authority for refusing to surrender his prisoners and for further keeping them in custody in the very argument that justifies the original arrest, until the purposes of the arrest have been secured.

The hour of two o'clock having arrived, the court adjourned to meet at half-past three o'clock.

## AFTERNOON SESSION.

The COURT re-assembled at half past three, Hon. R. M. Person, Chief Justice of the Supreme Court, in the chair.

The CLERK proceeded to call the roll of senators, when the following gentlemen were found to be present:

Messrs. Adams, Albright, Allen, Barnett, Battle, Bellamy, Brogden, Brown, Cook, Council, Cowles, Crowell, Currie, Dargan, Edwards, Eppes, Flemming, Gilmer, Graham of Alamance, Graham of Orange, Hawkins, Hyman, Jones, King, Latham, Ledbetter, Linney, Love, Mauney, McClammy, McCotter, Merrimon, Moore, Norment, Olds, Price, Robbins of Davidson, Robbins of Rowan, Skinner, Speed, Troy, Waddell, Warren, Whiteside and Worth—45.

Mr. SMITH, resuming his argument, said:

Mr. Chief Justice and Senators: Thanking you for the courtesy by which I am enabled to conclude the discussion of this case, I will resume at the point where I stopped when the hour for recess arrived. Senators will recollect that I was speaking in reference to the charge contained in one of the articles that the governor had violated the constitution and laws of the country by declining to surrender, upon the issue of the order by the chief justice of this state, the prisoners who had been arrested and held in the custody of the military officers. The judges of the supreme court, all, concurred in the opinion, as I have stated, that the effect of the declaration of insurrection in the counties of Alamance and Caswell, was to authorize—to legalize, so to speak—the arrest of suspected persons, without all those constitutional safeguards that are applicable to other cases in which arrests were made. And it was the opinion of the chief justice, that as soon as ordered, the writ of *habeas corpus* could run into the counties and the party was compelled to be surrendered and dischaiged upon the revision of the case by a judge of the supreme court. Now the view that we take of a state of insurrection, when declared to exist, in a county, is, that for the purposes of the case martial law prevails there, and all civil remedies are suspended. It is upon that ground only, that the arrest is lawful; and upon the same ground, it would be excusable to refuse to surrender the party who is in custody. And the right to arrest, with the grounds upon which it exists, necessarily involves that temporary detention of the prisoner which is essential to the consummation of the objects of the power declaring the locality in a state of insurrection. In other words, the constitutional right to immunity from arrest is the same in the county as the right to be set at liberty under the *habeas corpus*. It would be strange if a party could be arrested and could not be at all detained. It would be a singular omission, if martial law came in and authorized the arrest of parties and, at the same time, compelled them to be turned over immediately to a judge and liberated, and thus permitted to join the insurgent party. But that as we understand it, is not the correct view of martial law when it rightfully exists anywhere. Martial law supercedes all other law. It comes in as a sort of overruling necessity. It exists, not because it is recognized by law, but the emergency, the safety of the state, requires the exercise of something beyond, over, and above the ordinary legal tribunals of the country.

Now it is true that the privileges of the writ of *habeas corpus* cannot be suspended by law under the constitution of North Carolina, but the right to be released from an illegal arrest is *pari possee* with, and not to be extended an inch beyond the right to be protected under the constitution from any arrest at all except by a warrant issued according to law. The constitutional right to immunity from arrest is without any qualification, just as much as is the constitutional right to be discharged by virtue of the *habeas corpus*.

But whether this proposition be true or not, certanily the governor so understood it, because he regarded the opinion of the chief justice, as leaving it discretionary with him, if the public safety required that he should retain in custody the prisoners.

And so believing, and so understanding the judicial opinion pronounced, there is absent that guilty intent, that corrupt purpose, which subjects him to this mode of punishment, in declining to surrender the prisoners under the writ.

But, senators, these doctrines have been carried infinitely further in the government of the United States than they have ever been recognized in North Carolina. The privileges of the writ of *habeas corpus* cannot be suspended by the president of the United States. It is a right reserved to the congress of the United States, and has been, over and over, so decided. And yet, when these acts of arrest were being done, and when the president was refusing, upon the request of judicial authority, to surrender any of the prisoners, the attorney general of the United States, a man eminent for his legal learning and his high professional attainments, gave it as his opinion that, whenever a person was arrested by order of the president of the United States, no court in this country, federal or state, had the right to relieve him. He puts his whole argument on the ground that there are three co-ordinate and equal branches of the government; that the legislative, executive and judiciary are independent of one another in the exercise of their respective powers, and united and associated together constitute the sovereignty of the state. And the argument is, that if the president is compelled to surrender a prisoner held in custody under his order by a subordinate, it is elevating the judiciary over the executive department of the government, and it is allowing an appeal from the decision of the highest civil officer of the country—a chief magistrate—to the judges, a branch of the judicial department. Attorney General Bates gives his opinion in answer to the following questions of the president:

"In the present time of a great and dangerous insurrection, "has the president the discretionary power to cause to be ar-"rested and held in custody, persons known to have criminal "intercourse with the insurgents, or persons against whom there "is probable cause for suspicion of such criminal complicity?"

"In such cases of arrest, is the president justified in refusing "to obey a writ of *habeas corpus* issued by a court or a judge, re- "quiring him or his agent to produce the body of the prisoner, "and show the cause of the detention, to be adjudged and dis- "posed of by such court or judge?"

The attorney general held that the president had a discretionary power to arrest and forbid obedience to a writ of *habeas corpus*, and said:

"Unity of power is the great principle recognized in Europe; "but a plan of 'checks and balances,' forming seperate de- "partments of government, and giving to each department "separate and limited powers, has been adopted here. These "departments are co-ordinate and co-equal: that is, neither "being sovereign, each is independent in its sphere, and not sub- "ordinate to the others, either of them or both of them togeth- "er. If one of the three is allowed to determine the extent of "its own powers, and that of the other two, that one can in "fact control the whole government, and has become sovereign. "The same identical question may come up, legitimately before "each of the three departments, and be determined in three "different ways, and each decision stand irrevocable, biding "upon the parties to each case, for the simple reason that the "departments are co-ordinate, and there is no ordained legal "superior with power to revise and reverse their decision. To "say that the departments of our government are co-ordinate, "is to say that the judgment of one of them is not binding "upon the other two, as to the arguments and principles in- "volved in the judgment. This independence of the depart- "ments being proved, and the executive being the active one, "bound by oath to perform certain duties, he must be, there- "fore, of necessity, the sole judge both of the exigency which "requires him to act, and of the manner in which it is most "prudent for him to employ the power entrusted to him, to "enable him to discharge his constitutional and legal duty."

Now I am simply citing this opinion as that of the law adviser of the government of the United States, as to the relations between the judicial and executive departments of the country, and with that opinion published among the opinions of the attorney general—the legal adviser of the executive of the United States—certainly the present governor of North Carolina may be excused if following the opinion thus pronounced, he regarded himself as the judge in the exigency which existed as to whether these parties should be surrendered or detained. I admit it is a responsibility assumed by him for which he is amenable to this tribunal. You may enquire into the integrity of his conduct; but notwithstanding this investment of large and almost tyranical powers, the exercise of them is not itself an impeachable offence, unless accompanied with those improper motives and corrupt intentions which give to the act, and every other executive act the color which subjects him to an impeachment. If then, the executive, whether right or wrong—(I am not discussing the correctness of his opinion)—with these lights before him, with these views as to the meaning of the opinion of the chief justice himself, if he did not immediately surrender persons who were arrested and held, surely I may say in his behalf, that he ought not to be judged guilty of a corrupt purpose and intent, in doing an act which has so high a precedent and authority, as that which I have cited in its support.

It is said that there was not only an unlawful calling out of those troops, but an unlawful act of the executive in providing for their payment, and that this being done in controvention of an injunction issued by one of the judges of the state he has committed an impeachable offence, in that he incouraged and incited the paymaster of his army to pay over his funds in opposition to that fiat. Now, senators, the governor of this state is not subjected as such to the judicial fiats of the judges. To suppose that the injunction could be issued against him for an ordinary official act, is to say that if he disregarded it he could be put in prison, and the whole machinery of administration stopped. The governor is responsible, is is true, for those acts which appertain to his office, and those powers which are conferred upon it, but he is not responsible in the exercise of his functions as the chief magistrate of the state, to be controlled by *mandamus* or injunction, or otherwise from any of the judges. It is within the memory of us all, for it is an occurence dating only two or three years back, that an attempt was made, in the supreme court of the United States, on the part of the state of Georgia and the state of Mississippi, to arrest, by an injunction upon the president of the United States, the execution of those acts of congress under which reconstruction has taken place throughout the south, upon an allegation in the appeal, that those acts were in contravention of the constitution of the United States. But those bills were not entertained; leave was not given the parties to file them, on the broad ground that the courts had no right to issue an injunction to interpose between the executive of the country and the execution of the public laws of the country.

We submit that in this case they had no right to an injunction as against the governor of this state, and in fact no injunction was asked or granted against him. The injunction granted was against a subordinate officer—an appointee of his, but not an officer for whose conduct he is responsible. But if he had a right under the laws of North Carolina to call out these troops, he had a right to provide for their payment. There can be nothing criminal in executing that power because an injunction had been issued against a subordinate officer of the department, or any military officer of his appointment. I am fortified in this by the fact, that the record shows that no punishment was administered for disobedience of the injunction, but the whole matter was discharged upon its presentation the second time before the presiding judge. So that there was no breach of the injunction in that case, which induced the judge to proceed and punish anybody. The governor's right depends not upon whether it was issued, but upon his own authority, independent of the injunction, to draw his warrant and make the payment. If he had authority thus to appropriate the money in the treasury, which its payment over by the proper officers under his orders proves, the injunction granted upon *ex parte* statements contained in the bill against others, could not impair or abridge the powers belonging to the chief executive office of the state under the laws, nor is the governor in any respect amenable, by impeachment or otherwise, for the act.

But one of the articles alleges, as an impeachable offence, the arrest and detention of Mr. Turner, in the county of Orange, outside of the territory declared in insurrection.

This arrest cannot be defended upon the strict legal grounds on which the arrest of others rests, because it took place in a county in which the civil law remained in force. Let it be remembered, however, that the military movement put on foot was on a large scale and contemplated the over throw and breaking up of organizations of great strength and extending over many counties. Under such circumstances there will be occasional irregularities and excesses. which might perhaps have been avoided but which are incidental to such enterprises. They should not be allowed to loom up and assume an importance disproportionate to the matter of which they form a part. They are but eddies, ripples upon the surface of the great volume of events, as some mighty river, moving onward to the sea. If the dispersion of the illegal klans and the reinstating the dominion of law over a large territory from which practically it had been expelled, were objects commensurate in importance with the magnitude of the military operations inaugurated, and required them. the arrest wrongfully of a single per on, under great personal provocation. should not require an impeachment, when the grand military movement itself stands pproved, especially in the absence of a corrupt motive promping the act. The senate is not compelled to award a disgracel penalty simply because of an unintentional infraction of the iw.

Nor is there sufficient evidence that the arrest was made by ie orders of respondent. Those who executed the order of arrest declared that they were acting by the authority of

157

both the governor of the state and the president of the United States, and while the declarations were admitted as accompanying and qualifying the act, as part of the *res gestæ*, they are not competent to prove the truth of the independent fact that either of these executive officers did authorize or sanction what was done, in opposition to the positive averment in the answer that the arrest in Orange was neither authorised nor approved by the respondent.

I will now call your attention to some citations, in support of the positions maintained, which have been deferred until now in order that the train of argument marked out might not be broken in upon by their introduction at an earlier stage. I quote a recent work on martial law, from Finlason (page 140) where the law will be found briefly stated.

"It also follows, from the very nature of an emergency, of "which those only can judge who have to meet it and to deal "with it, that subjects to future censure by the crown for any "gross error or excess, (always assuming an honest intention "to meet the emergency, and to do no more,) the authority of "the executive or the officers of the crown entrusted with the "exercise of martial law, must necessarily be absolutely in the "sense that it is discretionary."

Then on page 148 he says:

"Yet on the other hand, under ordinary law, the meanest "magistrate or officer of justice is protected, if he acts honestly "in the exercise of a discretionary authority; otherwise it is "obvious that there would be no safety in actions in the exercise "of public functions, and no one would be willing to act on "them, the result of which would be fatal to the great objects "of government, the public safety. And if this immunity "attends the humblest officer of justice, how much more "would it in law be deemed to attend the exercise by the "executive of their high functions from which all others derive "their authority.

"The general principle upon which legal immunities rest, "namely, the public interest, which requires that those who

"are called upon compulsorily, by the obligations of public "duty, to exercise functions more or less discretionary, and "which it is for the interest of the public should be exercised "freely, with a sense of perfect freedom and independence of "judgment, without fear of legal liability for honest error. "and which is applied by the law of England, even in ordinary "times, under ordinary law, for the protection of the meanest "of its ministers, appears to apply *a multo fortiori* to those "who exercise the highest functions of the state, the functions "of supreme executive authority upon which depend the safety "of the state and the security of all the rest. And accord-"ingly so it has been held."

I desire also to refer to what is said by the chief justice of the United States in an opinion which he delivered as to the condition of a southern state declared in a state of insurrection. In a case known as the Mrs. Alexander'scotton case, [2 Wallace reports, 419.] which was a case in which claimant of the cotton alleged that though living in one of the southern states she was a loyal woman, and that therefore the armies of the United States had no right to confiscate her property as enemies' property the chief justice said:

"It is said that though remaining in rebel territory, Mrs. "Alexander has no personal sympathy with the rebel cause, "and that her property therefore cannot be regarded as enemy "property; but this court cannot inquire into the personal "character and dispositions of individual inhabitants of enemy "territory. We must be governed by the principle of public "law, so often announced from the bench as applicable alike to "civil and international wars, that all the people of each state "or district in insurrection against the United States, must be "regarded as enemies, until by the action of the legislature and "the executive, or otherwise, that relation is thoroughly and "permanently changed."

And in this connection, senators, I will say that the authority ited on the other side from another report, is totally at ariance with the principle announced in this decision as to when the state of insurrection determines. It is declared to be, in this opinion, not to be the right of each judge to determine the facts for himself, but of the executive and national authority as represented in the president and congress of the United States, whose decision upon these points the judiciary of the country must follow. And it would be very extraordinary if a judge sitting in Virginia were to declare an insurrection at an end, and another one sitting in North Carolina were to declare it in force, and we were to have a varying decision applicable to the views of each particular judge that might be called upon to pass upon the question. Far better is it to follow out the rule laid down by the chief justice, that there must be a power and authority somewhere to declare the whole insurrection at an end, which shall be binding upon and shall determine the fact for the judiciary in all parts of the country. Then we have a clear and distinct and permanent rule, one by which we may know our rights and our responsibilities.

I have said, Mr. Chief Justice and senators, all perhaps that it becomes me to say in connection with the defence. For their long and patient attention I owe to senators, and I give to them, my sincere thanks. If it shall have been my privilege to throw any light upon the subject that for seven weeks has engaged us in this investigation, I shall consider myself amply repaid for all the trouble and inconvenience to which I have been subjected.

In concluding a long, wearisome discussion, memory recalls an incident of which the occasion seems to justify a passing notice.

It is but a brief space since, at the close of our late civil war, a cloud of dark and threatening aspect hung over the southern horizon. The cause, to uphold which four years of unequalled, heroic, self-sacrificing efforts had been put forth, with its stained and tattered but undishonored banner upon the field of battle, had gone down in blood, and the conqueror stood with uplifted foot over the form of his prostrate foe.

At the moment of victory the president of the United States

fell, stricken by the assassin's hand, and a spirit of vengeance was roused throughout the north.

The bravest heart among us was appalled, and men knew not whether, in the madness of the hour, property and life would be demanded to expiate the offence of espousing the side of one's country. I had been honored by the suffrages of the people with a prominent place in the civil government of the Confederate States, during the entire conflict, and, well knowing how obnoxious I had thereby become to the re-established national authority, looked forward into the immediate future with gloomy forebodings. "*Treason must be made odious,*" was the fierce utterance which fell upon our startled ears from the lips of the successor of the fallen president! "*Treason must be made odious,*" was the echo back from the infuriated masses of the north! What is to be done? Who can help us in this emergency?

At this critical juncture, when every heart is despondent and sad, a deputation of our most honored and trust-worthy citizens, few in numbers, and the respondent among them, are seen on their way to Washington on an errand of conciliation and peace. Their patriotic efforts are crowned with success, and the respondent returns charged with the trusts of a mediation between an offended government and an offending people. He becomes, by appointment of the president, military governor, and is invested with almost imperial powers over the state. Possessing the confidence of President Johnson, and bound to him by the ties of a common political maternity, his judgment becomes the unquestioned passport to executive clemency, and an application endorsed with his approval commands a full immunity and pardon.

It is as fresh in my mind as an occurrence of yesterday, though more than five years has since elapsed, with momentous events in the nation's history, when I entered alone the chamber below, from which this impeachment, even before his conviction, has expelled the respondent, to ask his interposition and aid. I entered the room, full well remembering that I had been a life-long political opponent, and had no personal grounds on which to ask or expect an act of favor, and yet I knew there was no avenue to the ear of the president except through his provisional governor. My reception was kind and courteous, and my application endorsed without qualification, condition or terms, and soon a full pardon obtained and sent to me.

That was *my hour of darkness and trial*, as it was of thousands more of the southern people. Since, as before, I have been a political opponent of Governor Holden, and, if his views of public matters remain unchanged, shall be probably during the few remaining years of life.

But a change has come over the state and its people, mighty and sweeping, and to-day he stands arraigned before a body, largely of my own political opinions and adverse to his. The strong man has indeed become weak, and the weak man strong. The sword over ours, now hangs suspended over his head. It is *his hour of darkness and trial*, and with confidence in the manly independence and integrity of a profession that never hesitates in the path of duty, he has sought the feeble counsel and aid of a political foe. That profession represented in us,—whatever of obloquy or reproach may attach to the faithful discharge of its trusts, whatever outside popular clamor may assail—in our conduct of the defence will vindicate and assert its true dignity and its just claims to the unimpaired confidence of the virtuous and good. We will not falter in our course nor forfeit the confidence which has been reposed in us. Common gratitude, if no higher consideration, would exact this of me. I have endeavored throughout the trial to act and speak with the earnestness and candor becoming the gravity of the occasion and the interests at stake. It has been my sole purpose to point out and present the merits of the defence, and if at any moment I have over-stepped the limits of fair debate, it has been, I assure you, unintentional. And yet I feel how inadequate I have been to the task imposed. But my task is done, and graver responsibilities now devolve on you. Senators, it is a moment favorable to calm consideration. The tumultuous sea of party strife, whose tides have borne you into power, subsides into quietude, and the feverish excitements of the hour have passed away. Senators, you are *judges* now, partizans no longer, and it is for you to say if public justice demands the sacrifice of the accused. If so, the respondent, obedient to law and the decisions of its appointed judges, submits, unmurmuring, to a sentence that bows in sorrow, not himself only, but others also near and dear to his heart. Senators, judges, is this only alternative left?

The managers and their counsel demand condemnation. So demanded the managers of another prosecution, elsewhere tried, the conviction and condemnation of another son of our proud old state, in a more exalted station, where they charged him with the crime of interposing to save his mother land and her people from the avenger's wrath. In that trial, watched with the eager eyes of a nation from its inception to its final issue, right and patriotism prevailed over prejudice and passion, and the voice of party was hushed in the presence of justice! In pronouncing his opinion, said a senator who, after a life of conscientious duty performed, public and private, has gone to his reward, and whose good name will go down to posterity, associated with a sublime act of moral heroism;—"The people "have not heard the evidence as we have heard it. The re-"sponsibility is not upon them but upon us. They have not "taken an oath to do impartial justice, according to the con-"stitution and the laws. I have taken that oath. I cannot "render judgment upon their convictions, nor can they transfer "to themselves my punishment if I violate my own. And I "should consider myself undeserving the confidence of that "just and intelligent people who imposed on me this great "responsibility, and unworthy a place among honorable men, "if for any fear of public reprobation, and for the sake of se-"curing popular favor, I should disregard the convictions of "my judgment and conscience.

"The consequences which may follow, either from convic-"tion or acquittal, are not for me *with my convictions to con-*

"*sider.* The future is in the hands of Him who made and "governs the universe, and the fear that he will not govern "it wisely and well would not excuse me for a *violation of* '*His law.*"

And another, not less eminent, and still upon the stage of active life, with not less emphasis, in the conclusion of his opinion declares: "At the hazard of the ties of friendship and "affection, till calmer times shall do justice to my motives, "no alternative is left me but the *inflexible discharge* of 'duty."

These are noble sentiments, eminent examples of judicial probity and high moral courage, worthy of imitation.

Senators of North Carolina, may you, like Fessenden and Trumbull, forgetful of party strifes and party triumphs, rise to the dignity of the occasion and its grave responsibilities; rendering a judgment which shall merit and command the approval of your own consciences and of an enlightened and just public opinion, and bearing with you, from these walls to the walks of private life, the solace of a well performed act of public duty!

# FORTY-SECOND DAY.

SENATE CHAMBER, March 20th, 1871.

The COURT met at 11 o'clock, pursuant to adjournment, Honorable R. M. Pearson, Chief Justice of the Supreme Court, in the chair.

Proceedings were opened by proclamation made in due form by the doorkeeper.

The CLERK proceeded to call the roll of senators, when the following gentlemen were found to be present:

Messrs. Adams, Albright, Allen, Barnett, Battle, Beasley, Bellamy, Brogden, Brown, Cook, Council, Cowles, Crowell, Currie, Edwards, Eppes, Flemming, Gilmer, Graham of Alamance, Graham of Orange, Hawkins, Hyman, Jones, King, Latham, Ledbetter, Linney, Love, Mauney, McClammy, McCotter, Merrimon, Moore, Morehead, Murphy, Norment, Olds, Price, Robbins of Davidson, Robbins of Rowan, Skinner, Speed, Waddell, Warren, Whiteside and Worth—46.

Senator JONES moved to dispense with the reading of the journal.

The CHIEF JUSTICE put the question on the motion of Senator Jones, and it was decided in the affirmative.

Mr. BRAGG, of council for the managers, addressed the court. He said:

MR. CHIEF JUSTICE AND SENATORS: This is the forty-second day of this protracted trial, and I rejoice to be able to say, and no doubt you will rejoice with me in saying that it is now approaching its termination. To me has been assigned the duty of closing this discussion on behalf of the managers. All I regret is that the duty had not fallen to abler hands, especially as my physical condition has been such for several days as to hardly enable me properly to discharge it. In doing so I trust I shall conduct the discussion fairly. The managers ask at your hands for justice, and nothing more. I know that a great deal has been said in relation to this proceeding by several of the gentlemen who have appeared on the other side, which might indicate that possibly your minds would be so prejudiced that you would be unable to give the accused a fair and impartial trial. At one time you have been told that on a trial by political foes, of a political foe, no moral effect would be produced by a judgment on your part of conviction. At another time it has been intimated to you that consequences of a serious character might follow in case you thought proper according to your oaths and best convictions to pronounce a judgment of guilty. In fact every possible appeal has been made not only to your judgment, to your fairness, and to your mercy, but even to your fears. Senators, I have not the least doubt whatever that, notwithstanding all this, you will do as you have done heretofore—render a fair and just verdict, as you have given the accused a fair and impartial trial. If he be not guilty under the articles which have been preferred against him, in the name of God and of the people of North Carolina let him go free; but if he be guilty;—why in the name of all that is right and just, pronounce him so, without regard to consequences. The expense of this trial, so far as the accused is concerned, is to be borne by the state. Upwards of a hundred witnesses have been examined in his behalf. The utmost patience has been exhibited on the part of the court in listening to every sort of defence that could be made for him; and therefore when it is intimated that you will do otherwise than render a fair and impartial verdict, in his case, I must confess I have heard such intimations with some surprise.

Senators, this is no party trial, no trial in which the political foes of the accused seek to obtain over him a political victory, and punish him for political purposes. It is a trial in which the principles of civil and constitutional liberty, handed down to us by our forefathers, are involved, and the question is whether those great principles are to be maintained or whether hereafter they are to be regarded as a mere mockery.

Senators, have been told by learned counsel on the other side, that for the last ten years the great privilege of the *habeas corpus* has in a large portion of the country been regarded and treated as a mere by-word. I confess to some extent it is so, although I say it with sorrow. But I ask of you, senators, is it not full time that that state of things should cease? Is it not full time that examples should be made of public officers who have assumed to themselves powers and authorities not delegated by the constitution and laws? And for one, I shall be proud if North Carolina in this first impeachment, as it is said, of a governor of a state, shall let it be known not only to the people here, but to the people in other states, and the whole world, that those great principles of liberty and law of which I have spoken are hereafter to be held sacred and inviolable. You have been told that, during the rebellion, while war was flagrant, while the life of the nation, as some say, was at stake—a late president of the United States assumed to himself the power and authority to disregard the privilege of the great writ of *habeas corpus*. One of the learned counsel told you that in many instances he had done so without the assent of congress. He pointed you to the arrest of members of the legislature of a state, and to the arrest of individuals, the arrest and detention of a counsel who had merely applied for the writ to be sued out in a case of imprisonment under his, the president's, direction. I know all these things were done; and, asked the counsel, was President Lincoln impeached? No, he was not. But that was a time of war andunder very different circumstances; and whether President Lincoln was impeached or not, whether his acts were legal or illegal, censurable or praiseworthy, as some may say or think, it does not follow at all that the respondent, if he be guilty of the acts with which he is charged here, ought not to be impeached now. When he committed these acts five years or more had elapsed since the close of the terrible war through which we had passed. Is there never to be an end of these acts? Is bayonet law hereafter to be the law of the land? Is despotism to stalk through the country at its will and at its pleasure to arrest, hang and otherwise maltreat citizens? We are told that because these things had been done heretofore, under circumstances very different, that, therefore, they are to be done again. If that be so, all constitutional and civil liberty is at an end, and it is useless to talk further about it. Yes, senators, it is time that these things should cease. It is time that an example should be made. It is time that the people of this country should re-establish what was known as their constitutional rights and liberties before the unfortunate civil war which raged for four years, but which has long since terminated.

Before I proceed to the discussion of this case, it will be proper, I think, for me to state to senators what I consider to be the legal grounds taken in the defence here,—the grounds upon which a verdict of acquittal is asked. In the discussion of these questions, I shall necessarily have to repeat a good deal of what has been said before, and perhaps better said than I can say it. But I desire to do it in order to again present to your minds clearly and distinctly, as far as I am able, the points which have been made for the defence, and then I will follow with some on the part of the prosecution which I shall insist are involved in this case. I understand these positions to be assumed on the part of the defence:

1. That the respondent was by law invested with a discretion; that whatever he did was in pursuance of that discretion, given by the legislature, and that he is not amenable to this tribunal for any of the acts charged.

2. That by the Shoffner act, so commonly called, he was empowered to declare the counties of Alamance and Caswell in a state of insurrection; that having done so the legal effect thereof was to set aside all civil law, including the constitution of the United States and the laws thereof, as well as the constitution and laws of the state of North Carolina, and substitute, until the governor or legislature should declare the insurrection at an end, what they call *martial law*, to be exercised

and enforced by the governor of the state at his will and his pleasure; and that neither the judiciary nor any other department of the government could question such power by writs of *habeas corpus* or otherwise.

3. That even if that were not so, the effect of declaring these counties in a state of insurrection was, in a legal point of view, to put all the people therein in the attitude of insurrection; and that the respondent had rightful authority to arrest or cause to be arrested any and all ot them, by military force only, and to detain them as long as in his opinion the public safety or interest required it; and until that time the judiciary had no right to discharge any such prisoners by the writ ot *habeas corpus*.

4. That the effect of declaring a county in insurrection by the governor, under the Shoffner act, was and is legally conclusive of the fact that such insurrection did exist, and connot be contradicted or called in question before this court.

5. That though the acts complained of *were* unlawful, yet if they were necessary to be done, in the opinion of the respondent, to promote the public interest, he cannot be convicted on impeachment for doing them.

6. That a criminal intent is involved in every offence; and if the respondent honestly believed that he was acting legally, then he ought to be acquitted, notwithstanding the constitution and laws were in fact violated.

7. That the respondent is not responsible for the acts of his subordinate officers, however improper or illegal they may have been, unless he directly authorized or knowingly suffered such acts to be done.

Now, senators, I submit to you that this is a fair statement of the legal positions taken by the counsel for the defence. If it is not, then I am incapable, I confess, of making a correct statement of their positions of law. I have prepared this statement with some care. I have designed it to be correct, and I believe it is so. And I propose to say something in relation to these positions before I proceed to lay down certain ones of my own, and to discuss the various questions involved in these articles of impeachment.

The question was asked by one of the counsel, in reciting some cases of crime committed in one or other of the counties, whether the senate were prepared to justify that? If you convict do you necessarily justify the outrages, or any of them that were committed in either the one or the other of those counties? That is not the question. No senator within the hearing of my voice, I apprehend, justifies or will attempt to justify any of these outrages. Certainly I do not. I condemn them all, from the greatest to the least, and I say that those who have committed them are yet amenable, and ought to be punished for them, and I believe that every member of this body is in accord with me in that sentiment. But that is not the question here. The question here is, admitting that offences were committed against the law of the land by others, whether or not the accused himself, as the chief executive officer of the state, has not violated the law, and been guilty of great abuses in his office.

But now, let us see how far these positions of law, laid down here by the defence are tenable. In my humble judgment not one of them is tenable to the extent claimed. It is to me amazing that the accused in his formal defence to the articles of impeachment, drawn up with care, prepared by able counsel, should have thought proper to insist before such a body as this that, assuming, under the Shoffner act, he had a discretionary power to declare a county in insurrection, he is amenable to nobody, not even to this body, nor to any other department of the state government, for whatever offence he may have committed—for whatever abuse of office he may have perpetrated, for none of the illegal acts with which he stands charged here, because he had the discretionary power to declare counties in a state of insurrection, and power to suppress such insurrection. Why, senators, that question has already been discussed in a measure before this body. That would make the executive of the state, I was going to say, a tyrant. It would depend, perhaps, upon his conduct, but certainly it would clothe him with autocratic power. Will it be seriously contended that the legislature gave him, or had the right to give him, any such power? From whence could he get it? Certainly not from the constitution of the state, which defines and limits the powers of state government, the executive, the legislative and the judicial; and all powers not delegated, it is provided expressly by the constitution, are retained by the people. Then, from whence comes this power? Why it is a total mistake, a misapprehension of the principle laid down in the case which has been so often cited here—the case of Martin vs. Mott in 12 Wheaton's Reports. There it was stated that an executive officer, the president, having the discretionary power conferred upon him by the constitution and laws to call out the militia, in certain emergencies and for certain purposes specified, the judiciary could not call in question the fact whether the emergency existed which authorized him to exercise that power. That is all; but the officer exercising that power, it was held, would be amanable under the constitution for its exercise in an improper manner, or for its abuse. That is the true doctrine, undoubtedly. The judiciary, in the ordinary discharge of its duties and as another department of the government, could not call in question the exercise of that discretionary power at all—that is, as to whether the executive officer exercising it employed it on proper or improper occasions, or in a proper or improper manner. But in a court constituted like this, with power to try an officer upon articles of impeachment for abuse of his office, with what propriety can it be said that the constitution does not itself provide for that state of things, as it was clearly held by the supreme court of the United States it did, in the case to which I have referred? Oh, says one of the learned gentlemen on the other side, "That don't mean impeachment of the offenders. "It means by turning him out of office at the next election." Why, it means both, as every man of common sense, even without being a lawyer, must know. It means both; and when your law provides that for any abuse in office, any abuse of powers given—and there is abuse—why undoubtedly the constitution intended, and the law intended, that an officer guilty of such an abuse should be held amenable by impeachment. Why, according to that, the governor, who has the power of pardon, could not be impeached for a corrupt and improper exercise of that power. A judicial officer clothed with a discretionary power, as is often the case, could not be convicted for a corrupt and malicious or improper exercise of that power. I might go on and mention instance after instance, numberless, to show that such a position as is taken here by the accused cannot be sustained upon any principle of reason, of law, or of right.

It is a little remarkable, senators, that in another branch of the subject it is assumed, and urged with like earnestness, that this power of the governor, given under that act, was not discretionary, but was obligatory. You all remember it. An authority was attempted to be read by the learned gentleman who last addressed you [Mr. Smith,] to show that under certain circumstances the courts, in order to carry out the ends of justice, will sometimes construe the word *may* in a statute as if it had been *shall*; and it was said, so construing the act, had the governor omitted to do what he did, he would have been liable to impeachment for not executing the Shoffner act. And he asked with some feeling, "Will the legislature command the chief executive officer of the state to do a thing and then impeach him for doing it?"

Now, senators, I submit to those of you who are lawyers, and indeed to those of you who are not lawyers, that this was the position taken by the counsel for the respondent who last addressed you; and, strange as it may seem, it was urged and insisted upon, and authority cited to sustain it after, as it is within the memory of us all, the directly opposite position had been taken in the answer to these articles of impeachment, and elaborated in arguments by two at least of his associate counsel who had before addressed you—Mr. Conigland and Mr. Boyden.

Now nothing can be clearer than that both of these positions cannot be true. If the governor had a discretion given to him, by the act, under certain circumstances to declare the counties of Alamance and Caswell in insurrection, then it is very certain that no such provision made it obligatory upon him to do what he had a discretion to do or not to do. I submit to you that the counsel was mistaken not only as to the construction of the act itself, but as to the application of the authority cited by him.

But in connection with this part of the case, a matter has been brought into the discussion which it seems to me might as well have been omitted. I allude to the action of the present incumbent of the chief executive office of the state, touching the convention act passed at the present session of the legislature, and which he declines to execute upon the ground that it violates the constitution.

They say, "Would you impeach him for not carrying out or refusing to execute a law which he thinks to be unconstitutional, and yet impeach the accused, and convict him, for executing a law which it is insisted by his accusers was unconstitutional?" The cases are not parallel, nor does the point made touch but a small portion of the case of the accused. Whatever may have been the duty of the present executive of the state, I shall not undertake to discuss now. I have my own opinions about it, and they have been substantially expressed in certain resolutions now before the senate, which have been referred to by the counsel on the other side. There is, however, a marked difference between the two cases. One law is mandatory, the other is not. It I seems to me that no man of common sense can say that it was obligatory upon Governor Holden to do what it is claimed the Shoffner act authorized him to do. Had he failed to take such action it would have been a matter for which he could not have been impeached. It was solely in his discretion. The convention act is mandatory. There is the difference between the two cases.

But it has been asked whether you will pass a law and then undertake to punish the governor for executing it? Did this legislature pass the Shoffner act? A legislature passed the law, but not this one, and I shall have something to say about that hereafter. Now it may have been, and I shall endeavor to show it was so, upon another part of the case, that the governor and the legislature understood each other perfectly well when the Shoffner act was passed. They knew its purposes. They had a common design; and if the legislature passes an act undertaking to confer upon the governor of the state certain unheard of and unauthorized powers, and he is part and parcel of the whole transaction, while you cannot impeach your predecessors, are you to be precluded from impeaching the governor of the state who undertakes to exercise these powers, and moreover exercised them improperly? By no means. So, I apprehend, there is nothing in that position; and that seems to me is the main one here upon which the respondent must rest for his acquittal. It is the doctrine that martial law existed, and all other law was at an end, and that he was for the time being clothed with absolute power. There is no stopping short, when you take that position, that each and every part of the constitution of the United States and the laws of the United States, and the constitution of the state and the laws of the state, all—all cease to operate within the sphere or region of country where this martial law prevails, during the pleasure of him who is clothed with this immense power—the power of martial law.

What is martial law? Who has defined it? Who can tell what it is? Why, so far as we can get at it at all, it is the will of a commanding general, in time of war, within the lines of his army. That is it. One of the authorities read here quotes what the great Duke of Wellington said on the subject, that martial law was no law at all; neither is it any law at all—it is but the will of the commanding general for the time being. But all authorities at least agree that it can only be exercised in time of war—flagrant war—and not in such a state of things as is alleged to have prevailed in Alamance and Caswell. Was there any war there? There was no war except that made by the accused. Was there any resistance to the armed force sent by the governor? None. Were there armies there opposed to each other? No. Not a hand was uplifted against the force that he sent there. The people were counselled to keep the peace, to submit for the time being to these outrages, and they did submit one and all. That was the true state of things. Offences against the law, I admit, had been committed there, but there was no war. Yes, sir, it is gravely insisted that the effect of the Shoffner act, coupled with the declaration by him that Alamance and Caswell counties were in insurrection, was to clothe the governor of the state with these immense powers—the powor to set aside all constitutions and all laws during his pleasure; for one of the learned counsel insisted, when commenting upon a case cited by my learned associate, [Mr. Graham,] the Pennsylvania case, as it was called, that until the governor of the state, or the legislature of the state, had declared that the insurrection, so-called, had ceased, martial law continued; and he was compelled, log'cally carrying out his position, to say that the power included the right to suspend the privilege of the writ of *habeas corpus* as well as any other right of personal liberty secured or intended to be secured by the constitution—that the writ of *habeas corpus* itself, notwithstanding the decision of the chief justice of this state, did not run, legally speaking, to the counties of Alamance and Caswell, and he was necessarily compelled to take that position in order to sustain the one he had already taken, as to the existence of martial law, and by which he seeks to justify the action of the accused.

Now, senators, this is an important matter. If that position be correct, then it is useless to talk about free government any more. It that doctrine is to prevail, constitutions are not worth the paper they are printed on. But is it correct? It seems to me that to every man, lawyer or not lawyer, the simple statement of so monstrous a proposition is enough to show its absurdity and its untruthfulness. But I shall not be content with that. I shall undertake to show that by well settled law, by the decisions of our highest courts, and even by the authorities upon which the learned counsel relied to establish that position, the position is a false one. And with regard to that allow me first to ask the question, What is war? There may be war between two foreign nations, and there may be domestic or civil war. I admit that when there is organized armed resistance to a government to overthrow it, and the movement is one not of mere resistance to law, or even of mere local insurrection against law, but assumes the proportions of war against the government, then it becomes civil war—war actually exists and is recognized as such, as was the case in our late unfortunate contest. Then the rules of international law apply to it, and it is recognized by them as a state of war. But who and what part of the government of this country is authorized to make war or to recognize a state of war as existing?

The counsel on the other side who discussed this question mainly, referred us to English authorities and claimed that his position was supported by them. Now we all know the crown of England is invested with the war making power, and not parliament. But under our American system of government, the president of the United States, himself, cannot make or declare war, but congress only has that power. Has a state a right to make war? It is expressly forbidden by one of the articles of the constitution of the United States. No state is allowed to keep on foot troops in time of peace, and in another part of the same paragraph, leaving out the part which is inapplicable here—"or make war." Congress alone can do that. No state can authorize it; no petty governor can do it without making himself amenable and impeachable. Yet it is said we had a state of war in Alamance and Caswell counties. How ridiculous and absured to call the state of things which existed there a public war, so that martial law prevailed, so that the will of the governor became the law in these counties—nay outside also of these counties, in any portion of the state, where he choose to station his lawless force! And if this principle can be established and the accused shall go free here now, God only knows where and how and to what extent the exercise of that power will not be hereafter attempted. I wish, senators, to call your attention to a few authorities on this subject. I read from Wheaton's International Law, section 296, note 153.

" *Belligerent powers exercised in civil war.*—This question " has received a practical solution in a war on a vast scale— " the great rebellion in the United States, of 1861. This was " not an insurrection of professed citizens for a redress of " grievances, against a government whose general authority " they acknowledged, nor an insurrection or civil war for the " purpose of changing the government or dynasty of an ac- " knowledged common country. It was an attempt of a ma- " jority of the people in one section of the country to organize " themselves into a distinct and independent sovereignty, in " other words an attempt, by an act of revolution, to set up, " within the previously acknowledged limits of a previously " acknowledged common nationality, and of a government " acknowledged to be legitimate, a distinct and independent " nationality. As a question of law the nation could not but " regard this as rebellion and treason. It was a political " question, whether it should be acquiesced in and the inde- " pendence of the rebels recognized or the rebellion be sup- " pressed by force. The rebels organized a government com- " plete in all its parts—legislative, executive and judicial— " and set it in operation over the region covered by the great- " er part of eleven states, and declared that they should re- " gard any attempt to enforce the national authority within " their asserted limits as an act of international war; treating " the United States as a separate nationality."

So you will see from that what is a state of war, what constitutes a war, a civil war, between a government and a portion of its people, not a loose insurrection merely, opposing the government or the execution of its laws, but an attempt to overthrow the government itself. That constitutes a civil war.

But the idea that a mere paper insurrection in the county of Alamance or Caswell—(every senator within hearing of my voice knows that in point of fact there was no insurrection there whatever)—technically and in law constituted a state of war, is absurd. Call that a war!—war between whom? Who were the billigerent parties? War against the national government? The evidence is that there was not the slightest opposition to the enforcement of its laws, or in any other respect whatever. War against the state of North Carolina? Not at all. The courts all open, the law in operation, and there was no resistance to civil authority. Offences against the law had been occasionally committed, it is true—some of them outrageous in their character, if gentlemen please, but yet that did not constitute a state of war. But I have other authorities upon that subject, and will read now from 2 Black's reports, [page 666,] and from what is commonly known as the Prize Cases, decided in 1862, by the supreme court of the United States. In that case it became a question whether certain vessels that had been seized after the proclamation of President Lincoln declaring the southern ports in a state of blockade, were the subjects of lawful seizure and prize. It was decided that there was then a state of war. The only difference between some members of the court and others was as to whether the proclamation of the president, declaring that a state of war existed, was sufficient to authorize the seizure and condemnation of those vessels violating the blockade, until such a state of things had been first recognized expressly by an act of Congress—that is all. But as to the principles of international law applicable to a state of war, and to that only, there was no difference at all between the members of the court. I read from the opinion of Judge Grier:

"The parties belligerent in a public war are independent "nations. But it is not necessary to constitute war, that both "parties should be acknowledged as independent nationsor "sovereign states. A war may exist where one of the "belligerents claims sovereign rights as against the other.

"Insurrection against a government may or may not cul-

"minate in an organized rebellion, but a civil war always "begins by insurrection against the lawful authority of the "government. A civil war is never solemnly declared, it "becomes such by its accidents--the number, power and "organization of the persons who originate and carry it on. "When the party in rebellion occupy and hold in a hostile "manner a certain portion of territory, have declared their in- "dependence, have cast off their allegiance, have organized "armies, have commenced hostilities against their former "sovereign, the world acknowledges them as belligerents and "the contest a *war*. *They claim* to be in arms to establish their "liberty and independence, in order to become a sovereign "state, while the sovereign party treats them as insurgents "and rebels who owe allegiance and who should be punished "with death for their treason."

That is a state of war. And again:

"As a civil war is never publicly proclaimed, *eo nomine* "against insurgents, its actual existence is a fact in our "domestic history which the court is bound to notice and to "know."

And again, from the same opinion, I will read a passage or two on page 673.

"Under the very peculiar constitution of this government, "although the citizens owe supreme allegiance to the federal "government, they *owe* also a qualified allegiance to the state "in which they are domiciled. Their persons and property "are subject to its laws.

"Hence in organizing this rebellion, they have *acted as* "*states* claiming to be sovereign over all persons and property "within their respective limits, and asserting a right to absolve "their citizens from their allegiance to the federal government. "Several of these states have combined to form a new con- "federacy, claiming to be acknowledged by the word as a "sovereign state. Their right to do so is now being decided "by wager of battle. The ports and territory of each of these "states are held in hostility to the general government. *It is* "*no loose, unorganized insurrection having no defined bound-*" *ary or possession.* It has a boundary marked by lines of" bayonets, and which can be crossed only by force—south of" this line is enemies' territory, because it is claimed and" held in possession by an organized, hostile and belligerent" power."

Why, senators, there was not even in Alamance or Caswell *a loose, unorganized insurrection, having any definite boundary or position*,—nothing of the kind. And yet we are told that the state of things there was a state of war, and that all civil law was at an end, until it pleased the governor of the state to declare otherwise. I read still further from the opinion of another judge in that same case, Justice Nelson, as to what constitutes war in a legal sense.

"The legal consequences resulting from a state of war be-" tween two countries at this day are well understood and will" be found described in every approved work on the subject of" international law. The people of the two countries become" immediately the enemies of each other—all intercourse, com-" mercial or otherwise, between them is unlawful—all contracts" existing at the commencement of the war suspended, and all" made during its existence utterly void. The insurance of" enemies' property, the drawing of bills of exchange, or pur-" chases in the enemies' country, the remission of bills or money" to it are illegal and void. Existing partnerships between" citizens or subjects of the two countries are dissolved, and in" fine, interdiction of trade and intercourse, direct or indirect," is absolute and complete by the mere force and effect of war" itself. All the property of the people of the two countries" on land or sea is subject to capture and confiscation by the" adverse party, as enemies' property, with certain qualifications" as it respects property on land."

Now let us apply these principles to the people of Alamance and Caswell. Did they stand in the relation of enemies to the rest of the people of North Carolina? Were all contracts made between a citizen of one of those counties and a citizen of another county void? Was their property subject to seizure and confiscation? And yet, if the position taken by the learned counsel on the other side be true, all these consequences follow. And in that same opinion, senators, a case which has been referred to here as sustaining the position which the gentlemen on the other side have taken—the case of Luther *vs.* Borden, is referred to and explained. The opinion in that case was delivered by Chief Justice Taney, who was also on the bench of the supreme court at the time these Prize cases where heard before that court, and he concurred in the opinion of Judge Nelson from which I have read. Now let us see how that case is to be taken. What was the case of Luther *vs.* Borden? It is stated and explained here by Judge Nelson from whose opinion I have just read:

" The case of *Luther vs. Borden et al.*, [7 How., 45,] which " arose out of the attempt of an assumed new government in " the state to overthrow the old and established government " of Rhode Island by arms. The legislature of the old gov- " ernment had established martial law, and the chief justice in " delivering the opinion of the court observed, among other " things, that 'If the government of Rhode Island deemed the " 'armed opposition so formidable and so ramified throughout " 'the state as to require the use of its military force and the de- " 'claration of martial law, we see no ground upon which this " 'court can question its authority. It was a state of war, and " 'the established government resorted to the rights and " 'usages of war to maintain itself and overcome the unlawful " 'opposition.' "

" But it is only necessary to say that the term 'war' must " necessarily have been used here by the chief justice in its " popular sense, and not as known to the law of nations, as the " state of Rhode Island confessedly possessed no power under " the federal constitution to declare war."

So I state here now, that the legislature of North Carolina possessed no power under the constitution to declare war or authorize the governor of the state to do it. And I say further, in relation to that matter, that there could be no martial law rightfully declared or authorized by the legislature of North Carolina at all. The cases were very different. In Rhode Island there was an armed insurrection, an effort to overturn the existing charter government by force. It was opposed by force on the part of the state. What kind of a government and what sort of a constitution had the state of Rhode Island then? Why it had no written constitution except what was called the charter, granted by Charles II, simply authorizing them to establish a colonial government, undefined it its powers, unrestricted in many respects, and without those salutary prohibitions and safeguards which existed under our constitution. But how is it with ours? Look to your bill of rights, see the provisions there expressed that the privilege of the writ of *habeas corpus* shll not be suspended. See the provision there that the military shall always be kept in strict subordination to the civil power. See another provision that arrests shall not be made except upon warrants, taken out upon oath for probable cause. See the whole bill of rights; then the provision at the end of it, that powers not granted in the constitution are reserved to the people. So, I say, there could be no martial law in North Carolina, by legislative enactment, none even in the qualified sense as prevailed in Rhode Island during what was called there the Dorr rebellion. But in point of fact the legislature did not undertake to declare martial law here at all. They had no such power, and they knew it. And although they did assume very great powers. in some other respects, yet except by way of inference and argument insisted upon by the counsel on the other side, I deny that they attempted to exercise this power. They say that this matter of martial law necessarily results from what they did do. I say that no fair construction of the act would authorize any such conclusion, because such is not its language, and because it is to be supposed that the legislature did not intend to throw behind them all the provisions of the constitution intended to protect the liberties, lives and fortunes of citizens. But they merely intended to do what they did do, when they said that the governor, whenever in his judgment life and property were not safe in any county, might declare that county in a state of insurrection. They did not intend, (it ought to be at least charitably so supposed,) to set at defiance all those provisions of the constitution which were designed as safeguards of the citizen to protect him in these very rights which they said it was their purpose to protect by conferring this discretionary power. But to return to the subject of war, and martial law more particularly.

Perhaps I am piling Pelion upon Ossa with authorities upon that subject. But I will venture to read one more, (as English authority has been cited here,) and that from a very venerable father of law—I mean Coke—as to what is war. [3 Thomas Coke upon Littleton, page 40.] He concluds the subject as follows:

"Therefore, when the courts of justice be open, and the "judges and ministers of the same may by law protect men "from wrong and violence and distribute justice to all, it is "said to be time of peace. So when by invasion, insurrection, "rebellions or such like, the peaceable course of justice is disturbed and stopped so as the courts of justice be, as it were, "shut up, *et silent leges inter arma*, then it is said to be time "of war. And the trial hereof is by the records and judges "of the courts of justice; for by them it will appear whether "justice had her equal course of proceeding at that time or no, "and this shall not be tried by jury."

The same doctrine upon which I have been insisting is forcibly laid down in the case of Milligan, which has been so frequently referred to here, and which there was such a strenuous effort made on the part of one of the counsel on the other side to show was not law, but that the opinion of the courts, strange as it would seem, was not only not the law of the land, but that it was the mere *obiter dictum* of the judges concurring in that opinion.

Well, this is the first time that I ever heard the opinion of a court upon points directly involved in a case before it pronounced a mere *obiter dictum*. Now I have that case before me. I know a large portion of it has been read already and I would not trouble the senate with it again but for the elaborate effort that was made by one of the counsel on the other side to show that it had been entirely misapprehended, and that what we insisted upon here was not the opinion of the court but of certain judges thereof, and that it was not the law; that the question which they had undertaken to decide was not before them, was not presented, but that they had gone out of their way and decided a point not involved in the case. Is that so, senators? What was Milligan's case? I will dispose of it as briefly as I can.

"Lambdin P. Milligan, a citizen of the United States and a "resident and citizen of the state of Indiana, was arrested on "the 5th day of October, 1864, at his home in the said state, "by the order of Brevet Major General Hovey, military com-"mandant of the district of Indiana, and by the same authority "confined in a military prison, at or near Indianapolis, the "capitol of the state. On the 21st day of the same month he "was placed on trial before a "military commission," con-"vened at Indianoplis, by order of the said general, upon the "following charges preferred by major Burnett, judge advo-"cate of the north-western military department, namely:

"1. 'Conspiracy against the government of the United "'States.'

"2. 'Affording aid and comfort to rebels against the au-"'thority of the United States.'

"3. 'Inciting insurrection.'

"4. 'Disloyal practices,' and

"5. 'Violation of the rules of war.'

"Under each of these charges there were various specifica-"tions."

Milligan was brought before a military commission and was tried and convicted and sentenced, to be executed, and that sentence was approved by the president of the United States. He sued out a writ of *habeas corpus* before the circuit court of the United States, and his case being brought before that court, and there being a disagreement between the two judges holding the court as to whether he was properly or improperly convicted, or could be executed under the finding of the military court, as all lawyers know, upon that division of opinion between the judges, a decision by the supreme court of the United States was called for and was had in the year 1866.

The trial and conviction were during the war when every thing was in a state of heated excitement. These were the questions upon which the judges were divided:

"I. On the facts stated in the petition and exhibits, ought a writ of *habeas corpus* to be issued according to the prayer of said petitioner?

"II. On the facts stated in the petition and exhibits, ought "the said Milligan to be discharged from custody as in said "petition prayed?

"III. Whether upon the facts stated in the petition and "exhibits, the military commission had jurisdiction legally to "try and sentence said Milligan in manner and form as in said "petition and exhibit is stated."

So you see, senators, that the whole ground was covered, and not merely that arising under this act of congress of 1863, which allowed a suspension of the writ of *habeas corpus*—I mean the act of congress which required, as insisted by Mr. Boyden here, among other things, that after a certain time of detention, if a court passed and the party was not brought before that court and the charges against him inquired into, then he should be entitled to his discharge. In the meantime, however, Milligan had been tried by a military court, and he claimed his discharge not only under that act, but the whole ground was presented whether under any circumstances—that act or otherwise—a military commission sitting as this did, had a right to try, condemn, and have executed, a civilian, a man not connected with the army of the United States. Now the learned counsel, [Mr. Boyden,] says that nothing was in issue before the supreme court except as to whether this man had a right to his discharge under the act of 1863, having been detained by the military in the meantime so that he could not get before the circuit court and that that was the only question involved; that the court, in deciding upon the broad ground that martial law did not prevail in Indiana and authorize the trial, conviction and execution of this man by a military court, went out of their way and pronounced a judgment upon matters not involved in the case! Therein he is totally mistaken, as any gentleman who will take the trouble to read the facts of this case will see. Here in this volume of Wallace is the argument of counsel, occupying a hundred pages or more upon this very question among others, which was decided by the court. Well, what did the court decide? The first question raised in the supreme court was a question of jurisdiction. All the judges decided that the supreme court had jurisdiction. All agreed that the military commission had no right to try and convict him in the way they did. What was then the question about which there was some disagreement between the judges? Simply that the majority of the court held that under the constitution of the United States, even congress had not the power by any pretended law to authorize the trial and conviction of a man, situated as he was, by a military commission, whereas the minority of the court, composed of the chief justice and three other judges, said that although congress had not given such power—(that was expressly ruled)—yet that, in their opinion, congress in time of war, might give such power to try a civilian by military commission. That and other military commissions sat during the war, when the blood and the brains of men were in a seething state and had not cooled even when this decision was made. The majority of that court, however, has settled the law, as cited here, that not even the congress of the United States can by any law, even during a war, order a civilian to be tried by a military commission, but that every such man is entitled to a trial by a jury of his peers. That is a great principle of liberty which our forefathers incorporated into the constitution, and God forbid that it should ever be stricken out or silenced, or that the rights of the citizen under it should ever be impaired, diminished or taken away.

But take the dissenting opinion of the minority of the court, relied upon by my friend, [Mr. Boyden,] and let us see whether it warrants him in taking the position which he has. The chief justice says:

"We by no means assert that congress can establish and "apply the laws of war where no war has been declared to "exist."

Mark that—that not even congress could do that. Can the legislature of North Carolina do it? Can the governor do it?

"Where peace exists, the laws of peace must prevail. What "we do maintain is, that when the nation is involved in war, "and some portions of the country are invaded, and all are "exposed to invasion, it is within the power of congress to "determine in what states or districts such great and imminent "public danger exists as justifies the authorization of military "tribunals for the trial of crimes and offences against the dis-"cipline or security of the army or against the public safety."

That is all. They, the minority, held that congress had not authorized such tribunals, and they have told you when in their opinion congress may do it, differing from the majority in that respect, which we submit is the safer rule—the rule of liberty and of law.

We have had a great deal of English authority introduced upon the other side—as if it had, most of it, anything whatever to do with this case. Where is this power to be sought for in this country? In the constitution only. English authority, therefore, amounts to little or nothing upon questions of this kind. They have no written constitution defining the powers of government. The powers of that government are not limited in many respects as in our American systems, national and state. The power of the crown is vastly greater than that of the president of the United States. So that much of the authority cited upon the subject under discussion amounts to nothing. It does not follow that what the king of England may do can be rightfully done by the president of the United States, much less by a petty governor of a state.

Now as to this matter being one under the constitution, I read further from the same dissenting opinion of C. J. Chase.

"We have thus far said little of martial law, nor do we pro-"pose to say much. What we have already said sufficiently "indicates an opinion that there is no law for the government "of the citizens, the armies or the navy of the United States "within American jurisdiction, which is not contained in or "derived from the constitution. And wherever our army or "navy may go beyond our territorial limits, neither can go "beyond the authority of the president or the legislation of "congress."

One of our friends on the other side [Mr. Boyden] has produced, as one of the authorities relied upon here, Bishop on Criminal Law, which he declared to be "very high authority," and so much was he pleased at what he called this high authority that, when the question of insurrection was discussed, early in the trial of this case, he insisted, as senators will remember, that a whole chapter from it should be read to the senate notwithstanding it was stated then that it would be printed. He has again read it for your edification, and by this time, I trust, senators have it pretty safely fixed in their memories. Who is Mr. Bishop, that his opinion is to override the opinion of the judges of the supreme court of the United States? A Massachusetts lawyer, I believe, but certainly unknown to fame. I never heard of him, I confess, though that may be my own fault, until I saw first this book of his. He writes a book on criminal law and publishes it. In it is this remarkble chapter written during the war, no doubt, for the book is published in 1865. He tells you that these opinions that he puts in that chapter are his own opinions, and although he claims to deduce them from the constitution, they certainly differ widely from the constitution itself. He cites no authority whatever. He refers not to any of the fathers of the constitution or to the learned commentators who have written upon it—to Story or to Curtis or the *Federalist*—but he tells you these are his [Mr. Bishop's] opinions. They may be somewhat peculiar, he says, but nevertheless they are his. He utters them, he says, in no party sense—none whatever. Oh, no! but yet they are very extraordinary opinions and he seems to be aware of the fact. They were something new to the profession and they have never been recognized as law by any of the courts. Search this case of Milligan, decided one year afterwards. Do you see Mr. Bishop cited or relied upon there, although the case was argued by several of the ablest counsel in the land? It seems to have been regarded as the mere offspring of the heated season of the war, when, as we all know, opinions were put forward which would not bear the test of examination. Look at a later edition of his book, published since, with a reference therein to this decision in Milligan's case—and as to which he seems to have been somewhat nettled. In the third edition of his work, note 1 to the 65th paragraph, he says:

"Since this discussion originally appeared in the third edition "of the present work, the subject has been discussed before and "by the supreme court of the United States. Ex-parte Milli-"gan, 4 Wal. 2. There are in this case various expressions to "be found even in the opinions delivered from the bench not "in accordance with the doctrine of my text. Still I do not "think the text needs therefore to be in any way modified, "while yet it is important to examine the case somewhat in "this note."

And after such examination, with which I shall not trouble you, he says:

"There is much more which might be said about this case; "but the foregoing observations are sufficient to point to the "following conclusion concerning it. The court proceeded "throughout upon a misapprehension of the meaning of those "decisive statutory phrases which are a part of the fundamentals "of our language, and not of our language only, but of all "languages spoken by people who claim a share in the law of "nations, which is the common property of all civilized people. "The decision, indeed, if accepted as sound and followed here-"after, overturns a certain part of the English language and "of the language of the universal law of nations; and, with "it, a part of the law itself which is the common property of "mankind. The court is our supreme 'judicial tribunal,' "and no more. If it were a 'lexicographical tribunal,' it "would perhaps have jurisdiction of this question. As it is, I "deny that the decision is binding as law anywhere. See "Bishop First Book § 455, 456, Crim. Proced. 1, §1039, "1045. Even if it had jurisdiction, the fact that this main "point of the case was so evidently passed without a single "real thought, and without so much as a glance into the au-"thorities, would render it on familiar principles, nearly "valueless as a future authority. I shall not modify my own "text to suit the new *American*—not *English*,—which we find in "this case. My readers have the whole case before them in "the book of reports, and they can follow it as implicity as "they choose."

So, senators, you see who Mr. Bishop is, and what he thinks of the supreme court of the United States. He thinks that he. Mr. Bishop, knows much better what the law is than they do, and he does not hesitate to say so, though not in the best temper, and that is the "very high authority" with which my friend, Mr. Boyden, is so much in love. But even that authority, extraordinary as it is, and the opinions uttered by him, extraordinary as they are, apply only, as he himself says, to a state of war and not to a time of peace, and, as I have already shown, have therefore no application to our case.

Well, they refer you also to the opinion of Mr. Bates, while attorney general of the United States, which is most extraordinary of all. I regret that any lawyer, especially one who is now in his grave, should ever have penned such an opinion as that. What is it? Why that there are three independent departments in the government of the United States; that the president is one of them, and that he having in time of war exercised the power—which the supreme court, by the by, has since decided to belong alone to congress—of setting aside the privilege of the writ of *habeas corpus* and of arresting and detaining parties at his will, was the judge, solely, of what his powers were in that respect, and that no other department of the government could call in question his exercise of such authority. Why, what is the judiciary for? What are your laws in reference to *habeas corpus* for? For what was the great struggle in England for so many years against the crown, which claimed like authority? What security has any man if that doctrine is to prevail—that whenever a war exists, the president of the United States may not arrest whom he will and detain them as long as he pleases, and that no other department of the government can call his action in question? And, gentlemen of the senate, that opinion is cited here as authority to show that the governor of North Carolina can do likewise, because if it was not cited for that purpose, for what other purpose, I pray, was it cited? Yes, this extraordinary claim of power is set up here in connection with the pretended doctrine of martial law: and I say to you, senators, if such doctrines are to prevail, away with civil liberty, away with constitutional law; they are gone, they are worthless, and in their stead you inaugurate the law of one man's will—the will of a despot.

I have taken more time, perhaps, in the discussion of this question than I ought to have done. I have done so because I wanted to show its utter futility and baselessness. I believe, too, that upon that position rested mainly here the defense of the respondent; and if we have overthrown that, as I think we have completely, then, in a legal point of view, the respondent has little or nothing left to stand upon.

But this question is presented in a somewhat modified shape, in the next position taken by the counsel on the other side, and that is that the fact of declaring these counties in a state of insurrection was, in a legal point of view, to put all the people therein in the attitude of insurrectionists, and that the respondent had rightful authority to arrest or cause to be arrested any or all of them by military force alone, and to detain them as long at least as, in his opinion, the public safety or interest required it; and that, until that time, the judiciary had no right to discharge any such prisoners by writ of *habeas corpus*. Senators, is that position correct? I know that it was ruled by the chief justice, now presiding over this body, when the *habeas corpus* cases were before him, that he could not inquire into the fact whether insurrection did or did not exist; that sitting as a judge he was bound to take it that insurrection did exist, because he had no right to question the fact that it did, after a co-ordinate branch of the government, which was invested with a discretionary power to declare the counties in a state of insurrection, had done so. But with the other position which he took—(and it is with deference that I enter upon the discussion of that question)—I beg to enter here a respectful dissent. He *held* that the effect of it was to make every man, woman and child in those counties insurgents in point of law. I shall endeavor to show that it was an opinion formed and expressed, perhaps, with little consideration, and not sustained, as I believe I can show, by the very authorities upon which he relied for his decision. It seems to me that the mere statement of this position is enough to cause one to doubt its correctness. The idea that by a mere paper declaration of insurrection, every man, however innocent of any offence, in either of these two counties was in law an insurrectionist, liable to be seized and detained, without civil process or probable cause shown, or even without any charge made, is one that must strike very forcibly the mind of any man, whether he is a lawyer or not, as being extraordinary. Is there any such technical rule of law? If so, when does it apply—does it apply to such cases as we have now under consideration? Surely no rule of municipal law in a state,—lawyers will understand what I mean by that—creates any such state of things. The error of the chief justice was in applying a well known principle of international law, arising only out of a state of public war, to the case before him, as I shall endeavor to show you, but which had no proper application to a mere local insurrection in a state, (assuming that such insurrection existed,) which had not assumed the proportions of a war. Now, in that opinion the chief justice bases himself upon the opinion of the chief justice of the United States in the Mrs. Alexander Cotton Case. What was that? Mrs. Alexander lived in the state of Louisiana, upon the Red river. She was there residing during the late war. She had certain cotton in her possession. When the armies of the United States, under General Banks, made their celebrated campaign up that river, Mrs. Alexander's cotton was seized and it was carried to one of the western states, and there sought to be condemned as a lawful prize of war. That was in the year 1864. She made claim, as she had a right to do, in the circuit court of the United States. She claimed that she had always been loyal to the government of the United States, in point of fact, that the cotton was hers, that she had taken no part in the rebellion, and that, therefore, her cotton ought not to be confiscated. The case went to the supreme court of the United States, and it was there held that the cotton was a subject of seizure and condemnation, as a prize, upon the ground that when war exists, as between the belligerents, each is an enemy to the other, including all the inhabitants of the respective countries, and as an incident of war according to international law, the property of the inhabitants of the respective sections, at all events the property of those of us here who were called rebels, was a subject of seizure and condemnation—not by virtue of any act of congress, but upon the principles of international law as applied between belligerents in times of war. I wish to refer to that case. I read from page 419 of 2 Wallace—for it was upon this case alone that the chief justice in delivering that opinion based it:

"It is said, that though remaining in rebel territory, Mrs.

"Alexander has no personal sympathy with the rebel cause, "and thather property, therefore, cannot be regarded as enemy "property, but this court cannot inquire into the personal char- "acter and disposition of individual inhabitants of enemy terri- "tory.

"We must be governed by the principle of public law, so "often announced from this bench as applicable alike to civil "and international wars, that all the people of each state or "district in insurrection against the United States must be "regarded as enemies."

Now I put it to you, senators, whether the public law there referred to is not the law of nations, and whether it does not only apply to a state of recognized war between belligerents—whether that was not the meaning of the chief justice of the the United States, who delivered this opinion, and whether it could apply to such a state of things as existed in North Carolina, so as to put all inhabitants—every man, woman and child in those counties—in a state of insurrection, and make them public enemies and to be dealt with as such. Chief Justice Chase says we must be governed by the principle of public law so often announced from this bench, and he refers to the Prize Cases reported in 2 Black, and to the opinion of Judge Nelson, from which I have already read an extract, showing what were the consequences of a state of war, how each section of the country and their inhabitants became technically enemies, how all contracts and business ceased between them, how their property became liable to confiscation and seizure—all resulting from a state of war. But I will, with your permission, now read a little more from the same opinion of Mr. Justice Nelson, which is referred to by Chief Justice Chase in the Mrs. Alexander case, and upon which his opinion in that case is based:

"The ports of the respective countries may be blockaded, and "letters of marque and reprisal granted as rights of war, and "the law of prizes as defined by the law of nations comes into "full and complete operation, resulting from maritime captures, "*jure belli.* War also effects a change in the mutual relations "of all states or countries, not directly as in the case of the "belligerents, but immediately and indirectly though they "take no part in the contest, but remain neutral.

"This great and pervading change in the existing condition "of a country, and in the relations of all her citizens or subjects, "external and internal, from a state of peace, is the immediate "effect and result of a state of war; and hence the same code, "which has annexed to the existence of a war all these distur- "bing consequences, has declared that the right of making "war belongs exclusively to the supreme or sovereign power "of the state.

"This power in all civilized nations is regulated by the fun- "damental laws or municipal constitution of the country. By "our constitution this power is lodged in congress—congress "shall have power to declare war, grant letters of marque and "reprisal, and make rules concerning captures on land and "water."

And again he says:

"We have thus far been considering the *status* of the citi- "zens or subjects of a country at the breaking out of a public "war when recognized or declared by the competent power.

"In the case of a rebellion or resistance of a portion of "the people of a country against the established govern- "ment, there is no doubt, if in its progress and enlargement, "the government thus sought to be overthrown sees fit, it "may by the competent power recognize or declare the ex- "istence of a state of civil war, which will draw after it all the "consequences and rights of war, between the contending par- "ties, as in the case of a public war. Mr. Wheaton observes, "speaking of civil war, 'But the general usage of nations "'regards such a war as entitling both the contending parties "'to all the rights of war as against each other, and even as "'respects neutral nations.' It is not to be denied, therefore, "that if a civil war existed between that portion of the people "in organized insurrection to overthrow this government, at "the time this vessel and cargo were seized, and if she was "guilty of a violation of the blockade, she would be lawful "prize of war. But before this insurrection against the estab- "lished government can be dealt with on the footing of a civil "war, within the meaning of the law of nations and the con- "stitution of the United States, and which will draw after it "belligerent rights, it must be recognized or declared by the "war-making power of the government."

Has this pretended insurrection in Alamance and Caswell counties ever been recognized as war so that these tremendous consequences are to follow? Again it is said in the same opinion:

"No power short of this can change the legal status of the "government or the relations of its citizens from that of peace "to a state of war, or bring into existence all these duties and "obligations of neutral third parties growing out of a state of "war. The war power of the government must be exercised "before this changed condition of the government and people "and of neutral third parties can be admitted. There is no "difference in this respect between a civil or a public war."

Now I wish to know, senators, especially of those of you who belong to the legal profession, whether there be anything in this case—(and I should be willing even to lay the matter before his honor, the chief justice now presiding, after full con sideration,)—whether, I say, there was anything in the circum stances existing in the counties of Alamance and Caswell to bring after them all the consequences or any of the con- sequences of a public war or civil war, so as to make each one of these parties arrested, legally speaking, though not in fact, insurrectionists, and liable to be seized and arrested by military authority, and that without regard to the fact whether they were guilty or innocent of any offence. If that be so, it must be because there was existing war then and there in the sense known to the laws of nations. It can only be deduced from the principle of international law, as I have endeavored to show, applicable to a state of war only. But

I have shown you here that the state of North Carolina cannot make war upon any of its citizens, that one part of the people of a state cannot legally make war against another part. The governor, I admit, has power under the constitution to call out the militia to suppress an insurrection. He had those powers expressly given to him by the act of the legislature, if that could add to his power under the constitution. But to say that his proclamation produced or declared a state of war; to say that the effect of it was to put every man in Alamance and Caswell counties in the attitude of a law breaker and insurrectionist and at the mercy of the governor who chose to arrest him, is to say that which I think is not warranted by the law of the land and not sustained by any authority whatever. We ask in vain where, previous to the trial of these *habeas corpus* cases, any such ruling can be found as to the action of a state or of the United States government in undertaking to suppress insurrection—an insurrection not to overturn government, but merely to resist or prevent the execution of some particular law or laws of that government.

Why, take for instance, the Whiskey Insurrection in Pennsylvania in the time of Gen. Washington, referred to by one of the managers [Mr. Sparrow] in his opening speech here. What course, in the better days of the republic, was then pursued? Forces were called out; they were sent to that portion of Pennsylvania where there was open and armed resistance to the law; but was it considered that all the people in the insurgent district were public enemies and insurrectionists, and were they treated as such? No, they were treated, those only of them who were or had been in resistance, as misguided men. They, or rather a portion of them, were arrested upon warrants issued by the district judge of the United States, aided by the military authority, which was required in order to enforce the execution of the law. That was not the day of martial law or of military commissions. That was not the day of arresting men at the point of the bayonet without warrant or probable cause shown, merely because it suited the will of some man who was "clothed with a little brief authority." Such things were not done in the better days of the republic. Whether we shall ever know them again; whether we shall ever see that state of things restored, which every man must in his heart desire, depends somewhat, nay, very much indeed, upon the decision of this case.

There is another position taken kindred to the one I have been discussing: that the effect of declaring the counties in insurrection by the governor under the Shoffner act, was and is legally conclusive of the fact that such insurrection did exist, and that it cannot be contradicted or called in question here. Is that so? What authority is shown for it? None.

It is said that the chief justice, now presiding here, when the matter was before him in the *habeas corpus* cases, decided that he sitting as a judge could not enquire into it. He did so decide, and perhaps properly; but whether so or not is not here material to enquire. But has he decided so here—that is, that this court of impeachment is in like manner concluded? No; but in the progress of this case it has been virtually decided otherwise. You all recollect while the discussion was going on as to what constituted insurrection, and upon a question of evidence, and when it was objected on the part of the managers that in point of fact no insurrection existed, legally speaking, and according to the provisions of the constitution, and that the facts sought to be proved by the defence did not prove or tend to prove insurrection, it was said in reply: "It is proper, nevertheless, and altogether right to suffer these facts to go before the court upon the question of the intent and motives of the respondent." And it was, after elaborate discussion, so decided by the chief justice, and the decision was acquiesced in by the senate. And the chief justice in making his ruling, which you will find at page 475 of your printed proceedings, in substance said, that when the *habeas corpus* cases were before him, the question whether insurrection in fact existed was ruled out by him on the ground that the judiciary had no power to revise the action of the executive, but that it was competent for this court to do so, and to look into the official conduct of all the principal officers of the state. On the question of motives he ruled that the facts then proposed to be shown by the defence were competent, inasmuch as a criminal intent was charged upon the governor in declaring the counties in insurrection when there was none in fact, although such facts did not prove an open insurrection.

The whole matter is and must be an open one for a court of impeachment. How can this court be concluded from enquiring whether the governor of the state exceeded his lawful powers in declaring these counties in a state of insurrection? How, under the law, assuming that hehad such power, would you get at him for an abuse of the power that was conferred upon him, unless you could enquire into all the facts and circumstances under which he put these counties or attempted to put them in a state of insurrection? The proposition, it seems to me, cannot be maintained for a moment, and I dismiss it with these remarks.

The next position is that, though the acts complained of were unlawful, yet if they were, in the opinion of the respondent, necessary to promote the public interest, he ought not to be convicted upon impeachment for doing them. Is that a legal defence? The plea of necessity is set up—the plea of the public good, which it is even insisted is superior to all law—that is set up here as a defence; at all events if not pleaded by way of justification, it is offered by way of excuse. Bad men have been ever prone to offer such excuses for their evil deeds. That is an admission for the time being, at least, that the respondent has no law upon which to stand. Who is to judge of this necessity? Who has invested the governer of this state with any such power? From whence does he claim to derive such power as this? As I have said before, you are told, "other public men have done such things. He acted "as he thought for the best. He may have made mistakes, "he may have done things which he ought not to have done." Some of his counsel have said, "We are free to confess that he "has committed grave mistakes, but you should be merciful "and make allowances for the difficulty of his position, and "not convict him upon this impeachment." Another of them said in substance, "He is one of the best and purest and wisest "of men. He has done much service to the state. He has "at least suppressed this insurrection, and put a stop to the "commission of horrid crimes." Has he? Well, I have not heard much about that lately, except from another quarter. There it is said it is not suppressed, and that crimes of a certain kind are here an everyday thing; and while you are going on with the prosecution here, his excellency is in another place engaged in getting up a prosecution against you and the people of this state. For what? His counsel have told you here that he succeeded at least in putting down all these outrages, which now it seems are the subject of so much indignation, real or pretended, elsewhere.

Now any such plea as that—the plea of necessity and good intention—is a thing that addresses itself to your clemency and not your justice. Suppose that you were upon a jury—as you are the jury here. A man is charged with a heinous crime, say with murder. He is put upon trial, and by way of defence his counsel states, "This man that my client put to death was a law-"less, dangerous man, a nuisance to the public and a pest to "society. It was necessary that he should be put out of the "way, and my client therefore took his life, honestly believing "that the public welfare required it." Do you think you could acquit that man upon such pretences? Would you not, by all the rules of justice and of law, hold that he was guilty of murder? Now I grant that is a very strong case, an extreme case if you will, put by way of illustration merely, and to test a principle. But I cannot forget that the respondent here stands charged with some very great outrages—outrages upon individual citizens, and yet more upon the constitution and laws of the state, by him knowingly and wickedly violated time and again.

If these charges be true, how can you excuse him upon the plea of good intentions? There is a very bad place said sometimes to be paved all over with good intentions. If they really existed on the part of the accused, as to which, however, I shall have hereafter something to say, then I repeat that it is a matter which addresses itself to your clemency after he is convicted. You may or you may not subject him to all the pains and penalties of the law. But to say that he can set up any such excuses, true or false, by way of defence, is to go outside of the law. It would result in this—that every criminal, by erecting a self-constituted tribunal in his own bosom, could excuse himself from any of the consequences of the violation of law. That would be simply absurd. Yet when you come to examine it, that is one of the positions taken and seriously insisted upon by the counsel on the other side, with what reason you, senators, must decide.

Again, it is said that before you can rightfully convict the respondent, you must be satisfied and virtually so find that he had a criminal intent; that a criminal intent enters into every offence, and that if he had no criminal intent in what he did, you are bound to acquit him. Well, to a certain extent that is the law, but not to the extent claimed here. Every man is presumed to know the law. No man has a right, when arraigned for a criminal offence, to justify himself by saying that he thought he was doing right and did not intend to do anything wrong; but he is held to be amenable for his acts. That, as every lawyer knows, is a general rule, and none other could be safely adopted. I know that in a certain class of cases referred to by the learned counsel [Mr. Smith] who made this point more particularly, corruption or malice or improper intent as regards their official acts is not presumed but must be shown. What was the authority that he introduced? Wharton's American Criminal Law. It will be remembered that the reference was to judicial officers only. The doctrine is confined to them, as appeared also in the two cases that were read from our own reports on the same subject. It is there laid down, and correctly, that to convict upon an indictment a judge or a judicial officer of malfeasance in office, you are bound to show either corruption or malice, or something tantamount thereto—that a mere mistake in the exercise of his authority will not be sufficient to convict him upon an indictment. But even in such cases corruption or malice may be inferred from the circumstances of the case. But has it come to this, that no man can be convicted of an abuse in office, unless it appears by possitive proof that he intended to do wrong?—that no man can be convicted for any excess or abuse of authority, provided he shall set up a defence that he was acting honestly and thought he had a right to perpetrate the enormities committed by him? In truth the modified rule above referred to, does not apply to executive officers, certainly not to the extent that is claimed. Suppose a sheriff, for instance, to have a precept against me: I make no resistance; notwithstanding that, instead of arresting me in accordance with his authority and his duty, he knocks me down, ties me hand and foot, carries me off and puts me in jail: is he not responsible civilly and criminally? Can he excuse himself by any such plea as is set up here?

But I shall undertake to show you, senators, before I get through, that even assuming that such was the law, and that it applies in all its length and breadth to the governor of this state, yet that a guilty intent has been either positively proved or is to be presumed from the facts before you. The respondent is not that novice in legal and constitutional questions that the gentlemen would now have him to be, but, as you all know, is one who during the greater part of his life has devoted his time and attention to the study of such subjects. How, then, can he ask you to excuse him upon the plea of personal ignorance. We all know what the inference of law is upon the subject of criminal acts. A man kills another. Is he presumed to be innocent? No, he is presumed to be guilty of murder, of having taken the life of a fellow being with malice aforethought, until he shows to the contrary. So, wherever an act is done which is in violation of the law, the law infers a guilty intent until he who does the act proves to the contrary. The burden of proof is upon him, as we all know. If he makes such proof and the act be such a one as the law excuses, he is excused. If the proof be such as only to palliate the offence, then it is palliated. But the law never presumes that a man does an act in violation of the law innocently—never. Before I get through I shall endeavor to show that the exculpatory circumstances relied upon here did not exist, and that upon each and every one of these charges which are preferred here against him, the respondent ought to be convicted.

As I said, senators, the last point which was made on the other side was, that the respondent is not responsible for the acts of his subordinate officers, however improper or illegal they may have been, unless he permitted, authorized, or himself suffered such acts to be done. Now with one qualification that would be true, if the respondent could bring himself within the facts of such a case, and that qualification is that unless he afterwards sanctioned what they had done. For if he sanctioned and approved of their acts it makes him just as criminal as if he had himself ordered them to be done. It would be as grave an abuse in office as the chief executive officer of the state could commit. But I shall have something to say about this when I come to discuss the facts. I shall endeavor to show that upon the facts of the case there is no principle of law which will excuse the respondent. I shall endeavor to show that he knew of many of these abuses and outrages; that he either ordered or connived at them, and that the very military force that he used was an illegal one; and then I shall ask the senate to say whether, under the circumstances, the respondent is not responsible for the outrages committed by his subordinates.

Pending the argument of Mr. Bragg, the hour of 2 o'clock having arrived, on motion of Senator Robbins, of Davidson, the court took a recess until 4 o'clock.

## AFTERNOON SESSION.

The COURT re-assembled at 4 o'clock, Hon. R. M. Pearson, Chief Justice of the Supreme Court, in the chair.

The CLERK proceeded to call the roll when the following gentlemen were found to be present:

Messrs. Adams, Albright, Allen, Barnett, Battle, Bellamy, Cook, Council, Cowles, Crowell, Edwards, Eppes, Flemming, Gilmer, Graham of Alamance, Graham of Orange, Hyman, King, Ledbetter, Linney, Love, Mauney, McClammy, McCotter, Merrimon, Moore, Morehead, Murphy, Norment, Price, Robbins of Davidson, Robbins of Rowan, Skinner, Speed, Troy, Waddell and Worth.

On motion of Senator Merrimon, the court took a further recess until 7 o'clock in the evening.

---

## EVENING SESSION.

The COURT re-assembled at 7½ o'clock, Hon. R. M. Pearson, Chief Justice of the Supreme Court, in the chair.

The CLERK proceeded to call the roll of Senators, when the following gentlemen were found to be present:

Messrs. Adams, Albright, Allen, Barnett, Battle, Beasley, Bellamy, Brogden, Brown, Cook, Council, Cowles, Crowell, Currie, Edwards, Eppes, Flemming, Gilmer, Graham of Alamance, Graham of Orange, Hawkins, Hyman, Jones, King, Latham, Ledbetter, Lehman, Linney, Love, Mauney, McClammy, McCotter, Merrimon, Moore, Morehead, Murphy, Norment, Price, Robbins of Davidson, Robbins of Rowan, Skinner, Speed, Waddell, Warren and Worth—35.

Mr. BRAGG then resumed his argument on behalf of the managers. He said:

Mr. CHIEF JUSTICE AND SENATORS: Before proceeding

further, I beg to return my thanks to this body for extending to me the favor they have in postponing the discussion until this evening.

Just before I closed what I had to say this morning in stating other points made by the defence. I had reference to one, and the last in the series, as to how far the respondent, or a public officer, was responsible for the acts of his subordinates. And I stated that, as a general principle of law, the propositions laid down by the counsel for the respondent were in the main correct, with a certain qualification, which I then mentioned. I did not at that time wish to be understood as saying, as I am informed is the impression with some, that the respondent had brought himself within that principle of law. On the contrary, I intended to insist and thought I did say that he had not, and that upon the facts of this case he had totally failed to justify himself according to the principles of law as then enunciated. It was a mere statement of an abstract principle of law which, with certain qualifications, I admitted to be correct; but I did not mean then to say, or by any means to admit, as some I understand supposed that I did, that the agency made use of by the respondent was a proper one. On the contrary, I intended to be understood that the agency of which he made use in doing the acts, for some of which we seek to hold him responsible, was an illegal one; and that, therefore, he was in any point of view to be held responsible for the acts of such illegal agents. And that brings me now to the discussion of the question, whether this military force employed by him, and as to which there is much contained in the several articles of impeachment, was a lawful or unlawful force; for if it was unlawful, why then the respondent does not bring himself within the principle of law that I have stated, but they were all violators of the law, the agents as well as the principal.

Now, as to those troops sent into Alamance and Caswell, and a part of them sent to other parts of the state, it was but feebly insisted, as I thought, and I say it with all due respect to the counsel on the other side, that it was a lawful force—a part of the militia of North Carolina. We all know that, by the constitution of the state, the governor is made commander-in-chief of the militia, and in order to suppress riot or insurrection he is authorized to call out the militia; and we know further that, in the Shoffner bill, commonly so-called, about which so much has been said here, the governor was authorized to call out the militia of the state to suppress insurrection in any county when declared by him there to exist. Now, the question is, did he do that, or did he set on foot a force which was unknown to the law, and in violation of the law? The constitution of the state prescribes of what the militia shall consist—of every able bodied citizen of the state between the ages of twenty-one and forty. None other can constitute the militia according to law. But it is said that under this militia act of 1868 the respondent called out such a force as that and none other. I propose to invite your attention for a short time to that question. It is insisted that under this act of 1868, section 8, the governor had authority to call out this force. It reads:

"The governor is hereby authorized to accept and organize "regiments of volunteer infantry, not exceeding six, the same "to be apportioned as nearly as possible through the state, for "which purpose the state shall be divided into three divisions, "to be known as the eastern, middle and western divisions, "which divisions shall constitute a major-general's department. "If in the discretion of the governor it shall be deemed ad-"visable, he may also accept and organize volunteer battalions "of cavalry, not to exceed three, and one volunteer battery of "artillery, the same to be equally divided among the di-"visions named in this section."

Now, I might ask, supposing these troops called out were volunteer militia, in the sense of this law, whether this force was taken from the three grand divisions of the state, or from any one sub-division of the state as the law required? There is nothing of the kind to be pretended. But what is meant by this volunteer force which is authorized to be embodied and kept on foot by the militia act? Was it such a force as the governor raised and set on foot? By no means. This has been already made plain by my associate counsel. It was intended to be a permanent force—a permanent volunteer force, constituting a part of the state militia, and any gentleman who will take the trouble to look at our militia laws, as heretofore existing, will see thatt he same provisions as to a volunteer militia was contained in all those acts for a long period of time antecedent to the act of 1868. I have the revised code here before me, and in chapter 70, from sections 51 to 60 inclusive, the same kind of force is authorized to be raised, not as a temporary force, but as a permanent part of the militia organization of the state. The same substantially is to be found in the statutes revised in 1835, and for a long time before that. The same thing is to be found in the acts of congress of 1792 and 1795, providing for the organization of the militia of the several states, as will appear by an inspection of those acts. In other words, from the very commencement of the government this kind of force was authorized, not as a temporary one, not such a force as this Kirk regiment was, but as a part of the regularly organized militia of the state under the militia laws. Well, now, let us see what is Colonel Clarke's evidence on the subject of those troops. I beg to call the attention of the court to it. It will be found at page 1746 and 1747 of the printed record.

Col. Clarke, tells you that as a military man, he was sent for by Gov. Holden to advise with him as to the amount and character of the force to be called out, and that he then understood he was to have the command of the troops, and, to use his own language, of the whole affair; "that he had a great contempt for the militia as ordinarily organized, and was unwilling to have it understood that he was a mere militia colonel, and that it was determined at his suggestion to designate them "state troops." The men were to be regularly enlisted, as in the United States army, and individually sworn—that they were not to be drawn or drafted from any particular section of the state, but enrolled on voluntary enlistment, and that two regiments were so raised and mustered into the service of the state.

At that interview, which was early in the month of June, Col. Clarke further tells you that he heard nothing of Kirk or that he was to have any command, or that a force was to be raised from east Tennessee, or from the mountains in North Carolina, and he further says by way of reason for advising as he did, that he thought militia an ungovernable force, and unsuited for the purposes for which a military force was then wanted, and that he did not trouble himself with an enquiry into the legality of raising the troops,—he was not asked to do so, and he advised merely as a military man.

The colonel went on to state many other facts as to the character of these troops, and among other things that they signed regular articles of enlistment, modified only so far as to change the form of the United States soldiers' enlistment to that of an enlistment in the North Carolina state troops. And the adjutant general, Fisher, tells us that these men were to be sworn in, and he supposed that they took the oath—the officers he knew did. Colonel Clarke tells you the same, and that the men were regularly enlisted to serve for six months, or until discharged. Such a force as that a part of the state militia! It was a regular standing force, gotten up as any other army is gotten up, the officers and men all sworn, which is not required by law in the militia as to the men, although every militia officer who accepts a commission, as has always been the case, is required to take an oath of office. This act of 1868 as originally passed, required the men also to take the oath, but that was afterwards amended and stricken out by a subsequent act.

Now let us turn to the famous handbill of Kirk, which it was proved was written and caused to be printed by the respondent. It is to be found at page 283 of the record. And this, senators, has an important bearing, not only upon the question which I am now discussing, but upon other matters, going to show the motives by which the respondent was actuated after he had enrolled and set on foot this illegal force. You may recollect the terms of it. Perhaps it may be unnecessary that I should read it again, but I will venture to call your attention to it, although it may be fresh in your recollections:

"Rally union men in defence of your state." Rally union men? Why, he should have said "Rally militia," if this was addressed to the militia forces. The law required him to call out the state militia composed of everybody liable to perform militia duty, not what he might choose to call union men only. So you see it was a select force he wanted. "Rally soldiers of "the old North Carolina 2nd and 3d federal troops." Are they militia? "Rally to the standard of your old commander." Was he a militia man? Why he was not a citizen of North Carolina, and, therefore, could be no part of her militia. He was a Tennessean, as we have shown you here. I know it has been insisted by one of the counsel on the other side that notwithstanding the men were required by law to be citizens of the state, the officers were not, and that the governor might in organizing the militia, put officers over them from any other states. But with what reason and under what law? I want to know if the officers of the militia are not a part of the militia of the State as well as the rank and file? I want to know if the governor of the state can, at his pleasure, go outside of North Carolina and find officers and put them over the militia in this state? The law speaks of the officers as well as the men, and the officers are just as much a part of the militia as the rank and file. But to return to this remarkable manifesto:

"Your old commander has been commissioned to raise at "once a regiment of state troops." Mark the words; to raise a regiment of state troops, not a regiment of militia—not even a regiment of volunteer militia under the militia law. Those volunteers, under the act of 1868, were to be composed of citizens of the state generally who chose to volunteer, but to be apportioned, by the express provisions of the act, among the grand divisions into which the state was divided, the eastern, the middle and the western. What did he want with these gentle lambs of Kirk? He tells them, "To aid in enforcing "the law, and in putting down disloyal midnight assassins." Well, that was a very pretty expression for the governor of the state. "The blood (says he,) of your murdered country-"men, inhumanly butchered for opinion's sake, cries for "vengeance." Oh! for "vengeance" was it. It was vengeance that the governor wanted. "The horrible murders "and other atrocities of the rebel K. K. K. and southern "chivalry on grey haired men and helpless women call 'in thunder tones." On the militia? No, but "on all loyal "men to rally in defence of their state." "The uplifted hand "of justice—second and third federal troops—must overtake "these outlaws." And now for the finale. "One thousand "recruits are wanted immediately to serve six months unless "sooner discharged." Is that militia? "These troops will "receive the same pay as United States regulars." Yes, that was the bait held out in order to induce this ragged rabble from certain localities in North Carolina, and composed largely, too, of desperate men from Tennessee and other states to 'rally to the flag of their old commander," who was not a citizen of North Carolina, and known only to fame as a cruel, remorseless man. "Recruits will be received at Asheville, "Marshall and Burnsville, North Carolina." Recruits! Let them come from any quarter whatever in or out of the state, provided they were men of the description wanted, they were welcome, and were to receive pay and emoluments at the hands of the state.

Now, can it be pretended that this was a militia force? Will any man in his senses say so? We say that they were not drawn from the militia force at all, as the act prescribed. We say that many of them were under, and some over age, nearly or about three hundred of them my friend [Mr. Merrimon] states, and he has taken the trouble to examine these muster rolls. We say that a large portion of them were not citizens of North Carolina, at least two hundred of them, as the same muster rolls in evidence show. What business had they in the state of North Carolina? What right had the governor to recruit and organize a force of people who were not composed of citizens of the state, and then call them militia? Yes, they were "state troops," as he designated them, and raised as such, and not as ordinary militia, or even volunteers called out for a particular time or for a particular purpose. This force raised was in express violation of the constitutions of the United States and of the state of North Carolina. Article I, section 10, of the constitution of the United States expressly forbids any state to keep on foot troops, unless by the assent of the congress of the United States, as it also forbids any state to make war, or do anything else of the kind than repelling an invasion when the danger is imminent. These powers are expressly denied and refused to the states for the wisest of purposes.

Now, senators, I go further and say as to this matter that the governor of this state well knew, (and I will endeavor to show it,) that when he organized and set on foot this force, he had no right to do it under the constitution and laws of the state. A good deal has been said about motives, and that bears upon his motives. Let us see how that was? I beg now, therefore, upon that point to refer, senators, to the annual message of the respondent to the legislature of November, 1868. Among other things he says:

"Under the present militia law the executive is comparatively powerless to enforce the law."

That I deny—emphatically deny. He then proceeds:

"These laws should be amended so as to give the executive the authority to embody promptly such a militia force as will enable him to repress violence in certain localities, and maintain the peace."

Remember that the act under which he now attempts to justify, the militia act, was passed the 17th August, 1868. Well, it is very evident that the respondent, at the time of making that communication to the legislature, did not think that he had power to embody such a force as he did embody. He knew, therefore, that the militia act which authorized the organization, as a part of the militia, of certain volunteer regiments, did not authorize him to embody a standing force. He goes on to show wherein the militia, as organized under that act, was not an efficient force for the purposes for which he wanted it.

Again, on December 16th, 1869, he sends a special message to the legislature, partly on this very subject. I shall have occasion hereafter to use that more particularly, however, upon another branch of this discussion, but for the present I bring it to your attention as bearing upon this militia question and to show a knowledge on the part of the respondent that he had no such power as he now claims to have had, to raise these troops. He says:

" Allow me, respectfully and earnestly, to call you attention " to the necessity which exists for such amendments to the mil- " itia law as will enable the executive to suppress violence " and disorder in certain localities in this state, and to protect " the persons of citizens, their lives and their property."

There he again calls attention to this same militia law. It is a clear admission and declaration on his part, that he had no authority to raise such a force as this was. You see, senators, that this force was not only a force of the kind that I have stated, but the respondent well knew at the time he was raising it, that he had no power such as he claims to have had. In 1868 he admits he did not have it. In December, 1869, he admits he did not have it; and yet it is now claimed, contrary to the constitution and laws of the state, and contrary to the constitution of the United States, and to his own repeated admissions, that he had that power, and that he was acting legally in what he did. I submit to you, therefore, that it is manifest, beyond any sort of question whatever, that the whole of this force raised by him was raised in contravention of the law. There was a certain kind of militia provided in this act of 1868 called "detailed militia," but any one who examines the act will see that this was a very different force. That required a certain number of men, upon application of certain officers in any county, to be detailed from the militia, not exceeding fifty to each member of assembly. That, he says, was not a force that would answer his purpose, although he had by the act the control of it, and might send it to any part of the state. It is a little noteworthy that in the return which appears to have been made to one of these writs of *habeas corpus*—the writ sued out by Mr. Turner before his honor, Judge Brooks, at Salisbury, and after there had been great complaint about the character of this force, and what they had done—after it had been held up to the country as an illegal force which the respondent had raised—I say that when Kirk comes to make a return to that writ under the advice, no doubt, of counsel, the return is that Mr. Turner was arrested by Lieutenant Colonel Burgen of the "detailed militia." He had become alarmed about that matter. The force was then styled to be not "North Carolina state troops," but "detailed militia." That Burgen was ordered to arrest him "for alleged violations of law," and Kirk further stated in the return, "he is now detained on the charge of conspiring with divers other citizens of the state to overturn the government of the state of North Carolina. That was the vague and extraordinary return which was made and which is here upon your record. Now, it may be said that the respondent is not responsible for that. But it only goes to show how this thing as to the character of the force was shifting and changing.

The matter had been complained of from the first. It was notorious. It had been denounced as an usurpation on the part of the respondent to raise and make use of such a force as this. Casting about, then, to see where he could find some pretence of law, upon full consideration, satisfied by his advisers no doubt, that he could not sustain himself on the ground that this was "detailed militia," he then falls back upon this 8th section of the act of 1868, and they are called here now "volunteer militia."

Now, I think that we have successfully driven them from that position, and every senator must see that it was neither ordinary militia, "detailed militia," nor "volunteer militia," but a regular organized recruited force—a standing army, so long as it lasted—organized and equipped and set on foot by the governor for such purposes as he is charged with in these articles of impeachment. And therefore it is, senators, that I say he cannot justify here by alleging that these outrageous acts, proved to have been committed by such a force as this, were not done with his assent or his procurement or his connivance. And many of them he has since directly sanctioned.

Now what was the character of these troops? for that constitutes a part of the charges against the accused. We need not go into the details of the evidence on that subject.

Col. Clarke tells you that he had an utter contempt for the ordinary militia of the state. And no doubt he had, a thing by no means unusual with such military martinets.

But it is with the force that this man Kirk collected and brought down upon the people, that we have more particularly to do.

What was their character? What their discipline, conduct and behaviour?

We have all heard here—many highly respectable witnesses have fully described what their conduct was; that they were a lawless band of desperadoes, headed and officered by men who were worse than they were, if possible—men who had no control over the rank and file whatever—men who were themselves violent, and who did not feel restrained by any law or any decency. I know there has been some attempt here to set up a character for some of these officers. You have heard the evidence. What does it weigh? Who were the men who especially testified as to Kirk? Why men that belonged to the force which he commanded during the war. Three or four respectable witnesses here have told you what his character was. Have you any doubt about it? It was notorious throughout the land. Well, how did it happen that Kirk, especially, was sent for to raise and command this force? Col. Clarke tells you that he knew nothing about it. It was understood at the time he was here, early in June, that he was to command these regular forces. He refused to command the militia, or to be considered as a militia colonel. He wanted something higher than that, as he had an utter contempt for the militia of the state. He went off to Washington, and when he came back, lo! and behold here was Colonel Kirk and Lieut. Colonel Burgen—the last a man whom the learned counsel, [Mr. Smith,] says if he had had his deserts would have been shot—a sentiment in which I heartily con-concur. And yet he says the governor is not responsible at all for his acts. Well, we take it that when a public officer or a man undertakes to make use of such agencies as these, he is and ought to be responsible for their acts. He is just as much responsible for their villanies as would a man be who should turn loose a wild beast in a community for the mischief it might commit.

This, then, was the force which was organized by the respondent, officers and men, and sent abroad among the people of North Carolina to put down a pretended insurrection.

Senators, a great deal has been said about this Shoffner act. The learned counsel who last addressed you in behalf of the defense, [Mr. Smith,] would not even insist that that law was constitutional. He said it was an unwise measure, and ought never to have been adopted. He would not say it was constitutional, but he did insist, whether it was constitutional or not, the governor was excusable for acting under it, and not only excusable, but he insisted it was his duty to act upon it. I shall not enter again into the discussion of the constitutionality of that act. That question has been several times incidentally discussed before this body, and I think every senator whose mind is open to conviction must have concluded already that the legislature in passing it violated the constitution, if that act is to be construed in the manner in which the defence and the respondent insist that it ought to be construed and was construed.

But it is said that the respondent cannot be convicted for declaring counties in a state of insurrection under that act, because he acted in good faith and honestly, and did not know, and as governor had no right to know, that it was unconstitutional. Now, let us see how that matter is. I shall endeavor to satisfy the mind of every senator, and I think successfully, that the accused was instrumental in passing that act through the legislature, and that when it was passed he knew that thereby the constitution of the state was violated, or would be violated if that act was carried out in the manner in which he afterwards enforced it. And if so, I shall insist that these first two articles charging the respondent with falsely declaring those two counties in a state of insurrection are established, and that it is the duty of this senate to convict him on those articles as well as upon the others.

How do I connect him with the passage of that bill? I shall do it by a certain train of facts and circumstances which, when brought to the attention of this body and scrutinized, I think will be sufficient to satisfy every senator of the truth of the complicity which I charge. We have put in evidence the original bill as drawn and introduced into the senate. It was introduced on the 16th December, 1869. That original bill contained a clause authorizing the governor to call on the president to suspend, in this state, the privilege of the writ of *habeas corpus*. It was well known then, even to the respondent and to the last legislature, that that body could not suspend the privilege of the writ of *habeas corpus*, because there was an express prohibition against it in our own constitution. Hence it was that they incorporated into the original bill that provision. By whom was it introduced? By any man of prominence? Not at all. It was put into the hands of an obscure man, as is proved here—a man who was not capable of drawing such a bill. But it seems to have been carefully prepared by certain knowing parties, probably outside of the legislature, who understood what they were about, and what were the purposes of such legislation? How do I connect the respondent with it? I do it by this same special message, to which I have already referred, which he sent to the legislature on the 16th December,

1869, the same day on which this bill was introduced by senator Shoffner. I have read a part of this message to you relative to the militia. The recommendation as to that was part and parcel of what was to be done. Let us see further. Although the message is couched in general terms, it cannot be doubted at all, taking into consideration all the circumstances connected with this transaction, that the respondent knew perfectly well that this bill had been prepared, and when, where and by whom it was to be introduced. He says:

"Since my last annual message, dated November 16, 1869, "numerous outrages of the most flagrant character have been "committed upon peaceable and law-abiding citizens, by per- "sons masked and armed, who ride at night, and who have "thus far escaped the civil law. I have adopted such measures "as were in my power to ferret out and bring to justice all "breakers of the law, without reference to their color or to the "political party or parties to which they belong, and I am sat- "isfied the judges and solicitors in the various circuits have "been prompt, energetic, and impartial in the discharge of their "duties."

Now, throughout the whole history ot these matters the respondent never was without seeming fair pretext for anything that he designed to do covertly. We have had a great many proclamations read here. He might be called, and called truly, the "proclamation governor." He never was at a loss just before an election to issue a proclamation calculated to subserve his party purposes or the purposes of those with whom he was acting. On the 12th December, 1868, just before the presidential election, as it happens, (for it is put in evidence by him,) there was a flaming proclamation issued of three or four pages of printed matter, to the effect that he was credibly informed that large quantities of arms had been sent to the state of North Carolina, and that there was on foot a design to break up the government. Have you heard anything more of that matter since? And yet such a proclamation as that was issued. Why? Simply to alarm and create a false public sentiment in and out of the state. Much of the troubles that we have been enduring since his advent to power, and they have been many, have been brought about by this very system of issuing proclamation after proclamation, not intended or calculated to put a stop to the things complained of, but rather to foster and keep them alive and thus to inflame one class of the community against another. The respondent has been held up here as above reproach in every respect. My eloquent friend before me, [Mr. Conigland,] passed upon him a studied eulogium. Well, it was all admirable in a certain sense, but then it was not like the original—as little so as Hyperion to a Satyr. During the time of his predecessor in office, Governor Worth, we had peace and quiet in the State. From the time of *his* advent to office our troubles commenced, and they have been kept up ever since, and have not yet ceased. They were brought about mainly by his action, and that of those who have been and now are his coadjutors—one class of the population of the state arrayed against another, for party purposes and party ends, until at last a condition of things was brought about which was the fruit, necessarily, of his and their action, as surely following as the night follows the day—a state of things rendered not only possible, but, I am sorry to say, inevitably resulting from a bad system of government badly administered. That is the simple truth and the whole truth of the story. Now the respondent may be one of the best of men, at least in the opinion of some, but this I undertake to say, and say it confidently, that his administration of the state government has been the most disastrous, on the whole, that ever occurred in North Carolina, and perhaps I might add in any state whatever. Her treasury beggered, her credit gone, her people impoverished and ruined, and peculation and fraud, in high places and low places, stalking openly and unabashed through the land, and tolerated, connived at, if not participated in, by him. And yet he is held up here as a marvelously proper man, a man of virtuous deeds and life, and whose hand, when clothed with almost imperial power, was never raised against an enemy, and who never struck a political foe when he had the power to strike. What a marvel of magnanimity! Well, if that be the opinion of some, let it be so. It is not my opinion, and I think it is not the opinion of unprejudiced men all over the state, and I might add outside of the state, wherever the respondent is known.

But I am digressing from the subject which I was discussing. I was endeavoring to show that the real design of the respondent in that message was covered up. His purpose was to obtain the passage of the Snoffner act. His message came the same day with the bill. The bill, as I have said, had evidently been prepared before, and what was the action of the Senate after it was introduced? The rules were suspended, and the bill rushed through, without any amendment or debate, passing its three several readings on that day. Did not the governor know of it? Had he not seen that bill before? Did he not know what its provisions were? It seems to me, senators, you can come to no other conclusion.

Well, it goes to the other house. There it meets with some opposition. A portion of the political friends of the respondent were not quite so pliant and accommodating as those who happened to sit in this body. One of the counsel on the other side has read to us from the *Standard* a portion of the debate and certain proceedings upon that bill in the other house. Senators, I was a little surprised to hear the counsel give an account of what took place in the other house. I won't say I was gratified, but I did say to my friend who sat by me, [Mr. Merrimon,] in the language of the quotation which my worthy and eloquent friend, [Mr. Conigland,] who sits before me, used in his speech: "Now hath the Lord delivered them into our hands." (Laughter.) Yes, the bill was opposed there. One member said, "Why if that bill is passed you will inaugurate a civil "war here. You will establish drum-head courts matial to try and shoot men." The counsel who read these proceedings did not read what was said on the other side. He did, however, call your attention to the fact that one member,

Mr. Pou, of Johnston, a republican, offered an amendment that the military as thus to be raised should be held in strict subordination to the civil power. That is a part of the constitution—the state constitution prescribes and requires it. That was voted down. They succeeded, however, in striking out one obnoxious provision, and that alone—the provision in relation to the writ of *habeas corpus*. That was almost too strong for them to pass. My friend on the other side [Mr. Smith,] then asks, "What does this prove?" Not, says he, that the Shoffner bill was constitutional but that the legislature were thereby intending to confer upon the governor greater power than he possessed under the constitution or than they were authorized to grant. And he said that upon this debate, that being the construction of the bill, by its opponents, the respondent had a right to take it that that was the true construction of the act and to act upon it as the legislative intent, constitutional or not constitutional. That was in substance what he said—you heard it. Then I say, taking all that to be true, and doubtless the respondent was well informed of it, for it appeared in that paper which he read every day, his own organ—that is another reason why he knew what the purposes of this bill were and that it was in clear violation of those provisions of the constitution, so often referred to in this trial, touching the rights and liberties of the citizen. The counsel said that it was clear that the intention of the legislature was to give the bill that effect.

Now, senators, that was the first time in the course of a long professional life that I ever heard it urged in an argument that what was said in debate on a pending bill should be used to show that the legislature knew that they were violating the constitution, and that a public officer, knowing the facts, should seek to justify his conduct on that ground. And yet that is the position, if I am not mistaken, taken by the learned counsel, [Mr. Smith.] He has made, I grant, an exceedingly able effort, considering the nature of the cause which he had to defend, and if the defence has not proved successful, it has been owing rather to the cause itself than to any deficiency in the advocate.

If, then, the respondent was instrumental in getting up that bill; if he was duly apprised of its character and what transpired while it was pending in the legislature; if he intended from the first to exercise the power which he did exercise under it after it become a law; what becomes of all that has been said here as to his motives and as to his duty to carry out its provisions—as to his believing he had the powers under the act which he afterwards claimed and exercised?

Therefore it is that I submit it to senators, that the charges contained in the first two articles of impeachment—that the respondent declared these counties in a state of insurrection when he knew they were not in insurrection, are true, and that the senate ought so to find them. Nobody will pretend, I think, to dispute that every thing else charged in the articles is true, under the specifications as to illegality of this force, as to their conduct and behavior, and what they did as to the maltreatment of persons arrested; and connecting the respondent with the other matters charged in the way I have done—if I have been successful in doing that—it makes him guilty of declaring the counties in insurrection when he knew there was none, just as much as if he had done it without any color of authority whatever.

I will pass on, senators, to some of these other counts or charges—and in connection with them, also, I have a good deal to say as to the motives and conduct of the respondent. Article III is in relation to the arrest of Josiah Turner. As to that article, I might say that neither has the respondent nor the counsel shown any justification or excuse. The learned counsel to whom I have so often referred, who last addressed you, said in so many words that he had no justification for it. Another of the counsel, [Mr. Boyden,] did not pretend to justify it. Nobody, so far as I have heard here, has attempted to justify it. But you are asked to excuse the respondent upon their statement that there was no evidence here that the respondent had ordered the arrest to be made. In making that statement, our friends on the other side have certainly forgotten a great deal of the testimony. The respondent himself says that he did verbally order the arrest of Mr. Turner to be made if he was found in the county of Alamance or Caswell. He admits, however, that after Mr. Turner was arrested, he concluded to hold him, and did order his detention. In other words he sanctioned what had been illegally done by his subordinate officer. Was not that a great, gross abuse of his office? Remember that the county of Orange, where Mr. Turner was seized, had not been declared in a state of insurrection. He was seized without charges made, and without warrant or authority. He was hurried off from his family to Alamance county, and was thence carried to Caswell, where he was imprisoned and grossly maltreated. He was afterwards brought back to the county of Alamance and immured in a filthy and loathsome dungeon with a negro convict, who was there waiting to pay the penalty of his life for an outrageous crime. All these things were known to the respondent and yet he interfered not Indeed he says, after Mr. Turner was arrested that he sanctioned his detention. That makes him just as responsible as if he had ordered the arrest or had admitted that he had ordered it in the first instance. I shall insist, senators, that he did order the arrest, and that it was made in pursuance of his orders. Why do I say so? I say so, in the first place, on the testimony of John C. Gorman, who stated that he saw the respondent on the day of the election in the court house in Raleigh; that he heard him say, then and there, either that he had ordered the arrest or that he would order the arrest of Mr. Turner immediately, and he [Gorman] attempted to dissuade him from it. What else have we? It appears that Mr. Turner was arrested on the fifth of August—the day after the election. We have also certain mysterious telegrams which seem to have been passing about that time. Hancock, the commanding officer at Hillsboro', on the fifth, telegraphs his superior officer, Burgen, at the Shops, that he has a matter of great importance to communicate, but that he cannot do it without a violation of orders. Unfortunately, the telegrams at the Shops were spirited away just before they were sent for. The respondent knew, however, that he was charged with having this arrest made. He could have produced parties here to show that they had no orders if the fact had been so. It seems, however, that on that day one of these men, Hunnicut by name, was sent down from the Shops with a file of men to arrest Mr. Turner. What did he say there? He was one of the agents of the governor. He tells senator Graham, immediately after the arrest, "I arrested him by the "orders of Colonel Burgen, who directed me to do it pursuant "to an order received from the governor to that effect," and he added, "I have seen the order." Is there any doubt about that? And yet we are told that there is no evidence that the respondent had caused Mr. Turner's arrest. All the evidence goes to show that he did it; and all the evidence, so far as we have it here, goes to show that he directed it to be done at the time and place where it was done, and he himself avowed, after it was done, that he sanctioned it. According to every principle of law it makes him amenable for the act. Was there ever a grosser violation of duty, a greater abuse of official power on the part of a governor or a public officer than this was? I care not what may be said as to what had passed before that arrest between Mr. Turner and Governor Holden; that has nothing to do with it. Says the learned counsel, [Mr. Boyden,] Turner had invited an arrest. Suppose he had. Does that justify the governor or even excuse him? Did that justify or excuse such an outrage as this?—a violation of the constitution of the state and of every principle of law, that he had sworn to observe? By no means. And yet he detains Mr. Turner in the manner which I have stated up to the very last moment when he was discharged by Judge Brooks.

Senators, I am satisfied what your judgment will be on this charge. It cannot be otherwise than that he is guilty. One of the counsel on the other side spoke of this arrest and treatment of Mr. Turner in a tone of merriment. My venerable friend, Mr. Boyden, said: "Why suppose he did put him in "this dungeon with a man who was to be hanged, it only "afforded him an opportunity of giving some ghostly advice "to the condemned criminal. And after he was discharged "and came down to Raleigh, it gave him an opportunity of "being welcomed here and having a great to-do made over "him by his Kuklux friends." Well, senators, I have heard a good deal of that sort of language before. I have been connected with these matters growing out of the Kirk campaign in some degree ever since their commencement. And when my learned and elderly friend, [Mr. Boyden,] spoke of "Kuklux friends," I could but have vividly recalled to my recollection the state of things that existed here in the month of July last year. Then it was common to denounce my friends here who sit beside me, and myself and Judge Battle and Mr. Moore, as "Kuklux lawyers." I trust my friend has not forgotten it. He was then, as he is now, of counsel for the governor. In that day, when everything seemed to be going on swimmingly, before the election had taken place, and when his excellency was on the full tide of successful experiment, it was common to say to us in his organ, the *Standard*, in staring capitals, almost daily, "Beware! beware!" and what the learned counsel on the other side said about the reception of Mr. Turner here by his "Kuklux friends" has reminded me of that very pleasant state of things existing here when every man who undertook to raise his voice in behalf of constitutional liberty and law, did it, not only at the peril of denunciation, for that amounts to very little, but at the peril of having his own liberty put in jeopardy; and I say to you now, senators, that if that election had resulted differently, and if instead of your sitting here as you are to try the respondent upon the charges brought against him, things had gone otherwise, as he hoped and no doubt expected, I am not so sure that my associates and myself especially, and perhaps the other gentlemen associated with us at that time, would not have been placed in the same condition that Mr. Turner was. Amidst all this strife the people kept quiet, but they thought their day was coming. They thought the time would arrive when they would get redress, not by arms nor by force, but by that silent though potent means, the ballot, when justice would be done, and when those in high places would be brought to account at the bar of public justice for their evil deeds. That is all I have to say upon that charge.

Now, upon the next. That is of a similar character. It charges the illegal arrest and detention of sundry good citizens of the state by this military force that was illegally raised and set on foot in the manner I have stated. But those arrests were made in those two counties which had been declared in insurrection by the respondent. Well, how stands the case as regards them? Can the respondent offer any excuse for his conduct? At whose instance and by whose orders were these arrests made, and who were the parties thus arrested? Why, many of the very best citizens of North Carolina, and not a few of them, as you know, of prominence and position, were among the number—men who were not connected and never had any connection with these secret organizations, or anything whatever to do, direct or indirect, with these alleged outrages by disguised persons, as the evidence conclusively shows. I say that these arrests, at least in the outset, were made by the direct orders of the respondent himself—that he furnished the names of the parties to be arrested, and that Kirk was but the instrument of their seizure and imprisonment, and in the infliction of the gross indignities which they suffered. Why do I say so? I will endeavor to show you.

Remember that this force was gotten up in the latter part of June and early in July. Kirk and Burgen were found to be here about the 20th of June. This military movement, according to the evidence, had been determined upon about the first week in June. Why and for what purpose was it so determined? I had intended to say something upon that subject, though perhaps it would have come in more properly in an earlier part of this discussion, but I will advert to it presently. The respondent declared the county of Alamance in a state of insurrection on the seventh of March. He was authorized by the Shoffner act to call out the militia to suppress such insurrection, and the constitution gave him power, when insurrection existed, to call out a sufficient body of militia to suppress it and put it down. Now I will not undertake to say that when parties are actually in arms as insurgents or in insurrection, that the governor of the state, when he calls out the militia, may not cause the arrest of men under those circumstances, although it would be his duty to deliver them over to the civil authority as soon as need be, and not detain them at pleasure. But I undertake to say this, that where there is no insurrection of the kind, no force embodied or in arms, actual or threatened, under no such circumstances is he authorized to arrest any man except by due process of law for probable cause, and upon a magistrate's warrant. Those were the means pointed out by the constitution, and if necessary he was authorized to use the military in aid of the civil power. These men, however, were not insurgents in arms, requiring, as one of the counsel alleged in this discussion, that the governor should act promptly and not wait. At least the question was asked what would be the duty of the governor under circumstances of that kind? I concede that under such circumstances, as in the case of a peace officer who sees parties in the act of violating the law, he has the right to arrest them. But after the illegal act is done, I submit to you, especially to those of you who are lawyers, that a peace officer must resort to the regular process of law; and so must the governor. Did the respondent do anything of that kind? Nothing whatever.

But I asked just now, how was it that this force came to be raised? It seems there was a meeting of prominent political gentlemen here about that time. They were casting about for something to be done. The state election was near at hand. The political party to which they belonged was in imminent danger of overthrow, as every one within the hearing of my voice knows. Consultations were held; it was agreed upon that something must be done. There was no necessity at that time for these troops. The governor had procured United States troops to be sent to Alamance. The evidence shows that violations of the law, secretly and by disguised persons had ceased there. It is true that in the county of Caswell there had been two homicides committed after that time and some two or three persons chastised for alleged barn burnings or thefts, but the whole number of the offences proved to have been committed in the county by parties known or unknown, were not more than five or six. The great mass of the people in that county were in a state of perfect quietude. Some barns had been burnt; larcenies had been committed, and it was alleged that some of the parties charged with such offences had been whipped or punished; but not until the 8th day of July did the respondent declare the county in a state of insurrection. All this was doubtless done pursuant to an arrangement entered into here on or about the first week of June. Why did not the governor call his council together to advise him in this important matter? Why did he not consult with some persons whose opinions were worthy of being considered? Why did he consult only with senators Pool and Abbott, and other men of that class? It is worthy of remark, too, that in both of these counties a sufficient force of United States soldiers had been stationed before this Kirk invasion, and order and quiet prevailed. The insurrection, if you choose to call it an insurrection, had been suppressed. In fact it never existed, except in name. The president had been called upon and a large military force had been sent to North Carolina and stationed at different points of the state. This was a part of the programme, to overawe and silence the people of the state. They came expecting to find a civil war in existence, from what had gone abroad throughout the country, but which turned out to be a great mistake—at least they found it so when they got here.

Such was the state of things when this force under Kirk was ready and the governor prepared to enter upon the campaign. What do we hear next? Then comes the governor with one of his proclamations, that proclamation called the "Kuklux Klan proclamation," in which he rings the changes upon those words, and in which he enumerated many offences that nobody had ever charged before to have been committed by the Kuklux Klan. All these were paraded before the public and for what purpose? Why nobody at that day, and nobody now regards such a proclamation in any other light than as intended to effect the approaching election. On the 13th of July we find that Kirk, with a portion of his command, is at the town of Company Shops, in the county of Alamance, and there the men are mustered into the service of the state. Simultaneously an order goes out from the respondent directing Kirk to proceed to the town of Yanceyville and take possession ot the public buildings there and to take military possession of the county. What next? Why, upon their arrival there, notwithstanding there is no sort of opposition shown to them whatever, in a public meeting which was being held and addressed by the candidates for congress, Kirk makes an entry with his armed forces into the court house and commences seizing and does seize many of the most respectable citizens of the county. Was there any charge against them? None whatever, except that they were prominent men and belonged to a different political party from that of the governor. Did he direct their arrest? I say he did, and not only their arrest, but the arrest of others in the county of Alamance for similar reasons. Neither Kirk nor any of his men, except a few negroes, knew any of these parties, but the whole thing is made manifest by a part of the secret correspondence which took place between the respondent and this man Kirk, not found in his letter book where it ought to be found, but picked up in the court house at Graham, after he had left there, in the room which he had occupied. One of those letters was written as early as the 17th of July, another one on the 27th of July, and another on the 30th of the same month. Why were not these letters on his letter book? It has been stated to you here, and stated truly, that not a letter appears on his letter book to this man Kirk, except one, and one telegram, and that one letter tohim also passed through the adjutant-general's office. Where is all this correspondence, for correspondence there must have been? How did it happen, and who contrived that this man Kirk and his chief officers who resided in East Tennessee, should be found here about the 20th of June? Was he not written to? By whom? Who consulted with the respondent, who advised him? Colonel Clarke tells you that he knew nothing about that. It was advised no doubt by that little cluster of politicians which, I have stated to you, were here about the first week in June, and who it is proved were in consultation with the respondent.

I say that the respondent directed the arrest of John Kerr and others. I say that it was so stated in one of these letters. I say that while nothing of the kind appears in the order which he issued through his adjutant general, directing Kirk to proceed to Yanceyville, yet about the same time he privately furnished Kirk with a list of men to be arrested. He says in that letter, "the next list of persons who are to be arrested will be "handed to you by the judge advocate"—meaning of course of the military commission by which he intended to have them tried—thus showing that the first list had been furnished by himself. Kirk said to Judge Kerr, "I have nothing against "you; there is no evidence against you; I should not have ar-"rested you, but I was directed to do it by the governor. My "orders were to do it." Another one of these gentlemen said the same thing. Doctor Yancey, the coroner of the court, and sheriff Griffith, were also of the party that the governor directed should be arrested. Here, too, were the aged Doctor Roan and Mr. Bowe, the last a venerable citizen who had been especially recommended to the respondent by Mr. Donahoe, to whom he had written as to the state of things in the county, as a man having the entire confidence of the community, and who would do justice between the races there and to the public, and who could do a great deal towards quieting any disorder that might exist in the county, if clothed with authority to interpose his good offices for that purpose. But he is one of the first men the governor of North Carolina ordered to be arrested, and was arrested under circumstances of marked indignity. Was there any probable cause existing, any evidence then or thereafter produced against these gentlemen, some twenty or more in number? None whatever. Some two or three of them were afterwards examined and charges were brought against them of complicity in the murder of Stephens, and they were bound over to court, and subsequently discharged for want of evidence against them. But I mean to say that against the great mass of them there was no charge and no evidence whatever, and the governor knew it. He nevertheless orders his military satraps to go there and arrest these men without any cause or suspicion even, and without warrant. Why, to say the least of it, that was a gross abuse of his office. These men were not in arms, or offering any resistance whatever to the officers of the law. They could have been arrested by the civil authorities, any of them at any time—those against whom these charges, if any, had been then made, as well as those against whom there were no charges; and that being the case there was no necessity or excuse whatever for resorting to the military arm. No officer has a right to do that until the civil authority is resisted. So I say that the respondent caused the arrest of these gentlemen when he knew that there was no evidence against them. Out of his own wicked heart and for wicked purposes, he had them seized and detained and imprisoned until he was forced to surrender them.

But it is said that he is not responsible for these acts. Why? "Because other men have committed offences against the state." But these men had committed none, and from their characters and positions were not likely to have done so. There was not the slightest evidence that they had committed any, or that they were even suspected. He does not show that he had any information to that effect, but contrary to his duty, yes, his sworn duty, contrary to the laws of the land, he seizes these men and imprisons them. What is more, he prepares to try them by a military court and to shoot or hang such of them as that court might convict. That was his determination, senators. I submit to you that there can be no question as to his guilt upon that charge.

I come next to the two articles on the subject of *habeas corpus*. As to these it seems to me that upon the principle and the law heretofore discussed in this case, there can be no difficulty as to the decision that you are required to give. Soon after these gentlemen were arrested, as well in the county of Alamance as in the county of Caswell, writs were sued out before the chief justice of this state, alleging that they had been unlawfully seized and detained by this force, and asking for relief as they had a right to do under the laws of this state. Upon the first case that came before the chief justice—the case of Moore and others--there was a full and elaborate discussion by counsel on behalf of the petitioners as well as on the part of the respondent in this case. The counsel for the petitioners insisted that they were entitled to their discharge, and the counsel for the respondent insisted that they were not. Many of the questions which have been discussed here were then discussed before the chief justice. Finally, an opinion was delivered by him to the effect that the writ of *habeas corpus* was not suspended in North Carolina, and could not be, inasmuch as there was an express provision in the constitution of the state that it should not be suspended; and he held further that while under the circumstances, he would not issue a mandate to any officer to call out the *posse comitatus* for the purpose of delivering these prisoners--(for Kirk had declared that he would not deliver them except when compelled to do so by superior force or by the orders of his superior officer, the governor)—inasmuch as the governor was the commander-in-chief of the militia, the very force which would have to be called upon to enforce the execution of such mandate, yet, that he would issue an order to that effect and require that

that order, with a copy of his opinion, be served by the officer of the court upon the governor of the state himself. Well that was done. The governor took time to consider it. In the course of three or four days he made his response. What was that response? He declined to yield obedience to the order of the chief justice, pretending that he was justified by a portion of his opinion in doing what he did. But, senators, examine that opinion. Take what appears on the face of it, and say whether it bears any such construction as that? Inquire, if you will, why the governor undertook to override the law of the land and the great privilege of this writ. Who advised him to do it? Under what counsel did he act? Does it appear that he had any legal advice on the subject? He chose to act upon his own understanding of the law. He chose to contemn the decision of the highest judicial officer in the state, to trample under foot his authority. Was it not his duty to yield to that authority? Does not the chief justice say to him, substantially, in that opinion, "I have accorded full faith "and credit to your acts, now I will expect you will do the same "thing to mine. The judiciary has a right to supervise the "action of other departments of the government. It rests "with me to decide whether your action is legal or illegal, "whether you have a right to detain these parties or not; and "I hope you will not take the responsibility of doing it, upon "any extreme notion that the safety of the state requires you "to do anything of the kind." When the governor of the state had declined to yield obedience to that mandate, and when the motion was made in the first place to attach Kirk, his subordinate officer, the chief justice declined to do it. Why? Because the governor had assumed the responsibility. Counsel then moved to attach the governor, but the chief justice declined to attach him, because the governor occupied the position of a co-ordinate branch of the government of which the judiciary was another; but said that the responsibility rested with the governor, that he, the chief justice, had no means of executing the writ—that he had exhausted the powers of the judiciary, and that thereafter, he repeated, the responsibility was with the governor of the state. Notwithstanding all this, the respondent persisted in his course.

In that same opinion the chief justice held that the respondent had no right to try any citizen by any other mode than by bringing him before the civil courts of the country; that he could not lawfully institute a military commission to try these parties. Did he listen to that? No, he set it all at defiance. He trampled upon the law of the land and upon the judiciary. He set himself up as above both. He declared that he would detain these citizens as long as he thought proper. Even after this opinion was delivered, declaring that he had no authority to institute a military commission to try them, he went on and was engaged in organizing such a commission, which was to meet a few days before the election, and which, for some reason, was afterward postponed. He stated in one of these private letters to Kirk, "It will certainly meet "on the 8th of August," which was the week following the time he had originally set for the meeting. He then gave a partial list of the names of those who were to compose the court, and says, "The residue of this court will be made up out of your "regiment." I have given a brief statement of the history of this matter of *habeas corpus*, so far as the case of Moore and others is concerned.

A few days subsequent to that, a similar writ was sued out on behalf of John Kerr and a large number of others. The matter went through a similar train. The same conclusions were arrived at and the same result took place. Not one of them was surrendered. The respondent took the responsibility of holding them as he did Moore and others. Now what excuse can he have to offer? Was he acting legally? Why nobody will pretend that, unless the absurd position that martial law prevailed can be sustained. His own councel, with one exception, have not claimed anything of the kind. The utmost contended for was that he had a right to make the arrests. One of them, it is true, said that in cases of insurrection the governor had a right, by virtue of his power, to suppress insurrection, to detain an insurrectionist after his arrest for a "reasonable time." But who is to judge of the "reasonableness" of the time? Should the governor of the state assume this authority? Is he to be the judge of that? Is he, in other words, to hold such prisoners until it suits his pleasure to surrender them, or does the law vest that power in another tribunal, to wit, the judiciary of the state? Can there be any question about it? Can there be any question that this man now on trial before you knew that as well as any lawyer within the hearing of my voice, and especially after the chief justice had announced his decisions? I do not think there can be any sort of dispute about that; and yet it is insisted by the accused in his answer that he had a right to detain these parties until he thought he might safely surrender them—in other words, to detain them at his will and his pleasure. And if he did detain them, as the evidence abundantly shows, as long as he was able to do it, can it be said that he acted honestly about this matter?—that he acted from proper motives?—and how can they ask you to excuse him on that ground? Why, as I have stated before to you, if a man violates the law he is presumed to do it with a criminal intent until he shows to the contrary. But what evidence is there here that he acted from any proper motive? Let us enquire and see how that is.

In the first place, the respondent knew perfectly well that under the Shoffner bill the privilege of the writ of *habeas corpus* was not suspended. He knew that the original bill only authorized him to apply to the president, asking that the writ should be suspended by him or by congress. On the 14th of March, (the Shoffner bill having been passed on the 29th of January,) he sent a telegram to the members of congress from this state, to be laid before the congress of the United States, (which is an admission that he knew he had no such authority himself under the Shoffner act,) in which he says, "I have declared the county of Ala-

"mance to be in a state of insurrection." What further did he say? Why, that he cannot effect what he wants to effect without a suspension of the writ of *habeas corpus*, that the president had been applied to, but he was unable to do it under the constitution of the United States without the assent of congress, and he requests them to suspend the privilege of the writ. And for what purpose? He says substantially, "We "want military commissions—civil tribunals won't answer, we "want a speedier and sharper remedy than is furnished by any "civil tribunal. We want military commissions to try and "shoot the offenders." What! a plea of ignorance set up for a man who says that? From the beginning to the end, senators, he shows this fell purpose, and he follows it up to the last.

What else have we? He refused, as I have shown, to obey the mandate of the chief justice of the state. The chief justice having declared himself powerless, an application is made to another judge—the district judge of the United States. He issues his writs. What does the respondent then do? Does he yield? No! The writs having been issued on the 6th of August, on the 7th the respondent telegraphs to the president of the United States. And what does he say in that telegram? I want to call your attention to it. It is to be found on page 213 of the proceedings as reported, and is sent from the executive department at this place:

"*To the President of the United States:*

"SIR: The chief justice of the supreme court of this state, "sustained by his associate justices, has decided that I have "a right to declare counties in a state of insurrection, and to "arrest and hold all suspected persons in such counties. "This I have done.

"But the district judge, Brooks, relying on the fourteenth "amendment and the act of congress of 1867, page 385, chap- "ter 28, has issued a writ of *habeas corpus*, commanding the "officer, Kirk, to produce before him the bodies of certain pris-"oners detained by my order.

"I deny his right thus to interfere with the local laws in "murder cases. I hold these persons under our state laws, "and under the decision of our supreme court judges who have "jurisdiction of the whole matter, and it is not known to Judge "Brooks in what manner or by what tribunal the prisoners "will be examined and tried.

"The officer will be directed to reply to the writ that he "holds the prisoners under my order, and that he refuses to "obey the writ. If the marshal shall then call upon the *posse* "*comitatus* there may be conflict, but if he should call first on "the federal troops, it will be for you to say whether the troops "shall be used to take the prisoners out of my hands.

"It is my purpose to detain the prisoners unless the army "of the United States under your orders shall demand them."

Well, let us see how much truth and how much falsehood there is in this telegram in the first place. It is evidently an open defiance of the law. "I hold these prisoners," says he, "under our state laws, and under the decision of our supreme "court judges, who have jurisdiction of the whole matter." Was that true or was it false? I say there was not a word of truth in it. Hold these persons under the decision of the judges of the supreme court? Had not the chief justice, and the other judges concurring, as he said, decided that he had no right to hold them? And yet he telegraphs the president that the judges of the supreme court had decided that these persons for whom Judge Brooks had issued writs of *habeas corpus*, including Josiah Turner, jr., mind you, were held by virtue of a decision of the judges of the supreme court of North Carolina! He says further, without charging that Judge Brooks intended to take jurisdiction of murder cases, when in fact a great many of these men had been arrested, as I have shown you, not only not on charges of murder, but upon no charge at all: "It is not known to Judge Brooks in what manner or by "what tribunal the prisoners will be examined and tried."

Why put in that? Because if they were to be tried by a military commission, it was very plain that under the act of congress, Judge Brooks would have the right to interpose. Therefore it is that he says to the president, "Judge Brooks "does not know before what tribunal I am going to have these "persons examined and tried."

He intended then to have them tried, as he had already declared, before this military commission of his, which was to meet on the 8th of August; and it will be seen by an inspection of the testimony that about that time, or a few days afterwards, he issued an order to Kirk to bring all the prisoners over to Company Shops with the witnesses. And why? For the purpose of assembling this military court to try them. He then expected no doubt that he would be sustained by the president. It was declared all along that he was backed up by the president. His myrmidons had declared, when making their arrests, that they made them by order of the president and of the governor of the state. He professed all along to be acting in the name of and with the promised support of the president. Well, whether he was or was not, I don't know. I confess the circumstances are such that they do not show very favorably for the president of the United States. However, I do not wish to bring his name into this discussion. But certainly the public were assured that the accused had his sanction and authority. He then appealed to the president in the manner I have stated here to sustain him. He further says: "The officer will be directed to reply to the "writ that he holds the prisoners under my order, and that he "refuses to obey the writ." Now what comes? "If the "marshal shall then call on the *posse comitatus* there may be "conflict, but if he should call first on the federal troops it will "be for you to say whether the troops shall be used to take "prisoners out of my hands. It is my purpose to detain the "prisoners unless the army of the United States, under your "orders, shall demand them." That is, "I will resist, by force, "the marshal with his *posse comitatus*—he will not get them.

"I will use force against him. I will only yield when you "order the troops of the United States to take possession of "these men." Was there ever anything more defiant? Now, every lawyer knows that the marshal of the United States has the same powers as to summoning a *posse* to enforce a process of the United States as the sheriff of a county has. And yet here is this man who is held up as a model of virtue and a model governor, who telegraphs to the president of the United States, and asks: "Do not send any of your troops "here to enforce the execution of process from a United States "court—do not take these men out of the hands of my officer "with United States soldiers—let the marshal go and summon "his *posse* and let him attempt to take them. I am strong "enough to resist him, and I will do it." And he declares his determination to do it unless the president interferes, and he begs the president not to do it. But that was carrying the thing a little too far. The president referred this communication to his attorney general. His attorney general advised that it would not do, and a day or two after, through the secretary of war, the governor got a communication advising him to yield to the action of Judge Brooks.

Not getting support from that quarter, what next does the respondent do? The law under which Judge Brooks was acting gave to the officer of the respondent ten days after service of the writs within which to make his returns. The limit allowed by law was taken advantage of by the respondent. He refused to deliver these men or discharge them. In the meantime four of them were put in jail. One of them was ironed and the others were thrown into a loathsome dungeon without water or any other conveniences.

But what did the respondent in the meantime? When he found that those of the prisoners whom he had refused to liberate or to bring before the chief justice upon his mandate, had, with many others who had not sued out writs before him, to be carried before Judge Brooks, he took steps to procure the return of the chief justice from his home to this place for the purpose of resuming action upon these very cases, in which a few days before he had persistently refused obedience to his mandates. He addressed him a letter on the 15th of August, I believe, requesting his return. It appears from the evidence that the chief justice left here for his home a very short time before the election.

The CHIEF JUSTICE. The day before.

Mr. BRAGG. The day before the election, which was held on the 4th of August. After this correspondence had taken place between the president and the respondent, it appears that Mr. Ball was sent to the chief justice to know whether he could attend here, the respondent having changed his mind in the meantime, as he pretends, as to his duty in relation to these prisoners. Mr. Ball went and returned, and then Mr. Neathery, the private secretary of the governor, was sent off that night. The letter was written to which I have referred, dated the 15th of August, and he was dispatched post haste to procure the attendance of the chief justice here, in order that Mr. Kerr and others who had, after failure to get relief at the hands of the chief justice, applied for and obtained writs of *habeas corpus* from Judge Brooks, should be brought before the chief justice here, and not carried before the federal judge at Salisbury. That letter is also a rather remarkable one; and here again, senators, it seems to me that the respondent has not confined himself exactly to the truth. He says:

"In my answer to the notices served upon me by the mar "shal of the supreme court, in the matter of Adolphus G. "Moore and others, *ex parte*, I stated to your honor that at "that time the public interest forbade me to permit Col. George "W. Kirk to bring before your honor the said parties; at the "same time I assured your honor that as soon as the safety of "the state should justify it, I would cheerfully restore the civil "power and cause the said parties to be brought before you, "together with the cause of their capture and detention."

Now I say that in his answer he stated no such thing. He did not say anywhere in that answer, addressed to the chief justice, when this notice of the chief justice's decision had been served upon him, that he would bring the parties before him. On the contrary, I have before shown you that it was his purpose not to bring them before him but, in defiance of the opinion of the chief justice, to try them by a military commission as late as the 8th of August.

"That time has arrived, and I have ordered Col. George W. "Kirk to obey the writs of *habeas corpus* issued by your Honor."

Arrived! What, so speedily? Why, how was it that a few days before he could not do this thing? The safety of the state then required that he should hold these men in custody and try them by military commission; but somehow or other, in the meantime, the day had arrived when it would be safe for him to surrender these gentlemen in order that their cases might be disposed of by the civil authority. Well, there were several important matters that had occurred in the meantime. In the first place, the election had resulted differently from what was anticipated. In the next place, writs of *habeas corpus* had been issued by Judge Brooks, and that was another trouble. In the next place, he had telegraphed to the president and had found out that the president would not protect him in his violation of law with the army of the United States, and hence, within the short period which had elapsed, this very great change was brought about in the condition of things in the state, and he could now abdicate his usurped imperial power and yield obedience to civil authority and law. The truth is, senators, that it was a forced obedience, for he knew the time had arrived when he could no longer hold these men. He made a virtue of necessity—it was not his choice. The chief justice came down on the 18th, and what did he say to the respondent?

"Receiving the return after the delay to which you allude "of several weeks, is not to be taken as concurring on my part "in the necessity for the delay, or as assuming any portion of "the responsibility in regard to it."

He had before put the responsibility upon the governor. He was determined that it should rest there, and he told him so. Yet it is said here that upon these articles, the respondent had done nothing more than to arrest men whom he had a right to arrest; that he detained them for a reasonable time only, and that when he thought that he could surrender them with safety to the public interest and the state, he did so.

Senators, I think when you come to examine all the facts connected with that matter, some of which only I have brought to your notice, you will see that that sort of defence is entitled to little or no consideration at your hands.

Pending the argument of Mr. Bragg, the hour of ten o'clock, p. m., having arrived, on motion of Senator Graham, of Orange, the court adjourned to meet to-morrow at 11 o'clock.

## FORTY-THIRD DAY.

SENATE CHAMBER, March 21, 1871.

The COURT met at 11 o'clock, pursuant to adjournment, Honorable R. M. Pearson, Chief Justice of the Supreme Court, in the chair.

Proceedings were opened by proclamation made in due form by the doorkeeper.

The CLERK proceeded to call the roll of senators, when the following gentlemen were found to be present:

Messrs. Adams, Albright, Allen, Barnett, Battle, Beasley, Bellamy, Brogden, Brown, Cook, Council, Cowles, Crowell, Currie, Edwards, Eppes, Flemming, Gilmer, Graham of Alamance, Graham of Orange, Hawkins, Hyman, Jones, King, Latham, Ledbetter, Lehman, Linney, Love, Mauney, McClammy, McCotter, Merrimon, Moore, Morehead, Murphy, Norment, Olds, Price, Robbins of Davidson, Robbins of Rowan, Skinner, Speed, Troy, Waddell, Warren, Whiteside and Worth.

Senator JONES moved that the reading of the journal be dispensed with.

The CHIEF JUSTICE put the question on the motion of Senator Jones, and it was decided in the affirmative.

Mr. BRAGG, in behalf of the managers, in resuming his argument, said:

Mr. CHIEF JUSTICE and SENATORS: I am sensible that I have already occupied too much of the time of this body, it may be, unnecessarily, and I shall endeavor to be as brief in the remarks which I submit to-day as the nature of the case will admit.

I come now to the discussion of the last two articles preferred against the respondent, and it seems to me that in view of what I have said already, there can be little difficulty as to the judgment to which the senate shall come with regard to these articles.

The seventh article charges, in substance, the unlawful raising and equipping of a large military force, composed in large part of lawless and desperate characters, that the respondent sent them to the counties of Alamance and Caswell under the command of Kirk, Burgen and Yates, as their chief officers, who were from the state of Tennessee, and who were desperate men, and that without warrant or lawful authority, they seized, held and imprisoned divers of the good people of said counties, some of whom, including Josiah Turner, Jr., of the county of Orange, were thrown into a loathsome dungeon, and that to sustain the same band of armed and lawless men, the respondent made his warrant upon the state treasurer for large sums of public money for the unlawful uses and purposes charged

Now as to the first branch of this article, it is embraced substantially in other articles, as to which I have already presented my views very fully. The court is fully aware of all the evidence upon this subject. I need not go at length into the testimony by any minute comments upon it for the purpose of showing that the force was an unlawful one, or that it was of the character described in this article. But the principal point in that article, in addition to what is charged in other articles, is, as I conceive, the unlawful drawing of a warrant upon the treasurer for large sums of money to be appropriated for unlawful purposes. Now senators, if this force was an unlawful one, then beyond any sort of question, the respondent had no right in law to draw his warrant upon the public treasury for the purpose of sustaining and keeping it on foot. The constitution provides that no money shall be drawn from the public treasury unless it be duly appropriated by the legislative branch of the government. It has been said that the act commonly known as the Shoffner act, authorized the governor to draw from the public treasury such funds as were necessary for paying the militia, should they be called out according to the provisions of that act. That is not denied. There is no question about that. But then the question comes back again, whether this force was a militia force; whether it was such a force as was prescribed in that act. About that question, I suppose, there can be no sort of doubt. At all events, I have already presented my views upon that subject, and they can pass with the court for what they are worth. If senators shall conclude that this force was unlawful, then it necessarily follows that the governor, in drawing this money by means of his warrant, out of the treasury, violated the law, inasmuch as there was no appropriation of funds for any such unlawful purpose, and I have already undertaken to show you in wh: t I have said, not only that the force was unlawful, but that the respondent knew that it was unlawful.

Article VIII charges that to support the unlawful military force raised by him, he, by his warrant, caused large sums of the public money to be drawn from the public treasury in order to pay the officers and men composing it; that he appointed A. D. Jenkins, paymaster, to disburse the money for that purpose, and that an injunction was obtained from one of the judges of the state to prevent its disbursement—that he sought to evade the force and effect of the injunction, and to that end removed Jenkins from his place of paymaster and appointed John B. Neathery in his stead, and caused the money to be turned over to him to be disbursed, and it was disbursed accordingly, and that he thereby evaded the purposes of the writ of injunction. So it will be seen that the main point involved in that article is, whether he did the acts charged and did thus evade and disregard this injunction which, as chief executive officer of the state, it was his duty to respect, and, if necessary, cause to be enforced. The other matters have all been discussed. I submit, senators, that there can be no question upon that, when you to come to regard the evidence which has been offered upon that point. It seems that sometime in the month of July, the governor having given a military appointment to Mr. Jenkins, which, by-the-bye, he had no right to give to him, assigned him to the duties of paymaster to this illegal force. But prior to that time, when this man Kirk arrived here from the state of Tennessee, the evidence shows that there was then paid over to him upon the governor's warrant on the state treasurer, for what purpose it does not exactly appear, the sum of one thousand dollars. What has become of that money, we do not know. Of course he applied it to such uses as he thought proper or perhaps to such as he may have been directed to apply it. Soon after that, some sixty thousand dollars or more were drawn out at one time from the public treasury. Why was that done? Why was the respondent in such haste to get that money out of the treasury and into other, irresponsible hands? For though it appears from some orders put in evidence here that these disbursing agents of his were to give bonds, it does not appear from the testimony that any bond or bonds were given for the faithful taking care and disbursing of that money. Indeed it appears from the testimony that no such bonds were given. Those were then "flush" times, and everybody had plenty of money, except those who were honestly entitled to it. It could be drawn from the public treasury by the governor whenever he thought proper to draw his warrant. How far the treasurer in such a case as that would be responsible, it is not for me now to say. This money was drawn without lawful authority. It was placed in the hands of this young man as the agent or paymaster for unlawful purposes. But why was that large sum of money drawn out of the treasury at that time? There was certainly no immediate use for it. Was it not in anticipation that there would be objection raised to his getting that money out of the treasury at all? Why the whole country, at all events the state of North Carolina, was in a state of excitement. It was alleged, as we all know, as a part of the history of the day, that this body of troops raised by the respondent was unauthorized by law. It was commented upon in public and in private, before the chief justice in the *habeas corpus* cases, and the press of the state teemed with it. Senators, his purpose in drawing out that large sum of money was to prevent any interposition, as he hoped, by any citizen, as was afterward done by a writ of injunction. After all this trouble about the writs of *habeas corpus*, after the election, after the surrender of these men who had been detained by him, under compulsion as I have stated, and not by his choice, an injunction at last having been obtained at the instance of a citizen of the state against the public treasurer and against this agent or paymaster, young Jenkins, to prevent the disbursement of that money, or the paying out of any more money from the treasury—after that injunction had been issued and served, and that fund which he intended unlawfully to disburse in the payment of this unlawful force, was thereby tied up and stopped by the order of a court of justice, what then did the respondent do? Why he set about adopting some means—at whose suggestion it is not for me to say—to evade the operation of that injunction order. The evidence is, that he was fully aware of it, and he took means to evade it. This young man Jenkins dared not disburse the money himself. He was advised that he could not do it lawfully—that he would be guilty of contempt of court, and could be held amenable for it if he disregarded the injunction issued by his honor Judge Mitchell. What then were the means resorted to by the respondent to evade the injunction? He issues a military order, relieving this young man from the duty to which he had assigned him as a military officer and as paymaster, and appointed another, his private secretary, in his stead, and he then required young Jenkins to pay over the money to his successor. What are the circumstances connected with that transaction? Time and again, after he had made this new appointment, which was simultaneously made with the removal of young Jenkins, he applied to him to pay over this money to Mr. Neathery. The young man was doubtful as to whether he ought to do it. He was urged by the respondent time and again to do it. He whose duty it was, as chief executive officer of the state, to see that the laws were enforced and observed, was the man who covertly sought to evade and break the law, for we are to take it that that was the law, as his honor Judge Mitchell had issued the injunction, and until it was removed by him or some other judge, the respondent was bound to take it that it was lawfully done. On Saturday he wanted to know of young Jenkins whether he would pay over this money. On Sunday morning, even, he approached him again and wanted to know whether he would do it. On Sunday afternoon he was sent for again to the executive office, and there he found the governor's legal counsel in attendance with him. Young Jenkins was advised by one of them that he could safely turn over this money and not subject himself to the penalties of a contempt. It was remarked in his presence, by one of the gentlemen there—whether the governor or one of the others, he did not distinctly remember—that it was highly necessary to have the money paid over as the respondent had required, because there might be another injunction obtained to stop the money in the banks where it was deposited, and that it was necessary that it sho..ld be done at once to prevent that. Young Jenkins had been displaced. Finally, but reluctantly, he yielded to those urgent solicitations and to the commands of the respondent, and agreed to turn over the money. Neathery was sent for at nine o'clock Sunday night. There was haste in getting this fund into his hands and to get it out of the bank. Jenkins went to the bank and got the money that evening, by personal application to one of the officers. At the treasurer's office, at a late hour on Sunday night, they proceeded to count the money, and they got through counting and delivering it over to this new appointee of the respondent about 12 o'clock, and immediately thereafter the money was, by his orders, disbursed. Now can it be said that this was not a gross abuse on the part of the respondent of the duties of his office?

What is the answer made for him here? Why that an injunction cannot run from the judiciary against the governor of the state. That is not what is involved here at all. We do not pretend that there was any injunction against the governor, so that if he had violated it, he could have been put in contempt when brought before the judge. Not at all. It is unnecessary for me to discuss that point of law, but it is well settled in North Carolina that an injunction does properly run against the public treasurer, and by the same reasoning, *a fortiori*, it would run against this agent or paymaster of the governor, to restrain the paying out and disbursing unlawfully of any of the public money. But that is not controverted.

The gentlemen who represent the respondent, very well knew that they could not sustain any point of that kind—that is, that the injunction was not properly granted, and did not operate to all intents and purposes against the public treasurer, and against young Mr. Jenkins, who was the agent or paymaster to disburse this money. His advisers knew very well, as every lawyer knew, that if young Jenkins disbursed that money when there was an injunction resting upon him, he would be put in contempt and subjected to all the pains and penalties of a contempt. But he was told, "The governor has "power to remove you—the governor has removed you and "ordered you to pay the money to your successor. That will "be a sufficient answer when you are required to render an "account to the judge as to why you turned over this money. "That will excuse you from the pains and penalties of a con- "tempt;" and the judge so held afterwards, and properly held; for he did pay over this money virtually under compulsion, as I have stated; but whether on compulsion or not, he had ceased to be an officer in any sense of the word; had ceased to have any authority for detaining that money, by the action of the respondent, and it was accordingly turned over into the hands of another and a more pliant agent.

Senators, I wish to ask you now, in all seriousness, whether that does not amount to a high misdemeanor in office; whether on the part of the governor it was not an abuse of his office; whether it was not an evasion of the law—it being his duty not only to observe and respect the law, but to take care that it was enforced? If the governor of the state will not respect the law, who is expected to obey and respect it? So we say that upon that article there can be no sort of question as to what your judgment ought to be.

Senators, there are a few other remarks, somewhat of a general character, that I wish to make before bringing to a close what I have to say. It is alleged that there were a great many crimes committed, especially in the county of Alamance, and some in the county of Caswell. Nay, the respondent goes so far as to say in a part of his answer, that a majority of the white voters in these two counties belonged to this secret organization which was set on foot for the unlawful purposes which he alleges? Now we have evidence here as to the extent of these organizations in the county of Alamance from reliable sources, showing that the whole of their members never exceeded at any time two hundred. The purposes for which those secret organizations were set on foot have been stated by various witnesses. I have nothing to say about that now, except this: that the whole history of things in those counties—and I might say elsewhere—goes to show that all secret political organizations are in themselves dangerous, and ought, if possible, to be put an end to. I condemn, as fully as any man can condemn, the various acts which are complained of as committed there or elsewhere, whether they have been done by one secret organization or another. I am no apologist for any such thing, for while I may be considered as a party man, I beg to say, and I think every intelligent man within the sound of my voice will agree with me, that any and all such acts on the part of these organizations have redounded, not to the benefit, as has been alleged, of the political party to which I and many of you belong, but have been in the main of very great injury to that party. But I have said that this state of things in a great degree arose out of the state of the times. As for the county of Caswell, allow me to say that there is not a particle of evidence here to show that there was any organization of that kind within its limits. Some offences were proved to have been committed there, but comparatively few in number. Out of a population of some sixteen thousand or upwards, two homicides are alleged to have been committed in secret, one of them proved to have been done by disguised men, and the other committed by whom we know not. But let us take the whole number of offences that have been brought up here, chiefly from Alamance county, many of them very trivial in their character, but magnified to the greatest possible extent on the other side, and what do they show? It is evident that every offence, however trivial, where the personal rights of another had been invaded by any of these disguised persons, within the space of two years prior to July 1870, has been hunted up with the utmost industry and presented here with the highly colored comments of the gentlemen on the other side. Some of these offences look to be serious in character, and are serious no doubt, but not to the extent that has been represented either here or elsewhere. And again, I may remark somewhat in palliation, though not in justification, that these organizations, which were gotten up at first for the purposes, as alleged by some who belonged to them, of inflicting some kind of punishment upon men who had been guilty of wrong doing, when the laws of the country were not enforced against them were virtually dissolved, according to the evidence, some year or more before many of these offences were committed, and that in point of fact nearly the whole of those outrages were committed by small bands of irresponsible men who had belonged to these organizations, and for which the great mass of those who had belonged to them were not at all responsible. But, however that may be, still it was all wrong—there is no doubt about that. But on the other hand, other offences of a different character were also committed, the perpetrators of which were alleged to go unpunished. This whole state of things has resulted, in my humble opinion, from the evil counsels of certain men, who ought to have given other advice, and from the inefficient administration of the public justice of the state. Retaliations were spoken of, as if other acts of lawlessness were committed solely in retaliation of the outrages which have been charged to the Kuklux. And one of the learned counsel asks: "Why didn't you prove these other acts?" Why, it is sufficient for me to say, as senators know, that those acts, whatever they may have been, were not directly in issue here. It was proper and competent on the part of the respondent, as a part of his case, to prove all these alleged outrages on personal rights in those two counties, but it was incompetent and not proper for the managers to attempt to prove or prove separate and distinct crimes of a different character, and for and on account of which many of these personal outrages were committed. We have heard of barn-burnings, of thefts, insults to women, and of other offences of a heinous character, but they were not to be brought in issue here directly. It was only incidentally that these things could come up when a witness was put upon the stand and examined. In many cases they have admitted what they were punished for, and several had the candor to confess that they deserved what they got.

But I said that this bad state of things was measurably produced by inefficient action on the part of judicial and prosecuting officers. Let me call your attention, senators, to a piece of evidence that was introduced here towards the close of the trial—I mean the record of the criminal docket of two terms of the superior court of Caswell county. What does it show? A large number of cases of larceny and other crimes, and perhaps nine out of ten of them were settled by the judge, or perhaps I should say more properly, the solicitor, for that district, allowing parties to pay the costs of the prosecution and having judgment suspended, instead of their being subjected to punishment. The solicitor received his fees, but offenders went unwhipped of justice. You have seen the solicitor here as a witness. You have had an opportunity of seeing what manner of man he is, of forming an opinion as to his capacity, and as to how, in some respects, he performed his public duties.

Now it has been urged here by way of excuse rather than justification for the respondent, that there was no way of putting a stop to these offences. There was no means that the civil authority could adopt of breaking up these organizations and ferreting out and punishing these secret violations of the law. Suppose you had had an efficient judge and an efficient prosecuting officer in that district, such as those we used to have in North Carolina in former times, and such as we ought to have now, are you not satisfied that things would have resulted differently? Moreover, it was in the power of the governor to appoint courts of oyer and terminer there, and if the resident judge could not or would not enforce the law, or had not capacity to do it, he could have sent another judge there who would have done it: and if the state's counsel there was not competent to ferret out and cause to be brought to justice these offenders, it was in the power of the governor, under the law, to employ other counsel to do it. I appeal to every lawyer who hears me, I care not on which side of the senate he may sit, whether if that had been done, or if there had been a vigilant and efficient prosecuting officer there, and he had gone before the grand juries, as he would have a right to do, and set to work himself, and examined the witnesses, sending off, if necessary, for man after man and witness after witness, and causing a thorough and searching investigation into all these cases, this secret commission of crime would not have been broken up and the offenders brought to speedy and condign punishment? The difficulty was in the machinery of the law and in the want of its proper administration, for the evidence shows, despite of all that has been said to the contrary, that the grand juries were disposed to do their duty. The law was powerful enough to reach offenders. But to this day has the executive ever resorted to any such means? No, he resorted to a different mode. He preferred to resort to the military arm. He preferred to send troops there of his own, and to cause other troops to be sent there by the government of the United States by which this pretended insurrection was to be suppressed, and these crimes prevented. He preferred himself to become the executor of his own will, in his own way, and by the military arm, and to arrest, detain and imprison without regard to law, many men who were as innocent of crime as any of you, and then to organize and set on foot a military court to try them.

Senators, strong appeals have been made to you, and you have been warned not to listen to the promptings of political feeling. I again repeat that this is not a political trial. I again say that upon this trial depends, in a great degree, the preservation of the great principles of civil and constitutional liberty and law. And here I would say to those who belong to the political party in the minority here, that the same state of things might occur, (but I trust in God it never will occur, if these great principles are maintained and respected) when another political organization, that to which the majority of this body now belongs, shall get full control of every department of the government. It may be, let me now say to them, in justification of this prosecution, that when that party comes into power, if the present executive should be held to be guiltless and is excused, because it had been common to violate these fundamental principles of civil liberty and safeguards for the citizen. that another executive office—differing in political sentiment from the one now on trial, may undertake to exercise similar powers against his political opponents and commit like abuses. I do not believe that there will be any such attempt; but if there ever should be, let the author or asserter of them come from whatever political party he may, I for one will set a face of flint against him, as I have done against all such acts on the part of the respondent. I have lived too long not to value the principles of civil liberty. I have lived too long, and I trust have been too well educated in them, not to respect at all times and under all circumstances, those principles contained in our constitution and bill of rights, without which the mere forms of free government are a sham and a cheat.

But, senators, the case of the impeachment of President Johnson has been repeatedly brought to your notice. You have been told again and again that that was a mere political prosecution; that he was put upon his trial and sought tobe disgraced and turned out of his office merely on political grounds, and the learned counsel [Mr. Conigland] who sits before me, and who made such an eloquent appeal to you on behalf of the respondent, used this language:

"What man, Mr. Chief Justice and Senators, was ever "assailed with more ferocity than Andrew Johnson? During "the pendency of his trial the most disreputable means were "resorted to in order to secure his conviction. Those who "put trust in the calumny and vituperation poured upon him "must have regarded him as unredeemed by a single virtue, "yet he was innocent of all the crimes laid to his charge. This "of itself should satisfy us that public clamor and cries for "vengeance are not always evidence of guilt."

In another part of what follows, he undertakes to draw a parallel between President Johnson and Governor Holden, not only as men but as public officers, and he then says:

"President Johnson's only crime was the interposition of his "authority to save the prostrate bleeding south from utter "destruction."

Well, I shall not undertake to deny the most of what my friend said as to President Johnson. I think history, hereafter when it comes to be written in calmer times than those in which we live, will pronounce the same judgment that he has upon the merits of that case, but nevertheless I think the counsel was unfortunate in drawing the parallel which he undertook to draw between Mr. Johnson and the respondent. The charges against them are in no wise similar. Those against Mr. Johnson were in the main that he had attempted to violate the act commonly called the tenure of office act by removing Mr. Stanton, one of his cabinet officers, from office, which was a matter comparatively trivial. Such are not the charges brought against the respondent. And there was another fact my friend failed to recollect, that while Andrew Johnson was impeached for the reasons and under the influences assigned by him here, his client, who had been appointed by this same Andrew Johnson provisional governor of North Carolina, a position of almost imperial power, as another of the counsel has told us, was one of the men who, when this same President Johnson was sought to be immolated by his political foes for political reasons only, united in the attempt, and over his own hand in the public press of the country insisted that he should be impeached, degraded and driven from office. There is the parallel. Yes, this man whom he had thus taken up and placed in this prominent position, placed there against the remonstrances of many of his political friends, when the struggle came and he saw that Mr. Johnson was on the losing side, joined in the cry, crucify him! crucify him! and sought his political blood. Now I remember no such act in Mr. Johnson's life as that. Whatever else may be said of him, I feel sure that no act of his life can be found to furnish a parallel to the ungrateful act of the respondent towards him.

Now I know the warm, impulsive and generous nature of my friend who sits before me. No man is more his friend than I am. None can say that I mean to censure anything that he has thought proper to say here, or what any others of the counsel have thought proper to say on behalf of the respondent. I fully appreciate their situation, and his situation especially, and I say now and here that it was their duty, as members of our profession, to have appeared for him and to have rendered him all the service that they could fairly render in his defence. I know that if they have perhaps occasionally exceeded the bounds somewhat of the duty of counsel under the circumstances, and in some particulars, it is attributable to an honest zeal for their client, and in so far is to be commended. Judging from myself, and knowing that when the feelings of counsel become enlisted in the defence of a client they often go further in some respects than sober judgment and reason in calmer moments would perhaps prompt, I trust I shall be always ready to commend rather than to censure.

But, senators, the example of one or two prominent men,

who sat upon the trial of President Johnson has been brought to your notice as worthy of your imitation, especially the course and action of Senator Fessenden, now no more. No one approves more highly of the course of that distinguished senator than I do. I knew him personally, for I had the honor to serve for a time in the senate with him. It will be a monument to his memory, I believe, hereafter, that amidst all the clamor and all the excitement, indoors and out of doors, during that great trial, he listened only to the promptings of his judgment and of his conscience, and voted to acquit. But as I have said to you already, the charges preferred against the president and the circumstances attending his trial were very different from those to be found in this case. Understanding that it was the purpose of counsel, in referring to the course of Mr. Fessenden, and perhaps some other senator who voted for acquittal in that trial, to impress it upon this court that they did so merely on the grounds of the motives of the president, while in fact and in truth he had violated the tenure of office act in the attempted removal of Mr. Stanton, I took occasion to read what I had not read before, the reasons given by Senator Fessenden for coming to the conclusion that he did. I have that opinion here in the third volume of that celebrated trial. I have made an abstract in writing of the reasons given by him for his vote upon that occasion. They were briefly these,—and I hope senators will pardon me for reading them, though perhaps not strictly pertinent to the issue now before you. Senator Fessenden held—

1. That by the uniform practice of the government from the time of its inauguration, and the provisions of sundry acts of congress recognizing it as the proper construction of the constitution, the president had exercised the power of removing from office public officers, including those holding cabinet appointments. Without undertaking to decide whether this was the proper construction of the constitution he held,

2. That Mr. Stanton, having been originally appointed secretary of war by Mr. Lincoln during his first term, and remain-

ing in office without re-appointment after the commencement of his second term until his death, and so after president Johnson came into the presidential office, continuing in the office of secretary of war without any appointment from him, held the office of secretary of war at the pleasure of the president, and his case did not come within the provisions of the tenure of office act of March 2nd, 1867, and that the president was guilty of no misdemeanor in attempting to remove him, and that he had a legal right to remove him.

3. That he had a right to designate Gen. Thomas as secretary of war *ad interim.* These opinions disposed of all the articles up to the 10th, and that related to certain denunciations made of the then congress of the United States, or rather members thereof, in public speeches made by Mr. Johnson and reported and published in the public press.

4. These senator Fessenden considered to have been in bad taste, but not as constituting any crime or impeachable offence.

5. That the evidence failed to show that he was guilty of the 11th article, which charged an attempt to prevent the execution of the act of March 2nd, 1867, nor did it establish the truth of any of the specifications under that charge.

Now, you see the ground upon which Senator Fessenden acted. After a full discussion of the law as applicable to the questions involved,—and he was a distinguished lawyer,—he came to the conclusion, a rightful one as I believe, and one that will be justified by history hereafter, when the excitement which gave rise to those charges shall have passed away, that according to the law and the evidence the president had done nothing which constituted an impeachable offence, and therefore he voted to acquit him. What sort of a parallel is there between that case and this?

Senators, I have now, in a feeble way it is true, presented to you the views which, in the main, I desired to present upon this important trial. I have endeavored to discharge my duty here as one of the counsel for the managers, fearlessly but fairly. I hope I have said nothing here to give offense to any one. If in the heat of discussion here remarks may occasionally have fallen from me tending to wound the feelings of any person whatever, all I can say is that I regret that such words were spoken.

And now, senators, without further remark I commit this case to you. On you rests the responsibility of rendering a righteous judgement here. I know what that responsibility is. I know the solemn oaths that you and each of you have taken, and it is not for me to say what that judgement ought to be. I have my own views of it, and I have presented them fully to the best of my ability, but with you rests the responsibility. If, upon consideration, you conclude that the respondent is guilty of all or any of the articles of impeachment preferred against him, then I am perfectly satisfied, I am certain, that you will not hesitate, for any reason, to render that judgment. If, on the contrary, the prosecution has failed to make good any or all of the charges which have been made, then I am equally certain that it will be your pleasure, as I am that it will be your duty, to acquit him.

Senator FLEMMING offered the following order:

*Ordered*, That the senate, sitting as a court of impeachment, proceed to vote on the articles as presented by the house of representatives against W. W. Holden, Governor of North Carolina, on Wednesday 22nd inst., at eleven o'clock, and that a message be sent to the house of representatives informing that body of the day and hour designated.

Senator McCLAMMY called the ayes and noes.

A sufficient number of senators seconding the call, the ayes and noes were ordered.

The CLERK proceeded to call the roll on the adoption of the order of Senator Flemming, and it was decided in the affirmative by the following vote:

Those who voted in the affirmative are:

Messrs. Adams, Albright, Allen, Barnett, Battle, Beasley,

Brogden, Brown, Cook, Council, Cowles, Crowell, Currie, Edwards, Flemming, Gilmer, Graham of Alamance, Graham of Orange, Hawkins, Hyman, Jones, King, Latham, Ledbetter, Lehman, Linney, Love, Mauney, McClammy, McCotter, Merrimon, Moore, Murphy, Norment, Price, Robbins of Davidson, Robbins of Rowan, Skinner, Speed, Troy, Waddell, Warren, Whiteside and Worth—44.

Senator JONES offered the following order :

*Ordered*, That the time for filing written opinions in this case be extended to one week from the final decision.

Senator JONES. Mr. Chief Justice, some of the senators who intend to prepare and file opinions, think it would be hardly proper to commence the labor of preparation until after the arguments were finally closed. I think a week is as little time as will suffice, in view of our legislative duties, to enable senators to prepare opinions to their satisfaction. I hope there will be no objection to the order.

Senator EDWARDS. I would enquire, Mr. Chief Justice, whether the effect of adopting this order will be to keep the court open for another week ?

Senator JONES. I think not. I cannot see why it need delay the final adjournment. The opinions will be prepared and filed with the clerk and incorporated in the printed volumes.

Senator LOVE called for the ayes and noes.

A sufficient number seconding the call, the ayes and noes were ordered.

The CLERK proceeded to call the roll on the adoption of the order of Senator Jones, and it was decided in the affirmative by the following vote :

Those who voted in the affirmative are :

Messrs. Allen, Currie, Edwards, Flemming, Gilmer, Graham of Alamance, Graham of Orange, Hawkins, Jones, Latham, Linney, McClammy, Merrimon, Moore, Murphy,

Price, Robbins of Davidson, Robbins of Rowan, Skinner, Speed, Troy, Warren and Worth—23.

Those who voted in the negative are:

Messrs. Adams, Albright, Barnett, Battle, Beasley, Bellamy, Brogden, Cook, Council, Cowles, Crowell, Hyman, King, Ledbetter, Love, Mauney, McCotter, Norment, Waddell and Whiteside—20.

Senator ROBBINS, of Rowan, offered the following order:

*Ordered*, That the final vote in the articles of impeachment be taken without debate or explanation.

Senator COWLES called for the ayes and noes.

Senator GILMER. It strikes me, Mr. Chief Justice, that the order proposed is not necessary. Rule XIX reads thus:

" In taking the votes of the senate upon the articles of im-"peachment, the clerk will read the several articles suc-"cessively, and after the reading of each article, the clerk "will call the name of each senator, who shall rise in his place, "and thereupon the presiding officer shall put the following "question: 'Mr. —— how say you, is the respondent, "'William W. Holden, guilty or not guilty as charged in "'the —— article of impeachment?' Whereupon each sena-"tor shall answer 'guilty' or 'not guilty.'"

It seems to me, sir, that there can be no debate under the rule.

Senator ROBBINS, of Rowan. I am aware Mr. Chief Justice, that under that rule it would seem that there could not be debate. But there is another rule which says there may be debate prior to the vote. The object of the order which I have offered is to have the matter definitely settled, that we shall proceed to a vote without debate.

A sufficient number seconding the call for the ayes and noes, they were ordered.

The CLERK proceeded to call the roll of senators on the

adoption of the order of Senator Robbins, of Rowan, and it was decided in the affirmative by the following vote:

Those who voted in the affirmative are:

Messrs. Adams, Albright, Allen, Barnett, Battle, Beasley, Brogden, Brown, Council, Crowell, Currie, Edwards, Eppes, Gilmer, Graham of Alamance, Graham of Orange, Hawkins, Jones, King, Latham, Ledbetter, Lehman, Linney, Love, Mauney, McClammy, McCotter, Merrimon, Moore, Murphy, Norment, Price, Robbins of Davidson, Robbins of Rowan, Skinner, Speed, Troy, Waddell, Warren, Whiteside and Worth—41.

Those who voted in the negative are:

Messrs. Bellamy, Cook, Cowles, Flemming and Hyman—5.

On motion of Senator Linney, the court adjourned to meet at 11 o'clock, a. m., to-morrow.

# FORTY-FOURTH DAY.

SENATE CHAMBER, March 22, 1871.

The COURT met at eleven o'clock, a. m., pursuant to adjournment, Hon. R. M. Pearson, Chief Justice of the supreme Court, in the chair.

Proceedings were opened by proclamation made in due form by the doorkeeper.

The CLERK, William L. Saunders, Esq., proceeded to call the roll of senators, when the following gentlemen were found to be present:

Messrs. Adams, Albright, Allen, Barnett, Battle, Beasley, Bellamy, Brogden, Brown, Cook, Council, Cowles, Crowell, Currie, Dargan, Edwards, Eppes, Flemming, Gilmer, Graham of Alamance, Graham of Orange, Hawkins, Hyman, Jones, King, Latham, Ledbetter, Lehman, Linney, Love, Mauney, McClammy, McCotter, Merrimon, Moore, Morehead, Murphy, Norment, Olds, Price, Robbins of Davidson, Robbins of Rowan, Skinner, Speed, Troy, Waddell, Warren, Whiteside and Worth—49.

The DOORKEEPER announced the presence of the board of managers with their counsel, and the house of representatives, who proceeded to take seats within the chamber of the senate.

The CHIEF JUSTICE. The court is now ready to proceed to the final vote on the articles of impeachment presented against William W. Holden, Governor of the State of North Carolina. The doorkeeper is directed to see that order and silence is preserved in the gallery.

Senator JONES. Mr. Chief Justice, I give notice that if there be any demonstration of approval or disapproval in the galleries or lobbies, I shall move to have them cleared, except of the members of house of representatives,

The CHIEF JUSTICE. The clerk will read the first article.

Mr. Henry A. London, Jr., ASSISTANT CLERK, proceeded to read the first article in the words following:

### Article I.

That by the constitution of the state of North Carolina, the governor of said state has power to call out the militia thereof to execute the laws, suppress riots or insurrection, and to repel invasion, whenever the execution of the law shall be resisted, or there shall exist any riot, insurrection or invasion, but not otherwise; that William W. Holden, governor of said state, unmindful of the high duties of his office, the obligation of his solemn oath of office, and the constitution and laws of said state, and intending to stir up civil war, and subvert personal and public liberty, and the constitution and laws of said state, and of the United States, and contriving and intending to humiliate and degrade the said state and the people thereof, and especially the people of the county of Alamance, and to provoke the people to wrath and violence, did, under color of his said office, on the seventh day of March, in the year of our Lord one thousand eight hundred and seventy, in said state, of his own false, corrupt and wicked mind and purpose, proclaim and declare that the county of Alamance in said state, was in insurrection, and did, after the days and time last aforesaid, send bodies of armed desperate and lawless men, organized and set on foot without authority of law, into said county, and occupy the same by military force, and suspend civil authority, and the constitution and laws of the state; and did, after the days and times last aforesaid, and before the time of impeachment, in this behalf, through and by means of such armed, desperate and lawless men, arrest many peaceable and law-abiding citizens of said county of Alamance, then and there about their lawful business; and did detain, hold, imprison, hang, beat, and otherwise maltreat and injure many of them, to wit: Lucien H. Murray,

George S. Rogers, William Bingham, Alexander Wilson, Walter Thornton, William Redding, Thomas M. Holt, George Andrews, John Andrews, Frederick Blanchard, Adolphus G. Moore, John Roberson, James N. Holt, William Tate, Alexander Patterson, Jesse Gant, Lemuel Whitsett, Josiah Thompson, Sidney Steele, George Johnson, William Patton, Joseph Wright, Benjamin McAdams, Ruffin Andrews, Thomas Ray, Joseph Pritchard, Loften Tear, Joseph Thompson, Henry Cooke, William Andrews, M. N. Shaw, John Long, James H. Anderson, Joseph Gibson, Henry Pritchard, Joseph Nelson, James R. Murphy, Jr., William Kirkpatrick, Thomas Gray, Jefferson Younger, Frank Mebane, Clement Curtis, John W. McAdams, William Moore, William Clendenen, D. W. Weedon, David Moses, P. Thompson, David Moore, Monroe Fowler, Henry C. Hurdle, William Whitsett, Albert Murray, J. G. Moore, Joseph Kirkpatrick, W. V. Montgomery, John Trollinger, Jerry Whitsett, Calvin Gibson, John G. Albright, Robert Hannah, William Johnson, Henderson Scott, William Stockard, James Dickson, R. A. Albright, Thomas Lutterloh, John Grant, James Foust, John Curtis, A. Thompson, Robert Stockard, J. A. Moore, James T. Hunter, James S. Scott, John Smith, George Andrews, Milton Pickard, Henry Robertson, John R. Stockard, John Curtis, and Joseph Stockard, when in fact and truth there was no such or any insurrection in said county of Alamance. And he, the said William W. Holden, governor as aforesaid, well knew that such and said proclamation was groundless and false, and that there was no insurrection in said county, and that all civil authorities, both state and county, in said county, were peacefully and regularly in the full, free and unrestrained exercise in all respects, of the functions of their offices, and the courts were all open, and the due administration of the law was unimpeded by any resistance whatsoever, whereby the said William W. Holden, governor as aforesaid, did then and there, and in the way and manner, and by the means aforesaid, commit and was guilty of a high crime in office against the constitution and laws of said state, and the peace, interests and dignity thereof.

The CLERK, Mr. Saunders, proceeded to call the roll of senators, whereupon each senator arose in his place as his name was called, and the chief justice asked, "How say you, is William W. Holden guilty or not guilty, as charged in this article of impeachment?"

The calling of the roll having been concluded, the clerk announced the vote as follows:

*Guilty*—Messrs. Adams, Albright, Allen, Battle, Brown, Council, Crowell, Currie, Dargan, Edwards, Graham of Alamance, Graham of Orange, Jones, Latham, Ledbetter, Linney, Love, Mauney, McClammy, Merrimon, Morehead, Murphy, Robbins of Davidson, Robbins of Rowan, Skinner, Troy, Waddell, Warren, Whiteside and Worth—30.

*Not Guilty*—Messrs. Barnett, Beasley, Bellamy, Brogden, Cook, Cowles, Eppes, Flemming, Gilmer, Hawkins, Hyman, King, Lehman, McCotter, Moore, Norment, Olds, Price and Speed—19.

Whole number 49; two-thirds 33.

The CHIEF JUSTICE. The clerk reports thirty senators as voting guilty, and nineteen senators as voting not guilty on article I. So William W. Holden is acquitted on that article of impeachment. The clerk will read the second article.

The ASSISTANT CLERK, Mr. London, proceeded to read the second article in the words following:

### Article II.

That by the constitution of the state of North Carolina, the governor of said state has power to call out the militia thereof to execute the law, suppress riots or insurrection, whenever the execution of the law shall be resisted, or there shall exist any riot, insurrection or invasion, but not otherwise. That William W. Holden, governor of said state, unmindful of the high duties of his office, the obligations of his solemn oath of office and the constitution and laws of said state, and intending to stir up civil war, and subvert personal and public liberty, and the constitution and laws of said state and of the United States, contriving and intending to humiliate and degrade the said state and the people thereof, and especially the people of the county of Caswell in said state, and to provoke the people to wrath and violence, did, under the color of his said office, on the eighth day of July, in the year of our Lord one thousand eight hundred and seventy, in said state, of his own false, corrupt and wicked mind and purpose, proclaim and declare the county of Caswell, in said state, in insurrection, and did, after the days and times last aforesaid, send bodies of armed, desperate and lawless men, organized and set on foot without authority of law, into the said county, and occupy the same by military force and suspend the civil authority and the constitution and laws of the state, and did, after the days and times last aforesaid, and before the time of impeachment in this behalf, through and by means of such armed, desperate and lawless men, arrest many peaceable and law-abiding citizens of the said county of Caswell, then and there about their lawful business, and did detain, hold, imprison, and otherwise maltreat and injure many of them, to-wit: John Kerr, Samuel P. Hill, Wm B. Bowe, Nathaniel M. Roane, Frank A. Wiley, Jesse C. Griffith, J. T. Mitchell, Thomas J. Womack, A. G. Yancey, John McKee, A. A. Mitchell, Yancey Jones, J. M. Neal, Berzillai Graves, Robert Roane, James R. Fowler, M. C. Hooper, James C. Williamson, and Peter H. Williamson, when, in fact and truth, there was no such or any insurrection in said county of Caswell, and he, the said William W. Holden, governor as aforesaid, well knew that such and said proclamation was utterly groundless and false, and that there was no insurrection in said county of Caswell, and that all the civil authorities, both state and county, in said county, were peacefully and regularly in the full, free and unrestrained exercise in all respects of the functions of their offices, and the courts were all open and the due administration of the law was unimpeded by any resistance whatsoever, whereby the said William W. Holden, governor as aforesaid, did then and there, and in the way and manner and by the means aforesaid, commit and was guilty of a high crime in office against the constitution and laws of said state, and the peace, interests and dignity thereof.

The CLERK, Mr. Saunders, proceeded to call the roll of senators, whereupon each senator, as his name was called, arose in his place, and the chief justice asked: "How say you, is "William W. Holden guilty or not guilty, as charged in this "article of impeachment?"

The calling of the roll having been concluded, the clerk announced the vote as follows:

*Guilty*—Messrs. Adams, Albright, Allen, Battle, Brown, Council, Crowell, Currie, Dargan, Edwards, Gilmer, Graham of Alamance, Graham of Orange, Jones, Latham, Ledbetter, Lehman, Linney, Love, Mauney, McClammy, Merrimon, Morehead, Murphy, Robbins of Davidson, Robbins of Rowan, Skinner, Speed, Troy, Waddell, Warren, Whiteside and Worth —32.

*Not Guilty*—Messrs. Barnett, Beasley, Bellamy, Brogden, Cook, Cowles, Eppes, Flemming, Hawkins, Hyman, King, Lehman, McCotter, Moore, Norment, Olds and Price—17.

Whole Number 49; Two-thirds 33.

The CHIEF JUSTICE. The clerk announces thirty-two senators as voting guilty and seventeen as not guilty, so William W. Holden is acquitted on the second article.

The ASSISTANT CLERK, Mr. London, proceeded to read article III in the words following:

## ARTICLE III.

That the said William W. Holden, governor of the state of North Carolina, on the fifth day of August, in the year of our Lord one thousand eight hundred and seventy, in the county of Orange, in said state, did then and there unlawfully and without any lawful warrant and authority, and in defiance and subversion of the constitution and laws of said state, and in violation of his oath of office, and under color of his said office, incite, procure, order and command one John Hunnicutt and other evil disposed persons to assault, seize, detain and imprison and deprive of his liberty, a citizen and resident of the county of Orange, in the state aforesaid, and in pursuance of said incitement, procurement, order and command, the said John Hunnicutt and the evil disposed persons aforesaid, did assault, seize, detain, imprison and deprive of his liberty and privileges as a freeman and citizen of said county and state, for a long time, to-wit: For the time of ten days or more, the said Josiah Turner, junior, whereby the said William W. Holden, governor as aforesaid, did then and there commit a high misdemeanor in office against the constitution and laws of said state, and the peace, interest and dignity thereof.

The CLERK, Mr. Saunders, proceeded to call the roll of senators, whereupon each senator arose in his place as his name was called, and the chief justice asked, "How say you, is William W. Holden guilty or not guilty, as charged in this article of impeachment?"

The calling of the roll having been concluded, the clerk announced the vote as follows:

*Guilty.*—Messrs. Adams, Albright, Allen, Battle, Brown, Cook, Council, Cowles, Crowell, Currie, Dargan, Edwards, Flemming, Gilmer, Graham of Alamance, Graham of Orange, Jones, Latham, Ledbetter, Linney, Love, Mauney, McClammy, Merrimon, Moore, Morehead, Murphy, Norment, Robbins of Davidson, Robbins of Rowan, Skinner, Speed, Troy, Waddell, Warren, Whiteside and Worth—37.

*Not Guilty.*—Messrs. Barnett, Beasley, Bellamy, Brogden, Eppes, Hawkins, Hyman, King, Lehman, McCotter, Olds and Price—12.

Whole number, 49; two-thirds, 33; voting guilty, 37.

The CHIEF JUSTICE. The clerk announces that thirty-seven of the senators have voted guilty and twelve have voted not guilty. Thirty-seven being a concurrence of two-thirds or more of the senators, William W. Holden is convicted on the third article of impeachment.

The ASSISTANT CLERK, Mr. London, proceeded to read article IV in the words following:

ARTICLE IV.

That said William W. Holden, governor of the state of North Carolina, on the first day of August in the year of our Lord one thousand eight hundred and seventy, in the county of Caswell, in said state, did then and there, unlawfully and without any lawful warrant and authority, and in defiance and subversion of the constitution and laws of said state, and in violation of his oath of office, and under color of his said office, incite, procure, order and command one George W. Kirk, and one B. G. Burgen, and other evil disposed persons, to assault, seize, detain and imprison, and deprive of their liberty and privileges as freemen and citizens of said state, Jno. Kerr, Samuel P. Hill, William B. Bowe, and Nathaniel M. Roane, citizens and residents of the county of Caswell in the state aforesaid; and in pursuance of said incitement, procurement, order and command the said George W. Kirk, and the said B. G. Burgen, and the evil disposed persons aforesaid, did assault, seize, detain, imprison and deprive of their liberty and privileges as freemen and citizens of said county and state, for a long time, to-wit: for the time of one month and more, the said John Kerr, Samuel P. Hill, William B. Bowe and Nathaniel M. Roane, whereby the said William W. Holden, governor as aforesaid, did then and there commit and was guilty of a high misdemeanor in office against the constitution and laws of said state, and the peace, interests and dignity thereof.

The CLERK, Mr. Saunders, proceeded to call the roll of senators, whereupon each senator arose in his place, as his name was called, and the chief justice asked, "How say you, is William W. Holden, guilty or not guilty, as charged in this article of impeachment?"

The calling of the roll having been concluded, the clerk announced the vote as follows:

*Guilty*—Messrs. Adams, Albright, Allen, Battle, Brown, Council, Crowell, Currie, Dargan, Edwards, Gilmer, Graham of Alamance, Graham of Orange, Jones, Latham, Ledbetter, Linney, Love, Manney, McClammy, Merrimon, Morehead, Murphy, Norment, Robbins of Davidson, Robbins of Rowan, Skinner, Speed, Troy, Waddell, Warren, Whiteside and Worth—33.

*Not Guilty*—Messrs. Barnett, Beasley, Bellamy, Brogden, Cook, Cowles, Eppes, Flemming, Hawkins, Hyman, King, Lehman, McCotter, Moore, Olds and Price—16.

Whole number 49; two-thirds 33; voting guilty 33.

The CHIEF JUSTICE. The clerk announces that thirty-three senators voting guilty and sixteen senators having voted not guilty, this being a concurrence of two-thirds or more of the senators, William W. Holden is convicted on this article.

The ASSISTANT CLERK, Mr. London, proceeded to read article V., in the words following:

## ARTICLE V.

That the said William W. Holden, governor of the state of North Carolina, heretofore, to-wit: in the months of June, July and August, in the year of our Lord one thousand eight hundred and seventy, under the color of his said office, unlawfully recruited, armed and equipped as soldiers, a large number of men, to-wit: five hundred men and more, and organized them as an army and appointed officers to command, and use such armed men as he, the said William W. Holden, governor as aforesaid, under color of his said office, might from time to time order and direct; that during the said months of June, July and August, he, the said William W. Holden, governor as aforesaid, under color of his said office, placed a large number of said armed men under the immediate command and control of one George W. Kirk as colonel, aided by one

B. G. Burgen as lieutenant-colonel, one H. C. Yates as major, and sundry other persons as captains and lieutenants, and sent such last mentioned armed men under the immediate command of George W. Kirk as colonel, B. G. Burgen as lieutenant-colonel, H. C. Yates as major, and said sundry other persons as captains and lieutenants, into the county of Alamance, and by the procurement, order and command of him, the said William W. Holden, governor as aforesaid, under color of his said office, the said armed men last aforesaid, seized, held, detained and imprisoned in said county of Alamance and by the procurement, order and command of him, the said William W. Holden, governor as aforesaid. under color of his said office, the said armed men last aforesaid, seized, held, detained and imprisoned in said county of Alamance, one Adolphus G. Moore, a peaceable and law-abiding citizen of said county, then and there engaged about his lawful business; that the said Adolphus G. Moore being so seized, held, detained and imprisoned and deprived of his liberty, was then and there in the custody of the said George W. Kirk, acting as colonel, and commanding the armed body of men last aforesaid, by the order, command and procurement of the said William W. Holden: That the said Adolphus G. Moore, being so seized, held and imprisoned and deprived of his liberty, made due application to the honorable Richmond M. Pearson, chief justice of the supreme court of said state, as by law he might do, for the writ of *habeas corpus*, to the end, that he, the said chief justice, might duly enquire the cause of said seizure, detention and imprisonment, and deliver him from the same according to law. That the said chief justice issued the writ of *habeas corpus* at the instance of the said Adolphus G. Moore, directed to the said George W. Kirk, commanding him forthwith to produce the body of the said Adolphus G. Moore, before him the said chief justice, at the chamber of the supreme court in the city of Raleigh, in said state; that the said George W. Kirk was, on the seventeenth day of July, in the year of our Lord one thousand eight hundred and seventy, in the county of Alamance, duly served with the said writ of *habeas corpus;* that he made no return of or to the same, as required by law, and refused to produce the body of the said Adolphus G. Moore, before the chief justice according to the exigency of said writ, avowing and declaring that he had made such seizure, and detained and imprisoned the said Adolphus G. Moore, at the instance of and by the procurement, command and order of the said William W. Holden, governor as aforesaid, and would not produce the body of him, the said Adolphus G. Moore, before the chief justice, according to the exigency of said writ, unless compelled to do so by superior armed force, or by the express order and command of the said William W. Holden, governor as aforesaid, that such refusal of the said George W. Kirk to obey said writ, was made duly to appear before the said chief justice, whereupon the said chief justice made enquiry of the said William W. Holden, governor as aforesaid, if he had so ordered the said George W. Kirk, to so seize, detain and imprison the said Adolphus G. Moore; that the said William W. Holden, governor as aforesaid, made answer in substance, and to the effect, to said enquiry of said chief justice, that he had theretofore ordered and commanded the said George W. Kirk to so seize, detain and imprison and deprive of his liberty, the said Adolphus G. Moore, and that such seizure and detention was made by his order and command, whereupon the said chief justice, upon due consideration, solemnly adjudged in substance and effect that according to the constitution and laws of said state, the privilege of the writ of *habeas corpus* was not suspended, and that the said George W. Kirk, and the said William W. Holden, governor as aforesaid, were in duty bound to bring and produce the body of the said Adolphus G. Moore, before him, the said chief justice, according to the exigency of the said writ; yet the said William W. Holden, governor as aforesaid, unmindful of his most solemn oath of office, and his high duties as the executive of said state, and contriving, and then and there intending to deprive the said Adolphus G. Moore of his liberty, as a free citizen of said state, and to defy and subvert the constitution and laws of said state, declared that he had so ordered, and did still so order and commanded the said George W. Kirk not to obey the said writ so issued by the said chief justice, then and there declared to the said chief justice, that he, the said William W. Holden, governor as aforesaid, would not obey the said writ, or the command of the said chief justice, in that behalf, and that he would not allow the said George W. Kirk to obey the same and produce the body of the said Adolphus G. Moore, before the said chief justice, according to the exigency of said writ, until such time, as in his discretion, he might think proper to do so; that while the said William W. Holden, governor as aforesaid, so seized, held, detained, imprisoned and deprived of his liberty, the said Adolphus G. Moore, and so refused to obey the said writ, and to command the said George W. Kirk so to do, and so resisted the laws and the lawful authority of the said chief justice, he was by his own procurement, order and command, supported in that behalf by the means and use of said armed men so commanded and controlled as aforesaid, and so the said William W. Holden, governor as aforesaid, did, in the way and manner, and by the means aforesaid, procure, order and command the said George W. Kirk, so charged by said writ of *habeas corpus* to refuse to make due return of or to the same, and produce the body of the said Adolphus G. Moore, before the said chief justice, according to the exigency of the said writ, and to resist the same and the lawful authority of the said chief justice, and did himself, then and there in the way and manner and by the means aforesaid, resist the due execution of the said writ and the lawful authority of the said chief justice, and did then and there in the way and manner, and by the means and armed force aforesaid, suspend the privilege of the writ of *habeas corpus*, and did unlawfully and violently seize, detain, hold, imprison and deprive of his liberty the said Adolphus G. Moore, and for a long time, to-wit: for the space of one calendar month, after the said chief justice had adjudged such detention illegal, did continue to hold and detain and cause to be held and detained said Adolphus G. Moore, and did in the way and manner and by the means aforesaid, make the military supersede and prevail over the lawful civil power of the state, all of which acts, matters and things, the said William W. Holden, governor as aforesaid, did, in violation as aforesaid, of his solemn oath of office, and whereby he, the said William W. Holden, governor as aforesaid, did then and there commit high crimes and misdemeanors in office, against the constitutution and laws of said state, and the peace, dignity and interests thereof.

The CLERK, Mr. Saunders, proceeded to call the roll of senators, whereupon each senator arose in his place, as his name was called, and the chief justice asked, "How say you, is William W. Holden guilty or not guilty, as charged in this article of impeachment.

The calling of the roll having been concluded, the clerk announced the vote as follows:

*Guilty*—Messrs. Adams, Albright, Allen, Battle, Brown, Cook, Council, Cowles, Crowell, Currie, Dargan, Edwards, Flemming, Gilmer, Graham of Alamance, Graham of Orange, Hawkins, Jones, Latham, Ledbetter, Lehman, Linney, Love, Mauney, McClammy, McCotter, Merrimon, Moore, Morehead, Murphy, Norment, Robbins of Davidson, Robbins of Rowan, Skinner, Speed, Troy, Waddell, Warren, Whiteside and Worth—40.

*Not Guilty*—Messrs. Barnett, Beasley, Bellamy, Brogden, Eppes, Hyman, King, Olds and Price—9.

Whole number 49; two-thirds 33; voting guilty 40.

The CHIEF JUSTICE. The clerk reports forty senators as having voted guilty and nine as having voted not guilty, there being a concurrence of two-thirds or more of the senators, William W. Holden is convicted in this article.

The ASSISTANT CLERK, Mr. London, proceeded to read article VI, in the words following:

## Article VI.

That the said William W. Holden, governor of the state of North Carolina, heretofore, to-wit, in the months of June, July and August, in the year of our Lord one thousand eight hundred and seventy, under color of his said office, unlawfully recruited, armed and equipped as soldiers, a large number of men, to-wit, five hundred men and more, and organized them as an army, and appointed officers to command and use such armed men as he, the said William W. Holden, governor as aforesaid, under color of his said office, might from time to time order and direct; that during the said months of June, July and August, he, the said William W. Holden, governor as aforesaid, under color of his said office, placed a large number of said armed men under the immediate command and control of one George W. Kirk, as colonel, aided by one B. G. Burgen, as lieutenant-colonel, one H. C. Yates, as major, and sundry other persons as captains and lieutenants, and sent such last mentioned armed men under the immediate command of George W. Kirk, as colonel, B. G. Burgen, as lieutenant colonel, H. C. Yates, as major, and said sundry other persons as captains and lieutenants, in the county of Caswell, and by the procurement, order and command of him, the said William W. Holden, governor as aforesaid, under color of his said office, the said armed men last aforesaid seized, held, detained and imprisoned in said county of Caswell, John Kerr, Samuel P. Hill, Jesse C. Griffith, Frank A. Wiley, J. T. Mitchell, Thomas J. Womack, A. G. Yancey, John McKee, A. A. Mitchell, Yancey Jones, J. M. Neal, William B. Bowe, Barzillai Graves, Nathaniel M. Roane, Robert Roane, James R. Fowler, M. Z. Hooper, James C. Williamson and Peter H. Williamson, peaceable and law abiding citizens of said county, then and there engaged about their lawful business; that the said John Kerr, Samuel P. Hill, Jesse C. Griffith, Frank A. Wiley, J. T. Mitchell, Thomas J. Womack, A. G. Yancey, John McKee. A. A. Mitchell, Yancey Jones, J. M. Neal, William B. Bowe,

Barzillai Graves, Nathaniel M. Roane, Robert Roane, James R. Fowler, M. Z. Hooper, James C. Williamson and Peter H. Williamson, being so seized, held, detained and imprisoned, and deprived of their liberty, were then and there in the custody of the said George W. Kirk, acting as colonel and commanding the armed body of men last aforesaid, by the order, command and procurement of the said William W. Holden, governor as aforesaid; that the said John Kerr, Samuel P. Hill, Jesse C. Griffith, Frank A. Wiley, J. T. Mitchell, Thomas J. Womack, A. G. Yancey, John McKee, A. A. Mitchell, Yancey Jones, J. M. Neal, William B. Bowe, Barzillai Graves, Nathaniel M. Roane, Robert Roane, James R. Fowler, M. Z. Hooper, James C. Williamson and Peter H. Williamson, being so seized, held and imprisoned and deprived of their liberty, made due application to the honorable Richmond M. Pearson, chief justice of the supreme court of said state, as by law they might do, for the writ of *habeas corpus*, to the end that he, the said chief justice, might duly enquire the cause of said seizure, detention and imprisonment, and deliver them from the same according to law; that the said chief justice issued the writ of *habeas corpus* at the instance of the said John Kerr, Samuel P. Hill, Jesse C. Griffith, Frank A. Wiley, J. T. Mitchell, Thomas J. Womack, A. G. Yancey, John McKee, A. A. Mitchell, Yancey Jones, J. M. Neal, William B. Bowe, Barzillai Graves, Nathaniel M. Roane, Robert Roane, James R. Fowler, M. Z. Hooper, James C. Williamson, and Peter H. Williamson, on the twenty-sixth day of July, in the year of our Lord one thousand eight hundred and seventy, directed to the said Geo. W. Kirk, commanding him forthwith to produce the bodies of the said John Kerr, Samuel P. Hill, Jesse C. Griffith, Frank A. Wiley, J. T. Mitchell, Thomas J. Womack, A. G. Yancey, John McKee, A. A. Mitchell, Yancey Jones, J. M. Neal, William B. Bowe, Barzillai Graves, Nathaniel M. Roane, Robert Roane, James R. Fowler, M. Z. Hooper, James C. Williamson and Peter H. Williamson, before him, the said chief justice, at the chamber of the supreme court in the city of Raleigh, in said state; that the said George W. Kirk was, on the first day of August, in the year of our Lord one thousand eight hundred and seventy, in the county of Caswell, duly served with the writ of *habeas corpus;* but instead of making due return to the said writ, stated that "I hold the said prisoners under orders from W. W. Holden, governor and commander-in-chief of militia," and refused to produce the bodies of the said John Kerr, Samuel P. Hill, Jesse C. Griffith, Frank A. Wiley, J. T. Mitchell, Thomas J. Womack, A. G. Yancey, John McKee, A. A. Mitchell, Yancey Jones, J. M. Neal, William B. Bowe, Barzillai Graves, Nathaniel M. Roane, Robert Roane, James R. Fowler, M. Z. Hooper, James C. Williamson and Peter H. Williamson, before the said chief justice, according to the exigencies of the said writ, and thereafter the said George W. Kirk continued to hold and detain and deprive of their liberty, the said John Kerr, Samuel P. Hill, Jesse C. Griffith, Frank A. Wiley, J. T. Mitchell, Thomas J. Womack, A. G. Yancey, John McKee, A. A. Mitchell, Yancey Jones, J. M. Neal, William B. Bowe, Barzillai Graves, Nathaniel M. Roane, Robert Roane, James R. Fowler, M. Z. Hooper, James C. Williamson and Peter H. Williamson, for a long time, to-wit: for the space of one calendar month, the said seizure and detention of the said John Kerr, Samuel P. Hill, Jesse C. Griffith, Frank A. Wiley, J. T. Mitchell, Thomas J. Womack, A. G. Yancey, John McKee, A. A. Mitchell, Yancey Jones, J. M. Neal, William B. Bowe, Barzillai Graves, Nathaniel M. Roane, Robert Roane, James R. Fowler, M. Z. Hooper, James C. Williamson and Peter H. Williamson, by the said George W. Kirk, and the military force under his command, as aforesaid, having been made and continued as aforesaid, by the orders of the said William W. Holden, governor of the state aforesaid, he, the said William W. Holden, governor as aforesaid, well knowing that the privilege of the writ of *habeas corpus* was not suspended, and that the said John Kerr, Samuel P. Hill, Jesse C. Griffith Frank A. Wiley, J. T. Mitchell, Thomas J.

Womack, A. G. Yancey, John McKee, A. A. Mitchell, Yancey Jones, J. M. Neal, William B. Bowe, Barzillai Graves, Nathaniel M. Roane, Robert Roane, James R. Fowler, M. Z. Hooper, James C. Williamson and Peter H. Williamson were so detained without authority of law, whereby he, the said William W. Holden, governor, as aforesaid, did then and there commit high crimes and misdemeanors in office against the constitution and laws of said state, and peace, dignity and interests thereof.

The CLERK, Mr. Saunders, proceeded to call the roll of senators, whereupon each senator arose in his place as his name was called, and the chief justice asked, "How say you, "is William W. Holden guilty or not guilty, as charged in 'this article of impeachment."

The calling of the roll having been concluded, the clerk announced the vote as follows:

*Guilty*—Messrs. Adams, Albright, Allen, Barnett, Battle, Brown, Cook, Council, Cowles, Crowell, Currie, Dargan, Edwards, Flemming, Gilmer, Graham of Alamance, Graham of Orange, Hawkins, Jones, Latham, Ledbetter, Lehman, Linney, Love, Mauney, McClammy, McCotter, Merrimon, Moore, Morehead, Murphy, Norment, Robbins of Davidson, Robbins of Rowan, Skinner, Speed, Troy, Waddell, Warren, Whiteside and Worth—41.

*Not Guilty*—Messrs. Beasley, Bellamy, Brogden, Eppes, Hyman, King, Olds and Price—8.

Whole number, 49; two-thirds, 33; voting guilty, 41.

The CHIEF JUSTICE. The clerk reports forty-one senators as having voted guilty and eight senators as having voted not guilty. There being a concurrence of two-thirds or more of the senators, William W. Holden is convicted on the sixth article.

The ASSISTANT CLERK, Mr. London, proceeded to read Article VII, in the words following:

## Article VII.

That the said William W. Holden, governor of North Carolina, unmindful of his high duty to uphold and protect the constitution and laws of said state, and the good name, dignity and honor of the people thereof, and unmindful of the obligation of his solemn oath of office, under color of his said office did, in the months of June, July and August, in the year of our Lord one thousand eight hundred and seventy, in said state, without any authority of law, but in contravention and subversion of the constitution and laws of said state and the United States, and intending to provoke and stir up civil strife and war, recruit and call together from this state and the state of Tennessee, a large number of men, to wit: five hundred men and more, many of them of the most reckless, desperate, ruffianly and lawless characters, and did then and there organize, arm and equip them as an army of soldiers, and place the same under the chief command of a notorious desperado from the state of Tennessee, by the name of George W. Kirk, having falsely proclaimed the counties of Alamance and Caswell in said state in a state of insurrection, and did send large numbers of such armed desperate men into said counties, under the immediate command of the said George W. Kirk and two other desperadoes from the state of Tennessee, to wit: one B. G. Burgen and one H. C. Yates, and did there and then, without any warrant or authority, seize, hold, imprison and deprive of their liberty for a long time, to wit, for the time of twenty days and more, many of the peaceable and law-abiding citizens of said counties, to wit: John Kerr, Samuel P. Hill, —— Scott, John R. Ireland and many others; and seize, hold, imprison and deprive of their liberty, and hang by the neck William Patton, Lucien H. Murray and others, and did thrust into a loathsome dungeon Josiah Turner, junior, and F. A. Wiley; and to maintain, support and aid the lawless armed men so organized, armed and equipped, did, under color of his said office, from time to time, during the said months of

June, July and August, without any lawful authority, make his warrant upon David A. Jenkins, treasurer of the state, for large sums of money, to wit: for the sum of seventy thousand dollars or more, and cause and procure the said David A. Jenkins, the treasurer of the state, to recognize such unlawful warrant, and pay out of the treasury such said large sums of money to the agent or paymaster of the said William W. Holden, governor as aforesaid, for the unlawful uses and purposes aforesaid; whereby the said William W. Holden, governor as aforesaid, did then and there, and by the means and in the manner aforesaid, commit a high misdemeanor in office, in violation of the constitution and laws of the state, and of the peace and interests and dignity thereof.

The CLERK, Mr. Saunders, proceeded to call the roll of senators, whereupon each senator, as his name was called, arose in his place and the chief justice put the question, "How say you, is William W. Holden guilty or not guilty, as charged in this article."

The calling of the roll having been concluded the clerk announced the vote as follows:

*Guilty*—Messrs. Adams, Albright, Allen, Battle, Brown, Cook, Council, Cowles, Crowell, Currie, Dargan, Edwards, Gilmer, Graham of Alamance, Graham of Orange, Jones, Latham, Ledbetter, Linney, Love, Mauney, McClammy, McCotter, Merrimon, Morehead, Murphy, Norment, Robbins of Davidson, Robbins of Rowan, Skinner, Speed, Troy, Waddell, Warren, Whiteside and Worth—36.

*Not Guilty*—Messrs. Barnett, Beasley, Bellamy, Brogden, Eppes, Flemming, Hawkins, Hyman, King, Lehman, Moore, Olds and Price—13.

Whole number, 49; two-thirds, 33; voting guilty, 36.

The CHIEF JUSTICE. The Clerk announces thirty-six senators as having voted guilty and thirteen as having voted not guilty. There being a concurrence of two-thirds or more of the senators William W. Holden is convicted on this article.

The ASSISTANT CLERK, Mr. London, proceeded to read the eighth article in the words following:

## Article VIII.

That the said William W. Holden, governor of the said state, unmindful of the high duties of his said office, and the obligations of his solemn oath of office, and contriving and intending, and with a view and for the purpose of supporting and maintaining an armed military force in said state, which he had then and there recruited, organized and formed for illegal purposes, without the sanction of the constitution and laws of the said state, but in contravention of the same, did from time to time in the months of June, July and August, in the year of our Lord one thousand eight hundred and seventy, under color of his said office, in said state, without the sanction of the constitution and laws of said state, and in violation of the same, make his warrants as such governor upon the treasury of the said state, for large sums of money, to-wit: for the sum of eighty thousand ($80,000) dollars and more, to be used for the unlawful purposes aforesaid; that the said William W. Holden, governor as aforesaid, under color of his said office, then and there persuaded, commanded, incited and procured David A. Jenkins, treasurer of said state, to recognize such and said unlawful warrants on the treasury of said state, and to deliver such and said sums of money to such agents of the said William W. Holden, governor as aforesaid, as he the said William W. Holden, governor as aforesaid, might from time to time designate and appoint; that in pursuance of such warrants and orders of the said William W. Holden, governor as aforesaid, the said David A. Jenkins, treasurer as aforesaid, delivered to one A. D. Jenkins, called the paymaster, appointed by the said William W. Holden, governor as aforesaid, for such purpose, large sums of money from said treasury, to-wit: the sum of forty thousand dollars or more; that thereafter, to-wit: in the month of August, in the year of our Lord one thousand eight hundred and seventy, one Richard M. Allison, a citizen of the county of Iredell, in said state,, brought his suit in the superior court of the last named county, in his own behalf, and in the behalf of all the tax payers of said state, praying that a writ of injunction might then and there be granted, and issued according to law, restraining the said David A. Jenkins, treasurer as aforesaid, from delivering any sum or sums of money to the said William W. Holden, governor as aforesaid, or any other persons in obedience to such orders and for such purposes, and also restraining the said A. D. Jenkins, as such paymaster, or in any other respect or capacity from disbursing or disposing of said sum of money so in his said hands or any part thereof, for the purposes thereof. That the Honorable Anderson Mitchell, judge of said superior court, then and there granted the writ of injunction so prayed for, enjoining and forbidding the said David A. Jenkins, treasurer as aforesaid, from delivering any money from said treasury, in obedience to any such warrant or order, so made by the said William W. Holden, governor as aforesaid, and enjoining and forbidding the said A. D. Jenkins, as such paymaster or agent, from using or disbursing the said money or any part of it, so in his hands, to or for the use of said armed body of men for any of the purposes aforesaid; that the said David A. Jenkins, treasurer, and the said A. D. Jenkins, were each duly served with said writ of injunction, but nevertheless, the said William W. Holden, governor as aforesaid, wickedly intending to suspend and subvert the laws of said state, and to defy and disregard the lawful authority of said court, did afterwards, to-wit: after the month last aforesaid, persuade, incite, order, procure and command the said A. D. Jenkins to defy and disregard the said writ of injunction, and to deliver the said money so in his custody to another agent of the said William W. Holden, governor as aforesaid, to be used for the unlawful purposes aforesaid; that the said A. D. Jenkins, in obedience to such last mentioned order, command and procurement of the said William W. Holden, governor as aforesaid, and in disregard of such writ of injunction and the lawful authority of said judge, did deliver the said money so in his hands to another agent of the said William W. Holden, governor as aforesaid, to-wit, to one John B. Neathery, to be used for the unlawful purpose aforesaid, and the said William W. Holden, governor as aforesaid, did then and there in the way and manner, and by the means and for the purpose aforesaid, procure, order and command the said A. D. Jenkins so to disregard and disobey the said writ of injunction and the lawful authority of said judge, and did then and there, and in the way and manner and by the means and for the unlawful purpose aforesaid, defy, disregard, ignore, contravene, suspend and defeat the lawful purpose and effect of the writ of injunction so granted and issued by the said judge; and thereupon and thereafter the said William W. Holden, governor as aforesaid, the said sum of public money thus transferred as aforesaid to the hands of the said John B. Neathery, did order and cause to be paid out and disbursed by him, the said John B. Neathery, to, for and about the illegal purposes aforesaid, to-wit, the payment of the expenses in keeping on foot, sustaining and maintaining the said illegal military force as aforesaid; whereby the said William W. Holden, governor as aforesaid, was then and there guilty of a high misdemeanor in his said office in violation of his oath of office, and in subversion of the laws of said state, and the peace, interests and dignity thereof.

The CLERK, Mr. Saunders, proceeded to call the roll of senators, whereupon each senator, as his name was called, arose in his place, and the chief justice asked, "How say you, is "William W. Holden guilty or not guilty, as charged in this "article of impeachment."

The calling of the roll having been concluded, the clerk announced the vote as follows:

*Guilty*—Messrs. Adams, Albright, Allen, Battle, Brown, Cook, Council, Cowles, Crowell, Currie, Dargan, Edwards, Flemming, Gilmer, Graham of Alamance, Graham of Orange, Jones, Latham, Ledbetter, Linney, Love, Mauney, McClammy,

Merrimon, Morehead, Murphy, Norment, Robbins of Davidson, Robbins of Rowan, Skinner, Speed, Troy, Waddell, Warren, Whiteside and Worth—36.

*Not Guilty*—Messrs. Barnett, Beasley, Bellamy, Brogden, Eppes, Hawkins, Hyman, King, Lehman, McCotter, Moore, Olds and Price—13.

Whole number, 49; two-thirds, 33; voting guilty, 36.

The CHIEF JUSTICE. The clerk announces thirty six senators as having voted guilty and thirteen as voting not guilty. There being a concurrence of two-thirds or more of the senators, William W. Holden stands convicted on this article.

Mr. Manager SPARROW. Mr. Chief Justice, it having been announced by the presiding officer that the respondent, William W. Holden, governor of North Carolina has been convicted on six of the eight articles preferred against him, the managers, speaking through me as their chairman, and in the name of the house of representatives and of all the people of North Carolina, demand that the court proceed to judgment agaisnt the respondent in this his conviction.

Senator GRAHAM, of Orange, offered the following, which the clerk proceeded to read:

"THE STATE OF NORTH CAROLINA.

"THE SENATE OF NORTH CAROLINA,
"March 22, 1871.

"THE STATE VS. WILLIAM W. HOLDEN.

"Whereas, The house of representatives of the state of North "Carolina did, on the 26th day of December, 1870, exhibit to "the senate articles of impeachment against William W. Hol- "den, governor of North Carolina, and the said senate, after a "full hearing and impartial trial has, by the votes of two-thirds "of the members present, this day determined that the said

"William W. Holden is guilty as charged in the 3d, 4th, 5th, "6th, 7th and 8th of said articles:

"Now, therefore, it is adjudged by the senate of North Caro- "lina sitting as a court of impeachment, at their chamber "in the city of Raleigh, that the said William W. Holden "be removed from the office of governor and be disqualified "to hold any office of honor, trust or profit under the state of "North Carolina.

"It is further ordered, that a copy of this judgment be en- "rolled and certified by the chief justice as presiding officer, "and the principal clerk of the senate, and that such certified "copy be deposited in the office of secretary of state.

Senator JONES. Mr. Chief Justice, as there is no rule of the court requiring the ayes and noes, I ask that the vote on the order offered by the senator from Orange, [Mr. Graham] be taken by the ayes and noes.

Senator BARNETT. At the suggestion of one of the counsel for the respondent, I ask for the reading of section 12 of the act referring to proceedings on impeachment.

The CLERK proceeded to read in the words following:

"Upon a conviction of the person impeached, judgment may "be given that he be removed from office, or that he be dis- "qualified from holding any office of trust or profit under this "state, or both, but no other judgment can be pronounced."

The CHIEF JUSTICE. Is the court ready for the question?

Several Senators called for the question.

A sufficient number seconding the call for the ayes and noes, they were ordered.

Senator MOORE. Mr. Chief Justice, before the vote is taken, with the permission of the court, I would like to make a statement in regard to the vote I am about to cast. I would not object to the order offered by the senator from Orange, [Mr. Graham,] if it merely pronounced a judgment removing the respondent from his office. I think that under the evidence which has been elicited in the case the penalty providing for the disqualification of the respondent to ever hold office in this state is severe. Because that feature is included in the judgment, I shall be compelled to vote against the order.

The CLERK, Mr. Saunders, proceeded to call the roll of senators on the adoption of the order offered by Senator Graham, of Orange, and it was decided in the affirmative by the following vote:

Ayes—Messrs. Adams, Albright, Allen, Battle, Brown, Cook, Council, Cowles, Crowell, Currie, Dargan, Edwards, Flemming, Gilmer, Graham of Alamance, Graham of Orange, Jones, Latham, Ledbetter, Linney, Love, Mauney, McClammy, Merrimon, Morehead, Murphy, Norment, Robbins of Davidson, Robbins of Rowan, Skinner, Speed, Troy, Waddell, Warren, Whiteside and Worth—36.

Noes—Messrs. Barnett, Beasley, Bellamy, Brogden, Eppes, Hawkins, Hyman, King, Lehman, McCotter, Moore, Olds and Price—13.

Senator ROBBINS, of Rowan. Mr. Chief Justice, I arise to inquire whether the judgment of the court is not to be signed and certified in presence of the court before it shall adjourn *sine die*.

The CHIEF JUSTICE. The presiding officer is aware of no rule requiring that. He cannot see how the signing of it out of court will affect the validity of the verification if it is signed by the presiding officer and countersigned by the principal clerk. However, that is a matter for the senate.

Senator GILMER. In order to avoid any possible difficulty about the matter, I move that the clerk be directed forthwith to have a copy of the order prepared for yours and his signature.

The CHIEF JUSTICE put the question on the motion of senator Gilmer, and it was decided in the affirmative.

Senator MURPHY offered the following order:

"*Ordered*, That no opinion that may be filed in this case in

" accordance with the rule of the senate, allowing the same, " shall exceed twenty pages of the printed report in the trial."

Senator BROGDEN. Mr. Chief Justice, I don't see how the court can adopt with propriety an order of the kind just proposed. I propose myself to file an opinion, but I certainly should not know when to stop to make twenty pages of the printed report of the proceedings. I have no experience which will enable me to determine how many pages of foolscap will make that amount of printed matter. I think the order is unnecessary and should not be adopted.

Senator JONES. Mr. Chief Justice, after a consultation with some of the senators, who desire to file opinions, it was agreed that twenty pages of printed matter would be the outside limit which any senator would require for the opinion he should file. I am satisfied myself that the senator from Wayne, [Mr. Brogden,] will fall far short in his opinion, of the space allowed.

The CHIEF JUSTICE put the question on the adoption of the order of senator Murphy, and it was decided in the affirmative.

Senator GRAHAM, of Orange, offered the following order:

" *Ordered*, That the clerk of the senate be directed to have " prepared a printed and complete index of the proceedings on " the trial.

Senator LOVE. I ask the ayes and noes on the adoption of the order.

Not a sufficient number seconding the call, the ayes and noes were not ordered.

The CHIEF JUSTICE put the question on the motion on the adoption of the order offered by Senator Graham, of Orange, and it was decided in the affirmative.

Senator COWLES. Mr. Chief Justice, I desire, before the court shall finally adjourn, to say that I regret that the court did not take a day to mature and consider its judgment. I am by no means satisfied with the propriety of the disqualifying clause contained in the order of judgment adopted. I simply desire to make this statement and ask that it appear in the published proceedings.

Senator MOORE. Mr. Chief Justice, the order of judgment having been signed by the presiding officer and principal clerk, I move that the senate, sitting as a court of impeachment, do now adjourn *sine die.*

The CHIEF JUSTICE put the question on the motion of Senator Moore, and it was decided in the affirmative.

So the Court of Impeachment adjourned *sine die.*

# FINAL PROCEEDINGS OF THE HOUSE.

---

House of Representatives,

March 22d, 1871.

The Senate having, by message, given the house of representatives notice that it will proceed to vote on the articles of impeachment against W. W. Holden to-day at 11 a. m; therefore

*Resolved*, That at 11 o'clock the house resolve itself into a committee of the whole, and proceed to the senate chamber in the following order:

1st. Managers, two and two, headed by their chairman;
2d. The speaker of the house;
3d. The chairman of the committee ot the whole;
4th. The clerks of the house;
5th. The members, two and two;
6th. The doorkeepers.

Introduced by Mr. Robinson and adopted by house of representatives March 22nd 1871.

Report *of the Committee of the Whole, made to the House of Representatives, March 22d,* 1871.

The house having resolved itself into a committee of the whole, proceeded to the senate chamber at 11 o'clock to receive the vote of the senate on the articles ot impeachment, exhibited by the house of representatives against W. W. Holden, governor of North Carolina, for high crimes and misdemeanors in office. The committee having returned to their chamber, beg to report,

1st. That W. W. Holden was found guilty as charged in articles 3, 4, 5, 6, 7 and 8;

2d. The said W. W. Holden was found not guilty as charged in articles 1 and 2.

The respondent having been convicted on said 3d, 4th, 5th, 6th, 7th and 8th articles, the senate sitting as a court of impeachment proceeded to adjudge that the said W. W. Holden, governor, be deposed from office and forever disqualified from holding any office of profit or trust in this state. The committee ask to be discharged.

ERRATA.—The foregoing Report was hurried through the press by order of the Court, that each day's proceedings might be laid on Senators' desks the succeeding day. It was the purpose also of the Managers, at the close of the trial, to revise and re-print the entire Report. These two causes combined led to numerous typographical errors in this edition. Whether the work will be revised and re-printed remains with the Legislature. In the paging of the Report there are several errors; the most remarkable of which occurs in Gov. Graham's final argument—the numbers of the 16 pages 2303 to 2318, inclusive, have been repeated on the succeeding 16 pages, though the matter is in its proper order.

# APPENDIX No. 1.

## OPINIONS OF SENATORS.

### OPINION OF SENATOR L. J. MOORE.

I have taken an oath to return a verdict in this case according to the law and the evidence. I occupy substantially the position of a juror, bound by the same obligation and controlled by the same established rules of law. In accordance with my honest conviction, after long and earnest consideration, I am compelled to vote the respondent guilty on the 3d, 5th and 6th articles of impeachment. I know not how my vote will effect my political prospects hereafter, but this much I do know, that I intend to obey the dictates of my honest judgment, and trust to the people to vindicate me from the foul aspersions of those who would take advantage of my honesty and candor to subserve their own political advancement. If I go down because of my course in this trial, I shall do so in communion with my own conscience. If because I will not perjure myself, I must suffer political martyrdom, I say let me perish, for I had rather live an obscure life than occupy the highest position in the gift of the people, with the heinous crime of perjury resting upon my soul

The first article of impeachment charges substantially as follows:

Raising unlawful armed bodies of men and, without, cause declaring the county of Alamance in a state of insurrection, and afterwards unlawfully arrested Lucien H. Murray and some eighty-one other citizens of Alamance, and unlawfully detaining them, when there was no insurrection, and when

*

the civil officers of the law were in the full exercise of all their functions.

The second article charges the same as to Caswell—arresting John Kerr and seventeen other citizens of that county.

The fourth article charges the unlawfully arresting and detaining in the County of Caswell John Kerr and three other citizens.

Upon the above three articles I voted not guilty, for the reasons, I believed that under the provisions of the act to secure the better protection of life and property, ratified the 29th day of January, A. D. 1870. The governor had the right, "whenever in his judgment the civil authorities of any county were unable to protect its citizens in its enjoyment of life and property, to declare such county to be in a state of insurrection, to arrest all suspected persons, and do all things necessary to suppress the insurrection which did not come in conflict with the plain and express provisions of the constitution. The governor declared the counties of Alamance and Caswell to be in a state of insurrection. Claiming to act under this statute, and as the statute confides the question of insurrection solely to his judgment, and as I believe the very state of affairs existed in these counties which was contemplated by the statute, it is my pleasure to vote him *not guilty*. The question of the constitutionality of the act has no force on my mind. It was his duty, as the executive officer of the state, to rigidly enforce the law until declared unconstitutional by the proper court in its OFFICIAL CAPACITY, except the act had been palpably in violation of the constitution and it so appeared upon its face. A contrary doctrine to this would be ruinous; but think of it, to allow the governor to assume the judicial ermine and pass upon the acts of the legislature, as to their constitutionality or unconstitutionality, would be to consolidate the executive, legislative and judicial departments of the government into one, which doctrine is repugnant to every man who desires to see republican principles flourish and prosper.

The third article of impeachment charges substantially as follows:

The unlawful arresting of Josiah Turner, jr., in the county of Orange and imprisoning him.

Upon this article I voted guilty, because I believed from the testimony of Mr. Gorman that the governor knew of the arrest of Mr. Turner in Orange by his agent, or if he did not know it at the time, he made the act of his agent his own by endorsing it. This is too plain a proposition of law to admit of argument. The governor had the power and authority to have had Mr. Turner released after he learned he was so unlawfully arrested; this he could have done with a stroke of his pen, yet he refused to do it, but stood by and saw Mr. Turner thrusted into a dungeon with a condemned felon, and kept him so confined for the space of twenty days or more. I am not willing that the precedent should be established in North Carolina of the governor having the right to arrest and confine respectable citizens of the state without warrant or authority of law.

The fifth article of impeachment charges substantially as follows:

Refusing to obey the writ of *habeas corpus*, in the case of Adolphus G. Moore.

The sixth article charges substantially as follows:

Refusing to obey the writ of *habeas corpus* in the case of John Kerr and eighteen other citizens of Caswell county.

Upon the 5th and 6th articles I voted guilty, because the governor refused to obey the sacred writ of *habeas corpus*, which has been handed down to us by our forefathers, and which cost so much of the treasure and blood of our English ancestors. This writ, which has from time immemorial, been guarded with a jealous eye by the American people, and properly considered the great fundamental principle essential to the protection of civil liberty. The governor refused to obey this writ after it had been judicially decided by the honorable Richmond M. Pearson, chief justice of the state, that he, the governor, had no right to *disobey* the said writ, in which opinion the chief justice uses substantially the following language, that "he who runs may read :"

"I declare my opinion to be that *the privilege of the writ of habeas corpus has not been suspended by the action of his excellency.* THE GOVERNOR HAS NO POWER TO DISOBEY THE WRIT OF HABEAS CORPUS. *The judiciary has power to declare the action of the executive as well as the acts of the general assembly, when in violation of the constitution, void and of no effect. Having conceded full faith and credit to the action of his excellency within the scope of the power conferred on him, I feel assured he will in like manner give due observance to the law as announced by the judiciary.*"

Notwithstanding this plain announcement of the law from the chief judicial officer of the state, the governor refused to obey the exigencies of the said writ. How could I be expected to vote not guilty upon these articles with this light before my eyes? Had I done so, I would justly have become a by-word of reproach among men. I shall never commit myself as being in favor of giving any man the right, under any circumstances to violate this writ which is for the protection of the innocent. Yielding obedience to the writ of *habeas corpus* would not have had the effect of releasing the prisoners unless they were innocent. It is said that at the time the writs was served, the evidence against the prisoners could not be had. This only aggravates the offence of failure to obey the writ by arresting, in the first instance, without proper testimony. The right to be relieved from an unlawful detention, is a right dear to every true American citizen, and any one who, in this day of civilization and freedom would advocate contrary principles, must certainly meet with condemnation from all those who are true to the doctrines and teachings of our great government.

The seventh article of impeachment charges the unlawfully recruiting a large body of troops from this state and from the state of Tennessee, and placing in command of them one Kirk and other desperadoes from the state of Tennessee, for hanging by the neck William Patton and others, &c.

The eighth article charges, in substance, "The inciting and procuring the state treasurer to disregard the injunction restraining him from paying the sum of eighty thousand dollars or more out of the public treasury for the unlawful purpose of paying said unlawful troops.

Upon these two articles I voted not guilty. Such points as I have not put down as a portion of the substance of these articles, I believe I have fully answered under the head of other articles, and do not deem it proper or necessary to mention them here again. I am satisfied from the testimony that there were many men in the "troops" raised by the governor, who were under twenty-one and above the age of forty-five years. I also believe that many of the men enlisted were from the state of Tennessee, and that the conduct of "Burgen" was in keeping with his character, which no honest man will attempt to uphold. Yet the governor avows in his answer to these charges that these men were citizens of the state, and that the conduct of his inferior officers was without his sanction or approval, and he offered to show that he attempted the arrest of Burgen for his crimes against the prisoners. I am disposed to give the governor the benefit of the doubt in my mind as to his guilty knowledge, first, as to the age and place of residence of the men enlisted, and second, as to his approval of the outrages perpetrated upon Patton and others.

The act of the special session of 1868, entitled "An act to organize a militia of North Carolina," section 21, appropriates the sum necessary to carry out its provisions. It is under this act the governor claims to have acted. There was no evidence satisfactory to my mind that the governor invited the public treasurer to disregard the writ of injunction. I believe that I have given my reasons for voting as I did upon every important point raised by the articles and answer. If I have overlooked any one it is not from a desire to evade it. It has been now a week since the vote on the articles of impeachment was taken. I have reflected much upon the vote I gave and see no reason to wish I had voted differently. If I have erred it is a fault of the head and not of the heart. From the first day of this trial to the last, I have endeavored to disrobe myself of all prejudice and act in accordance with my honest conviction. "I have done so," and by this record I shall ever be willing to stand.

---

## OPINION OF SENATOR L. P. OLDS.

I vote in the negative, because the impeachment law has only two branches: 1st, in regard to vice; 2d, crime. The former includes drunkenness only, the latter something more serious. *The former cannot have intent; the latter has nothing else.* Hence impeachment for the latter goes on the sole ground of *wicked motive*, and thereon this whole case turns, as was ably shown by the respondent's counsel, and as is shown by common sense.

And hereon is based the entire charge, the like running through each article.

So then, taking up the 1st article, the allegation beginning at the 12th line, "intending to stir up civil war and subvert personal and public liberty, and the constitution and laws of said state and of the United States, and contriving and intending to humiliate and degrade the said state and people thereof, and especially the people of the county of Alamance," is true neither from *proof* nor *reason*. The mere fact of proclaiming in insurrection under a law enjoining it, is not proof; and fixing upon a fourth rate county where no enmities moved to banning it, refutes the second ground, that of reasonableness. Had Orange county, for instance, been chosen, where one of the prisoners lived who is embraced in the third article, it might have been imagined probably personal feeling actuated. But not so. Orange was treated as other unproclaimed counties, though no doubt infested with the organization. Article 1, therefore, cannot be sustained.

ARTICLE II. The same applies to this article, and the arrest of prominent men, if on grounds plausible to the governor, is no unusual thing, as it has occurred in all ages and places, and though always regretted when discovered to be at the expense of innocence, yet will probably be more or less seen as long as criminal laws exist. I was arrested during the late rebellion on account of sentiment, yet no great stir was made about it either by myself or the government so doing, as such complaint would have been answered by saying that public exigency so required. Besides no *civil* means existed whereby to complain, as the sacred *habeas*, so-called, had then played out in North Carolina, as in 1870.

ARTICLE III. I take this to be the strongest of the charges. Turner having lived in Orange, which, though as before intimated, very much disgraced by Kuklux, yet not falling under public rebuke. Hence, although he may have desired arrest as a good thing for him, and the respondent may have believed that the country would be benefited by such arrest, still no proof appears of an advised arrest, and it merely occurred as an incident of the times. Had the arrest been desired contrary to law, his presence in Raleigh where his business lay, might have been made any day; or, if as desirable as contended, Orange county might have been proclaimed insurgent, including this party. This was not done. The arrest was at a late day, and the inference is, leaving out proof, that no such arrest was directed.

ARTICLE IV. This article is mainly a repetition; and so in the 5th and 6th. The *habees corpus* is conditionally a very sacred thing, but when referable to one man, or a few men, it is less sacred than the rights of the entire people of a nation. And, moreover, when its application is to a class embracing "gentlemen" instead of poor whites and colored men, it loses its sanctity altogether and becomes simply ludicrous. I have been taught that "all men are equal," and that the duty of the citizen now-a-days is to the general government in a paramount degree; therefore when by a "species of wild justice," poor, ignorant, and especially colored men, are terrified and abused, we may expect a mild display of national punishment. I would refer to sections 4 and 5 of the Bill of Rights, touching the sanctity of our oaths in behalf of Union. It follows that the governor should protect "life and property" in states, and if so doing by the whole force of the state, it would relieve the general government from aiding by more general declarations of war. General rebellions may then be prevented, and would only in this way, for so soon as they get too strong for the state, they are strong enough for the Union, and it will be so in this country as long as it lasts; unless treason be nipped in the bud, its full blossom must be crushed by blood and treasure; and all good men certainly pray for as little sacrifice as possible.

Again; military law stops civil law for the time so far as its operation on accusations arising out of the emergency itself is concerned. Insurgents cannot be turned over to insurgents for judgment from the very reason of the thing. If then they are held till the public safety allows, it serves right and proper. This is the answer of the impeached.

ARTICLE 7. No doubt excesses were perpetrated by the soldiery, or rather some of the commanders. It is to be regretted. It was very much so when Wheeler's cavalry and Sherman's bummers came along in 1865, what one did not do the other finished, so said our citizens. It was never deemed advisable to meddle with them as it was all the result of war and confusion. So here, on a small scale, Burgen and others seemed to have conceived that old times were reviving and committed excesses. This the governor did not connive at, but rather opposed, and it was really true he would have punished for these outrages if permitted.

As to the class of troops and commanders employed as it was argued for defence that the force raised was purely volunteer, and the strict rules of ordinary organizations did not obtain, so, as in the past, we have seen all sorts of men were used by state and section fix ages from fifteen to seventy-five, and often of no character at all. Volunteers for emergency will always consist of all sorts of men; and as this military seemed to have been very effective, disclosing the Kuklux order and weakening it tor the present, we must in justice to the country at large not condemn too strongly. Where a surgeon cuts off a leg it is very bad, but is really worse to have the patient die from gangrene without it.

ARTICLE VIII. As an incident, money had to be used. If so, *no one man* before a judge of his own party views could be expected to stop the movement *in favor of all the people*, for if so, nothing could ever be done unless by universal consent, and at this day of the nation this is not to be expected.

I would say in concluding, that though errors of the head may have been committed, I cannot see any of the heart wherein all guilt lies. The governor has been blamed for not calling out the troops sooner; but his forbearance seems to have overruled him. But as his action, though late, has served to unearth the klan and prepare the government for *self-protection*, I cannot convict. My oath honestly taken to the union; my view of the comparative sacredness of *habeas corpus;* the persuasion that the nation, including north and south, may use this item of history to advantage in avoiding the danger and providing therefor, I feel proud of a consistency beginning with my first oath to the United States in 1839, again in 1865, and now in 1871, in the capitol of my native state. Being both religiously and civilly inclined to obey the solemnity of an oath, wherever truth and reason takes her stand, my feet shall also be found. I have therefore pronounced the words not guilty with unfaltering tongue.

---

## OPINION OF SENATOR R. M. NORMENT.

MR. CHIEF JUSTICE AND SENATORS: Being called upon to discharge one of the most important and responsible duties of my life, a duty the proper and conscientious discharge of which affects not only myself, my immediate constituents and the whole state of North Carolina, but also the character and reputation of the chief magistrate of the state, I feel it to be my solemn and bounden duty to enter of record the reasons which impels me to give the vote which I am about to cast upon the guilt or innocence of the respondent on the first and second charges preferred against him in the articles of impeachment.

I have endeavored, Mr. Chief Justice and Senators, throughout the whole of this protracted trial, to give a patient and careful hearing and consideration to *all* the *facts* which have been elicited in the investigation; I have listened with attention and with great pleasure to the able arguments of the learned counsel, both in behalf of the prosecution and of the defence; I have endeavored to divest myself of all prejudice and bias as far as it was possible for poor weak mortal man to do. I fear, however, that when I entered this jury box as one of the triers of this case, I was not as free from prejudice against the accused as I should have been and as I desired to be. The many reports, *exparte* as they doubtless were, which came to my ears through the public press before the meeting of this general assembly, and which, without intermission, have been industriously circulated almost up to the present hour, were well calculated to warp the judgment and bias the minds of jurors who belong to the political party of which those papers were the accredited organs. I fear, therefore, that I did not enter upon this investigation as free from prejudice as I should have been, but, Mr. Chief Justice and senators, when I took a solemn oath in this august presence to make a true deliverance between the state and the accused, I *determined*, God being my helper, to render a true and impartial verdict; I *determined* to *forget*, as far as possible, what I had heard from every other source, and look only to the sworn testimony of witnesses produced before this high court. The witnesses have been heard, and my mind has been convinced beyond the shadow of a doubt, that during the period intervening between the autumn of 1868 and the summer of 1870, the civil law was not adequate to the protection of life, liberty and property in the counties of Alamance and Caswell. Without going into the evidence in detail, it is sufficient to say that the sheriff of Alamance county, whose sworn duty it was to preserve the peace and bring the violators of law to justice, was, according to his own evidence, a member of a secret association who had banded themselves together, and under the solemn sanction of an oath not to betray one another, had taken the law into their own hands and had whipped, scourged, maltreated and *murdered* citizens of the county and destroyed their property and caused them to abandon their homes, for no other reason than that they had incurred the displeasure of this marauding midnight band of disguised assassins. It also appears from the evidence that *justices* of the *peace* and other peace officers in Alamance county, were also of this organized band; and it is in proof that there were upwards of sixty cases of murders, whippings, scourgings and forcible trespass, &c., &c., committed in this county, and not a single case of trial or punishment by the courts of law except, perhaps, a single instance in which some colored men were the offenders. This state of things was intolerable. It had brought disgrace upon the fair name of North Carolina, and was doing an injury which it would require years to repair. Public sentiment in Alamance and Caswell seemed not to discourage this state of affairs, and the infection seems to have been extending into other and adjoining counties. Civil law was inadequate to remedy the evil, and it became absolutely necessary to resort to other means to stay the tide of destruction or to give up the disaffected district to the tender mercies of a heartless band of disguised midnight executioners. The alternative was chosen; the military force of the country was called into requisition by the governor to suppress violence, to protect life and to save property, and for doing this he is impeached, and I am called upon to pass between him and his accusers, and for my verdict and upon my oath I do say, "he is not guilty of the first and second charges."

# OPINION OF SENATOR W. L. LOVE.

In order to avoid the charge of remissness, or indifference to public opinion, and forestall any insinuation that may arise in after years, that I voted on the great questions recently before the senate of North Carolina, involving the removal and degradation of the late governor, W. W. Holden, without due consideration, I avail myself of a senator's right to leave upon record, a reason or more, for my several votes as cast on the several "articles of impeachment," in the senate chamber on the 22d day of March, A. D. 1871. Brevity being a part of my nature, I shall endeavor to discharge the task of showing how I happened to vote the "strait ticket," and how I arrived at my conclusions, as the guilt of the respondent, by detailing the following illustration:

A certain minister in sacred things, very properly determined to induce each head of the several families in his pastoral charge, to establish the "family altar." By continual effort, in a few weeks, he had well nigh succeeded in this laudable undertaking. Among his many parishianers, there remained one, only one, obstinate, unruly and unmovable. Many were his excuses. It was inconvenient to assemble the several members of his household at every given hour. Their avocations were diverse, their engagements varied, and their hours of retiring necessarily very different. Besides, he was not educated—had a lack of language—was "slow of speech"—could not cull words and join them together, giving utterance to feelings of devotion—in fine he could not pray—could not "take up the cross." But the good *padre* knew no such word as fail. One by one he silenced the objections of this caviller--this wordly-minded member of his flock. One only remained—the lack of language—the want of ability to frame a prayer. But the family altar must be erected. The pastor was not to be outdone, and he prepared to put words into the mouth of *obstinate*. He prepared to write a prayer, which this Aaron should memorize, and in humble attitude repeat in the family circle every morning. This proposition was accepted, a compromise effected, a truce entered into, and the contest ended.

The prayer was written, brief, pointed, and the pastor went to his cloister, with a victorious tread, feeling that he had triumphantly wielded "the sword of the spirit," and had subdued the last resistant in his flock.

Obstinate, however, determined to evade the *letter*, and observe what he regarded as the *spirit* of the compromise. Being a great economist in point of time, he decided the following compliance with the terms of capitulation. Pasting the written prayer on a bit of bristol board, he tied the same to the post, at the foot of his bed, and at his hour for retiring, having called in the family, he would as he passed to his couch, reverently point to the prayer and exclaim,

"Oh Lord! them's my sentiments."

The application:

When the "articles of impeachment" were presented in the senate, I listened to their reading attentively. After the "articles" were printed, I read them repeatedly with much care. I received and read respondent's "answer" in like manner. I then listened for six weeks, without missing a roll call, to evidence and arguments *pro* and *con*, of managers and their counsel, and of respondent's counsel. Much of this I read and re-read, from time to time, after it was printed. When all was over, I mentally laid the "articles," and the evidence and argument offered in their support, on one hand, and the "answer," evidence and arguments offered *per contra*, on the other, and in reviewing the whole, my finger involuntarily pointed to the "articles of impeachment," and I as involuntarily exclaimed,

"Oh Chief Justice! them's my sentiments."

# OPINION OF SENATOR W. M. ROBBINS.

This is a case of great interest and importance, not only because it is the first instance in American history where the governor of a state has been impeached, but because it involves questions touching some of the fundamental principles of American law and liberty. The respondent stands charged, not merely with technical and petty violations of law, but with wilfully trampling under foot the most essential safeguards of individual right and public freedom. Among the allegations against him are these:

That he recruited and set on foot a large body of troops, such as he was not permitted to raise or to command, either by the constitution of the state or of the United States, they not being citizen-militia of North Carolina, but very many of them, including their chief officers, being mercenaries of a desperate character, hired from abroad, and many others of them being minors, extremely unfit to be conservators of public order, and perhaps for that reason, forbidden by the constitution of this state, from being enrolled among the militia;

That having thus organized a force not at all fitted to secure order and uphold the law, but admirably suited to be willing tools for the furtherance of his own designs, he unlawfully used large amounts of the public money for the support and maintenance of this unlawful military force;

That, by means of this force, he, without any warrant or authority of law, caused to be arrested, detained, and imprisoned, about one hundred peaceable citizens, against whom no charge of crime existed, and as to most of whom no evidence was produced by him upon which to found even a suspicion;

That some of these arrested men were threatened and tortured by his military agents, to extort from them confessions, and though this was made known to him he took no effective steps to prevent its repetition;

That he sought to raise the military above the civil authority;

That he persuaded and induced the paymaster of his troops to disobey an order of injunction, properly issued by a judge of the superior court, restraining said paymaster from disbursing the public moneys in his hands, on account of said troops, and having thus caused said moneys to be placed in the hands of a new appointee of his own, he procured the disbursement of the same to his troops, in evasion and contempt of the rightful authority of the judiciary;

That he refused to obey, and commanded and caused his military subordinates to refuse to obey writs of *habeas corpus* issued by the chief justice of the supreme court of North Carolina, on behalf of the citizens arrested and detained by him and his agents, and continued to hold said citizens in custody, and some of them in loathsome prisons, for many weeks after the service of said writs upon him and in defiance of the mandate thereof, he having ordered his military officers to resist with force, if necessary, any attempt on the part of the officers of the civil law to execute the said writs of *habeas corpus*.

The foregoing, I understand, from a careful study of the articles of impeachment, to be among the most flagrant acts of wrong and usurpation therein charged against the respondent. They are not arranged according to the order in which they are presented by the articles; but they constitute, I think, a fair summary of the principal allegations.

Certainly these are no light charges. Condensed into one sentence, they simply mean that the respondent lawlessly seized the sword and public purse, trampled down civil authority, overthrew the sacred muniments of liberty, and made himself a military dictator. Extraordinary as it is that such daring strides towards absolute and irresponsible power should have been attempted in one of our free North American states, and especially in one whose traditional love of liberty and jealousy of usurpation are so well known, the evidence produced before the senate has satisfied me of the fact beyond a reasonable doubt.

To come directly to the charges in the order and form in

which they are set forth in the several articles, I have settled down upon the conclusion that an article in a case of impeachment is properly to be regarded in the light of a charge with specifications; and if any of the several distinct and separate specifications of official misconduct contained in an article is sustained, and is sufficient in its character to make good the charge of high crime or high misdemeanor in such article, then an officer impeached must be found guilty on such article, though some of the specifications be not sustained; this principle to be applicable even where the specifications are not formally, but only substantially distinguished from one another, provided they are really distinct allegations and not so coupled and interwoven together that they cannot be considered as separate propositions.

This principle I have thought proper to lay down here, because upon it is based in some measure, my vote against the respondent upon the first two articles, which, except that they relate to acts done towards two different counties, are similar in form and substance.

Article I. charges a high crime, in this:

1. That the respondent, on the 7th of March, 1870, falsely and illegally declared Alamance county to be in insurrection.

2. That afterwards he sent unlawfully organized troops, of a desperate and lawless character, into that county, occupied it by said military force, and suspended the civil authority and the constitution and laws.

3. That he caused to be arrested, by said troops, eighty-two peaceable citizens of said county engaged in their lawful business.

4. That he permitted his military agents to injure and maltreat sundry of the persons thus arrested:

It being alleged that he did all this from corrupt and wicked motives and with evil intent.

If there were no other specification of crime in this article except the bare fact of the proclamation of insurrection, although I am well satisfied that there existed no semblance of any actual insurrection there, I should vote to acquit the respondent upon this article; because by the letter of the Shoffner act (so-called) the governor was authorized to do that, in a certain contingency of which he was to be sole judge, and I could not hold him bound to decide upon the constitutionality of an act of assembly; though, as this act was only to be enforced according to his *discretion*, it would have been wise in him not to have proceeded under it, as he would have been bound to proceed by a *mandatory* act, whatever might be his private opinion of its constitutionality.

But the Shoffner act evidently contemplated, in allowing insurrection to be proclaimed and militia to be used, not the overthrow or suspension, but the upholding and strengthening of civil authority in the disorderly county, and the term "insurrection" was used in the act to indicate a condition of disorder by no means amounting to insurrection in fact. This is shown by its provision respecting civil trials of offenders, the removal of trials upon the mere motion of the solicitor or the judge himself, and concerning costs. Evidently the civil tribunals alone were to have jurisdiction to try criminals, and the military were only to be used to assist in the apprehension of persons against whom proper civil process was issued, or persons found in the act of committing crime, protect the courts, if necessary, in the exercise of their functions, and afford security to those who might wish to bring complaints against offenders chargeable with outrages against person or property. This was the real purport of that act; and those who opposed its enactment, while they were right in doing so on account of several bad provisions in it, might not have contended so vigorously against it, had they not foreseen clearly that it would be used, as it has been, as a pretext for doing what the act itself did not warrant.

Upon the last three specifications in this article, and the proofs adduced, I cannot avoid deciding against the respondent. His troops were of an unlawful character; he had no right to arrest citizens not found in the commission of crime, without a civil warrant issued upon affidavit; and he had no right to permit their personal maltreatment in custody. Moreover, the evidence shows how completely he regarded the civil law set aside by his action, in that he appointed a military commission to try the arrested citizens—a step which he was apparently bent on carrying out, had not the result of the elections startled him, and an upright and fearless federal judge interfered and loosed the victims from the sacrifice.

Upon the question of the evil intent of the respondent, I can have no doubt. A great mass of testimony is before us touching the matter of outrages secretly committed against person and property in Alamance, by persons in disguise. Passing by what may be due to exaggeration, there remains enough to bring a blush of shame to the cheek of every true and thoughtful son of North Carolina. I wish here, as often I have done elsewhere, to pronounce my unqualified condemnation of these reckless and wicked deeds. It is no justification of them that they were usually perpetrated upon malefactors and incendiaries. But I am gratified to find, from the evidence, that they have long since ceased. Indeed, they are shown to have ended before the respondent sent his troops into Alamance. The respondent has also entirely failed to prove, by any credible testimony, that any forcible resistance was made to the constituted authorities, or that anybody contemplated an attempt to subvert or overthrow the existing state or federal government.

It is urged that the respondent, in all he did, was actuated solely by the good purpose to protect the poor and humble from outrage. After carefully weighing the evidence, including his numerous proclamations and his whole course of action in the premises, I am forced into the belief that the respondent and his aiders and abettors, in this state and out of it, were studious, not so much to repress the alleged outrages, as to utilize them for purposes of political thrift. What am I to think of his motives, when the proof before us tends so strongly to show that the respondent loved rather to make political capital by publishing to the world complaints of the wrongs of his devoted friends—the poor colored men—than to stop those wrongs by sincere efforts to that end? A proclamation of insurrection issued at the beginning of March, and followed up by nothing further till the end of June, and then followed up by bringing into the field such troops, commanded by such officers, governed by such orders, and used in such manner;—just upon the eve of a general election, though the outrages were mostly long past, and not alleged to have been very noticeable just then, and are really proven here to have ceased entirely;—what does all this show, but that the respondent was moved by political motives and a desire to influence the pending elections, and not by the high and pure purposes claimed for him here. In consideration of all these things, I vote the respondent "guilty" on this article.

Article II charges a high crime, with similar specifications to those of the preceding article, except that the proclamation of insurrection bears date July 8th, 1870, and relates to Caswell county; and nineteen citizens of said county are alleged to have been arrested, detained, imprisoned and maltreated.

Very few instances of crime are proven to have occurred in that county. One or two murders had been perpetrated, but they were and are still enshrouded in mystery. There seems to have been no ground whatever for proclaiming insurrection there. Upon the other specifications in this article and the evidence offered in support of them, my conclusions are similar to those I have come to upon the same specifications in the first article; and I vote the respondent "guilty" upon the second article.

Article III charges a high misdemeanor—in this:

That the respondent caused the unlawful arrest of Josiah Turner, of Orange county, and his detention for many days, accompanied by imprisonment and maltreatment.

Though the respondent denies ordering this arrest originally, the evidence strongly tends to show that he did so; and the fact of his ordering the detention and imprisonment of Mr. Turner, which is admitted must be held to make him a participant in the original wrongful act of his agents, even if he had not ordered it; besides that, upon general principles, he is responsible for all wrongful acts of his unlawful agents. I accordingly vote the respondent *guilty* upon this article.

Article IV charges a high misdemeanor in this: That the respondent caused the arrest, detention and imprisonment, unlawfully and without cause, of several citizens of Caswell county, John Kerr, S. P. Hill, W. B. Bowe and N. M. Roane, treating them with much contumely and violence. The proofs are conclusive, and I vote the respondent "*guilty*" upon this article.

Article V charges high crimes and misdemeanors, with many specifications, of which the principal ones, not laid down so directly in the preceding articles are, that the respondent attempted to subject the civil authority in Alamance to the authority of the military, treated the writ of *habeas corpus* as practically suspended by his own action, and refused obedience, and caused his subordinates to refuse obedience to this writ when issued by the chief justice upon the petition of A. G. Moore, of Alamance, arrested and detained by respondent's order. The evidence fully and conclusively sustains all these grave allegations. The constitution of North Carolina declares that the privilege of the writ of *habeas corpus* shall *never be* suspended. But it is useless to multiply words upon this point. Without this grandest of all its safeguards, liberty would be but an idle and meaningless name. And the attempt to inaugurate military rule in place of the civil power could only be tolerated by a people educated to endure the yoke of tyrants. I vote the respondent "*guilty*" upon this article.

Article VI charges high crimes and misdemeanors, and is in all particulars similar to the preceding, except in specifying that the wrong was done in Caswell county, and to certain citizens thereof, and it is sustained by the evidence. I vote the respondent "*guilty*" upon this article.

Article VII charges a high misdemeanor in this: That the respondent unlawfully drew from the treasury large sums of money and used the same in maintaining his unlawful military force. The evidence is direct and conclusive. I vote the respondent "*guilty*" upon this article.

Article VIII charges a high misdemeanor in this: That the respondent incited and induced the paymaster of his troops to evade and disobey a writ of injunction, lawfully issued by Judge Mitchell of the superior court, restraining said paymaster from paying out the public moneys in his hands, on account of said troops; and having thus procured said moneys to be turned over to a new appointee of his own, he caused them to be disbursed in evasion and contempt of said order of injunction. The evidence sustains the charge, and I vote the respondent "*guilty*," upon this article.

Such is the verdict I have felt compelled to render in this case. The proofs of the gravest official misconduct, on the part of the respondent, are overwhelming. It is a matter of unaffected regret with me that such a decision should have been pronounced against a man possessing amiable traits of private character, and towards whom I cherish no feelings of personal enmity. Loving party success more than his country's welfare, has proved his ruin. Nor is he himself less guilty from the fact that he probably perpetrated his wrongful acts at the instigation of wicked advisers, ready now to desert the man they counselled to his destruction. It is, moreover, an evil omen that the respondent committed these daring deeds of usurpation, not only without any apparent fear of interference by the partizans at the head of the federal government, but with the confident expectation of being sustained by them. All this but makes our duty the more imperative to record a judgment in this case which shall stand as a solemn landmark in history, to warn all our rulers against plotting to deprive us of those venerable heir-looms of liberty and popular rights which have descended to us from an honored ancestry, and which will, I trust, be cherished and preserved by the people of North Carolina, till Hatteras shall cease to battle with the waves and the granite sentinels of the Alleghany be driven from their stations.

---

## OPINION OF SENATOR R. W. KING.

The articles of impeachment preferred against W. W. Holden, governor of North Carolina, are eight (8) in number, more or less dependant one on the other.

It appears from the evidence that the general assembly of 1869 and 1870, passed an act, known as the Shoffner act, authorizing the governor, at his discretion, to declare a county or counties in a state of insurrection, and to call out volunteer militia for the purpose of restoring law and order in such counties, and for the purpose of bringing the violators of law to justice. It further appears that in the counties of Alamance and Caswell, sundry crimes had been committed, amongst which were murders. In both said counties, over forty colored persons, and more than twenty white persons had been whipped or otherwise ill treated; that it was impossible to execute the civil law; that in several instances the officers charged with the execution of the law were members of a secret, oath-bound organization which met in the woods during the night time, and there passed orders to whip, scourge, and, in some instances, to murder such citizens of the state as had incurred their displeasure, or were charged with some offence by a member of this murderous and treasonable organization.

It further appears from the evidence of persons at one time members of this secret organization, that each member was sworn to keep secret the proceedings of the "klan," and to aid each other in all their wicked and lawless acts; that it was required of every member of this organization to testify falsely in court in order to acquit a brother member, and to use all means to get on the jury in order to aid a member to escape the penalty of the law. These facts were testified to by members of this organization.

The governor was not allowed to prove the existence of this organization in other counties than the counties of Alamance and Caswell, or that outrages and murders had been committed by this organization in other counties of the state, and that members of the organization in other counties had testified to the fact that it was required either by the oath or explanation of the secret work of this "klan" that members should swear falsely to acquit each other in court, and to render false verdicts, if necessary, as jurors to enable a brother member to escape the penalty of the law.

It further appears in evidence, that the membership of this organization consisted exclusively of persons belonging to the democratic or conservative party, who perpetrated these outrages almost entirely on members of the other political party, clearly establishing the principle that no freedom of speech, or freedom of ballot was tolerated, or freemen permitted to think and act according to the dictates of their own consciences. In addition to this it appears that these facts were made known to the governor by citizens from every portion of the state, that outrage upon outrage was committed in the dead hour of the night, upon men, women and children. In many instances most brutal whippings were administered upon the bare backs of both white and colored persons; that in several cases persons were taken from their families by disguised men in the darkness of night, and not even allowed to give their wives and little ones a last farewell, the next day their bodies were found hanging to a tree, and in one instance near the court house in the town of Graham, in the county of Alamance; in another instance a colored man who was proven to be occasionally insane, was taken from his house and family in the night, and his body was found some weeks afterwards in a mill pond with a rock tied to it.

In another instance, a state senator was murdered in the court house at Yanceyville during the sitting of a public meeting in the day time: it further appears that no person has ever been punished by the civil authorities for any of said offences.

In view of all these facts which was made known to the governor, and in view of the appeals made to him for protection of life and property, under the act known as the Shoffner act, passed to meet such a state of affairs, there is no reason to believe that the governor acted upon bad, corrupt, or improper motives.

ARTICLE 3d.—arrest of Josiah Turner, jr., of the county of Orange. Upon this charge there is no direct evidence that the governor ordered the arrest of "Turner." It appears in evidence that "Turner" used every means to incite the respondent to arrest him, and that for this arrest, if illegal, the respondent is liable in a civil action. This charge partakes more of a private than a public offence, and as the law does not mention what offences are impeachable, I am of the opinion that impeachment for an offence of this kind was not contemplated by the law.

ARTICLE 4th. This charge appears to be the same as charged in article 1st and 2d, except that it alleges the arrest and detention of sundry persons. It appears that the governor was authorized to arrest persons in counties declared in insurrection

ARTICLE 5th. This article, the same principal is involved, as in articles 1, 2 and 4, with the additional charge "that the governor failed to surrender the parties arrested, in pursuance to writs of *habeas corpus* issued by the chief justice, until sometime after the demand was made, and the writs served."

Upon this charge many authorities were read, showing that parties could be held until after a regular term of a court. It is clear that parties arrested could only be tried by the civil courts; at what time, whether immediately, or at such time as the safety of the state required? There are conflicting opinions entertained by the legal profession, and in view of the fact that a learned judge of the United States court has recently decided that an arrest by the military was another mode of arrest, and could be legally made, and the parties held for trial by the military, I am of the opinion that the respondent is entitled to the benefit of the doubt; and further, that in my opinion he acted in *good faith* from *good motives*, and that if he was in error that it was an error of judgment, and not from wicked and corrupt motives, and that he could have had no motive to oppress and otherwise ill-treat good citizens of the state.

Article 6th contains the same charges as article 5th—refers to failing to surrender the prisoners arrested in the county of Caswell. Same reason given for acquittal, as in article 5th.

Article 7th contains the same charges as the 1st and 2d articles, with the addition that said Wm. W. Holden made drafts on the treasurer of the state for large sums of money to pay off the militia organized under the act known as the Shoffner act. Same reasons for his acquittal as is given in other articles; and that he was authorized to draw on the treasurer. Said act of the general assembly was admitted in evidence, and that there is no reason to believe that he acted wickedly or corruptly, and unless he did so act from corrupt, evil, and bad motives, he is not liable to impeachment even if said act known as the Shoffner act is unconstitutional.

Article 8th charges, as in No. 7, that said Wm. W. Holden, governor, did draw large sums of money from the treasury for the purpose of supporting said military force, and that said Wm. W. Holden, governor, did cause A. D. Jenkins, paymaster, to turn over the funds in his hands to another agent of the governor for the purpose of defeating an injunction issued by his honor Judge Mitchell, one of the judges of the superior court.

It does not appear that any injunction was served on the governor, or that the governor refused to obey any injunction or order of the judge.

If he had been guilty, I take it for granted that the judge would have taken action against him for contempt.

I am therefore of the opinion that this charge is not sustained, and that there is nothing in the additional charge in regard to the injunction that makes the respondent guilty.

In conclusion, I must say that the respondent acted in the

matter of calling out the volunteer militia under extraordinary circumstances; that not only the writ of "*habeas corpus*" was suspended by this oath bound secret organization, but all civil law was powerless to protect the life and property of the citizens; that many of the outrages committed were of the most revolting character, both contrary to christianity and civilization; that this secret insurrection was more dangerous and formidable than open insurrection or rebellion; that the fact that they wore hideous disguises and were bound together by horrid oaths to keep secret the outrages committed, and to commit perjury, both as witnesses and jurors, to relieve from the penalty of the law any of the members of this organization; all tending to prove that some extraordinary measures were required to put down this organization of disguised murderers and assassins, and the fact that civil officers who did not belong to or encourage this organization were afraid to discharge their duty, and that the persons who were whipped or scourged by these desperate and wicked men, did not dare to appear and testify even when they knew the parties, believing from what has occurred in different portions of the state, and by the evidence of members of the klan, which was offered by the respondent's counsel and decided to be *competent evidence* by the chief justice, (but was ruled out by a vote of the senate.) Upon a full and fair examination of all the evidence and articles of impeachment, and arguments of the learned counsel, I am of the opinion that the accused should be acquitted upon all the charges, and more especially upon the grounds that if he committed error, it was not from bad, corrupt, or wicked motives, but from mistaken judgment under most extraordinary circumstances. To justify the conviction of the governor, there must be specific allegations of some crime or misdemeanor involving moral turpitude, gross misconduct, or a wilful violation of law, and the proof must be such as to satisfy the conscience of the truth of the charge.

I have therefore voted *not guilty* on each and every charge.

## OPINION OF SENATOR W. W. FLEMMING.

The importance of the issue that the senate as a court of impeachment is called upon to decide, no one can doubt. The result all must feel. For it behooves each senator to decide between the people of North Carolina, as heard through their representatives, and the chief executive of that people. I have therefore thought fit, in justice to myself, to those who have honored me with their confidence and placed in my hands the scales of justice, to take advantage of the opportunity afforded in thus filing my opinion.

In the first place, I look upon this body, not simply as a court, governed by the same strict rules of evidence, confined to the same narrow channels as an ordinary court of law, but differing in so much that senators must decide alike the law and the facts, augmented with great discretionary power, more nearly allied to what is known to the system of jurisprudence as the courts of equity, where the rigid rule of law is set aside that the appeals of humanity may be heard, the demands of justice satisfied. Further, there having existed a confidence between the accuser and the accused, a presumption arises that no intentional injury would be done either by the one party or the other; but as injury is ofttimes the result of the best motives, the intent is to be carefully considered, and this is the province of this court, for it is considered capable of giving proper credence to all questions of fact, and drawing the nice distinctions between testimony and evidence, in consequence of which I favored the admission of all testimony having a tendency to throw light upon either the subject matter or the intent, for according to the rules laid down by learned writers, the exclusive principle ceases, and in the language of the law, *cesante ratione cesat lex*. Again the respondent does not occupy the position of an ordinary criminal. It is a well settled principle of law, that intent is the essence of all crime, and that every violation of law is *prima facie* evidence of intent, thus throwing the *onus probandi*, or burden of proof, upon the accused. To this there are, however, three expressed exceptions, to-wit, infants, idiots and insane persons, who from want of reason, can have no intent. There is, however, one other exception, not springing from the same cause, but arising from the wisdom and foresighted policy of the law. It is the case of an executive officer, whose acts are always supposed to be prompted by the best motives until the contrary is shown. I shall not speak of the expediency of this except as upon reflection it must force itself upon every one. However, it may here be well to observe that no executive is to be held amenable for the execution of a law whether it be mandatory or permissive, and should an executive fail or refuse to execute a law on the grounds that it is unconstitutional, he does so at his own peril; for if an executive might at his own option execute the law, it would combine within one of the co-ordinate branches of government the executive and judicial functions, which is so dangerous to republics that the best and wisest statesmen have universally agreed that they ought to remain forever separate and distinct. There is one other reason which I will state why an executive should carry into effect the enactments of the legislature, for as each member is sworn to support the constitution, they are supposed to pass no law, which after mature deliberation they did not consider constitutional. Hence, I have favored the exclusion of such matter only as in my opinion would encumber rather than aid, tend to obscure rather than make clear.

I now come to the consideration of the eight articles of impeachment, and that I may be the more brief, shall confine myself to the following classifications:

Articles first, second and fourth, may be considered as contained in the first, under the following heads:

1st. It is alleged that the respondent declared the counties of Alamance and Caswell to be in a state of insurrection, no insurrection existing.

2d. That the respondent raised, armed and equipped, large

bodies of lawless and desperate men, and sent them to Alamance and Caswell without authority of law.

3d. That the respondent, in said counties, caused to be arrested, detained, imprisoned and otherwise maltreated good and lawful citizens contrary to the law of the land.

Article third alleges that the respondent caused to be arrested Josiah Turner, junior, in the county of Orange, without due process of law.

Articles fifth and sixth allege,

1st. That the respondent caused to be arrested and detained certain good and lawful citizens of Alamance and Caswell without authority of law.

2d. That the parties so arrested and detained, applied to the chief justice for a writ of *habeas corpus*, which was granted, and that the respondent, through George W. Kirk, refused to obey the writ and make return thereto.

3d. That upon proof that the commands of the writ had been disregarded, and the avowal of the respondent that the same was done by his order, the chief justice adjudged and declared that the writ of *habeas corpus* was not suspended, and caused a writ to issue demanding the body of the persons named in the said writ, directing the marshal of the court to serve the same upon the respondent, together with a copy of his opinion; that the respondent still refused; thus by means of an armed force, suspended the privileges of the writ.

Article seventh alleges that the respondent made warrants upon the treasury for large sums of money without authority of law.

Article eighth alleges that the respondent caused A. D. Jenkins to violate the writ of injunction for unlawful purposes. All of which is alleged to have been done with evil intent and for the purpose of subverting the civil law, and with a total disregard for the constitution, which has for its leading object to obtain for the government means of coercion without resort to force.

It now remains, in the first place, to enquire, did the respondent declare the counties of Alamance and Caswell in a state of insurrection? This is admitted. Did an insurrection exist in said counties? I shall not decide the question of what is an insurrection, nor consider it in its technical sense, but refer at once to the language of the statute under which the respondent claims to have acted. Chapter 27th, section 1st, laws of 1869-'70, reads as follows: "That the governor is hereby authorized and empowered, whenever in his judgment, the civil authorities in any county are unable to protect its citizens in the enjoyment of life and property, to declare such county to be in a state of insurrection." Thus we find the governor clothed with full power to declare, at his own option, any county to be in a state of insurrection. Then did the respondent wilfully abuse the power conferred? The facts as set forth disclose that both life and property were unsafe, and that it was beyond the power of the civil law to bring the offenders to justice, establishing an insurrection within the purview of the statute. In the next place, did the respondent raise, arm and equip large bodies of men and send them to Alamance and Caswell? This is admitted. Were they lawless and desperate? They seem, with few exceptions, to have obeyed orders, which is considered, in military, the first requisite of a soldier. Were they raised and sent to Alamance and Caswell without authority of law? The act above referred to empowers the governor to call out the militia to aid in the suppression of the insurrection. Was this militia? Chap. 22, laws of the special session of 1868, entitled, "An act to organize a militia of North Carolina," provides for a militia, a volunteer militia and a detailed militia; for the detailed militia, certain qualifications are required that are not prescribed for volunteers—age, residence, and that each member must be a qualified elector of the state; none of which requisites are mentioned in the 8th section, authorizing volunteers; and the reason a good one, that while the governor may accept the services of persons under or over the ages required, he cannot compel the same to serve.

As to what name the volunteer regiments were called by, even did the statute express the maxim, *de minimus non curat lex*, might well apply. Thus I am of opinion that the force was legal; if not, the language of the statute is such that, without evil intent, it might be so construed. Lastly, under the first head, I come to consider the right to arrest, detain and maltreat. 'Tis here we call into service that faculty which makes the theory of law so beautiful, and well calculated to maintain right and suppress wrong,—this close discrimination, the balance pivot on which rests the scales of justice. What power had the respondent a right to exercise over the insurrectionary counties—for no one will deny he had a right so to declare them under the law?—power to arrest and detain all insurgents in an ordinary insurrection, those who are found in open arms against the authorities; but in Alamance and Caswell, no one being in open insurrection, who had the respondent a right to arrest? Certainly, all those who are guilty of aiding in bringing about that state of things, which the statute declares to be an insurrection. It being proved that disguised men under cover of night committed the most heinous offences, there could be no crime in arresting any one of their number; but as they concealed their persons by disguises and acted in the night time, who they were no one could tell, and only strong suspicions could attach to any one; and if the respondent had caused persons to be arrested and detained from the proper motives, thus far he might well be acquitted of brutality; for section seventeen of the bill of rights declares that no man ought to be deprived of his liberty, &c., save by the law of the land. The Shoffner bill suspends the law of the land, so far as it declares and is not directly in conflict with an expressed law of a higher nature, substituting these for the military law. The maltreatment, as proven to have been inflicted upon some of the prisoners, I need not say is shocking to humanity. Yet, as it is not proven that the respondent ordered or approved of the same, he is, therefore, not to be condemned for the act of a subordinate exceeding this authority.

Article 3d alleges that the respondent caused to be arrested Josiah Turner, junior, in the county of Orange, without authority of law. It is admitted that Josiah Turner, junior, was arrested in the county of Orange, but that it was done neither by the order or approval of the respondent. The facts here are to be inquired into, was it done by the order of the respondent. While the declaration of the officer in command would not be sufficient to convict the respondent—as knowledge of man proves that in order to give importance to their acts, they will intimate and even declare their authority to have been derived from the highest possible source. Yet this, accompanied with the declaration of the respondent in the presence of Mr. Gorman, together with the immediate arrest, leaves the fact beyond doubt.

Articles fifth and sixth alleges:

1st. That the respondent caused to be arrested certain citizens of the counties of Alamance and Caswell without authority of law. This is set forth under article first.

2d. That being so arrested and detained, they applied to the chief justice for the writ of *habeas corpus*, which was granted; that the respondent, through George W. Kirk, refused to obey the writ or make return thereto. It is admitted by the respondent that the writ was obtained and that George W. Kirk, by his order, refused to obey the same, consequently the respondent refused to obey the writ for *facit per aliam facit per se* is the language of the law. Then did the respondent have any right or authority to disobey the writ, as the writ of *habeas corpus* demands the production of the body of the person detained. Any disobedience carries with it a suspension of the writ, and the 21st section, bill of rights, expressly states "that the privileges of the writ of *habeas corpus* shall not be suspended." Could the respondent have been mistaken as to his powers? No law or statute confers such authority, and in addition, the chief justice, the expositor of the law, had declared the writ of *habeas corpus* was not suspended. Yet, after being served with the above declared and adjudged opinion, the respondent did, by means of armed force, suspend the only safeguard to individual liberty, the great writ of *habeas corpus.*

The seventh article alleges that the respondent made warrants on the treasury without authority of law. The law is contained in 21st section of 22d chapter, special session 1868.

It now remains to inquire into the eighth article. I shall only inquire as to the right of the respondent to disregard the writ of injunction. Finding no precedent, as no immediate necessity arose for the total disregard of the mandate of a judge of the state, save the payment of troops who were aiding in the crime of suspending the highest writ known to the law, I am of opinion that the respondent could have been actuated by no other motive than that of carrying out his own purposes, regardless of civil authority in any part of the state, which is criminal in any officer of trust.

Thus I have endeavored to give the reasons which have governed my action, without going into the minute detail of evidence, or encumbering my opinion with numerous references—I hope, also, without being carried away from the immediate subject, by discussing the propriety of placing into the hands of one man arbitrary powers, or expressing a just abhorrence of acts in themselves unpardonable, and with which, it is to be hoped, North Carolina may never again be afflicted, nor her representatives be called upon to condemn. And while the conclusion to which I have arrived differs in some particulars from that of my personal and political friends, I am willing to accord to them motives as pure, intentions as just and honorable as I am conscious have actuated myself.

Hoping, then, that our action may be a lasting rebuke to misrule and to the lust of ungoverned ambition; that it may inspire the virtuous with a new attachment to liberty, and a yet stronger determination ever to support the just administration of the laws within the borders of our noble state; and lastly, having made every possible allowance for that misguided and erring judgment which, without necessarily supposing evil intent, may, in part, have led to the crime which we condemn,

I shall not hesitate to vote guilty on the third, fifth, sixth and eighth articles; that the respondent be removed from office, and that he be forever disqualified from holding any position of trust within the gift of that people he attempted to dishonor, or under that law he so wantonly violated.

---

## OPINION OF SENATOR J. A. GILMER.

In arriving at a just conclusion for a proper vote on each of the articles, I have carefully attended to all the suggestions of counsel for as well as against the guilt of the respondent. Representing in this senate, as I do, the people of Alamance, among and against whom a number of the misdemeanors and crimes alleged were committed, I have sought to throw off all influences and impressions which were, of course, obtained from a thorough acquaintance with that people, their habits, views and condition during the period through which they were under the ban of the respondent's proclamation of 7th March, 1870, and have, in good faith, endeavored to decide the issues involved in this trial, as I have been sworn, "truly and impartially," and "*according to the evidence.*"

Though not required by law or precedent to be charged with the same nicety and particularity of words and circumstances, the eight articles of impeachment are, in my opinion, analagous to bills of indictment under our criminal code, (see C. J. Pearson's opinion, page 940 of this trial,) and therefore I have been obliged to vote upon each article *as a whole,* and "as charged" in the whole article.

In this view I apprehend I may not have the entire concurrence of other members of this court, of eminent legal ability, yet in the celebrated trial of President Johnson this question was raised and clearly decided by C. J. Chase, then presiding, and his opinion seems to have been unanimously assented to by the United States senate. On page 480, 2d volume of the trial, C. J. Chase says:

"In conformity with what seemed to be the general wish "of the senate when it adjourned last Thursday, the chief jus- "tice, in taking the vote on the articles of impeachment will "adopt the mode sanctioned by the practice in the cases of "Chase, Peck and Humphries.

* * * * * * * *

"The chief justice has carefully considered the suggestion "of the senator from Indiana, (Mr. Hendricks) which appeared "to meet the approval of the senate, that in taking the vote "on the 11th article, the question should be put on each "clause, and has found himself unable to divide the article as "suggested. The article charges *several facts, but they are so "connected* that they make but *one allegation*, and they are "charged as constituting *one misdemeanor*."

Believing my duty and the law to be as above recited, I have unhesitatingly voted that the respondent is "guilty" *as charged* in each of the eight articles, respectively, except the first, upon that one I have voted he was not guilty *as charged.* In such vote, I should regret to be misunderstood. Upon inspection of the first article, it will be seen that it is therein distinctly charged that the respondent

1st. Did, on the 7th of March, 1870, of his own false, corrupt and wicked mind and purpose, proclaim and declare that the county of Alamance, &c., was in insurrection; and

2nd. Did send illegal and disreputable bodies of armed men into said county, and suspended civil authority therein; and

3rd. Did by and through such illegal means, arrest many peaceful and law-abiding citizens in said county; and

4th. Did detain, imprision, hang, &c., and otherwise maltreat the same, giving their names.

Now, as to the respondent's guilt, as charged, in the above recited 2nd, 3rd and 4th sub-divisions or clauses of the first article, I have entertained no doubt, and had my views of the law permitted me thus to separate those three clauses, excluding the first, I would, unhesitatingly have voted "guilty," as it will be seen I *did* vote, upon the identical charges reproduced in the seventh article. It is upon the first of the above clauses of the first article that my opinion has been undecided, and *that* being a part and evidently the most prominent part of *the* "high crime" charged in the first article, which I had to vote upon as "one allegation," I gave the respondent the benefit of my indecision. It will be remembered that the extraordinary "Shoffner act," as it is called, was passed on the 29th January, 1870. The respondent's proclamation in regard to Alamance county was on the 7th March, 1870. This "Shoffner act," though in my opinion unconstitutional, *allowed* the respondent, "whenever *in his* "*judgment* the civil authorities in any county are unable to " protect its citizens in the enjoyment of life and property to " declare such county to be *in a state of insurrection.*"

Now, it is shown in the evidence, that the impressions made on the mind of the respondent, in regard to the security of life and property in Alamance county, were derived from men, citizens of that county, who, like the Messrs. Albright, were both his party and confidential friends, and some of whom officers in the judicial administration of the county. These men doubtless detailed to him *their* views of the extent of crime and terror in the county. Is it therefore unreasonable to suppose that, *thus informed*, the respondent may have concluded, that as far as Alamance county was concerned, there was this insecurity? If this was *his judgment*, he had he right so to proclaim, under said "Shoffner act." Now, it is not a question for me, in this connection, to decide whether there was or was not an *insurrection*. Technically speaking, there was, indeed, no insurrection nor anything like an insurrection, in either of the counties, nor could any *proclamation* of the respondent possibly make one, unless it had theretofore existed.

The constitution of North Carolina here steps in for the

guidance of the respondent, and according to *its* behests should he have acted. It says "the governor shall have "power to call out the *militia*, to execute the law, to *suppress* "riots and *insurrections*, &c. Article XII, section 2." For *no other* purposes, though, can he even use the lawful militia in arresting citizens of the state. After issuing his proclamation, (the legal effect of which, *under the "Shoffner act,"* was simply a declaration on his part, that, *in his judgment*, life and property were insecure in Alamance county,) the respondent proceeded further at his own peril. It was his duty *next, to see to it* that there really was an *insurrection* before he exercised any such powers over the *militia* in regard thereto. Is it not probable, from his long delay in making any use of the militia thereafter, that he *then* knew he had gone as far as he could, legally? I incline to the opinion, from the *evidence* in the cause, that the plan of sending for Kirk to recruit the force that afterwards appeared on the stage, had not then been determined on, and was only so determined on, under the counsel and advice of others, when, as a part of the same plan, the county of Caswell was also proclaimed to be in a state of iusurrection, while in said county the proof shows he had no reason to suspect the existence of any conspiracies, nor, from any representations coming therefrom, that there was any insecurity whatever. For these latter reasons I voted that the respondent was "*guilty*" as charged in the second article.

But little space in this opinion, as I conceive, after the exhausting arguments and high authority cited by the managers in the course of the trial, can be given to the remaining articles. No sufficient justification has been shown for the illegal arrest of Turner, and indeed nothing, except the fact that it was done in a moment of passion or great excitement. I have therefore voted "guilty" on the 3d article.

The fourth, fifth and sixth articles may be considered together. They unitedly charge the unlawful arrests of numbers of peaceful and law-abiding citizens of both counties, and their imprisonment and detention, all by the means of an unlawful force of reckless armed men, under command and direction of respondent's agents, sent and instructed thereto, and also the refusal of the respondent through his said agents, to obey the mandates of the writs of *habeas corpus*, issued by supreme judicial authority in the state, in the cases of Moore and of others. There being no *insurrections*, the effort of the respondent to supplant the civil authority by the military, and by this means to make arrests, *at all*, without warrant, was in violation of sections 9 and 17 of the declaration of the rights of the people. His manifest purpose to try, at least, a portion of such arrested persons, was directly in the face of sections 12 and 13 of the same instrument. His refusal to obey the writs of *habeas corpus* was simply annulling the dearest and most positively declared of those rights, to-wit: "The "privileges of the writ of *habeas corpus* shall *not* be suspended." See section 21—also section 18. And the *means* employed by the respondent, (not even by himself regarded as *militia*, but as "state troops,") by which these infractions of the organic law were consummated, were, in my opinion, by reason of their manner of organization and mustering in, their ages and their citizenship, clearly illegal. See constitution, article XII, section 1, and laws 1868, chapter 22. Upon the fourth, fifth and sixth articles; therefore I have voted guilty.

The foregoing reasons will mainly apply to the seventh article, which charges, in addition to the raising of the same illegal force, (whereby said unwarranted arrests were committed in both of said counties, and cruel and inhuman treatment was inflicted upon some of such arrested persons,) also the drawing from the treasury of the state large sums of money for their compensation. If the force were thus illegally organized, it was unlawful to pay them such sums, as was shown to have been done through the agency of respondent. He is therefore "guilty" as charged in this article.

In order to secure such unlawful payments, it is shown, as charged in the *eighth* article, that highly improper official acts were committed by the respondent, in contempt of another highly remedial writ, issued by other competent authority in the state, whereby, in my opinion, he is "guilty" as charged.

## OPINION OF SENATOR R. K. SPEED.

The facts in the above opinion of Senator Gilmer, are, as I understand them ; and I concur in the reasoning and adopt the conclusions.

---

## OPINION OF SENATOR W. A. ALLEN.

The charges contained in the eight articles of impeachment under which the respondent is arraigned before the bar of the senate for trial, may be conveniently arranged as follows:

*First.* That the respondent falsely, corruptly and wickedly proclaimed and declared the counties of Alamance and Caswell, in a state of insurrection.

*Second.* That he unlawfully and without warrant, and in subversion of the laws and the constitution arrested, detained, imprisoned and otherwise maltreated peaceable and law abiding citizens of said counties.

*Third.* That he unlawfully and without warrant, arrested the Hon. Josiah Turner, jr.

*Fourth.* That he unlawfully and in subversion of law and the constitution, suspended the privilege of the writ of *habeas corpus.*

*Fifth.* That he unlawfully recruited an army of desperate and lawless characters and equipped them as an army of soldiers, and unlawfully made his warrants upon the treasurer of the state for large sums of money for its support and maintainance.

*Sixth.* That he wickedly, intending to suspend and subvert the laws of the state, incited, ordered, procured and commanded

A. D. Jenkins to defy and disregard a *writ* of injunction, issued by one of the superior court judges of the state.

The foregoing, I think, are the material charges under the different specifications against the respondent. My purpose is to examine into the truth of these charges candidly and according to the solemn obligations of the oath I have taken, to try the respondent impartially. I have no revenge to gratify in this matter, and no unkind personal feeling to promote. I enter upon the discharge of the high, solemn and important duty, with feelings of pain and mortification. That North Carolina, my native state, should be the first state in the Union to prefer articles of impeachment against her governor, is a matter of pain and mortification to the good citizens of the commonwealth. With every disposition to judge charitably, and at the same time justly, I approach the investigation.

Did the respondent falsely, corruptly and wickedly proclaim and declare the said counties of Alamance and Caswell in insurrection? The answer of the respondent admits that he proclaimed and declared the said counties in insurrection, and the only question on this branch of the investigation, therefore is, as to whether he did it falsely, corruptly and wickedly. In other words, were the said counties in insurrection when so declared by the respondent, for I take it that the corrupt and wicked purpose necessarily follows if it appears that the proclamations are untrue, unless the contrary appears from the evidence, and the burden of proof is on the respondent to show this. As I understand the position of the respondent, it is not pretended by him that these counties were in insurrection according to the general legal understanding of that term, but it is insisted that the "civil authorities" in these counties were "unable to protect the citizens in the enjoyment of life and property," and that, therefore, the respondent was authorized by the act of the general assembly, ordinarily known as the "Shoffner" act, to proclaim and declare said counties in insurrection. Did this act so authorize the respondent? Every act of the legislature must be construed to be consistent with the constitution, unless the contrary clearly appears. In using the term "insurrection" in the "Shoffner" act, as it is familiarly called, I suppose, therefore, that the legislature used it in the same sense in which it is used in the constitution, and as there is nothing in the constitution indicating that the framers of that instrument intended to give the word "insurrection" any other than the ordinary signification, it seems clear to my mind that the term "insurrection," as used in the act of the legislature, was intended to mean an "insurrection" in its usual sense. If these propositions are correct, it will follow that the enquiry is, whether these counties were in "insurrection" in point of fact according to the usual legal meaning of that term? I have already said that, as I understood the position taken by the respondent, he does not pretend that such was the case. The act of the legislature, under which the respondent undertakes to justify, recites "That the governor is hereby authorized and empowered, whenever in his judgment the civil authorities in any county are unable to protect its citizens in the enjoyment of life and property, to declare such county to be in a state of insurrection, &c. The commission of a great number of crimes in a county will not, I submit, under the wording of *even this statute*, justify the declaration of insurrection while the "civil authorities" are unmolested and uninterrupted in the administration of public justice, and the execution of the laws is unresisted. This view, to my mind, is irresistible, for to conclude that the "civil authorities are unable to protect its citizens in the enjoyment of life and property," while they are uninterrupted and unresisted in the exercise of their power, is to admit a weakness in the administration of the laws inconceivable, and such a conclusion could only have the effect to bring into contempt the administration of the laws by civil authority, and would justify either the abolition of the system, or the removal of the weak and imbecile authorities, as it might appear that the one or the other was at fault. I conclude that a state of insurrection cannot exist where the "civil authorities" are in the full, free and unrestrained exercise of power. The proof in this case is full that there was no resistance to the execution of the laws in Alamance and Caswell. The courts were regularly held, and the officers say that they could execute any process or warrant in their hands. There was no resistance to the *execution* of the laws. Alamance and Caswell were not, therefore, in "insurrection" in point of fact, and if this be so then it follows from the premises herein laid down that the respondent's proclamation was false as charged, and that he knew it to be so.

*Secondly*. Did the respondent unlawfully arrest, detain, hold, imprison and otherwise maltreat, many of the peaceable and law-abiding citizens of said counties? The respondent in his answer admits the arrest and detention of the persons named in the articles of impeachment. Were these arrests made unlawfully and without warrant, is, therefore, the question for investigation? If there was no insurrection existing in the territory in which the arrests were made, it must most certainly follow that they were unlawfully made, unless made by peace officers in the ordinary discharge of their duties, or by due process issued by some magistrate. The provisions of our law are clear, distinct and emphatic in reference to this matter, and cannot be misunderstood. If the arrests were made under warrants, or in due course of law, it is matter of defence, and it devolved upon the respondent to show the authority under the plea of justification. The mere fact that violations of the criminal law were committed in these counties is not a sufficient justification. There must be resistance to the execution of the laws. No such proof has been offered in evidence. I conclude, therefore, that the second charge has been established according to the rules of evidence obtaining in courts of justice.

*Thirdly*. Did the respondent without any lawful authority arrest the Hon. Josiah Turner in the county of Orange?

The answer to this article admits the detention, but denies that the respondent ordered the arrest. The question presented here is one of fact, as a justification in law can hardly be said to have been pretended even faintly. The proof is satisfactory—indeed full and complete.

The fourth charge is an exceedingly grave and serious one. The privilege of the writ of *habeas corpus* has ever been held among the dearest rights of the citizen of the United States. Without the right to have the legality of the *caption*, *detention* and *imprisonment* of the citizen inquired into, the liberty of which we so much boast, becomes a mere empty sound, without any foundation. Indeed, it becomes a false and hypocritical cry. Our revolutionary fathers who framed the constitution of the United States duly appreciated this great and important right, and guarded it by inserting it into that instrument among the prohibitions upon the powers of the congress, paragraph 2, sec. 9, of art. 1: "The privilege of the writ of *habeas corpus* shall not be suspended, unless when in cases of rebellion or invasion the public safety may require it" The present constitution of North Carolina emphatically says, "the privilege of the writ of *habeas corpus shall not be suspended*"—a positive prohibition without exception. The right to suspend this great privilege, even by the highest authority of the United States, is utterly inconsistent with a time of peace, and the framers of our fundamental law have cautiously guarded the right of the citizen in this particular. Except in "cases of rebellion or invasion when the public safety may require it," the privilege of this great *writ of right* can never be suspended. Only in a time of war can any authority in the United States exercise this power. If our state constitution were entirely silent on the subject it is believed that the constitution of the United States is sufficient to prohibit any state authority from its exercise without the express consent of congress. In the second paragraph of section 10 of the 1st article of the constitution of the United States, the following language occurs: "No state shall, without the consent of congress, lay any duty of tonnage, *keep troops*, or ships of war in time of peace, enter into any agreement or compact with another state, or with a foreign power, *or engage in war*, unless actually invaded, or in such imminent danger as will not admit of delay." It will, therefore, be seen that the states are forbidden "*to engage* in war, and as the right to suspend the writ of *habeas corpus*, at most, exists in even the United States authorities *only* "when in cases of rebellion and invasion the public safety may require it," surely it can hardly be contended that any state authority which is forbidden to "engage in war" can exercise this power, which is only incident to a state of war—"*rebellion or invasion.*" No more serious charge could be brought against the respondent. Is the charge sustained by the proof in the case? Did the respondent suspend the privilege of this *great writ of right?* That he did refuse to obey the writ, I think, is admitted in the answer of the respondent. On pages 30 and 31 of respondent's answer, the following language will be found: "Furthermore this respondent admits that the said Adolphus G. Moore applied to the honorable Richmond M. Pearson, chief justice of North Carolina, for the writ of *habeas corpus*, to the end set forth in said fifth article, and that the said chief justice caused the said writ to be issued and directed to the said George W. Kirk, commanding him to produce the body of said Moore, at the time and place alleged in said fifth article, and this respondent further admits that the said writ was served on the said Kirk, and that the said Kirk made no return thereto, and refused to obey the same, and that this failure on the part of said Kirk to make return to said writ and to produce the body of said Moore in obedience thereto, was done by the order of this respondent as governor of North Carolina: I take this to be an admission that he refused to obey the writ, and having an organized military force under orders to resist the execution of the writ, it amounted in point of fact to suspending the writ. Was the respondent authorized to do this by the constitution and laws of the state? I have undertaken to show that the constitution of the United States forbids the exercise of this extraordinary power by any authority of a state. I have unquestionably shown that the constitution of North Carolina positively forbids the suspension of the writ. How then can the respondent justify the exercise of the power? He undertakes this task by asserting that these counties were in insurrection. In my argument upon the first charge, I undertook to show that there could not be a state of insurrection where the "civil authorities" were in the full, free and unrestrained exercise of their powers, and were not resisted in the execution of the laws. I also referred to the proof in this case to show that there was no resistance to the execution of the laws in Alamance and Caswell, and that the "civil authorities" were in the full, free and unrestrained exercise of their powers. If my conclusions were correct the defence on this point necessarily fails. But it is contended that the act of the legislature conferred upon the respondent a discretionary power, and that we cannot go behind the proclamation to ascertain how the fact is in reference to the question of insurrection. I do not believe, as I have heretofore in this opinion undertaken to show, that any such arbitrary power was intended to be conferred by the act of the legislature even as to the proclamation of insurrection. The respondent can not in this way justify an act in direct violation of the constitution. The history of the legislature on this subject negatives any such idea as that the act was intended to confer upon the respondent the power to suspend the privilege of the writ of *habeas corpus* in direct violation of the words of the constitution. All that can be contended with any kind of plausibility, is that the act authorized the respondent to declare a *constructive* insurrection subject to the prohibitions of the constitution of North Carolina. But it is said insurrection did exist for the purposes of the action of the respondent, and that in cases of insurrection a suspension of the writ is a necessary incident. If this were so in ordinary cases, still I maintain that it could not be so in North Carolina under the present constitution, because the power to suspend is positively forbidden. I am free to admit, however, that if the respondent had exercised even this excess of authority with a view to the public good he might be excusable.

How is it in this case? It is perfectly manifest that the respondent exercised this excess of authority for the purpose of promoting partizan ends, and not even to suppress crimes, much less an insurrection. This is manifest from the fact that he arrested individuals against whom not even the suspicion of crime rested. The conduct of the respondent in reference to this charge can not be considered otherwise than as a most flagrant violation of the constitution and laws, and as exhibiting a wickedness of purpose rarely ever equalled in the history of civilization. I am pained to feel compelled to use such strong language, but my indignation at such a flagrant abuse of power I feel ought not to be suppressed. The liberty of the citizen in this honest old commonwealth is too dear to be placed at the mere discretion of any petty tyrant who may happen to be clothed with a "little brief authority." The framers of our fundamental law have been too cautious to preserve and guard the right secured and extorted from tyrants by the best blood of a noble ancestry, for us thus lightly to deal with the subject. The respondent had the right, and it was his duty under the act of the legislature which has been relied on for his defence, whenever he thought it was necessary to aid the "civil authorities in any county to protect its citizens in the enjoyment of life and property," to organize a legal force, such as the law authorized him to organize under the militia laws of the state, and send them in aid of the "civil authorities," and in subordination to civil authority. For the 24th section of the first article of the constitution of our state emphatically says: "A well regulated militia being necessary to the security of a free state, the right of the people to keep and bear arms shall not be infringed; and, as standing armies in time of peace, are dangerous to liberty, they ought not to be kept up, *and the military should be kept under strict subordination to, and governed by the civil power.*" Crimes were committed, it is shown, in the counties of Alamance and Caswell of a character calling for extraordinary diligence on the part of the "civil authorities," and it was the duty of the governor of the state to use all proper power to aid the civil authorities in bringing these culprits to justice, but the language used in the proclamations of the respondent exhibit a partizan feeling unworthy of the high dignity of the office to which the people of the state had called him, and discloses a motive utterly inconsistent with honesty of purpose.

But I have perhaps said enough on this charge, and I therefore pass to the fifth charge embraced under the head of 7th article of the impeachment, and this and the charge contained in the 8th article, I shall notice very briefly, as I have taken more time in considering the preceding than I intended. I have already said that the governor would have been justified in raising or rather organizing the militia in aid of the civil authorities in Alamance and Caswell. He could do nothing more than to send such force as he might by law be authorized to organize in aid of the civil authorities. George W. Kirk, he knew to be a desperate character, and offensive in every respect, and that the respondent employed him for the purpose of stirring up strife, and to produce civil war in our state, by provoking the good people of the state beyond endurance, I do not believe any honest man can doubt. That he had no power, as he did to call into his service, citizens of another state, organize them into an army and use them for the perpetration of untold outrages and cruelties on our citizens, as the evidence shows that he did, and draw his warrants on the treasurer of the state to pay for their services out of the hard earned taxes ot the people, every man who understands the constitution and laws of the state I think must admit. I will not therefore say more on this charge, but will pass to the last and sixth charge contained in the eighth article.

Did the respondent, "wickedly intending to suspend and subvert the laws of the state, and to defy and disregard the lawful authority" of the court, "persuade, incite, order, procure and command A. D. Jenkins" to defy and disregard the writ of injunction," and to deliver the money in his hands to another agent of the respondent to be used for the unlawful purposes alleged in the 8th article?

I shall enter into no details of the evidence to justify my vote on this charge. It is satisfactory to my mind, and I believe to every unprejudiced mind, and I can see no legal justification for it. Having discharged what I conceive to be simply a high and solemn duty, I offer no apoligy to any one, and can only say, if I have erred in my opinion of the law it is an honest error, and being in the interest of individual liberty may be pardonable in a devoted friend to the personal liberty of the citizen.

---

## OPINION OF SENATOR C. H. BROGDEN.

This cause should be decided upon the reasons and presumptions which by law apply to all other criminal accusations. It should be decided upon the great and everlasting principles of truth and justice.

The house of representatives of the state of North Carolina, did, on the 20th day of December, 1870, exhibit to the senate eight articles of impeachment against William W. Holden, who has been put on trial in this senate, sitting as a court of impeachment, to answer the accusations as set forth in said articles.

The law declares that, "The court for the trial of impeach- "ment shall be the senate."

"A court is defined to be a place wherein justice is judically "administered."

Before entering upon this trial, each senator took an oath, "truly and impartially to try and determine the charges in "question, under the constitution and laws, according to the evi- "dence."

This cause then should be "truly and impartially tried and "determined, under the constitution and laws, according to all "the evidence," which should be fully and fairly considered.

The articles of impeachment allege that William W. Holden "did commit high crimes and misdemeanors in office, against "the constitution and laws of the state, and the peace, dignity "and interests thereof."

It is necessary to correctly understand the true meaning and application of those grave and important allegations.

"A crime or misdemeanor, is an act committed or omitted, "in violation of a public law, either forbidding or commanding "it. This general definition comprehends both crimes and mis-"demeanors, which, properly speaking, are mere synonymous "terms; though, in common usage, the word "crimes" is made "to denote such offences as are of a deeper and more atrocious "dye; while smaller faults, and omissions of less consequence, "are comprised under the gentler names of "misdemeanors" "only." Blackstone, Book 4, page 3.

It may be remembered, that although it has been alleged, it has not been shown that the respondent did commit any "high crime," as defined by our constitution, or by any criminal statute law of North Carolina. It has not been alleged that he has committed treason, which is, indeed, a "high crime," and it is clearly defined by section seven of article four of our state constitution, which declaresthat "treason against the state "shall consist only in levying war against it or adhering to its "enemies, giving them aid and comfort." Neither has it been alleged that the respondent has committed murder, arson, burglary or rape, which are also "high crimes." It has not been even pretended that he has committed either one of those "crimes." But he has been accused of "intending to stir up "civil war, and subvert personal and public liberty and the "constitution and laws of this state, and of the United States, "and contriving and intending to humiliate and degrade this "state and the people thereof, and especially the people of the "county of Alamance, and to provoke the people to wrath and "violence."

There is no statute law for inflicting any kind of punishment on any person merely for *intentions*, and the question arises whether it can be a crime or misdemeanor in a single person, without combination or conspiracy with others, to contrive and intend means without executing the schemes. To contrive and intend is an intellectual process, and when not executed by acts done cannot be punished as a crime, however unworthy or vicious. Shall we vainly attempt to do something infinitely more than any other human tribunal on earth has ever attempted to do, and that is to punish a man for what may be his supposed thoughts and intentions? Shall we undertake the punishment of the thoughts, opinions, purposes, conceptions, designs, devices and contrivances of men when not carried into acts? All such allegations are contrary to that reason which is said to be the soul of the law.

But instead of acting unlawfully as it has been alleged, the respondent, it seems, was sustained by the laws under which he acted.

Sections two and three of article twelve of our state constitution declares that "the general assembly shall provide for the organizing, arming, equipping and discipline of the militia, and for paying the same when called into active service. The governor shall be commander-in-chief, and have power to call out the militia to execute the law, suppress riots or insurrection and to repel invasion."

Under this requirement of the constitution, the general assembly passed "an act to organize a militia of North Carolina," ratified the 17th day of August, A. D. 1868. Said act declares that "the militia shall consist of companies, regiments, brigades and divisions as now required by law."

"The regulations of the United States army shall be adhered "to as near as practicable in organizing the militia of this "state."

"The governor is hereby authorized to accept and organize "regiments of volunteer infantry, not exceeding six."

"The said detailed militia shall be under the command of "the governor and be subject to his orders, and may be sent "to any portion of the state by him."

" Any officer of said detailed militia shall have power and it " shall be his duty to use such force as may be necessary to over- " come resistance, in quelling riots or making arrests, and not " otherwise."

Much has been said about accepting as volunteers in the militia service some persons who were non-residents of the state, and not of the age prescribed by law for militia duty. There is no law in this state to prevent or exclude volunteers on account of their age or residence, if the proper officers think such volunteers are capable of performing the duty required of them.

As to what has been said relative to calling the volunteer militia state troops, instead of militia, it is only necessary to remark that the name was changed upon the suggestion of Judge Clarke, who was colonel of the first regiment, as he testified before this court.

The facts have been conclusively proved by scores of reliable witnesses during this trial, that the most barbarous and atrocious crimes and outrages were committed on peaceable and unoffending citizens by large bodies of armed and disguised midnight murderers and assassins, commonly called Kuklux. That wicked and lawless organization, not having the fear of God before their eyes, and moved and instigated by the devil, continued to murder, shoot, hang and scourge men, and yet none of the guilty perpetrators of those terrible, hideous and horrid crimes and outrages were ever punished by the civil law.

That was indeed an extraordinary state of affairs. It has been proved that the Kuklux organizations had ten different camps in operation in the county of Alamance alone. It has been also proved that Albert Murray, the sheriff of Alamance, was chief of the Kuklux camp No. 1, in said county, and he so stated in his examination on oath. It has been also proved that some of the conservative magistrates of the county were members of the Kuklux organization, and that the deputy sheriff was also a Kuklux.

Each member of the Kuklux organization was required to take the following unlawful oaths:

"You solemly swear in the presence of the Almighty God that you will never reveal what is now about to come to your knowledge, and you will never reveal the names of the men that initiate you, and that you have not, and do not belong to the Red Strings, U. L. or H. of A. M., or other political society or party whose aim and intention is to destroy the rights of the states and of the people, and to elevate the negro with the white man, and you are opposed to all such organizations. So help you God."

2d oath. "You now further swear in the presence of the Almighty God, that you will be true to the principles of the brotherhood and to the members; that you will never reveal any of its edicts, orders, or principles to any person, not even a known brother, or that you are a member yourself, or who are members, and that you will obey all calls and summons of the chief of your camp when in your power to do so; and should any member reveal any of the acts, orders or secrets of this brotherhood, that you will assist in punishing them in any way that the camp may direct, and that you will not initiate or allow in this brotherhood any radical or any one who sympathizes with them or has radical views, it in your power to prevent. And should you know or see any brother or his family imposed upon by any radical or negro, you will go to their assistance and render them all the aid in your power, or should you know them to be in imminent danger, you will immediately inform them and go to their assistance, and should you hear the word of alarm given, that you will go immediately to ascertain the cause and tender all the aid in your power. So help you God."

6th. There shall be six (6) regular initiated members in this district before they have a right to form a camp and organize.

7th. All members are requested to be suitably disguised and ready for all occasions.

8th. All members are honor bound to induce all true conservatives to join the brotherhood; in no case to mention such to another.

9th. The word of distress shall never be used by any member only in cases of imminent danger or peril.

The following letter to Gov. Holden from five prominent citizens of Alamance, justices of the peace and the clerk of the superior court, will explain itself:

GRAHAM, N. C., February 28th, 1870.

*His Excellency* W. W. HOLDEN, *Governor of North Carolina:*

DEAR SIR:—We are under the painful necessity of informing you of the commission of the most atrocious murder ever committed in any community. On the night of the 26th inst., a body of disguised men came into our town at about one o'clock, broke into the house of Wyatt Outlaw, and took him to the public square near the court house and hung him to the limb of a tree, where he was found hanging the next morning, his neck broken, with a piece of paper writing pinned to him, "Beware you guilty, both white and black." This body of disguised men were seen by three of the undersigned, and are estimated to consist of from seventy to one hundred in number. Outlaw was an industrious mechanic, well to-do and prospering. No crime can be alleged against him except that he is a colored man, a republican, and has presumed to hold the office of town commissioner for two terms, once by your appointment and the second by an election of the people. On the same night these disguised men broke into the house of Henry Holt, a colored man. Holt escaped, but they left word with his wife that if he did not leave by next Saturday night they would hang him, and cut a cord from his bed with which they hung Wyatt. Within the last two weeks brutal outrages have become common, almost nightly, and people have become so terrified that they dare not report the outrages committed on them. Every republican in the county who has stood up for his own rights and that of the freedmen is in danger. The civil authorities are powerless to bring these offenders against law and humanity to justice. Out of the numberless cases occurring in the county, not one has yet been indicted, much less punished, and we know of no way in which these bands of lawless men can be put down and punished except by the strong arm of the military. Our people are not only alarmed, but many are in great danger. If these disturbances are not arrested many will have to seek safety from home.

We respectfully submit to your excellency to take such steps as will insure the quiet of the county and the safety of all citizens.

Very respectfully,

H. A. BADHAM,
J. W. HARDEN.
P. R. HARDEN,
HENRY M. RAY.
W. A. ALBRIGHT.

Under such extraordinary circumstances, it was highly necessary to resort to extreme measures to suppress such diabolical crimes, as it sometimes becomes necessary for the surgeon to amputate an arm or a leg to save the life of the patient. Extreme cases justify the application of extreme remedies.

The governor issued proclamation after proclamation in vain. The Kuklux organizations still continued to murder, hang, shoot and scourage peaceable and law-abiding citizens. The sworn testimony before this court has shown that more than twenty white citizens, and more than forty colored citizens were cruelly beaten, scouraged, shot and hung, by bodies of armed and disguised murderers and assassins, and none of whom were punished for their atrocious crimes.

On the 29th of January, 1870, the general assembly passed "An act to secure the better protection of life and property."

The first section of said act declares as follows:

"That the governor is hereby authorized and empowered,

whenever in his judgment the civil authorities in any county are unable to protect its citizens in the enjoyment of life and property, to declare such county to be in a state of insurrection, and to call into active service the militia of the state to such an extent as may become necessary to suppress such insurrection; and in such case the governor is further authorized to call upon the president for such assistance, if any, as in his judgment may be necessary to enforce the law." This act and "an act to organize a militia of North Carolina," ratified the 17th day of August, A. D. 1868, authorized the governor as commander-in-chief to organize and call the militia into active service.

It has been alleged that the respondent acted in violation of law. But it may also be affirmed that extraordinary cases may sometimes justify extraordinary means and remedies, as when it becomes absolutely necessary for the surgeon to amputate a leg or an arm in order to save the life of the patient.

In speaking of the insurrection in the state of Pennsylvania, in the year 1794, Aaron Bancroft, in his life of George Washington, president of the United States, page 144, says:

"The secretary of the treasury, the secretary of war, and the attorney general, were of opinion that the president was bound by the most sacred obligations to use the means placed at his disposal, faithfully to execute the law. They therefore advised him to try the power of the government to coerce submission; and from policy and humanity to march a force into the insurgent counties too strongly to be resisted."

The president did not hesitate to do his duty. Without exerting the means of prevention in his power, he could not see the laws prostrated, and the authority of the United States defied.

On the 7th of August he issued the proclamation which the law made a pre-requisite to the employment of force. In it he gave a recapitulation of the measures of government, and of the opposition of the insurgents, and thus proceeded: "Whereas, it was in his judgment necessary, under the circumstances of the case, to take measures for calling forth the militia in order to suppress the combinations aforesaid, and to cause the laws to be duly executed, and he had accordingly determined so to do; feeling the deepest regret for the occasion, but withal the most solemn conviction that the essential interests of the Union demanded it; that the very existence of government, and the fundamental principles of social order were involved in the issue; and that the patriotism and firmness of all good citizens were seriously called upon to aid in the suppression of so fatal a spirit." The proclamation closed by ordering all insurgents, and all other persons whom it might concern, on or before the first day of the ensuing September, to disperse and retire to their respective homes. Orders were on the same day issued to the governors of New Jersey, Pennsylvania, Maryland and Virginia for their respective quotas of twelve thousand men, which at a subsequent period was increased to fifteen thousand, who were to be held in readiness to march at a minute's warning.

Reluctant to draw the sword upon his fellow citizens, the president at this awful crisis, determined to make one more attempt to reclaim by mild entreaty his deluded countrymen. The attorney general, Judge Yates, and Mr. Ross, were commissioned to bear to the insurgents a general amnesty for all past crimes, on condition of future obedience; but the clemency of the government was again spurned, and its power disregarded.

The insurgents, forming an opinion from the language of democratic societies, and from the publications in anti-federal newspapers, seem to have entertained the supposition that their disaffection was generally felt by the citizens of the United States, and that the attempt to suppress them would issue in a revolution of the government.

That the executive of Pennsylvania might act in unison with the national administration, Governor Mifflin had also issued a proclamation, and appointed commissioners to join those of the nation.

The faction opposed to the government insidiously attempted to obstruct the execution of the orders of the president, but without effect; the community expressed unequivocally the determination to support the government and to execute the laws. The personal influence of Governor Mifflin surmounted the obstructions which arose from the insufficiency of the militia laws of Pennsylvania; the officers and men of the respective states obeyed the summons with an alacrity that exceeded the expectation of the most sanguine, and the required number of troops was seasonably in readiness to obey the orders of the commander-in-chief.

The command of the expedition was given to Governor Lee, of Virginia, and the governors of Pennsylvania and New Jersey commanded the militia of their respective states under him. This force moved into the insurgent counties and bore down all opposition. Thus by the vigor and prudence of the executive, this formidable and alarming insurrection was, without the sacrifice of a life, subdued.

The president attributed this insurrection, in a great degree, to the influence of the democratic societies. This opinion he expressed in his private letters and in his public communications to the legislature. In a letter to Mr. Jay, he observed, "That the self-created societies, who have spread them-"selves over this country, have been laboring incessantly to "sow the seeds of distrust, jealousy, and, of course, discontent, "hoping thereby to effect some revolution in the government, "is not unknown to you. That they have been the fomenters "of the western disturbances, admits of no doubt in the mind "of any one who will examine their conduct. But, fortunately, "they have precipitated a crisis for which they were not pre-"pared; and thereby have unfolded views which will, I trust, "effect their annihilation sooner than it might have happened."

Gen. WASHINGTON had the firmness and independence to denounce these societies to the national legislature, and to lend his personal influence to counteract their designs, thereby bringing upon himself their resentment.

In 1794, fifteen thousand men were called into active service from the states of New Jersey, Pennsylvania, Maryland, and Virginia, to suppress the insurrection in certain western counties in Pennsylvania, although there had not been even one single individual murdered, hung, shot or scourged, by the insurgents in said counties.

In North Carolina, organized bodies of armed and disguised men, under the name of Kuklux, have committed the most atrocious outrages upon scores and scores of peaceable citizens, at their own homes and in the darkness of night; and yet no person has been punished for any of those horrid crimes.

On the 26th of February, 1870, Wyatt Outlaw, colored, a citizen of Alamance, was taken from his house in the town of Graham, by disguised persons known as the Kuklux, and hanged by the neck until he was dead, on a tree near the court house.

On the 21st day of May, 1870, John W. Stephens, white, state senator from the county of Caswell, was murdered in open daylight, in the courthouse in the village of Yanceyville.

On the 13th of May, 1870, Robin Jacobs, colored, living near Leasburg, Caswell county, was murdered at night by a band of Kuklux.

But it is deemed to be unnecessary, at present, to recapitulate the voluminous mass of evidence brought out before the senate during this impeachment trial, which shows that about seventy citizens, white and colored, were scourged, shot, hung and murdered by bodies of armed and disguised Kuklux.

T. M. Shoffner, a republican senator in the general assembly of this state, from the counties of Alamance and Guilford, was compelled to sacrifice his property, and, to save his life, to make his escape from said county, on account of his opposition to the Kuklux, and his devotion to the government of the United States.

The governor was authorized by law to exercise his own judgment and discretion as to the necessity for declaring the counties of Alamance and Caswell to be in a state of insurrection.

North Carolina is not the only state that has passed laws authorizing the governor, in certain contingencies, to declare any county to be in a state of insurrection.

The legislature of the state of New York, in 1845, passed "an act to enforce the laws and preserve order," similar to "an act to secure the better protection of life and property," passed by the legislature of this state in 1870.

The act of the state of New York vested discretionary power and authority in the governor to call out the militia and to declare any county to be in a state of insurrection. By authority of that act, Governor Silas Wright, of the state of New York, did declare one county to be in a state of insurrection, in 1846, but no proposition was ever brought forward to impeach, or even to censure Gov. Wright, for exercising his discretionary power in declaring a county in insurrection.

"For the law will not cast an imputation on that magistrate whom it entrusts with the executive power, as if he was capable of intentionally disregarding his trust."—Blackstone, Book 1, page 185.

Circumstances sometimes arise which excuse or justify a resort to extreme measures, as when a large and destructive fire is rapidly spreading in a town or city, it may become necessary to demolish and destroy a valuable house in order to check and stop the rapid progress of the fire and to save many other valuable houses. A man's wife or child or some other person may be dangerously sick, and he sends for a physician to come and assist the patient; the physician sends his prescription to the apothecary for quinine, which is generally used for chills and fevers, but the apothecary sends strychnine, which is administered to the patient and causes immediate death. Of course no reasonable man would then allege that the man who first sent for the physician was guilty of any crime. It was his intention to assist in restoring the patient to health.

All public servants, and especially all high public functionaries, must necessarily exercise more or less discretionary powers.

The legislative, executive and judicial departments of our government, each and all, exercise many discretionary powers in the performance of their various duties.

In deciding upon this grave and important question of impeachment, it would be well for us all to bear in mind that charitable and divine advice of St. Paul, which says:

"Let all bitterness, and wrath, and anger, and clamour, and evil speaking be put away from you with all malice."

---

## OPINION OF SENATOR R. F. LEHMAN.

I do not intend to examine in detail the several articles of impeachment; I have not the leisure for such a task, if I had the inclination. I will, however, consider according to my ability, and as a reason for my vote, some of the legal questions involved in this trial. And, first as to the nature of this proceeding. By the constitution of the state, it is expressly provided, "that the judicial power of the state shall be vested in a court for the trial of impeachments, a supreme court, superior courts, courts of justice of the peace and special courts." It is conceived, therefore, that impeachment is a judicial proceeding for the trial of a real crime, and not political, and that the senate, when sitting as such court exercises judicial functions according to existing law. The house of representatives, through its managers, appear before us in the character of accusers, and senators, constituted as a court, perform the functions of a complete supreme judicial tribunal from whose decision there is no appeal. It is the constitutional mode of bringing great offenders to justice for offences of an official criminal character, tending to the subversion of social order, and the regular administration of justice, which by reason of their quality and magnitude are beyond the ordinary process of law, and which the supreme legislative power is alone competent to prosecute with effect. Impeachment, as a mode of criminal procedure, should be resorted to only in extreme cases, when the presumption is great and danger imminent, and whenever the people are satisfied that their ruler has acted in excess of power, and meditated a subversion of their liberties; but every accusation against such ruler, to be well founded, must have or allege a substantial crime for its basis—a crime known to the common or statute law. I take it to be well settled in England, that a court of impeachment must administer the same law as the criminal court, and that the evidence on an impeachment must be the same as on an indictment. "An impeachment is a prosecution of the already known and established law." 4 Blackstone Com. 259. Hence the respondent in this case may, as a matter of right, claim the full benefit of the rule in criminal cases, "that he may only be convicted when the evidence makes the case clear beyond a doubt." In the impeachment trial of the Earl of Macclesfield, which occurred in England about the time of the formation of our federal constitution, it was maintained by the respondent, who was himself an eminent lawyer, that he had committed no act for which he could be indicted, and therefore he had committed no impeachable offence. This case was distinctly put upon the ground, that an act to be impeachable, must be indictable, and amount to a breach of the common law. In Lord Melville's case, determined in 1806, who was impeached for malversation in office, the question was submitted to the common law judges, "whether the acts charged were unlawful so as to be the subject of information or indictment." The judges determined that question in the negative, and this being intimated, he was acquitted. These two cases are the most elaborate on the subject and contain throughout, on all the points presented, a precision of statement, so as to render them worthy to be adopted as precedents, and were determined at a period of time in English history, when party rancor had subsided and the political mind enjoyed a stat rest. And this brings us to a consideration of our own stat the language of which is: "That every officer in the st shall be liable to impeachment for. 1st. Corruption or otl misconduct in his official capacity. 2d. Habitual drunkenne 3rd. Intoxication while engaged in the exercise of his offi 4th. Drunkenness in any public place. 5th. Mental or phy cal incapacity to discharge the duties of his office. 6th. A criminal matter the conviction whereof would tend to brin his office into public contempt." The second, third, fourt and fifth sub-divisions are not the subjects of any particul charge. The sixth sub-division is an accumulative sentenc and gives a definite meaning to the number and character of tl crimes that are impeachable, or in other words, every officer ma be impeached tor any of the offences enumerated, and for an act that may be the subject of an indictment, and none other Having thus disposed of the preliminary questions I proceed to consider in their order the first and second articles Do the facts proved establish the existence of an "insurrec tion" in the counties of Alamance and Caswell? It appears by the evidence that peace officers were ready, and that the courts were open to hear criminal accusations, and to redress wrongs. No officer of the law was resisted. The processes of the courts were unobstructed. It also appears that there existed secret combinations of men, having a common design, to obstruct the fair administration of justice by threats, terrorism, violence, acts of outrage, assassination and murder, who. disguised, and masked, and with arms in hand, rode about under cover of night, to commit these murders and various outrages, to the common terror of the colored population, if not generally to that of those who differed politically from them. This association had its lines of communication, its signs, passwords and grip, and by its rules denied membership to an avowed republican. It assumed the powers of government by bestowing on its members the right to punish, and by promising protection to those who should carry out these unlawful acts of vengeance. So great was the terror that, in the instances in which the perpetrators of the crimes were known, witnesses could not be induced to testify against them, while in the majority of cases, even had there been a disposition to discover them, the identity of the parties could not be recognized. These are the facts. Do they constitute an insurrection within the meaning of the constitution? It is reasonable to suppose that the framers of that instrument employed the term insurrection in the sense affixed to it by the laws of the United States, and as defined in adjudged cases. The governor is empowered to call forth the militia, first, to execute the laws; second, to suppress riots or insurrections, and third to repel invasion. Now, almost the same powers vested in the governor, as commander-in-chief, are by the constitution of the United States, fixed in congress, "to provide for calling forth the militia, to execute the laws of the Union, suppress insurrections, and repel invasions." Congress, to give effect to this provision, passed an act Feb. 28, 1795, of which sections two and three read as follows: "That whenever the laws of the United States shall be opposed, or the execution thereof obstructed in any state by combinations too powerful to be suppressed by the ordinary course of judicial proceedings, or by the powers vested in the marshals by this act, it shall be lawful for the president of the United States to call forth the militia of such state or states as may be necessary to suppress such combinations, and to cause the law to be duly executed," etc. "That whenever it may be necessary in the judgment of the president to use the military force hereby directed to be called forth, the president shall forthwith, by proclamation, command such *insurgents* to disperse," etc. It is well known that this act of 1795 was passed to meet the state of things then existing in particular sections of certain states, and to clothe the president with the power of the government to execute the laws. This act passed in review before the United States supreme court in 1820, while chief justice Marshall presided, in the case of Houston *vs.* Moore, 5 Wharton, 15. Mr. Justice Johnston and

Story delivered opinions. Mr. Justice Story said: "No doubt has been here breathed of the constitutionality of the provisions of the act of 1795, and they are believed to be, in all respects, within the legitimate authority of congress." The act gives the term insurrection a legislative definition, to-wit: That whenever the laws shall be opposed or the execution thereof obstructed in any state by combinations too powerful to be suppressed by the ordinary course of judicial proceedings. A law may be said to be opposed when it is not obeyed, or when one acts contrary to it or resists it either by physical means, by argument, or by other means. It is obstructed when its execution is hindered by a combination of party spirit, of force or otherwise. This recited act was passed to meet the state of things then existing in the interior of Pennsylvania, which was proclaimed, declared and adjudged to be an insurrection, and reference has been made to it to ascertain the meaning of the term in question, as well as to show that the act of January 29, 1870, under which the governor acted is substantially the same in purport. It provides "that the governor is hereby authorized whenever in his judgment the civil authorities in any county are unable to protect its citizens in the enjoyment of life and property to declare such county to be in a state of insurrection, and to call into active service the militia of the state to such an extent as may become necessary to suppress such insurrection, etc. The general assembly, by this act, has defined what facts should constitute an insurrection. Both acts seek to provide against combinations too powerful to be overcome by the ordinary course of law; each act aims to remove the obstructions that may be interposed to the due execution of the law. Both laws were framed to cover the particular state of things then existing in the localities, for which they were intended, and in each the unlawful acts committed were of such a character as to render the life and property of the citizen insecure; to loosen the bonds of society, and to obstruct the due execution of the law. In the one case, by open resistance; in the other, by means *suigeneris*. It is clear to my mind from the evidence that life and property were insecure, that the very state of things contemplated by the Shoffner act existed in these counties, but in my opinion this act conferred on him no power in the matter of calling forth the militia, which he did not before possess under the constitution. It was a useless piece of legislation in that respect. It is assumed therefore as a postulate, that every officer upon whom devolves the exercise of constitutional powers and duties must in the first instance for himself, determine their nature and extent, otherwise he would be a mere machine, acting only when he is acted upon. The governor of the state under the constitution, article 3, section 8, article 12, section 3, has an equal if not greater power than the president, and especially since it is a distinct grant of power to the executive department, the governor, from the very nature of the duty to be performed, must be the exclusive and final judge whenever a necessity exists for calling out the militia. This view of the question is fully sustained by chief justice Pearson in Kendall *vs* Inhabitants of Kingston, 5 Mass. 524. In Martin *vs.* Mott, 12 Wheaton, 29, it was held "that the president of the United States in exercising his power of calling out the militia in certain cases was the exclusive and final judge when that exigency had arisen." Like every other officer, he is liable for any wilful abuse of his discretionary authority, but on principle, no good reason can be assigned why an executive officer should be held to stricter accountability in a judicial tribunal like this, for a mistake in judgment, than a judicial officer, if he were the accused and indicted. But before dismissing the question immediately under consideration, it may be well to look at it in the light of authority, as expressed in adjudged cases. I am also fully aware that as a rule of interpretation the term insurrection should receive the same meaning affixed to it in the books, but upon examination it will be found that this source affords very little aid on the subject, for neither the offence of treason nor insurrection seem to be well defined in the English elementary works and adjudged cases. This being so, the rule is scarcely binding. It must also be remembered that both these crimes are of a political nature, and the adjudged cases, as well as the legislation upon the subject, clearly indicate the political views entertained by those who administered the law. Besides, our constitution was intended for the people, and adopted by them as a plain instrument, easily to be understood, and without any technical distinctions. To proceed. For example, Hawkins says: "Those also who make an insurrection in order to redress a public grievance, whether it be a real or pretended one, and of their own authority attempt with force to redress it are said to levy war against the King, although they have no direct design against his person, inasmuch as they insolently invade his prerogative by attempting to do that by private authority which he by public justice ought to do, which manifestly tends to a downright rebellion; or where great numbers by force attempt to remove certain persons from the King, or to lay violent hands on a privy councillor; or to revenge themselves against a magistrate for executing his office, etc." This definition, with slight modifications, fits our case; and if certain witnesses for the respondent are to be believed, it would require but little ingenuity to show that these combinations of men in their acts and purposes exhibited every element of the crime of treason against the government of the United States. The distinction between treason and insurrection is not easily made by definition. To view it in the light of authority, an insurrection is an open resistance to the lawful authority of the government by opposing a particular law or class of laws, without design wholly to renounce its authority, while treason is an open and avowed renunciation of the authority of the government with the view of changing its jurisdiction and rulers. An insurrection is not necessarily treason, but every treason includes insurrection. The former is aimed at a particular law, measure or policy; the latter is directed against the existence or life of the government itself. It may be assumed as judicially settled in this country, that any combination of men to resist by force the execution of any law, will be *treasonable;* but if the design is not to oppose the execution of the law in all cases, but only in a particular case, such as preventing the arrest of A B, it would only constitute a riot or murder if any one were killed. In treason there must be the overt act of levying war—the employment and exhibition of force, which are the indispensible elements of the crime. But the definition prescribes the quality of the evidence to ascertain the degree of the crime, rather than the quantity or manner of the force to be applied. It is a rule of evidence for the courts. For example: supposing a body of men to be in a position to execute their treasonable purpose, without the aid of military weapons or the employment of force, would it need the presence of such weapons or force to complete the crime? On the trial of Aaron Burr for treason, Chief Justice Marshall in declaring his opinion, uses the following significant language: "No adjudged case has, or it is believed can be produced from those books in which it has been laid down that war cannot be levied *without the actual application of violence to external objects.*" If it be true that according to the books to constitute the crime of treason, or insurrection, there must be the "military array," "the posture of war," "the open resistance to constituted authority," the doctrine is more surprising than instructive, and the *books* need be *revised* and *improved.* For if it be so, it would only require unanimity of sentiment on part of the people to oppose the law or to establish a revolutionary government. It would be more effectual than to measure arms with the government. To illustrate: Supposing a state convention, relying on the almost unanimous consent of the people, should pass an ordinance contravening the authority of the general government in the state, and that all the United States officers in it, through fear, pressure of public sentiment or inclination, should omit to perform their duties, so that the employment of force or violence would be wholly unnecessary to accomplish the purpose. This example presents a case in which there is neither a *levying of war* nor a *rising* against constituted authority according to the books, and yet the law and the government are as effectually subverted as if "weapons" had been used to establish this kind of revolutionary government. The purpose is accomplished, in the language of Chief Justice Marshall, "without the application of violence to external objects," for the simple reason that the use of such violence was unnecessary, the object being effectuated by the force of public opinion. Now, when we reflect that these offences are eminently crimes of motive, and of a political nature, as well as justifiable when the government or its laws are deemed oppressive and odious, it would be difficult to point out a more effectual mode of annulling the power of the government, than the one indicated, without incurring the pains and penalties of treason. I don't believe the doctrine. In my judgment it would be *undeveloped treason* and *insurrection consummated.* But let us admit that the act in question is unconstitutional, nevertheless the governor had the constitutional right and it was his sworn duty to pass upon its construction. His judgment, as evinced by his acts, was that it is constitutional. Our constitution provides that the executive, legislative and judicial functions of the government shall remain separate. By this division of governmental powers into separate departments it follows that the officers who are appointed to discharge the duties of these respective departments are free to act, within the limits of that instrument, and their particular branch, without control from any other, if they act fairly, honestly and within the line of their duty. It will readily be perceived that in a system of government in which powers are thus apportioned and distributed among the several departments, certain duties are imposed upon the several divisions, as well as upon the officers of each. It is in short a government of duties as well as powers, and whenever any officer is called upon to discharge such duty he is, at the same time and instant, also compelled to pass upon the question of constitutional construction. This decision may or may not be conclusive from the very nature and extent of the duty to be performed, and it may or may not be subject to review by another department. A law which is *ipso facto* void is a nonentity, and the executive, as well as every other officer, has an equal right with the legislature and the judiciary to construe the constitution, because the oath to support that instrument is not peculiar to judges, but every officer is required to take it. It defines his powers,—an officer may be wrong in the construction of the law, but if he has acted honestly though erroneously, he will be protected, and the rule embraces the humblest magistrate as well as the highest official civilly as well as criminally. For if this protection were denied, men in accepting office, would shrink from the performance of their necessary duties, in great emergencies, and thereby defeat the due discharge of the functions of government. Our institutions, in theory, as well as in practice, seek a free and untrammelled exercise of every duty, devolving upon constitutional officers, and hold them responsible only when they are guilty of gross misconduct or wilful corruption. The decision of every branch, as of every officer, is entitled to respect, and the judiciary should ;pronounce a law unconstitutional only when the violation is self-evident, but in all cases of doubt it should pronounce in its favor. It is true that a law may prescribe a mere ministerial duty, though void, it should be executed by such ministerial officer on grounds of public convenience, unless it involves political consequences in contravention to the supreme law of the land. For the reasons stated I have concluded that the governor acted honestly when he declared these counties in a state of insurrection; that his judgment is exclusive and final when such a necessity exists; that there was an insurrection within the meaning of the act of assembly; that the governor had a right to pass upon its constitutionality, and if his judgment was erroneous he acted honestly and for the public good, and therefore should be protected from criminal liability. And with this view of the case it is deemed unnecessary to consider the fourth, seventh and eighth articles which contain mere matters of inducement properly belonging to the first and second articles, and probably to the sixth, on the principle that if he had a right to do what is well charged in the first and second articles, the gist of the charges which are criminal and impeachable in the fourth, seventh and eighth articles would follow as necessary incidents to the complete exercise of the powers of the former—and I don't mean by this to justify the illegal manner and desperate character of the force employed, but the conduct of the respondent must not be weighed in golden scales, and I have grave doubts whether he was circumscribed in the choice of means. For in the language of Lord Coke, "When the law granteth anything to any one, *that* also is granted without which the thing itself cannot be." The law always contemplates the beneficial execution of every power, and it grants whatever is necessary to execute it. A commander would cut a very sorry figure if he were required to suppress an insurrection without the power of arming or equipping men, with no means to pay them or facilities to arrest insurgents.

The third article will now briefly be considered. It charged the illegal arrest of Mr. Turner, in the county of Orange,—a county not declared in insurrection. There is some evidence that the respondent believed, and acted on that belief, that Mr. Turner "was at the bottom of all these troubles." Mr. Turner, on the other hand, positively denies, that "he was king of the Kuklux," or ever belonged to, or had any knowledge of these illegal organizations. He admits, however, that in a jocular conversation in his office, with three or four gentlemen, he was introduced as "king of the Kuklux." He neither denied, nor admitted it, but remarked that that was "what Holden said." "It was in this way the thing came about." The senate, by its rulings, excluded every species of testimony tending to show the existence of these organizations, and their connections outside of Alamance and Caswell counties. On principle this was wrong. The respondent was deprived of a full defence by this exclusion. It is admitted, that according to the evidence, the arrest of Mr. Turner was illegal, but there is enough to show that the respondent, honestly, though erroneously, believed him to be, the head and front of this insurrectionary movement. It was an error of judgment which, under the circumstances, should excuse him from criminal liability. If the respondent believed him to be a member of this conspiracy, which had manifested itself in the form of an insurrection, and that he was principal actor in it, he had a right to proceed against him as an insurgent, in any county in the state, however remote he may have been from the scene of the insurrectionary movement. The whole state was his jurisdiction as to insurgents. He was about twenty miles from the insurrectionary district when arrested. His proximity and position were such, that had he been one of them, to enable him successfully to co-operate with them—he was constructively present. Upon the whole I am not fully satisfied, and must give to the respondent the benefit of the doubt.

The fifth and sixth articles, charge the refusal to obey the writ of *habeas corpus* in the specified cases. The first question that presents itself, as a preliminary one, in considering the nature of the offences charged, is, does the constitution itself provide for military government as well as civil? If this question is decided in the affirmative, it will follow as a corollary that the civil protection thrown around the one, by the constitution, cannot be made to apply to cases, coming within the limits of the former—both powers should be complete in themselves, on the principle that "when a general power is given or duty enjoined, every particular power, necessary for the exercise of the one, or the performance of the other, is given by implication." If our constitution has granted the power of creating a military government, whenever the exigency may arise, for that purpose, then the following sections of Art. 1, of that instrument, cannot apply, and are meant to be regulated by the civil branch in a state of peace, and can have no application to a state of war, or insurrection, when the government, in order to suppress it, is, or should be, under martial law. The sections are as follows:

Section 17. "No person ought to be taken, imprisoned, or disseized of his freehold, liberties or privileges, or outlawed or exiled, or in any manner deprived of his life, liberty or property but by the law of the land."

Sec. 21. "The privilege of the writ of *habeas corpus* shall not be suspended."

Sec. 24. "A well regulated militia being necessary to the security of a free state, the right of the people to keep and bear arms shall not be infringed: and as standing armies in time of peace are dangerous to liberty, they ought not to be kept up, and the military should be kept under strict subordination and governed by the civil power."

The language of the seventeenth section is, substantially that of Magna Charta, and it was held that it did not apply to the military power of the English government. But the chief justice says, "The privilege of the wait of *habeas corpus* cannot be suspended." What good can the military avail when their action at every step may be embarrassed by this writ. It belongs and pertains exclusively to the judicial department, and can be employed only when the judicial power has jurisdiction. But while this writ is an arm of the judicial power, and always effective in a state of peace, it cannot reach a party held by the military power, if it be true that it is separate and independent from the civil, for the reason among others, that the judiciary has not the means to prosecute it, unless it infringe upon the rights and invade the functions entrusted to a distinct branch of the government, acting independently and under well defined powers. Even at common law, in case of military arrest, the judiciary had no jurisdiction to proceed by *habeas corpus*, and by parity of reasoning it has no authority, when all the powers of government are distinctly apportioned, as under our constitution—all equal in degree but not in power. The governor controls the militia as head of the executive and political department, and there is no single grant of power to the judiciary, by the constitution under which it may govern that officer, when he calls into service the militia, embracing the whole power of the state; and if the governor, as commander-in-chief, refuses to obey the writ, the judiciary is powerless, and without means to enforce its decree. He necessarily acts under a law peculiar to his department, arising from the nature of the power to be exercised, but which is nevertheless a necessary part of the law of the land, for its object is to be promotive of the public good in restoring peace and tranquility. In Luther *vs.* Borden, 7 How., it is said, "unquestionably a state may use its military power to put down an armed insurrection too strong to be controlled by the civil authority." In the same opinion, it is also held, that a state may declare martial law, which, as I understand it, would be equivalent to an act of war, yet all war making power is denied to the states, severally, and belongs to the general government. This was the case, it will be remembered, of the Dorr rebellion. This decision was put on the ground that a "State may be said to be invaded when she is pressed on all sides by domestic enemies, and that an overruling necessity may be allowed for the time being to suspend an express provision of the constitution." It must not be forgotten, however, in this connection, that the legislature of Rhode Island, by its charter, had the power, and in pursuance of it, did declare martial law, and the doing of which, was recognized by the government as "an overruling necessity." Now the president, either on his own motion, or upon the application of the governor, in all cases of resistance to the laws of the United States, is empowered to send troops into the state, and the governor would in such cases, act as a subordinate to the president, who may order the executive, as well as militia officers, and their refusal to obey would be an offence against the laws of the United States. Houston *vs.* Moore, 5 Wheaton, page 15, and 12 Wheaton, Martin *vs.* Mott, 19. It appears that the governor did apply to the president for aid, and my first impression was, that he was acting under orders from the president, as commander of the militia of the Union, leaving to the governor the appointment of the officers and the training of the militia, but the letter of the respondent to the president of August 7th, 1870, rebuts it, and he appears to have acted on his own authority as governor. But I am relieved from pursuing the inquiry further on this subject as to whether under the constitution there can be military government, even for a temporary purpose. The Chief Justice in *ex parte* Moore *et al.*, 64 N. C. Rep. said: "I declare my opinion to be, that the privilege of the writ of *habeas corpus* has not been suspended by the action of his excellency; that the governor has power under the constitution and laws to declare a county to be in a state of insurrection, to take military possession, to order the arrest of all suspected persons, and to do all things to suppress the insurrection, but he has no power to *disobey* the writ of *habeas corpus*, or to order the trial of any citizen otherwise than by jury. According to the law of the land such action would be in excess of his power." It necessarily follows, that if the "privilege of the writ" cannot be suspended under any circumstances that martial law, as understood in a legal sense, and recognized in legal precedents, cannot prevail in North Carolina, so that in times of civil commotion, the laws and the judicial tribunals can only be appealed to for relief, and if these are obstructed, the militia may be ordered out only to strengthen the civil authorities, to enforce their processes. There can be no courts martial; no military commissions for the trial of citizens, and if the military make arrests, the imprisoned must be delivered to the proper tribunal for trial, according to the common law. Viewing it in the light of a cotemporaneous construction, our present constitution is eminently a peace instrument, for it contains no war powers that are *available*, and such was evidently the intention of its framers when they, by almost a unanimous vote, rejected the amendment, denying to the person restrained of his liberty to inquire into the lawfulness thereof, "in war," "insurrection" or "invasion." See proceedings of Constitutional Convention, 1868. But the chief justice says "the governor may order the arrest of all suspected persons, and do all things to suppress the insurrection." The use of the word "order," it would seem might carry with it the meaning, that such suspected persons may be arrested without warrant; and the power to arrest without warrant, might be said to embrace the power to detain as long as in the opinion of the governor, the public safety required it. For what avails the power to arrest, if the next moment the prisoners may be discharged by the judiciary for the want of evidence, when in truth the circumstances were such as to render powerless every effort to obtain the necessary proof to warrant a detention. To make arrests under such circumstances, would be the doing of a very useless thing, when at every step it could be thus embarrassed and delayed by the slow process of the courts, and in the end result in the discharge of the prisoner. Would not the commander-in-chief make but poor headway in suppressing the insurrection, if the insurgents could mock his authority by suing out the writ of *habeas corpus*. It is true that the military arm of the state in this emergency, would be so completely crippled, that the governor would have to stand idly by and see them gain strength and power, with no means to overcome them, other than to make orders of arrest one moment and jail deliveries the next, until the United States should happily intervene to relieve the judicial sport. I have thus endeavored to present the respondent's case, in as strong a light as possible from his own standpoint, to show that his difficulties in a trying emergency are fully appreciated. But the disputed question, as it stands, is not one of fact or error of judgment, it is one of law. The facts are fully admitted on both sides, as set forth in the certified opinion of the chief justice and the reply of the respondent of July 27th, 1870. The former says, "he (the governor) has no power to disobey the writ of *habeas corpus*." The latter, in his response says: "no one subscribes more thoroughly than I do to the great principles of *habeas corpus* and trial by jury. Except in extreme cases, in which beyond all question the safety of the state is the supreme law, these privileges of *habeas corpus* and trial by jury should be maintained," etc. "I do not see how I can restore the civil authority until I suppress the insurrection," etc. "It would be mockery in me to declare that the civil authority was unable to protect the citizens against the insurgents, and then turn the insurgents over to the civil authority." The motive of the respondent is evident, for he says, "the civil authority and the military are alike constitutional powers." The one begins where the other fails to answer the purpose of its creation. He is willing to assume the whole responsibility. He declines to obey the writ on the ground of an overruling necessity. He, too, had the right to put his own construction on the constitution in the first instance, and act accordingly until its provisions were expounded by a competent tribunal, but thereafter he was legally and morally bound to receive his law from the court, and recede from his position. He was told in plain terms that to disobey was to override an express provision of the fundamental law. If the repondent had this right, other functionaries, who may come after him, must have the same right, and there is an end of all good government. If he can set aside one provision of the constitution to-day, another occupying the same position may set aside all of them to-morrow, and government becomes a contemptible sham. If he can substitute his own will as the supreme law of the land in one case, his successor may do it in all cases, and there is an end of representative government and civil liberty. To avoid such usurpations of authority constitutions are made, representing the collected will of the people who make them; made to be observed by all as limitations upon *them*, as well as upon governments, but not so much as a measure of the rights of the people, as a rule of conduct for rulers. Looking at the matter in the light of history for the past ten years, may we not fully conclude that it was the intention of the framers of that instrument and the people who ratified it, to place the privilege of that inestimable writ beyond the power of legislative, executive or judicial control for all time, and without diminution? They had not forgotten, and it was yet fresh in their minds, that they had recently passed through a struggle, in which the light of civil liberty was almost extinguished amid the tumult of war. They solemnly resolved, that under no circumstances, shall this "one light" be put out again by their consent. Can any intention be clearer than this? Shall we, then, on a solemn occasion like this, furnish men of opposite political views with a precedent *argumentum ad hominem* for future action, and then give them a pretext to invade our rights in the hour of defeat, and to say "you have set us the example,"—you suspended the writ; you disobeyed it and justified it on the ground of an "overruling necessity." Shall we illustrate our principles by such an obnoxious and practical example, and thus add another precept to a catalogue that is already abundantly full? For these reasons, among many others, I was constrained, however painful the duty, to vote "guilty" on these two articles because the respondent, after having been informed in the most unequivocal language as to the law, *knowingly, deliberately, wilfully* and *unlawfully disobeyed* it, with no mistake of fact to excuse him; no error of judgment to protect him, but holding the key to the position he boldly and calmly contemplates the probable consequence of his own acts.

---

## OPINION OF SENATOR McCLAMMY.

As a senator sworn in this behalf, I have to submit my judgment, arising from the facts and arguments presented to this court during the trial.

It appears from the evidence before the court, that there were sundry violations of the law, in Alamance county, during the year 1868–'69, embracing two murders and numerous whippings. There were also two murders committed in Caswell county, and in both counties running through the same time, there were instances of barn burnings. The perpetrators of these outrages against the peace of the state, were, it appears, acting against each other,—were taking retaliatory steps. It is proved that there existed secret societies of various names—one composed almost entirely of blacks, and operating in the interest of a political party, and others composed of whites, and having also, perhaps, political objects. It is not by any means established that those secret organizations had any pur pose to subvert the government, but were rather organization, like vigilance committees, to punish those offenders against the law and against society who were not punished in the courts. It does not appear that there existed anything like a struggle between the races. Republican negroes were, it is in evidence, treated in the same manner in Alamance and Caswell as in other parts of the state, whenever their alleged crimes did not render them obnoxious to the communities in which they resided, and in general the two races were found there occupying much the same relation to each other as in other sections of the state. It is in evidence that the respondent issued frequent proclamations calling on the people of these counties to maintain order, and that he subsequently proclaimed said counties in a state ot insurrection, that he on or about the 21st day of June, 1870, organized a military force by appointing Geo. W. Kirk colonel, who called for recruits in the following proclamation, printed from a document proven to have been in the handwriting of the respondent:

"RALLY UNION MEN!"

"IN DEFENCE OF YOUR STATE.

"Rally, soldiers of the old N. C. 2d and 3d federal troops, "rally to the standard of your old commander. Your old com- 'mander has been commissioned to raise at once a regiment "of state troops to aid in enforcing the laws and in putting "down disloyal midnight assassins.

"The blood of your murdered countrymen, inhumanly "butchered for opinion's sake, cries from the ground for ven-

"geance. The horrible murders, and other atrocities com-"mitted by rebel K. K. K. and "southern chivalry" on grey "haired men and helpless women, call in thunder tones on all "loyal men to rally in defence of their state. The uplifted "hand of justice, N. C. 2nd and 3rd federal troops, must over-"take these outlaws"—under which proclamation he organized a regiment claiming to be state troops, over two hundred (200) of whom were from other states, and three hundred and ninety-nine (399) under the age of twenty-one. These troops he distributed at several points, but chiefly in these two counties. It appears also that there was besides, and prior to the organization of this force, a company of U. S. regulars in each of these counties under instructions to enforce the law, and amply sufficient to do so if there had been any resistance thereto. That these state troops proceeded to arrest divers persons named in the articles, and to detain them against their will—the persons being incarcerated and badly treated and in some instances subjected to torture. Some of these parties petitioned for and were granted the great writ of *habeas corpus* which was served on the military officer having the petitioners in confinement, who refused to obey the writ. That the respondent sanctioned this refusal of his military subordinate, claiming that the writ of *habeas corpus* was suspended, that civil law had been subverted in these counties, and that he would use the military to restore it. That he ordered the arrest of Josiah Turner, jr., in Orange county, which had not been declared in insurrection, and by his officers, kept the said Turner a prisoner for several days. That he, without warrant of law, drew large sums of money from the treasury for the payment of these troops, and that he disregarded a writ of injunction forbidding the paymaster to pay said troops, and ordered him to turn over the money in his possession to another for the purpose of having it disbursed according to his unlawful orders before the second party be enjoined. On this statement of facts, it is claimed by the managers that the respondent is guilty of the various charges contained in the articles.

The respondent replies that he was authorized by the act of assembly "to secure the better protection of life and property," ratified the 29th day of January, 1870, to declare the said counties in a state of insurrection; that the courts were unequal to the duty of enforcing the law, and that he was obliged to resort to a military force to preserve order; that the parties arrested were members of a secret organization, having for their object the overthrow of the government, and that they could not be otherwise dealt with than by the means and in the manner he used; that the peace of the state demanded he should keep as military prisoners the persons arrested until the proper time arrived for surrendering them to the civil authorities, and claims that his military force was rightfully organized as militia troops. It is to me perfectly apparent that a case is made out against respondent unless his defences thereto justify him.

I shall first examine the articles charging him with the commission of a high crime in declaring the counties in a state of insurrection. To my mind the authorities cited are conclusive that there can be no secret insurrection, that to constitute insurrection there must be open armed reisistance to the existing government by some of the persons owing allegiance thereto. Now the facts are, in Caswell two men are murdered, and in Alamance two murders are committed and sundry persons of a low character are flogged. That these outrages were committed in secret, signifies only that the perpetrators thereof feared the law, rather than defied it, that so far from defying civil law they sought to evade its expected penalties by all the ruses their ingenuity could invent. If insurrection be a flagrant opposition to and defiance of the existing government, the course of those who committed the outrages has none of the "outward and visible" signs of insurrection. These infractions of the law were committed by members of secret associations, but it does not appear that the objects of these associations were resistance to established government, and the commission of such acts as partake of the nature of insurrection. They did not undertake to subvert the existing government—the courts were not interfered with—process could at all times be served—persons accused of crime could be tried and punished if a jury of their countrymen had found them guilty, and the forms of law at least remained. It is true, the respondent claims that the spirit of our beneficent institutions had departed, and that juries always failed to convict men belonging to these organizations. If that were so, (an assertion not sustained by evidence) the fault was in the mode of trial, and in an evidence of the inefficiency of human devices to attain a perfect administration of justice. It is alleged that witnesses and jurors would not do their duty—would perjure themselves, and the criminals would escape "unwhipped of justice." Yet if this was so, the very act which the respondent claims gave him authority for his action, provides for the removal of the trial of these very offenders to other counties than those in which the offence was committed. But to my mind, while the existence of such a state of society is to be deplored, and while it is to be regretted that the sacred institution of trial by jury should ever cease to operate as a wholesome check on crime, yet this does not constitute insurrection, nor does the commission of any number of offences, whether punished or not, having a different nature from insurrection, constitute that offence. The respondent however, relies on the "Shoffner act." Without entering into a discussion of the constitutionality of the act, and only characterizing it as an unwise grant of discretionary power, perhaps beyond the scope of legislation under the constitution of North Carolina, I am of opinion that the respondent was, by the terms of the act itself, forced to exercise a proper discretion. Now, not regarding the subtle distinctions that the learned counsel have argued at such length, a dispassionate consideration of the facts forbid me to view the conduct of the respondent as being the result of a desire to execute the law. It is apparent to my mind that he was actuated by motives that should not govern the executive of a state. He did not have at heart the discharge of the duties incident to his office, so much as other designs, which were totally incompatible with those duties. His interest—his object is plainly shown by the facts. Col. Clarke, it was arranged, was to have had charge of the military organization, but this arrangement was set aside, because he was a man of too much character to answer the purposes of respondent, and was replaced by a person of notorious bad reputation, imported into this state as a proper tool to accomplish sinister purposes. To secure fitting material for the execution of the vile project, an illegal force is raised, partly from the lawless regions of Tennessee, and these troops well suited to obey such a leader in such an enterprise, are sent into a county where no insurrection exists—where no outrages are being committed—and where there is a strong force of United States troops already quartered, under the pretext of suppressing insurrection—but with the real intent to control the election. Now what was the conduct of this officer and his troops—as showing the intent of their commander, the respondent? They arrested without warrant, without bail and on no charge, the political opponents of their commander; they incarcerated these prisoners against whom there was not a particle of evidence and who were not even suspected of crime, in foul cells; they broke up public meetings of peaceable citizens by the seizure of the best and most esteemed members of the community; they took forcible possession of the court house, and turned the officers of the law out of their appointed places of business; they threatened to burn the town of Yanceyville, and resorted to all the means their ingenuity could devise to precipitate a conflict between the citizens and the soldiers—to exasperate them or to terrify them and prevent a free expression of the popular will at the polls. Such was the object, such the means employed for its consummation; and such the conduct of the respondent who, by a stroke of his pen, could have countermanded the orders that subverted civil liberty.

The constitution of North Carolina, art. 1, sec. 21, says that "the privilege of the writ of *habeas corpus* shall not be suspended." The evidence under art. 5 is, that the respondent had in control, under the guard of a military force, sundry citizens deprived of their liberties without due process of law: that they petitioned for the writ, and the respondent, in his answer to art. 5 of the articles of impeachment, admits that said arrests and detention were approved by respondent as governor of North Carolina. No greater crime against the state exists, in my judgment than this, save alone treason.

This writ is the palladium of our liberties. Without it our lives would be at the mercy of our officers; with it our boasted freedom is indeed a reality. Destroy its power and our cherished institutions are emasculated of their virtue. The beneficient operations of this legacy gives to the humblest citizen an equality before his fellows with the most powerful officer. No people are worthy of, or can maintain their independence who do not guard with a jealous care every avenue to this tower of their strength. The respondent, failing to remember its sanctity, admits that he undertook to render it inoperative. In this he is guilty, in my judgment, of a high crime. The governor is sworn to execute the law, not to make it nor to expound it. The troops which he had in the field being illegally organized, the treasurer was enjoined from using public moneys in paying them off. The duty of the governor, as of every citizen, is to obey the law, respect the order of the court. If *he* evades the law, and defies the order of the court, who in all the land will give to the law a willing obedience? Yet in this instance the respondent did evade the law, and by illegal means, caused to be withdrawn from the treasury the enjoined funds which he wished appropriated to the payment of his unlawful soldiery; calls into existence an illegally organized body of troops, uses them for an unlawful purpose, and violates the law to pay them for their services. Under this charge there can be no doubt of his guilt. The remaining charges relate to the arrest of citizens of Alamance and Caswell counties. Of the large number arrested there were none taken under warrants properly made out, but they were seized at the instance and by direction of respondent with utter disregard of the provisions of the constitution. If there had been insurrection and these men had engaged therein, his acts might have been lawful, but there was no insurrection and the capture and detention of these parties were without the sanction of the law. Among them were numbered some of the truest and most deserving citizens of North Carolina; these, with their neighbors, were arrested on the mere motion of his excellency without warrant, and as far as this court can discover, without a scintilla of evidence implicating them in any violation of the law. Had they engaged in any criminal undertaking, their apprehension might be excused; but there is not even an insinuation that most of them had committed any offence known to the law. As for the members of the secret organizations shown to have existed in these counties, they do deserve harsh punishment from the hands of inexorable justice. Not even can the respondent entertain for them a greater aversion than myself. But these societies were the fungus growth of the times, and in checking them it was criminal in the respondent to deprive innocent citizens of their dearest rights. The constitution and the laws are worth nothing if they can be violated with impunity at the arbitrary will of one man. They are intended not merely to limit power in quiet times, but rather to prevent encroachments on the liberties of the people when "reason forsakes her throne, and passion rules the hour."

## OPINION OF SENATOR R. Z. LINNEY.

There are periods in the history of all governments when the subjects have for a time been oppressed, that outcries of reform have arisen from the populace. It may also be truly said that when the demagogue, joining in the popular clamor, excites the prejudices of the people, the arrows of vengeance may be hurled against an innocent officer. The stream, which for a time is impeded, at last breaks down and rushes over the barriers, and carries everything before it. When in this deluge, the ark itself is in danger, the patriot endeavors to confine the torrent within its proper banks and directs its impetuosity; and, in so doing, may call upon himself the faults of the times, insomuch that the most virtuous members of society in official place may be sacrificed. Such, in darker ages, was the "course of time." I have such confidence, however, in the rectitude of the intentions and of the staid judgment of the people of North Carolina, that they are not, in my opinion, to be censured for their selection of a victim; for when they contend for a principle, they lose sight of the individual. Whatever may be the results of the impeachment of Governor Holden, the house of representatives, reflecting the popular will, were actuated from motives no less pure than at least a virtuous indignation at the supposition of his guilt. The impeachment of the governor was demanded by the voice of sovereignty in the state. Good men almost everywhere could not believe either that the constitution and laws of the state justified the perpetration of outrages upon the liberties of the people, or that the governor was actuated from misguided and ill-regulated public spirit. While they were willing to pass over almost any crime in silence, which originated in an inordinate zeal for the good of the commonwealth, they could not believe that such flagitious crime, as has received his sanction and encouragement, originated in anything save selfish capacity. Those members, in my opinion, who wished to reflect public opinion, could not avoid taking the action they did in this matter. In the trial of this cause, however, our character is materially changed. While the public has indicated its will in the matter through the house of representatives, the senate, sitting in its judicial character, can only look upon that will as desiring to be exercised to the extent of securing the application to this cause, of the principles and safeguards provided for every human being accused of crime. In exercising the power given the senate as a judicial tribunal, I think the idea suggested during the trial, that we were bound by no rules of law or evidence save that of our own will, was erroneous. Being both judges and jurors, deciding both law and fact, we would necessarily fall into that class of whom Bacon says their office is "*jus dicere*" and not "*jus dare.*" Let it never be said in North Carolina that this is not an alter of justice! Let us in this, an unusual proceeding with us, double the guards of justice so that in all tempests, party rage and party hate, may be kept from doing a demon's work by the irrefragible rules of law. With this view of our responsibility as a member of the court of impeachment, I have endeavored to apply to this cause the same principles and safeguards in passing both upon the law and facts that I conceive to be provided for every human being accused of crime.

Articles 1st and 2d charges substantially, that the accused corruptly and wickedly declared the counties of Alamance and Caswell to be in a state of insurrection, whereas there was no insurrection; that he took military possession of those counties by armed bands of lawless and desperate men, organized without lawful authority; and that he made unlawful arrests of peaceable citizens, whom he imprisoned, beat, hung by the neck, and otherwise maltreated.

Section 16th of an act ratified the 10th of April, 1869, regulating proceedings of impeachment, enumerates impeachable offences. Corruption or other misconduct in his official capacity, is therein declared to be an impeachable offence; and the sixth item of this enumeration declares "any criminal matter, the conviction thereof would tend to bring his office into public contempt," to be an impeachable offence.

The allegations are admitted as to the arrests without warrant, and the taking military possession of those counties under a proclamation that these counties were in a state of insurrection, but the wicked intent denied. An unauthorized arrest by an officer certainly makes the officer guilty of such criminal matter as expressed in section 16 of the act regulating impeachment—the conviction thereof would tend to bring his office in public contempt. From those who have been elevated to positions of power and honor, the public expect (and of right should expect) that devotion to law and order, and exemplary conduct, as would, even as an example, tend to restrain evil doers. Nothing would, in point of fact, have so great a tendency to bring his office in public contempt than for the chief executive to become himself a violator of law, and a co-worker with the wicked and disorderly to punish the innocent and unoffending. But to look at these arrests only as they become illegal and assume the nature of crimes or misdemeanors, I conceive to be the duty of every member of the court. In the case of the arrest of the five Knights; viz: Darnel, Cobert and others (the investigation of which case, more perhaps than any thing else, caused the passage of the *habeas corpus* act of Charles II.) I find the following quotation in the *habeas corpus* proceedings therein had, as the opinion of Chief Justice Markham to Edward IV: "The King cannot arrest a man upon suspicion of felony or treason as any of his subjects may." No verbal order of the King nor any under his sign, manuel or privy signet, was a command, said Seldon, "which the law would recognize as sufficient to detain any of his subjects; a writ duly issued under the seal of a court, being the only language in which he could signify his will," and further, "that even if the first commitment by the King's command were lawful, yet when a party had continued in prison for a reasonable time, he should be brought to answer; liberty being a thing so favored by the law that it will not suffer any man to remain in confinement for a longer time than of necessity he must." "If the King command me," said one of the judges under Henry IV, "to arrest a man, and I arrest him, he shall have an action of false imprisonment against me though it were done in the King's presence."

All these authorities show that an unauthorized arrest subjects the officer to a criminal charge. They further show that the signature of some member of some branch of the judiciary, and that only, can impart vitality to any process in the hands of an officer which justifies him in making an arrest.

And the only reason the king was not regarded an offender with the person whom he might order to make an arrest was, in consequence of the fiction of law, "the king can do no wrong." In this country, however, the higher the officer in authority, the greater the offence. That these arrests were unauthorized is evident, for the reason that they were made in form and manner, as is expressly prohibited by section 17 of the declaration of rights, which says: "No person ought to be taken, imprisoned or disseized, or outlawed, or in any manner deprived of his life, liberty or property, but by the law of the land;" and section 15 provides "that general warrants, whereby any officer or messenger may be commanded to search suspected places without evidence of the act committed, or to seize any person or persons not named whose offence is not particularly described and supported by evidence, are dangerous to liberty and ought not to be granted." There are certain axioms in our constitution, a disregard of which must necessarily have its origin in a mind bent on the exercise of arbitrary power and the subversion of the liberties of the citizen. I could not vote to convict any officer of "misconduct in office" for a failure, through inadvertence, to observe all the formalities of the law. There are, however, certain self-evident principles in the organic law of the state, whose truth, scope and requirements are so evident at first sight that no process of reasoning or demonstration can make it plainer. There are, on the other hand, questions so abstruse and complicated that to construe them properly would require the application of that astuteness and learning seldom found other than in the exercise of the judicial mind. A failure to place the same construction on them that the courts might do, could not of itself be regarded a proceeding from corruption. Inadvertence, however, cannot excuse the accused for disregarding an axiomatic provision of the organic law of the state. Section 15 of the Bill of Rights contains just such principles as, in my opinion, the breach of which must have grown out of corruption in office. I apprehend that under this section, if any magistrate of the state were to issue a general warrant he would be guilty of a malfeasance in office as would render him unfit for the position, the functions of which he pretends to exercise. The order of the governor would be of less validity; for while process signed by a magistrate who had no jurisdiction in the matter would protect the officer in the prudent execution of it, from a criminal prosecution, an order issued by the governor could not. That he who enjoys the highest office within the gift of the people of the state, and orders the arrest of citizens in a way less formal than an arrest under a general warrant—not even giving the names of the persons—designating them by the term suspected persons, when by an axiom of our state constitution, which it was his duty to support, such arrest would have been illegal if ordered by a member of the judiciary, is guilty of misconduct in office, it seems to me there can be no doubt.

There is another point of view in which these arrests become illegal. Even criminals are entitled to protection from torture. An arrest under legal process for crime does not clothe the officer making the arrest with absolute power as to the treatment of the criminal. The assaulting some and hanging others to extort confessions, was an unwarranted as well as a cruel and brutal act.

It was given for law, by Senator Sumner, in his opinion at page 251. 3d vol., that (among other things) the introduction of arbitrary power was a high crime and misdemeanor.

I understand an arbritrary exercise of power to be, to rule at will or discretion; rejecting the fixed rules of law. From all I was able to gather from the testimony, I have no hesitancy in saying the will of the respondent was the only law meted out to those counties during the time they were held by the state troops under Kirk.

At page 833 of American Criminal Law, by Wharton, extortion is denominated an offence against society, and is defined to be "the taking of money by an officer by reason of his office; either when none is due or where none is yet due." The testimony discloses the fact that one Burgen, an officer of the troops, released prisoners for money and brandy. The offence of extortion finds a place among the outrages perpetrated by the troops during this military movement of the accused in those counties.

Corruption or other misconduct in office is made an impeachable offence by statute in this state. Wharton, on American Criminal Law, teaches that "if a public officer, intrusted with definite powers to be exercised for the benefit of the community, wickedly abuses or fraudulently exceeds them, he is punishable by indictment, though no injurious effects result to any individual from his conduct." This, that author denominates the offence of misconduct in office. The crime consists in the public example in perverting those powers to the purposes of fraud and wrong, which were committed to him as instruments of benefit to the citizen and of safety to public rights. Here I propose to notice an interrogatory, put by the chief justice, at page 476 of this trial. "Whether the executive is liable to impeachment for exceeding an act which is constitutional, should he falsely, corruptly and wickedly proclaim the state of things set out in the statute to exist, when, in truth, such a state of things did not exist?" Under Wharton's definition of misconduct in office, such would be an impeachable offence. Misconduct in office is expressly declared to be an impeachable offence, and the interrogatory put in substance finds an answer in the definition of that offence. If misconduct in office as a criminal offence does not necessarily consist in exceeding the powers conferred, but in perverting those powers to the purposes of oppression and wrong, it seems to me the executive would be guilty of misconduct in office were he falsely and corruptly, under the Shoffner act, to proclaim an insurrection to exist when the courts were in the full and undisturbed exercise of their functions, and no insurrection did exist. Great responsibilities are necessarily associated with the grant of great powers; and if he, upon whom great powers have been conferred, chooses to abuse them from corrupt motives and for the accomplishment of ends foreign to the legitimate purposes of the law, he is certainly guilty of misconduct in office. If then, the citizens of Alamance and Caswell were, at the time of these arrests and wrongs perpetrated upon them, entitled to share in the immunities which I hope, as evil as the times may have been, every freeman of the state was entitled to, the accused is guilty, at this stage of my enquiry, of such corruption and misconduct in office as should convict him on the 1st, 2d and 4th articles.

The 3rd article charges the unlawful arrest of Josiah Turner, jr., in the county of Orange, by the procurement and order of the accused. The arrest was effected in a way unauthorized by law, and was attended by every aggrivating circumstance without a palliative. Here we are presented with an instance of the wanton exercise of arbitrary power with but few equals in civilized countries. This citizen had employed the press (at least apparently for the purpose of correcting the abuses of the times, though severe in its denunciations of official malfeasance,) it purported to fill the office to which Lord Baker assigns truth. "Truth the daughter of time, not of authority, is constantly warning the community in what their interest consists, and that to protect, not to encroach upon these interests, all governments are formed." The testimony to my mind disclosed the fact that shortly after an article appeared in the *Sentinel* containing a severe denunciation of the governor, the editor was arrested and deprived of his personal liberty for a period of eleven days and otherwise maltreated. It further discloses the fact that about the time said article appeared, the governor expressed the intention of arresting the said Josiah Turner, jr. Orange had not been declared to be in a state of insurrection, and Turner accused of no crime. The defence then set up in justification of the arrests made in Alamance and Caswell could not apply here. Here is an instance in which power, tenacious of retaining its authority, increased its exactions until the liberty of the citizen was disregarded. To acquit on this article would be to permit an officer to exercise these dangerous exactions of power with impunity. The accused seeks to throw all the responsibility on the troops, answering that they made the arrest without his order. It is admitted in the respondent's answer that when informed of the arrest he ordered his detention in the counties declared to be insurgent counties. It is a well settled principle of law that an agency may be confirmed and established, and in fact created by a subsequent adoption and ratification. The case of Lane *vs.* Dudley, 2 Murph., decides that if one person sell the horse of another and warrant his soundness, without the consent of the owner, who afterwards accepts the purchase money without any knowledge that the warranty had been made, the owner shall nevertheless be answerable on his warranty. This case rests on the idea that there can be a subsequent ratification of an act of an agent without even any knowledge of the acts of the agent. If then we apply this rule to the conduct of the accused, he must necessarily be responsible for the arrest of Turner. The case here is stronger than that decided in the case referred to. In that case the acceptance of the money for which the horse was sold was a ratification of the act of the agent who made the warranty without the consent of the principal, or even his knowledge that such warranty had been made. Here the act of the illegal arrest of Turner was ratified by the accused in his ordering his detention with knowledge of the illegal arrest. As a general rule, however, the principal is not responsible for the criminal acts of the agent. There is an exception to this rule. Where the criminal acts of the agent are expressly commanded, the principal then becomes responsible for them. I cannot see the difference, at least so far as the animus of the accused is concerned, in the arrest of Turner by Hunnicutt, at the express command of the accused, and the ratification of that arrest by ordering his detention after the illegal arrest came to his knowledge. Suppose Turner had resisted the arrest and had been slain, and the accused, when informed of it, instead of punishing this officer had approved it by the act of ordering his troops to protect the officer who committed the deed from arrest, would he not have become an accessory to this foul murder? He must with equal certainty be *particess criminis* of the illegal arrest of Turner as charged in article 3rd.

Besides there is authority raising a strong presumption of a criminal intent on the part of a principal in the employment of dangerous and mischievous persons as agents. He who rejects the powers of the civil law, or well disciplined U. S. troops, commanded by men of character, and substitutes in their stead raw troops, controlled by ignorant and desperate men, (unauthorized by law,) was certainly actuated from some base and criminal motive. And, in my opinion, the use of such instruments at all shows an illegal purpose in view.

If it were really so, as proclaimed by the governor, that Alamance and Caswell were in a state of insurrection, and that the effect of the governor's proclamation of that fact was to place every citizen of those counties *ex lex*, I cannot see how that would justify the arrest of Turner, a citizen of Orange. The defence set up by the accused that he only ordered his detention in those counties, certainly cannot avail the accused anything. I know of no better rule of argumentation—no better test by which the soundness of any proposition may be ascertained than by examining the effects produced by the adoption of the proposed theory. What then would be the results of admitting that the accused was justified in detaining Turner in the insurgent counties, so called, when he was not a citizen thereof? If he could detain one in that manner, I suppose numbers could not change the principle. All then that would be necessary to deprive any or all persons of the state, who might have incurred the displeasure of the executive, of their absolute rights, personal liberty, &c., would be to declare some section of the state to be in insurrection and decoy the wanted victim into it. Thus the liberties of the people would be placed at the entire control of the executive. The stability and strength of the safeguards by which the Carolinian has ever been taught to believe he was protected, would depend upon the passion, temper or caprice of the executive. To such a doctrine I cannot subscribe—a rule of argumentation that leads to such deplorable results, ought at once to be abandoned. I therefore vote guilty on article 3.

Articles 5 and 6 charges, among other things, the refusal of George W. Kirk, by the order and command of the accused, to surrender citizens unlawfully held by him as prisoners to the civil authorities in obedience to the writ of *habeas corpus.*

The constitution declares, in section 21st of the Bill of Rights, that the privilege of the writ of *habeas corpus* shall not be suspended. There is no contingency upon the happening of which, nor any emergency in which it can be suspended by state authority. Nor is it necessary that there should be. Ample means are furnished in the federal constitution for any emergency in a state. Sec. 4th, of article 4th of the constitution of the United States, is as follows: 'The United States shall guarantee to every state in this Union a republican form of government, and shall protect each of them against invasion, and on application of the legislature, or of the executive, (when the legislature cannot be convened) against domestic violence." Here was the proper remedy for the accused to have employed in correcting every species of violence in the state which the courts could not reach. And I am unable to see how he who affects such admiration for and fidelity to that instrument as the accused could prefer, the exercise of arbitrary power unauthorized anywhere, to the exercise of powers afforded in the section referred to for the protection of the states. There cannot be such a thing as martial law in North Carolina, (set up by state authority) for the writ of *habeas corpus* cannot be suspended. And since there can be no suspension of the writ, there are none who are exempt from the penalties of attachment who disobey it. There is no private economical relation of life that can deprive either party to that relation of the privilege of that writ, nor is either party exempt from the penalties of attachment who disobeys it. An instance is laid down by Lord Bacon of an *habeas corpus* issuing against the husband in favor of the wife, and the court held that while the wife could not be removed from the husband, yet she was entitled to the writ in order to gain that freedom which would enable her to commence proceedings of divorce, and it was contempt in the husband not to obey the writ. The same author gives an instance in which a *habeas corpus* was directed against the Bishop of Dunham, who returned that he was invested with royal privileges as such, and on that account would not surrender the prisoner, for which he was fined £4,000. Indeed, I believe it has been held in England and America, ever since the *habeas corpus* act of Charles II, to be in contempt of a court not to obey the writ by proper return. And no position in life exempts him who thus disregards the authority of the courts from the penalties of an attachment. Chief Justice Gascoigne ordered Prince Henry, afterwards King Henry V, to be carried to prison for contempt of court—such was the character which he then bore and the majesty of the laws which he sustained. And Hume relates no incident more to be admired by the patriot and more worthy the emulation of modern judges. Here we have authority proving that no one can put himself in contempt of the authority of the courts as he does who disobeys the writ of *habeas corpus* without incurring severe penalties. The husband could not do it when issued in favor of the wife. Bishops, under the claim of royal prerogative, could not exempt themselves from the penalties that liberty requires should be meted out to him who disregards the writ of *habeas corpus*. No officer in a republic ever enjoyed the prerogatives of King Henry V, while a prince. When he entered the court of chancery, the Lord Chancellor and keeper of the great seal arose from his wool sack and veiled himself while he received the prince, the bar standing. Yet such was the majesty of the law that he, about whose reception so much formality was due, was not exempt from imprisonment for contempt of court. How, then, can it be that in this advanced age of civilization, a governor of a state can put himself in contempt of the highest judicial tribunal of the state with impunity? That he cannot do it without being guilty of misconduct in office, is, it seems to me, an axiom of common sense. The arrest of the five knights which contributed largely to the passage of the *habeas corpus* act of Charles II, had the effect, not of establishing any new principle more than was already secured by magna charta, but that cut off the abuses by which the government's lust of power, and the servile subtlety of the Crown lawyers had impaired so fundamental a privilege. And if these abuses had not been thus lopped off possibly another effort like that of the insurgent barons at Runnemeade would have been necessary to the protection of the personal liberty of the citizen. In my humble judgment, the conviction of the accused will tend to lop off the abuses by which the accused's lust of power in North Carolina had rendered inoperative the powers of the judiciary in the execution of the writ of *habeas corpus*. And believing the attempted exercise of arbitrary power on his part was for the purpose of wrong and oppression instead of the protection of public rights, I am driven to the necessity of voting guilty on those articles.

Article VII charges the organization of an army of desperate men, and unlawful warrants made by the accused upon the treasurer of the state for large sums of money for the unlawful purpose of supporting this lawless band of armed men. The organization being unauthorized, money drawn from the treasurer for their support must also have been unauthorized. I, therefore, believing the same illegal purpose was in view, vote guilty on Article VII.

Article VIII charges that the Hon. Anderson Mitchell, one of the superior court judges, issued writs of injunction which were served upon the treasurer and paymaster restraining them from paying money to the troops. That thereupon the accused caused the writ, and its objects to be thwarted by the removal of the paymaster, enjoined and appointing another. Thus the efforts of a tax-payer in behalf of himself and the tax-payers of the state, to have the legality of the expenditure of large sums of money for an illegal purpose, enquired into, were arrested. It is the duty of all persons, and especially officers, to obey process of this character until the matter in controversy has been determined by the exercise of the judicial mind, and he who disobeys it is in contempt of the authority of the court. It was claimed that the accused could not be enjoined, and that being the case he had the legal power to thwart its purposes. I cannot see how the question of his power to do it, is of itself a defence. It is misconduct in office for an officer to use the powers conferred if used for the purposes of fraud and wrong, instead of the protection of public rights. The efforts of a tax-payer to enquire into the legality and justice of this wholesale expenditure of the public funds, were certainly commendable. And the officer who would interpose his powers to frustrate these noble ends, is certainly guilty of misconduct in office. The way to the courts was plain and easy. And the very fact that the accused resorted to artifice to prevent the passing upon these matters by the courts argues a perversion of the powers given him, if indeed he possessed such power—so I vote guilty on the VIII article.

The conclusion I have reached in reference to the 1st, 2d and 4th articles proceeded on the theory that the citizens of Alamance and Caswell were entitled to all the privileges of other citizens. It now remains to be seen what was the legal effect of the proclamation of the accused declaring those counties to be in a state of insurrection. The position was taken and supported by the authority of Judge Bond in the *habeas corpus* proceedings in the case of B. G. Burgen, that the sword is due process of law to insurgents. But what if these citizens were not insurgents? That decision rests on the idea that by the Shoffner act, the governor was the sole and exclusive judge of that, and that a judge would have no right to question the truth of the governor's proclamation. This I believe was the course that case took. It seems to me the only question here presented is, since the Shoffner act left a discretion with the judge—has allowed him to say when there is an insurrection—has this tribunal a right to enquire whether that proclamation was false.

The language of the statute is " the governor is hereby authorized and empowered, whenever in his judgment, the civil authorities in any county are unable to protect its citizens in the enjoyment of life and property, to declare such county in a state of insurrection, and to call into active service the militia of the state," &c. We have already seen the offence of misconduct in office is the perversion of the powers given an officer, for the purposes of fraud and wrong which were committed to him as instruments of benefit to the citizen and safety to public rights. If then the proclamation of insurrection can never be questioned in an impeachment trial, how could an investigation ever be had into the conduct of a governor who should pervert the powers given him by that statute?

Section 9th of article 3rd of the constitution, gives the governor, with the advice of the council of state, the power to convene the general assembly in extra session. Suppose these powers should be used for the purpose of annoyance to the members, would the governor not be guilty of misconduct in office? Or should he abuse the pardoning power or any other power, would he not be guilty of misconduct in office? So under the act referred to. If the act gave a discretion to the governor, it does not follow that he could not abuse that discretion. He could not declare the counties to be in a state of insurrection when there was no insurrection. What then is insurrection? I am, with the lights before me, unable to find that insurrection is not treason. Whether insurrection is treason, becomes necessary to be known in this trial, for the reason that our constitution has defined treason to consist only in levying war against the state or adhering to its enemies, &c.

It all insurrections are treason, then it must necessarily follow that nothing less than a levying of war is an insurrection. Wharton's American Criminal Law, I believe, enumerates seventeen offences against society, among which insurrection is not tound. He also recognizes two offences against the government, viz: treason and the violation of the neutrality laws. Then since a riot or rout is one grade in the scale of offences below insurrection, it must follow that insurrection is not an element of any of that class of offences against society. Then are we not to look to that class of offences against the government for insurrection? In so doing it will be seen that though all treason is not insurrection, yet all insurrection is treason.

Hallam, at page 574, says, "in the earlier ages of our law, the crime of high treason appears to have been of a vague and indefinite nature, determined only by such arbitrary construction as the circumstances of each particular case might suggest. A petition was, however, presented to Edward the III, by Parliament, requesting, among other things, that the King would, by his council and the noble and learned men of the land, declare what should be held treason; whereupon a statute was passed defining treason; and among other things, counterfeiting was made treason. Hallam, in commenting upon that statute says: "It is a strange conjunction of offences to make counterfeiting, which is for the sake of private fraud, rank among all that really endangers the established government, with conspiracy and insurrection. Thus it appears that insurrection is the very essence of treason, else why would that author complain that counterfeiting was by that statute assigned a position in the scale of crime equal to insurrection when it was made treason. All tumultuous assemblages of persons that do not amount to levying war can only be a riot or rout. If these assemblages assume such magnitude as to silence the courts, they may then become insurrections. This not being the case in those counties, the governor declared an insurrection to exist when there was none. And even if such were the case,

I cannot see how that could have the effect of nullifying that section of the Bill of Rights, which declares that the privileges of the writ of *habeas corpus* shall not be suspended. The maxim, *salus populi supremer lex or necessitus quod cogit, defendit* cannot justify the governor in the exercise of arbitrary power in a time of peace under the circumstances of this case. In all cases the officer or person claiming to act under the pressure of necessity, real or supposed acts at his peril. As necessity compels so necessity alone can justify it. It does not make legal what would otherwise be illegal. So that when the accused undertook to exercise the powers which necessity under circumstances requires, he did it at his peril. It is only real necessity that can justify it, and not that ideal necessity which is the daughter of inordinate ambition and an insatiate lust of power. Believing that no insurrection existed and no such pressure of circumstances as justified a resort to the exercise of arbitrary power, I cannot see how any one could vote otherwise than guilty on all the articles. To vote otherwise it seems to me, would be to turn the crimes of an individual into public guilt. I prefer to convert those offences which have thrown a transient shade upon our state government, into something that will reflect a permanent lustre upon the honor and justice of this commonwealth.

---

## OPINION OF SENATOR E. J. WARREN.

It is not disputed that all the articles charge, by proper and sufficient amounts, impeachable offences. I do not propose to examine them in their order, or with any great particularity. Some of them, the third article for instance, may be easily disposed of. That Turner was arrested as charged, and not as alleged in the answer of the respondent, does not admit of a doubt. Nor can it be questioned that he was arrested without cause and in open defiance and contempt of the law. Indeed the answer itself sufficiently shows *quo animo* the arrest was made.

Article IV charges the arrest of John Kerr and others in the county of Caswell, which had been declared in insurrection. Articles V and VI charge the arrest, detention and imprisonment of persons in the counties of Alamance and Caswell, by order of the respondent, and that he caused to be disregarded writs of *habeas corpus* issued in their behalf by the chief justice of the state, and thus suspended the privilege of the writ. The facts are admitted. But it is said in behalf of the respondent, that having, under authority conferred upon him by the constitution and what is called the Shoffner act, declared the counties of Alamance and Caswell in insurrection, he had the right to arrest the parties without process and by his military agents—that he had the right to detain them until in his judgment it was proper to surrender them to the civil authorities—that the court of impeachment cannot go behind respondent's proclamations to ascertain whether in fact there were insurrections in said counties or not; and that, as it must be taken as a fact that insurrections did exist there, the privilege of the writ of *habeas corpus* was *ipso facto* suspended in those localities, and the writ could not run.

Had there been an insurrection in the counties named, arrests by a lawful military force, without process, would have been proper, of those engaged in open resistance to the laws—the military being used in such case in aid of the civil authority, and acting in subordination to it. The functions of the military, under such circumstances, may be likened to those of persons acting in aid of a peace officer, whose duty it is to part the combatants in an affray, and to arrest them on the spot. He may call upon the bystanders to assist him, and no process is necessary for his protection or theirs. But there was no such state of things in Alamance or Caswell. There was no time when civil process could not be obtained and executed by the proper officers of the law. The courts were open, the civil authorities were in the unobstructed exercise of their functions, and there was, in judgment of law, a state of peace. There is no justification or excuse for making the arrests in the mode resorted to. Nor is there any for the detention of the prisoners in military custody. Legally, supposing their arrest proper, there could have been no means for detaining them one instant longer than was necessary to prefer charges against them before a civil tribunal. The allegation on the part of the respondent, that his purpose was to deliver them to the civil authorities as soon as he could safely do so, is disproved by evidence which is absolutely overwhelming. It is established, as far as human testimony can establish anything, that his determination was, in defiance of law, to organize military tribunals for the trial of men, against some of whom suspicion was never breathed by any man but himself; and their detention was to this end. The respondent could not have been ignorant that the trial and execution of any one of his prisoners, whether innocent or guilty, would have been murder in the eye of the law. The right of the parties to be delivered over to the civil authorities for examination, to the end that they might be discharged if innocent, or committed or bound over to appear before the proper tribunal, if sufficient cause was shown, was as sacred as the right of trial by jury, or any other right which belongs to the citizen.

But it is said this court is bound to take the fact to be that there was insurrection in the counties named, or at least such a stateof things as was in the contemplation of the legislature when it passed the Shoffner act. The doctrine goes to this extent, that, supposing a county to be in a state of profound peace, without a crime or criminal within its borders, if the governor chooses to declare it in insurrection, a court of impeachment cannot try him and convict him of official misconduct. It is only necessary to state the proposition to show its absurdity.

Yet this doctrine is not so entirely without a show of reason to support it, as the other proposition of the counsel for the respondent, to wit: that the privilege of the writ of *habeas corpus* was suspended in Alamance and Caswell by force of the executive proclamations declaring them to be in a state of insurrection. The provision of the constitution is emphatic and without qualification: "The privilege of the writ of *habeas corpus* shall not be suspended." It is equivalent to saying that neither in peace nor in war shall the privilege of the writ be suspended. In the convention of 1868, which framed the constitution, Mr. Rodman, now a justice of the supreme court, moved to strike out the clause above cited, but his motion did not prevail. Subsequently, upon the third reading of the declaration of rights, he made the same motion and accompanied it with a motion to amend section 17 (now 18) by adding thereto the following words: "The remedy shall not be suspended except in case of war, insurrection or invasion." The yeas and nays were ordered upon this motion and amendment, and resulted in yeas 6, nays 72; showing conclusively the sense of the convention on this subject. Besides, in the case of Adolphus G. Moore, Chief Justice Pearson declares his opinion to be that the privilege of the writ of *habeas corpus* was not suspended by the action of the governor, and that the governor had no power to disobey the writ, or to order the trial of any citizen otherwise than by jury. It is a significant fact that a copy of the opinion in that case was delivered to the respondent as early as the 23d of July, and that on the 3d of August, he wrote to Kirk that the court-martial for the trial of the prisoners would "meet one day next week." The respondent's declaration that he was sustained in his action by the opinion of the chief justice, and his averment now to the same effect in his answer to article V, tends to cast suspicion upon the motives which governed him in all the conduct for which he stands impeached. It is impossible for human reason to be so perverted and at the same time sane, as thus to interpret the opinion in this respect.

I have already said there was no justification or excuse for making the arrests in the manner in which they were made. I go further. In many, if not most of the cases, there was no justification or excuse for making them at all. Take, for example, the case of Judge Kerr. Malice itself could not have invented an excuse for his arrest and imprisonment, except the base and despicable one of political expediency. The detention of the prisoners and the refusal of respondent to obey the writs of *habeas corpus* were in violation of his known and sworn duty. Thus to make the military suspend the civil power is a crime without a parallel in American history.

But it is urged as a circumstance favorable to the respondent, that in fact he did not cause any of the prisoners to be tried by a military court. It is not charged that he did so. It is difficult, however, to perceive how this helps his case. That he proposed so to try them; that he persisted in his purpose after its illegality was most clearly declared; that he partially organized his court; that, as late as August 7, he appealed to the president of the United States to withold aid and support from the judiciary of the United States; that he abandoned his purpose only when the attorney general of the United States (whose advice the president followed) pointedly rebuked him; that even then he sought to oust the jurisdiction of the federal judge, are facts admitting of no dispute. It is beyond controversy that from March 10, 1870, when he wrote to the president asking the suspension of the privilege of the writ of *habeas corpus* to the end that "criminals might be arrested and tried before military tribunals and shot," to the close of the dismal drama, he was "fatally bent on mischief."

In his answer to article VII, the respondent denies that the men composing his military force "were many of them of the most reckless, [illegible] and lawless characters from the state of Tennessee," and avers "that the said men were citizens of North Carolina at and immediately before the organization of said militia, and if any of them were at the time of said organization citizens of the state of Tennessee, the same was unknown to this respondent." The phraseology of the avowment is peculiar. "At and immediately before" seems to imply that respondent was aware that they had not for any appreciable time been citizens of the state. The proof is that many of them were citizens of Tennessee, and there is no proof that they had become citizens of North Carolina. That respondent knew they were from Tennessee, and also knew that some of them were desperate and lawless is sufficiently apparent. In addition to this the force was not only unlawful to a great extent in the materials of which it was composed, but as a whole it was unlawfully raised and organized. It was not militia in any sense of the word, and was not authorized by the constitution, or colorably by any law. It follows that respondent's warrants upon the treasurer for the payment of this force were made without lawful authority.

As to the eighth article, it is only necessary to say that the evidence sustains the allegations, and establishes official misconduct on the part of the respondent, in that, in his official capacity he caused to be evaded and disregarded the proofs of a court of competent jurisdiction.

Much of what has been said is applicable to the charges contained in the first and second articles. One of the charges in each of those articles is, that respondent declared the counties of Alamance and Caswell in a state of insurrection, whereas he well knew there was no insurrection in either of them. The word "insurrection" as used in the constitution has a well settled meaning—a meaning which, if not established by judicial decision is well understood by every scholar and every jurist, and it is not competent for any legislature to declare that to be insurrection which is not insurrection within the meaning of the constitution. There was no insurrection in either of said counties, and I am fully satisfied by the evidence that none was intended. That there were conspiracies is certain, but none of them were for the purpose of making insurrection. It is to be presumed that the respondent knew the state of things in those counties as we know it now. But he says he is justified in what he did by the Shoffner act. That act undertook to authorize him to declare a county in insurrection whenever in his judgment the civil authorities were unable to protect its citizens in the enjoyment of life and property. This act presents the only difficulty in the case and furnishes the respondent his only ground of defence. It is not for a judicial tribunal to declare that the purpose of the legislature is to violate the constitution, but it is clear to my mind that the act undertook to vest in the respondent a power which, by the constitution, he is not permitted to exercise. In other words, I hold that the act was unconstitutional and void. The question then is, whether the respondent is impeachable for exercising the discretion given him by an unconstitutional act, provided he received it in good faith, and without dishonest and corrupt motives. I am free to say I think he is not. Then the only inquiry is, whether he did exercise that discretion *bona fide*. There is much evidence bearing upon this question. I have already referred to some of it, and stated the inferences which are to be legitimately drawn from it. I do not think the evidence is sufficient, however, to establish the fact that the respondent corruptly declared the county of Alamance in insurrection; and if that was all the article charged, I should have voted "not guilty" upon that article. More than this: had the respondent done only what was allowable under the Shoffner act, I should have voted his acquittal. It is not necessary, for the explanation of my views, that I should say anything about the proclamation as to Caswell.

But these articles charge further: 1st, that the respondent sent an unlawful military force into said counties and took possession of them; 2d, that this force, by his order, made many arrests of peaceable and law-abiding citizens without process; 3d, that he detained, imprisoned and maltreated a large number of persons, naming them. I consider the charge of corruptly issuing the proclamations as inducement to the other allegations, or at most, as one of several specifications of crime contained in the articles. I am very strongly inclined to the opinion, that no formal conclusion is necessary in articles of impeachment, as in the case in indictments. Holding, therefore, as I do, that the agency employed by the respondent was altogether unlawful, I have no question as to his responsibility for whatever was done by it. It follows, if these views are correct, that he is guilty under these articles, as he is, in my judgment, under all the others.

In conclusion, I avail myself of the opportunity to express my abhorrence of the secret political societies which existed in Alamance, and which, I am convinced, exist there no longer. Without undertaking to say what their original purposes and objects were, it is certain that they became mischievous in the extreme. They committed many most heinous crimes. They did not, so far as we know, assassinate Stephens, but they murdered Outlaw and probably Puryear. They whipped and scourged many for actual or pretended offences, and some out of a spirit of wantonness or revenge. They established in Alamance a reign of terror. They supplied, as far as they could supply, pretexts for the oppression of our people, to those who sought them. They disgraced us in our own eyes and in the eyes of the world. If any man, who loves North Carolina, shall hereafter write the history of these times, his cheeks will burn with shame, when he recounts the atrocities committed in Alamance.

In all this lawlessness, whether in Alamance or Caswell, I could find a justification or excuse for the lawless acts of the respondent, I would most cheerfully say so. One crime cannot be set off against another. However much turbulent and misguided men may have taken the law into their own hands, he was not at liberty to do so. They were citizens, and were entitled to the benefit of those provisions of the constitution, which protected even the guilty from arrest, imprisonment, trial and punishment, otherwise than by the law of the land.

NOTES—1. The case of the Earl of Lancaster (Edward II and III,) about which there was some controversy, was in point for the purpose for which it was cited by one of the counsel for the managers. It is true that Mr. Hume (vol. 1, page 533) says: "all the attainders, also, which had passed against the Earl of Lancaster and his adherents, when the chance of war was turned against them, were easily reversed, during the triumphs of their party." This was cited by one of the counsel for the respondent, and the inference was drawn (a fair one) that the attainders were reversed, not because they were against law, but because the party of Lancaster was in the ascendant. But the historian is not to be so understood. He says elsewhere (page 518, same vol.) as follows: "In those violent times, *the laws were so much neglected*, on both sides, that even where they might, without any sensible inconvenience, *have been observed*, the conquerors deemed it unnecessary *to pay any regard to them*. Lancaster, who was guilty of open rebellion, and was taken in arms against his sovereign, *instead of being tried by the laws of his country*, which pronounced the sentence of death against him, was condemned *by a court martial*, and led to execution."

2. It will be seen by reference to Judge Battle's Habeas Corpus Cases, pages 101 and 102, that upon the question of the legality of the arrests made by the respondent, I am in accord with Judge Brooks.

## OPINION OF SENATOR L. C. EDWARDS.

I have read, with much attention, the paper containing Judge Warren's reasons for his vote upon the articles of impeachment, prepared by the house of representatives against Gov. Holden, I approve of, and adopt them as my own.

L. C. EDWARDS.

# INDEX.

INDEX. III

www.ingramcontent.com/pod-product-compliance
Lightning Source LLC
Chambersburg PA
CBHW031349290326
41932CB00044B/682

*9783337172596*